Stress, Strain, and Vietnam

STRESS, STRAIN, AND VIETNAM

An Annotated Bibliography of
Two Decades of Psychiatric and Social
Sciences Literature Reflecting the Effect
of the War on the American Soldier

Norman M. Camp, Robert H. Stretch,
and William C. Marshall

Bibliographies and Indexes in Military Studies,
Number 1

GREENWOOD PRESS
New York • Westport, Connecticut • London

Library of Congress Cataloging-in-Publication Data

Camp, Norman M.
  Stress, strain, and Vietnam : an annotated bibliogaphy of two
decades of psychiatric and social sciences literature reflecting the
effect of the war on the American soldier / Norman M. Camp, Robert
H. Stretch, and William C. Marshall.
     p.   cm. — (Bibliographies and indexes in military studies,
ISSN 1040-7995 ; no. 1)
  Includes index.
  ISBN 0-313-26272-1 (lib. bdg. : alk. paper)
  1. Vietnamese Conflict, 1961-1975—Psychological aspects—
Bibliography. 2. Vietnamese Conflict, 1961-1975—Social aspects—
Bibliography. I. Stretch, Robert H. II. Marshall, William C.
III. Title. IV. Series.
A3226.C35 1988
[DS559.8.P7]
016.959704'3—dc19   88-30138

British Library Cataloguing in Publication Data is available.

Library of Congress Catalog Card Number: 88-30138
ISBN: 0-313-26272-1
ISSN: 1040-7995

First published in 1988

Greenwood Press, Inc.
88 Post Road West, Westport, Connecticut 06881

Printed in the United States of America

The paper used in this book complies with the
Permanent Paper Standard issued by the National
Information Standards Organization (Z39.48-1984).

10 9 8 7 6 5 4 3 2 1

Copyright Acknowledgment

Annotations appended with references from the *Journal of Social Issues* are reprinted
with permission of the Society for the Psychological Study of Social Issues.

"The past is not easily forgotten. Perhaps the truest measure of how the nation learns the 'lessons of Vietnam' will not be how well it remembers that experience, but how wisely." *The Vietnam Experience: A Nation Divided* by Dougan, Lipsman, & the editors of Boston Publishing Co., 1984, p. 183.

To Marshall, Lee and Dean;
to AnneMichell and Micah;
and to Laura and James.

Contents

Preface

Our principal objective in writing this book was to collect and summarize the published observations, research findings, opinions, and conclusions of mental health professionals, social scientists, and other trained observers regarding the effects of the war in Vietnam on those who fought it. The 851 compiled references span from 1965, when large numbers of American combat troops were first committed in Vietnam, through 1987, almost 15 years after American combat activities had ceased.

The word stress in the book's title refers primarily to physical, social, and psychological challenge and is meant to characterize the collection of hardships, deprivations, fears, losses, and psychological disequilibrium suffered to various degrees by everyone who went to--and especially who fought in--Vietnam. Stress also refers to the bewilderment, loneliness, shame, and stigma experienced by every returning soldier because of the nation's blame and neglect. Further, it includes the angst of those who feared being sent to war but were ultimately exempted, the anxious worry of those who waited for soldiers to return, the grief of those whose soldiers never returned, and the turmoil and outrage of all who opposed the war, especially those who took risks in speaking out.

Strain applies to situations in which an individual's resiliency is taxed beyond its limits. In the case of Vietnam, it refers to the more or less permanent and perhaps disabling psychological alterations of the reaction patterns, attitudes, relationships, and future prospects of many who answered America's call to arms. It also includes the persisting psychological repercussions of those who didn't serve but worry that they should have, the sadness and emptiness of those whose losses from the war seem irreparable, and the pain and struggle of those who seek to reach someone who came home and yet never returned. More generally, the concept of strain seems to apply to the political uncertainty and social tensions of a nation still repressing much of the pain and disillusionment associated with the radical, divisive, and decadent Vietnam period. Like the veteran with a psychiatric disorder that distorts his reactions and limits his creative adaptations, America may remain vulnerable until the bitter past is examined, becomes understood, and contributes to its wisdom. In that regard, as we emerge from the Vietnam era, it seems critical to grasp as thoroughly as possible the collective discoveries and interpretations from the social and behavioral sciences, for although historians may tell us the "how" and the "when," our development as a nation will be especially advanced as we come to understand the "why" that is rooted in individual and group psychology.

The idea for compiling this annotated bibliography arose in 1982 as the by-product of research on psychiatric need and the delivery of (Army) psychiatric services in Vietnam. It stemmed from my discoveries that an electronic bibliographic search could not reach back to the years of the war (1965-73), that the majority of relevant articles for that period did not provide abstracts, that innumerable reports and presentations were published in edited volumes and therefore were not referenced independently, and that a great amount of very significant material was published in a wide array of sources. This diversity of sources is attributed to the fact that interest in the bio-psychosocial factors influencing Vietnam war stress, strain, and recovery is shared by professionals ranging across many disciplines. Thus, as a part of my research interest in psychiatry in Vietnam, I began to collect and abstract references that described or explained the stress of soldiering during the war, the various forms of adaptive failure (i.e., psychiatric and behavioral disorders) seen among the deployed troops, and the types and results of the mental health interventions that were used to prevent psychiatric depletion of the combat forces and to aid disabled troops.

Fortunately, R. H. Stretch, a colleague at Walter Reed Army Institute of Research, was simultaneously studying Vietnam veteran stress and residual symptoms among active duty, reservist, and civilian populations, and he agreed to develop a section of the bibliography pertaining to veteran adjustment and psychiatric conditions.

Subsequently, we recognized that to fully understand either battlefield stress and breakdown or reentry stress and maladjustment, we not only must appreciate the combat environment of Vietnam, but also should consider the influences of military and government institutions more generally, as well as the changes in the American social and political climate from which these soldiers came and to which they returned. Accordingly, we decided to include a third section whose references could provide a backdrop or context for those in the first two, which bear more directly on soldiers in Vietnam and returning veterans.

As the work extended beyond even our most ambitious estimates, we became convinced of its potential for being more than a reference source for behavioral science researchers and military historians. We thus undertook to write and organize the manuscript so that it might serve a broader readership by being a psychosocial digest of the tumultuous late '60s-early '70s period as it related to the drawn-out and controversial war in Southeast Asia.

More specifically, we sought to make the reference collection comprehensive, albeit within certain bounds, and to provide abstracts that succinctly highlight the authors' critical findings, observations, and opinions so one could easily survey the psychosocial impact of the war through the panorama of professional study and interpretation. We hope the resulting composite will increase the reader's awareness of the personal and social cost of this war, as well as serve as a guide for further research into the treatment of Vietnam's casualties and the prevention of new ones in the next war.

The constraints of time and space have required that this work not be exhaustive but instead concentrate on the fundamental psychological tasks and adaptations of those participants who took the greatest risks and had the least to gain--the infantry soldiers. For example, an important and burgeoning literature has evolved surrounding the POW experience; however, because of the relatively small numbers and unrepresentative qualifications (e.g., high levels of education and training) of those who underwent that particular ordeal, we included only a few selected review articles, which can point the interested reader to other sources. Additional subject areas pertaining to service in Southeast Asia that we treated similarly were stress, performance, and illness among Navy personnel serving off the coast of Vietnam; the various activities comprising the air war; and the toxic effects of the Agent Orange herbicide used in Vietnam.

As to the scope of our sources, we included mostly psychiatric, social, and behavioral science publications. These were augmented with personal narratives of those who served, descriptions and reactions of war correspondents, and historical reviews of the war and the period that include observations and analysis of their effect on the combat soldier.

We elected to limit our selections to materials published in generally accessible sources--primarily periodicals, journals, books, monographs, and government reports. We excluded news reports, unpublished manuscripts, novels, articles from military publications, and articles intended for distribution within the Veterans Administration. We also did not include articles from the popular press unless they were written by behavioral science professionals or unless the authors presented firsthand observations from Vietnam of an especially insightful nature.

We found it quite a challenge to decide the best way to classify the collected references. The resultant topical arrangement includes three major parts (service in Vietnam, veteran adaptation, and social and institutional context), each of which is then divided into chapters, which are arranged to lead from the more general to the more specific. Placement of a reference within this system often involved compromise, primarily because many works included multiple aspects of war experience and reaction. Every effort was made to place a work in the part that represented its major emphasis. Whenever a publication belonged equally in two or more parts (or chapters), it was placed in the more general or earlier part (or chapter). For example, if a work equally describes aspects of the Vietnam experience (Part I) and of the veteran experience (Part II), it was placed in the Vietnam service section. It should be mentioned that it was very tempting to create many more chapters than are found in our final arrangement. However, we concluded that additional chapters would only suggest artificial and confusing demarcations in the spectrum of stress and strain from Vietnam.

Finally, although we have sought not to editorialize as we constructed and arranged these annotations, we acknowledge that we have not been entirely able to avoid bias, especially in deciding which aspects of an author's work to highlight. We sincerely regret any distortions in our representations of the referenced works and accept full responsibility for our abstracts. Similarly, the opinions expressed in this volume are the private views of the authors and are not to be construed as official or as reflecting the views of the Department of Defense or the Department of the Army.

N. M. Camp
(Vietnam class of '70-'71)

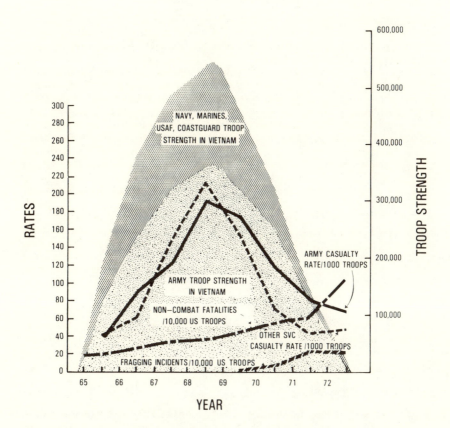

Figure 1. Rates for Combat Casualties (Those Killed or Wounded in Action), Noncombat Fatalities, and Fragging Incidents Among U.S. Troops in the Vietnam Theatre. Printed by permission of N. M. Camp and C. M. Carney from ongoing research on Army psychiatry in Vietnam. Data sources: Troop strengths and casualty rates from Department of Defense, OASD (comptroller), Directorate for Information Operations, 15 March 1974; noncombat casualty rates from U.S. Army Center for Military History, U.S. Casualty Data from Vietnam/Southeast Asia, 1961-74, Washington, DC; fragging incident rates from Crisis in Command: Mismanagement in the Army by R. A. Gabriel and P. L. Savage, 1978, New York: Hill and Wang, table 3.

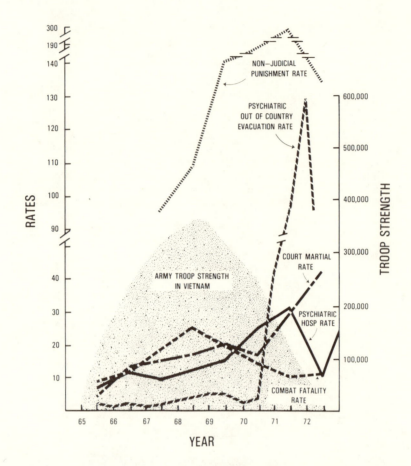

Figure 2. U.S. Army Rates for Combat Fatalities and for Indicators of Psychiatric and Behavioral Dysfunction per 1000 Troops per Year. Printed by permission of N. M. Camp and C. M. Carney from ongoing research on Army psychiatry in Vietnam. Data sources: Army troop strength and combat fatality rates from Department of Defense, OASD (comptroller), Directorate for Information Operations, 15 March 1974; nonjudicial punishment rates and court martial rates from Law at War: Vietnam 1964-1973 by G. S. Prugh, 1975, Washington, DC: U.S. Government Printing Office, appendix K; psychiatric out-of-country evacuation rates from "Medical and Psychiatric Treatment Policy and Practice in Vietnam" by F. D. Jones and A. W. Johnson, Jr., 1975, Journal of Social Issues, 31(4), figure 2; psychiatric hospitalization rates from A Summary of Source Data in Military Psychiatric Epidemiology by W. E. Datel, 1976, Alexandria, VA: Defense Documentation Center (Document AD No. A 021-265), figure 19.

Acknowledgments

Our appreciation for support in the formative stages of this project is extended to David H. Marlowe, Ph.D., chief of the Department of Military Psychiatry, Walter Reed Army Institute of Research (WRAIR), Washington, D.C. We also wish to thank Linette Sparacino, Dick Pickle, and Veronica Davis of WRAIR, and Virginia Velasco of Walter Reed Army Medical Center, for their considerable assistance in locating primary sources as well as in preparing the early versions of the manuscript. We offer our special thanks to Calvin Kytle for his encouragement and astute advice. Finally, we would like to express our unending gratitude to Jane and Larry Gold for their expert and vitally important assistance in the completion of this work.

Introduction

The reader will notice that each annotation is followed by a parenthetical code. These codes designate the source of the annotation: (C) = Camp; (S) = Stretch; (M) = Marshall; (A) = author's published abstract or summary; (MA) = modified author-- that is, author's published abstract or summary modified or edited to ensure stylistic consistency with the rest of the bibliography or to further emphasize some aspect of the original publication that has particular relevance to this bibliography.

Annotations appended with (A) that belong with references from the Journal of Social Issues are reprinted with the expressed permission of the copyright holder, the Society for the Psychological Study of Social Issues.

Several authors included in this bibliography are represented by multiple publications. We found, however, that this sometimes revealed inconsistencies in the authors' use of initials preceding their surname in the titles. To reduce any possible confusion and to ensure a more concise and usable index, we have used an author's full initials in all such cases whenever it could be ascertained that the two names did indeed identify the same person.

Finally, the following special terms, acronyms, and sources appear repeatedly throughout the text and are defined below:

DSM-III -- American Psychiatric Association. (1980). Diagnostic and statistical manual of mental disorders (3rd ed.). Washington, DC: Author.

Flashbacks -- A symptom of PTSD in which individuals report periodic vivid and intense recollections of some aspect of the apparently traumatizing events. In the more intense episodes, they may feel (and sometimes act) as if they were reliving the experience.

Fragging -- The phenomenon by which American enlisted soldiers attempted to assassinate their superiors using fragmentation grenades or claymore mines, devices that destroy the evidence with the consummation of the act.

MMPI -- Minnesota Multiphasic Personality Inventory.

Psychic numbing -- A fundamental PTSD symptom group in which individuals report or demonstrate reduced interest in, responsiveness to, or involvement with people and activities in their environment.

PTSD -- Posttraumatic Stress Disorder, a specific and characteristic set of mental and psychological symptoms that arise in response to exposure to exceptional physical or mental (i.e., traumatizing) stress. The label is not always used precisely by the authors represented in this bibliography. It was only officially recognized with the publication of the DSM-III (pp. 236-238) in 1980; prior to then, PTSD was also variously referred to as delayed stress reaction or response, gross stress reaction, combat or war neurosis, and, with respect to symptomatic Vietnam veterans, post-Vietnam syndrome.

Rap groups -- A modified type of group therapy that originated as an experiment by a consortium of Vietnam veterans and mental health professionals. Rap groups began as a series of self-help meetings whose purpose was to promote personal and group exploration of issues affecting the participants' postservice adjustment and reintegration. They were unorthodox group therapy sessions in that they had less formal boundaries for time and membership and required attending professionals to function as facilitators rather than as therapists.

Short-timers syndrome -- Mounting and perhaps disabling psychological symptoms observed in combat zone soldiers who are nearing their expected date of return home. These symptoms typically include a preoccupation with worries, fears, and anxieties--especially regarding personal safety--as well as associated mood swings and social withdrawal.

I   VIETNAM SERVICE

American troops of all kinds participated in the war in Vietnam with its stated goal of assisting the South in defending itself from a communist takeover from the North. Too late, however, it became evident that the United States had ensnared itself in Vietnam's simultaneous and protracted nationalistic opposition to foreign domination, civil war, and social revolution. Almost 3 million American men and women served in Southeast Asia through the 8 years (1965-73) of the war. An estimated 1 million faced combat or other hazardous circumstances. Officially, 58,132 were killed or missing in action, over 304,000 were wounded, and an estimated quarter of a million Americans lost an immediate family member to the war. For the first few years, morale and sense of purpose for those serving in the Vietnam theatre was high, and troop attrition due to psychiatric or behavioral dysfunction was exceptionally low. However, the war dragged on, the enemy proved to be more resilient and committed than anticipated, and the American people became passionately divided about the war (the numbers of those opposed dramatically increased following spring 1968, when the communist troops defied predictions of imminent defeat by staging theatrewide surprise "Tet" offensives). Ultimately a very large proportion of U.S. troops demonstrated in various ways their inability or unwillingness to accept the risks of combat, acknowledge the authority of military leaders, or tolerate the hardships of an assignment in Vietnam (see figs. 1 and 2, pp. xv and xvi). Matters worsened appreciably in late 1970 when a Vietnamese-based heroin market began to flourish and large numbers of U.S. soldiers became heroin users. It was only after reliable urine drug screening technology became available that the military could begin to comprehend and react to this widescale problem of self-inflicted soldier disability.

References in this section provide research results, observations, or opinions that reflect on the nature of the stresses of serving in Vietnam as well as on soldier adaptation or failed adaptation and its psychiatric management.

1   Combat Theatre Stress and Adaptation

Anderson, C. R. (1976). The grunts. Novato, CA: Presidio Press.

Draws upon Anderson's personal combat experiences in Vietnam to reconstruct in Part 1 a composite of the actions of one U.S. Marine infantry company (160 men) on a 58-day combat operation in 1969. Anderson interrupts the chronology of the account with brief, contrasting descriptions of the activities of his stateside countrymen, who were far from the war. In Part 2, he presents a general description of pre- and postwar experiences of the typical "grunt" who served in Vietnam as examined against the backdrop of American society in the late 1960s. (C)

Balkind, J. J. (1978). Morale deterioration in the United States military during the Vietnam period. Dissertation Abstracts International, 39 (1-A), 438. (University Microfilms No. 78-11333)

This thoroughly referenced historical review documents the severe breakdown in morale and effectiveness of the U.S. military (enlisted and officers) in Southeast Asia, as well as throughout the rest of the Army, during the period of the latter half of the war (1969-73). Especially reviewed are the unprecedented increases for rates of combat refusals, combat atrocities, heroin use, assassinations (or threats) of military leaders, racial conflicts, desertion and AWOL, and indicators of pervasive careerism among military leaders, as well as the emergence of the GI antiwar movement. Balkind contends that military social scientists failed to conceptually grasp and anticipate the effects of U.S. combat mission ambiguity, the consequences of guerrilla warfare, and the potency of the antiwar movement in undermining military morale. (C)

Bey, D. R., & Zecchinelli, V. A. (1974). G.I.'s against themselves: Factors resulting in explosive violence in Vietnam. Psychiatry, 37, 221-228.

Describes individual, group, and circumstantial factors that culminated in violent behaviors toward other American troops in 43 cases examined in the 1st Infantry Division between July and December of 1969. The composite picture is that of a young, immature, action-oriented soldier who is constitutionally fragile (secondary to a history of limited or punitive upbringing, marginal intellect or education, and incomplete social skills). Early in his Vietnam tour this soldier not only remained apart from sustaining peer groups (or worse, was an object of group scapegoating) but also failed to form an identity consistent with the military and its mission. He thus ultimately succumbs to using the available weaponry and his heightened combat reactions to vent accumulated frustrations (attendant to the hot, hostile, and deprived environment) that reach a flashpoint because of his exaggerated passivity and the unavailability of alternate release behaviors such as AWOL or sick call attendance. Additional group dynamics noted are individual violent behaviors serving to express group tensions (including derivatives of latent homosexuality aroused by the intense closeness of peer groups), as well as the usual group sanction of violent behaviors in a combat theatre. Case examples are provided. (C)

Blank, A. S., Jr. (1982b). Stresses of war: The example of Vietnam. In L. Goldberger & S. Breznitz (Eds.), Handbook of stress (pp. 631-643). New York: Free Press.
    From a vantage point of having served in Vietnam as an Army psychiatrist and having later evaluated over 1,000 Vietnam veterans, Blank catalogs the compounding collection of stresses to which the soldiers of Vietnam and the returning veterans were often subjected (in what he refers to as a "holocaust experience"). He also elaborates a rough taxonomy of their consequent clinical and adjustment problems. (C)

Bloch, H. S. (1970c). The psychological adjustment of normal people during a year's tour in Vietnam. Psychiatric Quarterly, 44, 613-626.
    Describes and analyzes patterns of adjustment by American military personnel who serve a tour of duty in Vietnam. Bloch draws upon his casual experiences there as well as on clinical observations while treating psychiatric casualties from combat and other stresses. He emphasizes the need to view these adaptive patterns developmentally and psychodynamically ("to view each person's adaptation to powerful affectual issues of separation and abandonment, fears of death and disfigurement, and the experience of frustration in the continuum of the person's earlier adaptive experiences"). He considers that certain unusual behavioral phenomena among U.S. troops (such as the "short-timers syndrome") can be understood as characterologic ways they "buttress themselves against the waves of strong internal reactions to external stresses." (C)

Bond, T. C. (1976). The why of fragging. American Journal of Psychiatry, 133, 1328-1331.
    Presents a study of 28 men convicted and confined for using explosives in assaults on superior officers during the Vietnam war. There were several predominant characteristics in this group, including deprivation and/or brutality in family backgrounds, poor self-image, lack of critical self-observation, use of externalization,

and feelings of insecurity or vulnerability. Drug use joined with these and several other factors related to their situation in Vietnam in a lethal combination that led to an indirect assault with an explosive device on a leadership figure perceived as powerful and threatening. (MA)

Bourne, P. G. (1970a). Men, stress, and Vietnam. Boston: Little Brown.
     Presents a series of essays regarding observations, experiences, and speculations from Bourne's year-long tour in Vietnam (1965-66) as a psychiatrist member of the Walter Reed Army Institute of Research field study unit. Topics include sociopolitical aspects of foreign policy planning, the biochemical and psychosocial correlates of combat stress, psychosocial considerations of the Vietnamese culture with relevance for U.S. goals and methods, and a comparative study of neuropsychiatric incidence rates for the U.S. Army and that of the Republic of Vietnam. (C)

Bryan, C. D. B. (1984, June). Barely suppressed screams: Getting a bead on Vietnam war literature. Harper's, pp. 67-72.
     Through highlighting common elements found in the literature produced by participants of the Vietnam war, Bryan seeks to understand its personal and social impact, especially as distinguished from previous American wars of this century: "The generic Vietnam war narrative charts the gradual deterioration of order, the disintegration of idealism, the breakdown of character, the alienation from those at home and, finally, the loss of all sensibility save the will to survive." He contends that what has yet to be adequately portrayed in the literature is the "moral disparity" surrounding this war and consequent to its execution. (C)

Cosmas, G. A., & Murray, T. P. (1986). U.S. Marines in Vietnam: Vietnamization and redeployment, 1970-1971. Washington, DC: Government Printing Office.
     Produced by the History and Museums Division, Headquarters, U.S. Marine Corps, and part of the official history of U.S. military activities in the Vietnam war, this volume covers the period of the transfer of military responsibilities to the armed forces of South Vietnam in the provinces bordering on North Vietnam and the eventual withdrawal of Marines from the combat theatre. It includes a section (chap. 20, pp. 343-369) detailing the mounting morale and discipline problems within Marine units in Vietnam, which mirrored those seen in other branches during this demobilization phase of the war. Finally, it covers the following problems (and attempts at their resolution): combat atrocities, "friendly fire" accidents, combat refusals, racial strife, drug abuse, "fraggings," and dissent. (C)

Cragg, D. (1982). Viet-speak. Maledicta--International Journal of
Verbal Aggression, 6, 249-261.
     Defines 63 terms of U.S. troop lingo that evolved during the
Vietnam war. This specialized dictionary of soldier slang centers
around an anonymous piece published in the February 1971 edition
of The Army Reporter, in which the story of Little Red Riding
Hood is modified to use terms and expressions that were "passed
on from much older times and wars (and) that found new life in
Vietnam; loan words from the Vietnamese language, often mispro-
nounced and misunderstood by Americans; words borrowed by the
Vietnamese from us and garbled in the most interesting ways;
French, Chinese and Japanese borrowings; military jargon; peculiar
nonce words and expressions; and wholesale appropriations from
the lexicon of general American slang that through usage became
the exclusive property of Vietnam veterans." (C)

Dowling, J. (1967, May/June). Psychologic aspects of the year in
Vietnam. U.S. Army Vietnam Medical Bulletin, pp. 45-48.
     Describes vicissitudes of mood and adjustment in soldiers
assigned for a 1-year tour with the 1st Cavalry Division in Vietnam in 1966-67. Specific phases are designated as (1) apprehensive
enthusiasm, (2) resignation (depression), and (3) anxious appre-
hension. Elaboration of daily stressors is pointed more toward base
camp routines than toward combat itself. Dowling comments that
generally both psychotics and character-behavior disorders are
most likely to require psychiatric attention in the first few
months of the tour as a consequence of their inability to adapt to
this especially stressful environment. (C)

Faris, J. H. (1977). An alternative perspective to Savage and
Gabriel. Armed Forces and Society, 3, 457-462.
     Seeks to correct some assertions by P. L. Savage and R. A.
Gabriel (1976) in their review of the military "disintegration" of
the U.S. Army during the Vietnam period. Faris argues that
primary group bonding in Vietnam, although weakened by replacement policies, continued to be viable. The critical problem arose
instead because these primary groups became alienated from the
military and society: "primary groups can only be effective when
linked through immediate leaders and orientation to secondary
symbols, to the military organization and the broader society." In
the case of Vietnam, one sees not only the inadequacy of military
leadership, as emphasized by Savage and Gabriel, but also the
critical lack of powerful secondary symbols (e.g., presidents
Johnson and Nixon were not inspirational leaders for American
youth) and the serious disenchantment of soldiers as they perceived a lack of sacrifice among draft-immune peers. Further,
strong evidence indicates the presence of such primary groups
among the soldiers in Vietnam in the group forms of defiance

highlighted by Savage and Gabriel (e.g., "fragging" assassinations of leaders and communal drug use). (C)

Forrest, D. V., Bey, D. R., & Bourne, P. G. (1972). The American soldier and Vietnamese women. Sexual Behavior, 2, 8-15.

Describes the co-mingling of the cultural characteristics of the Vietnamese, especially the women, with the cultural and developmental characteristics of the American soldiers at their interface during the peak of the American ground forces buildup. The portrayal of American-Vietnamese sexual liaison is one of brief, stereotyped, commercial, and mutual exploitation. Elements of aggression far outweigh those of loving in the exchange. Some couples, however, develop protracted intimacy and seek marriage. Forrest's clinical experience with a select group of these yielded an impression that both the American soldier and his Vietnam girlfriend found each other because of personality characteristics of an immature nature, and that bureaucratic obstacles to marriage are constructive in forcing a test of their resolve. (C)

Fulghum, D., Maitland, T., & the editors of Boston Publishing Co. (1984). The Vietnam experience: South Vietnam on trial. Boston: Boston Publishing Co.

Part of a multivolume series providing a historical account of America's war in Southeast Asia and liberally illustrated with photographs and detailed maps, this volume describes events in and surrounding this "standing down" phase of the war (mid-1970 to 1972) when public opposition was at its peak, military morale and indiscipline were at crisis proportions, and the success of the "Vietnamization" policy of turning over the primary military role to the South Vietnamese was questionable. As U.S. combat presence declined, the more offensive large-scale search-and-destroy operations gave way to primarily defensive small unit patrols. Further, "(the Army) sometimes seemed to be little more than a ragtag band of men wearing bandannas, peace symbols, and floppy bush hats, with little or no fight left in it." Combat refusals, drug problems, and racial strife often proved unresolvable. Punishments tended to be increasingly lenient as commanders openly acknowledged that they considered their primary responsibility to be to return their men safely home rather than to hunt the enemy or to carry out a tactical mission. This phase in the war ended in 1972 with a massive invasion attempt from the north by the North Vietnamese army. Its success was blunted only by extensive use of U.S. air support and left little doubt that South Vietnam would be lost with the complete withdrawal of American personnel. (C)

Gabriel, R. A., & Savage, P. L. (1978). Crisis in command: Mismanagement in the Army. New York: Hill and Wang.

Seeks to demonstrate through both historical review and cross-cultural comparisons that the military failures of Vietnam were symptomatic of an inadequate Army officer corps, both organizationally and ethically. Review of the data from Vietnam includes considerations of such phenomena as assassination of officers ("fragging"), combat refusals, falsified reports, atrocities, racism, drug abuse, and other features of the war that served to erode military morale and performance. (C)

Gillooly, D. H., & Bond, T. C. (1973). Assaults with explosive devices on superiors: A synopsis of reports from confined offenders at the U.S. Disciplinary Barracks. Military Medicine, 138, 700-702.
    Reports results of interviews with 24 confinees of the Army disciplinary barracks at Ft. Leavenworth, KS, regarding the circumstances and emotions behind their assaulting superiors with an explosive weapon. Most of these attacks occurred at a base camp, in darkness, and with unauthorized weapons. Among the offenders, 87.5% acknowledged being intoxicated and 90% had had direct confrontational interactions with the victims up to 3 days prior; 67% had made no effort to avoid getting caught. They reported feeling scapegoated by the victim, who generally was perceived as insensitive to the frustrations of his subordinates. (C)

Herrell, J. M. (1969, November/December). Birth order as a patient variable in combat zone psychiatry. U.S. Army Vietnam Medical Bulletin, pp. 29-33.
    Reports studies of case records of 1,256 randomly chosen patients of the psychiatric treatment team near Saigon (935th KO Detachment) in 1968 comparing source of referral, diagnostic type, and disposition with the variable of firstborn versus later-born. Significant findings include that firstborn were more likely to be self-referred, diagnosed as either a situational problem or as no psychiatric disease, and returned to duty. The later-born were more likely to be referred by command, typically sent for administrative separation purposes, diagnosed more often as a character and behavior disorder or as psychotic, and hospitalized or recommended for administrative separation from the Army as characterologically unfit. Implications for further research are discussed. (C)

Jones, F. D. (1967, November 15). Viet duty causes varied "psychoses." U.S. Medicine, pp. 2-6.
    Summarizes a presentation by Army psychiatrist Jones, who served in Vietnam with a combat division and later with a field hospital in Saigon (1966). Jones describes patterns of adaptation and maladaptation by U.S. soldiers over the 1-year combat tour. Overall, most soldiers are successfully managing despite the mul-

tiple stresses of loneliness, boredom, cultural alienation, and sporadic combat stress.   (C)

Kirk, D. (1975). Tell it to the dead: Memories of a war. Chicago: Nelson-Hall.

Provides a war correspondent's impressions of the war in Southeast Asia. Kirk's exposure, which lasted for the full duration of American involvement there, ranged from vantage points within South Vietnam that cut across the various levels of military organization. He also reports from within Cambodia and back in the States at the end of the war. His bias is acknowledged as he comments on "the futility of a struggle that had really proven nothing except, possibly, man's cruelty toward man." Most of the book focuses on the withdrawal years of the war (after 1969), with the political events in the United States (President Nixon's suspension of bombing in the North and pursuit of peace negotiations with North Vietnam) and the associated rapid decline in troop morale accompanied by their unwillingness to accept combat risks or deprivation. Kirk illustrates the pervasive dissension within the military as expressed in wholesale problems of low morale, combat avoidance, indiscipline, drug abuse, and racial conflict. He also gives witness to the prevalent belief among the American military that the North Vietnamese were patiently waiting until the Americans departed before they seized a quick and decisive victory over the South.   (C)

Lewis, L. B. (1985). The tainted war: Culture and identity in Vietnam war narratives. Westport, CT: Greenwood Press.

Provides a sociological analysis of the influences of the Vietnam war on those who fought (i.e., evidence of a world view, belief system, or meaning system), as represented in published personal accounts. Lewis seeks especially to explain how various social forces shaped the participant's belief system as he struggled to fight in a war in which disorder and the absence of a clear purpose were increasingly prominent. Lewis posits that the Vietnam soldier's expectations were established by his childhood exposure to media portrayals of World War II heroics (e.g., John Wayne movies). When these models failed to fit actual combat experience and, especially, when the situation became more ambiguous in Vietnam, his disillusionment rose and he increasingly despaired of finding meaning in his experience. His return to the United States, the final phase of his war experience, was made even more difficult by society's refusal to acknowledge his sacrifices for his country.   (M)

Lewy, G. (1980). The American experience in Vietnam. In S. C. Sarkesian (Ed.), Combat effectiveness: Cohesion, stress, and the

volunteer military (pp. 94-106). Beverly Hills, CA: Sage Publications.

Examines the state of the American forces in Vietnam with
regard to various indicators of mounting indiscipline and morale
deterioration, and presents data to refute these as indexes of
force degradation. For example, while drug use was prevalent, the
percentage of drug users was not much higher there than in other
theatres of command. Lewy also challenges the allegation that
young blacks were fighting and dying in disproportionate numbers
due to military racial discrimination. Regarding "fraggings," he
points out that the killing of officers by their own men has taken
place in other wars, and even in the 1970s it occurred in other
theatres of command. Similarly, he states that acts of combat
refusal are not uncommon in war and that it is unusual for any
conflict to lack at least one full-fledged mutiny. As for disciplinary issues, Lewy notes that combat-related desertion was rare
in Vietnam for the simple reason that there was no place to go.
Most lengthy AWOLs involved noncombat troops stationed in rear
areas. It is estimated that opposition to the war accounted for no
more than 10%-15% of all absence offenses. He contends that the
erosion of discipline in the latter years in Vietnam was caused in
part by such factors as the soldiers' feelings that those at home
did not appreciate their sacrifices and a growing permissiveness in
American society, accompanied by an increase in social pathology
and widespread social attitudes of disrespect toward authority and
law enforcement. Combat performance there was damaged by the
demobilization, when "no one wanted to be the last man killed in
Vietnam." A related issue was soldier discontent resulting from
idleness and boredom as combat activity diminished. Other issues
that affected morale were the short tours of duty, lower standards
for enlisted men obtained through the draft, and diminished
leadership quality, aggravated by the administration's policy
prohibiting the deployment of experienced reserve and national
guard officers. Lewy also posits that leadership quality was
detrimentally affected by the replacement of the "gladiatorial"
officer type (devoted to "duty, honor, and country") with the
"managerial nonparticipant" (valuing efficiency and career
enhancement). (S)

Linden, E. (1972, January 8). The demoralization of an army:
Fragging and other withdrawal symptoms. Saturday Review, pp.
12-17, 55.

Presents a journalist's account of a visit to Vietnam during
the phasedown period to investigate the deteriorated morale of
U.S. troops. Through case examples and other observations, Linden
provides a dynamic description of the layers of circumstance and
meaning that he believes combined to produce the "class war" between soldier and leader, often with "fragging" as its final result.
Linden reports that fraggings and threats of violence were com-

monly used as a means of controlling officers and NCOs by intimidating the intended victim and his peers. This is contrasted with
World Wars I and II and the Korean conflict, in which an assassination of an inexperienced or overzealous junior officer may have
been attempted during intense combat by his troops who perceived
him as dangerous. Only 370 cases of fragging were reported among
the almost 5 million GIs who fought in World War I, whereas 363
cases were tried and 118 were listed as "possible" in the low-
intensity conflict of Vietnam in 1970 alone. Linden refers to
fragging in Vietnam as "prevalent, passionless, and apparently
unprovoked, representing the grisly game of psychological warfare
that GIs use." In addition to its greater frequency, Vietnam war
fragging more often occurred in rear areas. Linden explains that
rear echelon troops are "acutely aware of the authoritarian nature
of the system and the privileges and luxuries enjoyed by officers;
yet they see little justification because both officers and enlisted
men are doing essentially nothing." He surmises that for most GIs,
fighting the war in Vietnam in its latter stages was so meaningless and bewildering that it took on a dreamlike quality. This
unreality paved the way for acts like "fragging the sarge" and
"snorting skag" (heroin), which would otherwise be unacceptable in
other environments. (M)

Moskos, C. C., Jr. (1980). Surviving the war in Vietnam. In C. R.
Figley & S. Leventman (Eds.), Strangers at home: Vietnam veterans
since the war (pp. 71-85). New York: Praeger.
     Provides a sociological assessment of certain historical events
that fostered demoralization of American troops in Vietnam and
disrupted their cohesion, especially the 1-year rotation system by
which each soldier knew the exact date he would singly leave
Vietnam. The consequent rapid turnover thus hindered the development of primary-group ties and led to "short-timers syndrome,"
in which a soldier in the last few months of his tour became
increasingly less effective. Combat group cohesion was also negatively affected by cleavage and conflict. Differing attitudes between young enlisted men and career noncoms and officers sometimes led to "fraggings" (assassinations) of superiors suspected of
being racist, too zealous in enforcing antidrug regulations, or too
"gung-ho" in combat situations. In discussing ideology and military
effectiveness, Moskos argues that the decline in military order in
Vietnam was also affected by the general weakening of morale
that usually accompanies an army coming to the end of a war.
Soldiers arriving in Vietnam after 1969 differed appreciably from
their predecessors in that they were coming from a society that
had become increasingly hostile toward the war. Yet despite all
the problems faced by American forces in Vietnam, Moskos notes
that the American Army there did not disintegrate, did not suffer
mass defections, and was not receptive to subversive political
forces. (S)

Parrish, M. D. (1981). Man-team-environment systems in Vietnam. In F. D. Jones (Ed.), M. D. Parrish, MD: Collected works 1955-1970. Alexandria, VA: Defense Documentation Center (Document AD No. A 108-069).

From his observations as the senior Army psychiatrist in Vietnam in 1967, Parrish discusses the challenge of welding the individual to his task group and its available technology so as to achieve maximum effectiveness in a specific combat ecology. He considers the man-team-environment (ideally "symbiotic") to be "the ultimate weapon for work or war," and he examines various environmental features and personnel policies that may degrade combat team performance, whether a surgical team or an infantry unit. He argues that the individualized replacement system in Vietnam is the least disruptive to the "team's" task adaptation (i.e., it assimilates new members with the least disequilibrium to the group's effectiveness). (C)

Pasternack, S. A. (1971). Evaluation of dangerous behavior of active duty servicemen. Military Medicine, 136, 110-113.

Presents results of a records review of enlisted patients referred to a large Navy hospital in 1969-70 for psychiatric hospitalization associated with acts of violence ($N = 27$) or threats to commit them ($N = 7$). Of the first group, 22 were hospitalized after violent incidents in Vietnam against fellow soldiers. Although there was considerable diversity, common trends included psychotic or near-psychotic mental states with severe and brittle underlying character pathology. Family backgrounds included extensive chaos with parental alcoholism, mental illness, criminality, or brutality toward the patient. These patients had been poor students, socially inept, and rigidly defended with projection, denial, and reaction formation; they sought combat service to prove their masculinity. Tension release through drinking, drugs, sexual activity, or combat was common. All 7 who only threatened violence had recently returned from Vietnam. They differed in being capable of delaying action to weigh alternatives but had other features in common with the overtly violent group. Apparently feelings of rejection by society because of being Vietnam veterans evoked intense emotions from childhood rejections by parents. Pasternack urges recognition of premonitory signs of violent behavior and offers a checklist for assessing dangerousness. (C)

Prugh, G. S. (1975). Law at war: Vietnam 1964-1973. Washington, DC: U.S. Government Printing Office.

Describes the legal issues arising between U.S. military personnel and the people and legal institutions of the Republic of Vietnam through the period of the war. Prugh includes general descriptions of the patterns of war crimes investigations, black market activities, currency violations, and the drug problem.

Appendix K provides numerical data on U.S. Army disciplinary actions in Vietnam by year of the war. (C)

Renner, J. A., Jr. (1973). The changing patterns of psychiatric problems in Vietnam. Comprehensive Psychiatry, 14, 169-181.
    Provides observations regarding the epidemiology of psychiatric and related difficulties in Vietnam from the vantage point of a Navy psychiatrist serving aboard the USS Repose hospital ship in 1969. Renner argues that military psychiatrists have been premature in asserting that the war in Vietnam produced fewer psychiatric casualties than previous wars. While the number of men hospitalized and evacuated because of psychiatric problems has decreased, there has been a concurrent increase in disciplinary problems (including high rates for racial disturbances and attacks on superiors), drug abuse, and the number of men entering medical channels diagnosed as character disorders. In Renner's estimation, the prevalence of these often hidden casualties indicates a high level of psychological distress among U.S. troops (e.g., the Navy and Marine Corps dishonorable discharge rate rose 53% in Vietnam from 1968 to 1969). He catalogs the numerous features of the combat theatre late in the war that have served to erode social structures, psychological defenses, and especially the military identity of the typical soldier. Although most soldiers are still able to tolerate the consequent low morale, guilt, and disillusionment, many others succumb and become involved in regressive and delinquent behaviors. (C)

Rose, E. (1982). The anatomy of a mutiny. Armed Forces and Society, 8, 561-574.
    Compares and contrasts mutiny-like incidents, primarily from this century, and includes references to the Vietnam period. Rose presents his deductions regarding its general social etiologic dynamics, the nature and form of the mutinous act itself, and the systemic aftermath of such collective antimilitary insubordination. Further, he considers Vietnam unique because of both the prolonged nature of the soldiers' collective challenge to military authority (a "macromutiny") and the conciliatory encounters ("working it out") that often transpired there between officers and their men. (C)

Stanton, M. D. (1972b). Understanding the Vietnam veteran: Some social-psychological considerations. In L. J. Sherman & E. M. Caffey, Jr. (Eds.), The Vietnam veteran in contemporary society: Collected materials pertaining to the young veterans (sec. III, pp. 17-21). Washington, DC: Veterans Administration.
    Describes the experiences and psychological reactions of soldiers who serve in Vietnam based on data derived from inter-

views of recent returnees who were reassigned to a stateside post. (C)

Sterba, J. P. (1971). Cover your ass. In R. A. Falk, G. Kolko, & R. J. Lifton (Eds.), Crimes of war (pp. 445-458). New York: Random House. (Originally printed as: Close up of the grunt: The hours of boredom, the seconds of terror. New York Times Magazine, 1970, February 8.)

Provides observations on the shifting demographics and particularly on the attitudes of the soldiers who went to fight in Vietnam in 1969. Sterba notes how the rapidly unfolding political events in the United States had caused the romance and idealism of the early war to be replaced by a "hated, dreary struggle" in which the soldier's overriding preoccupation was that of self-protection: "These were the grunts of the class of 1968--they had come out of that America some of their commanders had seen only from the windows of the Pentagon. They were graduates of an American nightmare in 1968 that stemmed mostly from the war they had now come to fight--the year of riots and dissention, of assassinations and Chicago, the year America's ulcer burst." (C)

2   Combat Stress
and Adaptation

Austin, F. H., Jr. (1969). A review of stress and fatigue monitoring
of naval aviators during aircraft carrier combat operations: Blood
and urine biochemical studies. In P. G. Bourne (Ed.), The psychology and physiology of stress: With reference to special studies
of the Viet Nam war (pp. 197-218). New York: Academic Press.
     A study of blood plasma phospholipid fractions in 27 Navy
attack carrier pilots flying highly stressful combat flights over
North Vietnam during 1966 revealed an apparently distinctive
pattern of response compared with normal and other stress states.
The phosphatidyl glycerol level responded to this type of stress
more markedly and consistently than the other fractions. A discriminant functions formula was developed to facilitate identification of the stress type and degree of subject response up to and
including psychophysiological exhaustion and collapse. (C)

Austin, F. H., Jr., Gallagher, T. J., Brictson, C. A., Polis, B. D.,
Furry, D. E., & Lewis, C. E., Jr. (1967). Aeromedical monitoring of
Naval aviators during aircraft carrier combat operation. Aerospace
Medicine, 38, 593-596.
     Reports findings from a study (building on the preliminary
work of Roman, Older, & Jones, 1967) that monitored the physiologic correlates of stress and fatigue as related to performance in
32 Navy carrier pilots flying high-risk attack combat missions over
North Vietnam during a 22-day period in October 1966. In-flight
electronic recordings (electrocardiogram, respiration, and acceleration) were augmented with biochemical analysis of pre- and
postflight blood and urine. Among the findings is that the selected
elevation of the phosphatidyl glycerol and phosphatidic acid fractions of the plasma phospholipids during combat periods represents
a different pattern from that found in past stress studies and controls, and the authors consider this a characteristic biochemical
response pattern for combat flying stress. (See also Austin, 1969.)
(C)

Bey, D. R. (1972a). Change of command in combat: A locus of
stress. American Journal of Psychiatry, 129, 698-702.
     In the military, a change of command is particularly stressful
for the members of the unit involved. A comparison of units, some
of which showed few increases in the indexes of organizational
stress and some of which showed great increases, revealed a relationship between the administrative style of the departing com-

mander and the amount of stress experienced by the unit. Bey describes methods used in the Army's 1st Infantry Division to help
prevent excessive stress during the replacement period. (A)

Bey, D. R. (1972b). Group dynamics and the "F.N.G." in Vietnam: A
potential focus of stress. International Journal of Group Psychotherapy, 22, 22-30.
    Describes problematic elements in the development of primary
combat group cohesion when solitary soldiers joined already functioning combat units in Vietnam in 1968-69. The replacement period is routinely stressful to the new arrival ("fucking new guy")
and to his unit. The dynamics involved are similar to those involved when a new member is admitted to an established therapy
group. The stress is greater in the instance of a combat unit
because of the vitally interdependent relationships the task requires. Failure to integrate a new man into a combat unit is illustrated by a tragic case example. Bey describes a program that
was instituted to help the unit commanders see how they--through
empathy, admission of more than one replacement at a time, orientation, and assignment of a sponsor for the new man--could
reduce the stress for the FNG and ensure the unit's integrity and
continued effectiveness in the stress of battle. (C)

Bourne, P. G. (Ed.). (1969a). The psychology and physiology of
stress: With reference to special studies of the Viet Nam war. New
York: Academic Press.
    Presents collected works regarding the reactions of indi-
viduals facing the stress of the Vietnam combat environment
(American and South Vietnamese military). This includes the
organization and record of Army psychiatry in the early years of
the war; the results from monitoring changes in plasma phospho-
lipid fractions, testosterone metabolites, and urinary 17-OHCS
levels associated with combat stress; measurements of prestress
psychological vulnerability; results of studies of the physiological
effects of environmental stressors such as heat and humidity; and
descriptions of sociologic influences on the fighting forces. (See
also Allerton, 1969; Austin, 1969; Bourne, 1969b, 1969c; Glass, 1969;
Rose, Bourne, Poe, Mougey, Collins, & Mason, 1969; San, 1969;
Strange, 1969; Tischler, 1969; Wallen, 1969.) (C)

Bourne, P. G. (1969b). Military psychiatry and the Vietnam war in
perspective. In P. G. Bourne (Ed.), The psychology and physiology
of stress: With reference to special studies of the Viet Nam war
(pp. 219-236). New York: Academic Press.
    Synthesizes the findings in this volume regarding stress on
soldiers in the field, lessons from previous American wars, and
findings from Bourne's research studies in Vietnam in 1965-66.

Bourne highlights how "a slowly shifting emphasis, culminating in the Vietnam experience, has led to a conceptualization of the psychiatric casualty as an adaptive failure of a basically temporary nature rather than a disease entity." He notes that most patients in Vietnam have been categorized as having character and behavior disorders, but that, regardless of the presenting symptom, typically shaped by social or cultural factors, "the critical issue is that the man has ceased to cope with and function in the combat environment." He alludes to findings contained in the book that help to clarify how individual predisposition contributes to the breakdown of a combat soldier, and he comments, "It is only under very unusual circumstances, when combat is extremely heavy or when he becomes excessively tired, that a healthy man will become a psychiatric casualty. . . . Significant psychiatric attrition has been in Vietnam and presumably will be in the future, largely confined to those who bring some psychological liability with them to the combat zone." Regarding findings from his research in Vietnam, Bourne concludes that "for the average soldier physiological homeostasis is maintained at the expense of realistic appraisal of the danger." (C)

Bourne, P. G. (1969c). Urinary 17-OHCS levels in two combat situations. In P. G. Bourne (Ed.), The psychology and physiology of stress: With reference to special studies of the Viet Nam war (pp. 95-116). New York: Academic Press.

Reviews and synthesizes findings of several studies: steroid excretion levels of helicopter medics (Bourne, Rose, & Mason, 1967) versus their anxiety levels as measured by the Multiple Affect Adjective Check-List (Bourne, Coli, & Datel, 1966), compared with a similar study of steroid excretion levels of a group of isolated Special Forces troops (Bourne, Rose, & Mason, 1968) versus their anxiety levels measured in a like fashion (Bourne, Coli, & Datel, 1968). (C)

Bourne, P. G. (1970b). Military psychiatry and the Vietnam experience. American Journal of Psychiatry, 127 (supplement), 481-487.

Reviews the record of military psychiatry in the Vietnam theatre for the early years of the war. Bourne attributes the exceptionally low incidence rate for serious psychiatric conditions (averaging 6% of all medical evacuations from Vietnam compared with 23% in World War II) to the limited 1-year tour for soldiers, the availability of communication with home, ample opportunities for compensatory pleasures ("R&R, bars, brothels"), and the sporadic nature of the combat (brief mobile engagements with immediate withdrawal to secure areas). He also credits the sophisticated leadership of the commanders as well as the use of modern combat psychiatry principles by the general medical officers. Despite the relatively low psychiatric rate, Bourne notes that the experience has allowed the correlates of psychiatric attrition in combat to be further defined, and for the first time the physiological responses of those who have successfully adapted to combat have also been studied. From his perspective, combat reactions represent "an adaptive failure, often of a very temporary nature" which, as a "dynamic state . . . is potentially reversible at any point in its development." (C)

Bourne, P. G. (1971). From boot camp to My Lai. In R. A. Falk, G. Kolko, & R. J. Lifton (Eds.), Crimes of war (pp. 462-468). New York: Random House.
    Seeks to explain the recently reported atrocities by American soldiers in Vietnam. In so doing, Bourne draws on his experiences as a research psychiatrist there (Bourne, 1970a) as well as on his study of adolescent identity transformation in basic training (1967). He posits that combat excesses such as those reported in Vietnam are the result of the concatenation of (1) the "militarization process" from basic training (in which the soldier is forced to reject his civilian identity, which emphasized personal initiative, and replace it with an obedient institutional identity of the military organization), and (2) the brutalizing "socialization to war itself and specifically to killing, which occurs once he arrives in Vietnam." He feels that the sum of these sequential experiences leads the soldier to abandon his previous values and beliefs and leaves him particularly vulnerable to unquestioning obedience to the orders of superiors. (C)

Bourne, P. G., Coli, W. M., & Datel, W. E. (1966). Anxiety levels of six helicopter ambulance medics in a combat zone. Psychological Reports, 19, 821-822. (This research is reported in more detail in P. G. Bourne, W. M. Coli, & W. E. Datel (September 1965-August 1966). U.S. Army Medical Research Team Vietnam: Annual progress report (pp. 69-76). Washington, DC: Walter Reed Army Institute of Research.)
    Anxiety scale scores from the serial administrations of the Multiple Affect Adjective Check-List were significantly correlated with type of daily activity (combat mission, work, or day off) for six helicopter ambulance medics over 21 consecutive days through January-February 1966. (C)

Bourne, P. G., Coli, W. M., & Datel, W. E. (1968). Affect levels of ten Special Forces soldiers under threat of attack. Psychological Reports, 22, 363-366.
    Serial weekly administrations of the Multiple Affect Adjective Check-List were obtained from 10 Special Forces soldiers in Vietnam in May 1966 during a phase when enemy attack was felt to be imminent. Results compared anxiety, depression, and hostility

levels. Scores and participant observations corroborated that hostility was the dominant affect expressed. (C)

Bourne, P. G., Rose, R. M., & Mason, J. W. (1967). Urinary 17-OHCS levels: Data on seven helicopter ambulance medics in combat. Archives of General Psychiatry, 17, 104-110. (This research is reported in more detail in P. G. Bourne & W. M. Coli (September 1965-August 1966). U.S. Army Medical Research Team Vietnam: Annual progress report (pp. 59-66). Washington, DC: Walter Reed Army Institute of Research.)

Reports 24-hour levels over a 3-week period that included combat flying, noncombat flying, and nonflying days for each subject. Results showed little variations from overall mean, and levels did not correlate to objective measurement of danger. The chronic mean level for each subject was lower than predicted on the basis of weight alone. Interviews revealed subjects used an extensive range of effective psychological defenses to perceive risk situations as less dangerous, thus enhancing feelings of omnipotence and invulnerability and allowing a high level of adaptability to unit mission. (C)

Bourne, P. G., Rose, R. M., & Mason, J. W. (1968). 17-OHCS levels in combat: Special Forces "A" team under threat of attack. Archives General Psychiatry, 19, 135-140.

Examines the influence of combat exposure on 11 members of a Special Forces team camped in the central highlands of Vietnam in 1966. The authors found no significant daily increases in urinary 17-OHCS levels as a result of exposure to combat stress except for the 2 officers whose levels were higher than those of the 9 enlisted men. This led to the speculation that combat stress can be increased by social influences such as in the leadership expected of officers. (C)

Bunting, J. (1972). The lionheads. New York: George Braziller.

This novel about combat in the delta region of Vietnam concludes with an operation by riverborne troops directed at a suspected location of an enemy battalion. Although by some standards the operation is a success, an enemy ambush of one U.S. battalion leads to intense conflict at various organizational levels about the tactical decisions made during the mission. The narrative vehicle allows Bunting to reflect on the ethics and goals of the combat operations in Vietnam from the multiple perspectives of the participants involved. (C)

Cash, J. A., Albright, J., & Sandstrum, A. W. (1985). Seven firefights in Vietnam. New York: Bantam Books. (Originally published by the Office of the Chief of Military History, U.S. Army, 1970.)

Provides accounts of Army combat activities in Vietnam based on official U.S. Army records: daily journals and files, afteraction reports and interviews conducted soon after the events by historical officers in Vietnam, and interviews and correspondence conducted later by the authors themselves. The seven incidents detailed occurred between November 1965 and May 1968. (C)

Dougan, C., Weiss, S., & the editors of Boston Publishing Co. (1983). The Vietnam experience: Nineteen sixty-eight. Boston: Boston Publishing Co.

Part of a multivolume series providing a historical account of America's war in Southeast Asia and liberally illustrated with photographs and detailed maps, this volume concentrates on the pivotal year in which America's resolve turned against the war effort in Southeast Asia. It describes the full spectrum of the tactical, strategic, social, and political repercussions stemming from the broadscale enemy offensives that were staged to coincide with the 1968 Vietnamese Tet holidays. In the early hours of January 30, the eve of a holiday truce, the enemy launched massive, coordinated assaults on nearly every population center and major military installation in South Vietnam. The unprecedented magnitude and ferocity of the attacks stunned the South Vietnamese and their American allies and, although they ultimately failed in military terms, resulted in an unqualified political success because they served to convince Americans that the war was unwinnable. Included in this volume are descriptions of the fighting in and around Saigon and the U.S. Embassy; the extended house-to-house combat by American forces to recapture the former imperial capital of Hue, a city rich in historical, symbolic, and strategic significance; and the unsuccessful 77-day siege of the 6,000 U.S. Marines dug in at Khe Sanh by 20,000 to 40,000 North Vietnamese regulars. (C)

Doyle, E., Lipsman, S., & the editors of Boston Publishing Co. (1982). The Vietnam experience: America takes over. Boston: Boston Publishing Co.

Part of a multivolume series providing a historical account of America's war in Southeast Asia and liberally illustrated with photographs and detailed maps, this volume concentrates on the political and strategic military decisions behind the "build-up" of men and materiel from March 1965, when the decision was first made to commit American ground troops to Vietnam, through 1967. In the process of assuming the primary fighting responsibilities for the South Vietnamese, the number of U.S. military personnel in South Vietnam rose during that period from 29,000 to over half a million. Although leaving the more detailed depiction of the

American fighting man's experience during this early phase of the
war for its companion volume, A Contagion of War (Maitland,
McInerney, & the editors of Boston Publishing Co., 1983), this
work includes descriptions of combat activities such as the
Marines' first major search-and-destroy mission (Operation Star-
light); the fighting between the 1st Air Cavalry Division and North
Vietnamese regulars in the valley of the Ia Drang; and the activities of the Mobile Riverine Force as it cruised the Mekong Delta
for Viet Cong strongholds. It also includes sections on the development of air war strategy and the beginnings of protest in the
United States and internationally. (C)

Doyle, E., Weiss, S., & the editors of Boston Publishing Co. (1984).
The Vietnam experience: A collision of cultures. Boston: Boston
Publishing Co.
        Part of a multivolume series providing a historical account of
America's war in Southeast Asia and liberally illustrated with
photographs, this volume concentrates on the full scope of consequences of America's 2-decade attempt to promote economic and
social development, political reform, and modernization in South
Vietnam. The work especially considers how the massive U.S. financial, military, technical, and cultural involvement in South
Vietnam's war with the North profoundly altered the land and its
people, society, and culture. Extensively described is the effect of
this cultural clash on the American serviceman assigned there--
both generally, as in his reactions to being assigned to fight in a
culture so different and often paradoxical to his, and more specifically, as in the stress of conducting counterinsurgency warfare
within it. Two chapters of the book--"The American Way of War"
(pp. 122-147) and "An Environment of Atrocity" (pp. 148-169)--
provide detail in regard to the latter. (C)

Fox, R. P. (1974). Narcissistic rage and the problem of combat
aggression. Archives of General Psychiatry, 31, 807-811.
        Based on clinical contact with Marine Vietnam returnees of
1967 through 1969, Fox argues that overly aggressive combat behavior in Vietnam, as well as similar difficulties post-Vietnam,
represent an individual's psychological deviation from the group-
controlled and -sanctioned adaptive aggression, which was the
norm for a member of a functioning combat team. Such overly aggressive soldiers apparently regressed to a state of vengefulness
motivated by a narcissistic rage, which overshadowed group necessity. Fox posits that the intense buddy relationship that typically
develops between combat soldiers constitutes a range of narcissistic mirror transferences that leave each individual soldier, to
varying degrees, especially vulnerable to such reactions should his
"other self" be killed. He notes that, should a soldier avenge this
loss, he typically is devoid of concern for the victim. Moreover,

the act does not provide relief but instead leads to new anxieties related to fear of retaliation and leaves the soldier more narcissistically vulnerable. Fox conjectures that, although this is undoubtedly a common battlefield process, Vietnam participants are more affected because of the political controversy surrounding that conflict. (C)

Gault, W. B. (1971). Some remarks on slaughter. American Journal of Psychiatry, 128, 450-454.
   Based on his clinical contacts with Vietnam returnees as an Army psychiatrist, Gault presents his observations and conclusions about the influences inherent in the military culture as they interacted with certain individual, circumstantial, and mechanical features in Vietnam to contribute to excessive and misdirected violence against civilians by relatively normal young men. He specifically lists "the universalization of the enemy; the 'cartoonization' of the victim; the dilution of responsibility; the pressure to act; the natural dominance of the psychopath; and the ready availability of firepower." Case examples are provided. (C)

Glass, A. J. (1969). Introduction. In P. G. Bourne (Ed.), The psychology and physiology of stress: With reference to special studies of the Viet Nam war (pp. xiii-xxx). New York: Academic Press.
   Provides a brief history of the evolution of modern combat psychiatric doctrine; considers explanations for the exceptionally low rate of psychiatric attrition to date in Vietnam; reflects on the apparent swing within military psychiatry to a predisposition model of understanding combat breakdown; and summarizes the psychophysiological research data in this volume as "confirming clinical impressions that an event is only stressful when it is perceived as such, and that 'ego' defenses, depending on their effectiveness, correspondingly control the endocrinological response to stressful situations." (C)

Glasser, R. J. (1971). 365 Days. New York: Braziller.
   Through a series of fictionalized vignettes, Glasser, an Army doctor assigned to an evacuation hospital in Japan in 1968 and 1969, portrays the medical and psychological struggles of the casualties of the war as well as the reciprocal anguish of those designated to provide their medical support. Noteworthy is a chapter devoted to the provision of combat psychiatric care in Vietnam (pp. 124-149). (C)

Harvey, F. (1976). Air war: Vietnam. New York: Bantam.
   Surveys the various combat and support components that constitute America's air war capability in Vietnam. In recounting

his travels during the buildup period of the war, journalist-pilot Harvey offers descriptions that range from the complex carrier-based launch-and-retrieval operations of supersonic and heavily armed naval jet aircraft, which fly missions over heavily defended targets in North Vietnam; through the varieties of armed and un-armed helicopter missions conducted throughout South Vietnam; to the slow, low-flying, unarmed propeller planes, which fly recon-naissance missions or spray defoliants over South Vietnam. In addition to describing the capabilities and combat requirements of the various aircraft, Harvey reconstructs his facility visits and interviews with crewmembers, and portrays their various hardships, dangers, and adaptations. (C)

Hendin, H., & Haas, A. P. (1984a). Combat adaptations of Vietnam veterans without posttraumatic stress disorders. American Journal of Psychiatry, 141, 956-960.
Discusses the characteristics of 10 veterans who did not develop PTSD following intense combat in Vietnam. The authors found that these veterans differed from others with stress dis-orders in that during combat each had exhibited calmness under pressure, intellectual control, acceptance of fear, and a lack of excessively violent or guilt-arousing behavior. These qualities are believed to be part of an adaptation uniquely suited to preserving emotional stability in an unstructured, unstable context. (S)

Hersh, S. M. (1970, March). My Lai 4: A report on the massacre and its aftermath. Harper's, pp. 53-84. (Excerpted from a book of the same name by Random House, 1970.)
Presents a journalist's reconstruction of the situational preconditions and events surrounding the March 16, 1968, slaughter of hundreds of Vietnamese civilians by members of Charlie Com-pany, 1st Battalion, 20th Infantry Brigade of the Americal Division in Quang Ngai province of South Vietnam. (C)

Hicken, V. (1969). The American fighting man. New York: Macmillan.
Compares impressions and accounts of the dominant individual characteristics of American soldiers, sailors, and Marines across time to fashion a descriptive composite of "American fighting qualities." Hicken's observations from the Vietnam war are limited to the first half, the predominantly optimistic years: "so pro-foundly strong is the sense of duty among American fighting men in Vietnam that even the most hardened and cynical observers come away convinced." (C)

Howard, S. (1976). The Vietnam warrior: His experience, and implications for psychotherapy. American Journal of Psychotherapy, 30,
121-135.
    Describes the circumstantial and psychologic experiences of
the combatants in Vietnam. Howard, who was a Marine battalion
surgeon in Vietnam in 1968, also shows how the combat experiences continue to affect the lives of these men and emphasizes
the critical nature of the therapeutic relationship when treating
Vietnam veterans' adjustment difficulties. Specifically, the therapist needs to become unusually honest in examining the countertransference reactions, such as the emergence of his own violent
impulses, that are aroused in trying to help the veteran manage
his guilt stemming from real events and behaviors. (C)

Just, W. (1978). Ain't nobody been walking this trail but Charlie
Cong. In A. R. Millett (Ed.), A short history of the Vietnam war
(pp. 73-80). Bloomington: Indiana University Press. (Originally
published in the Washington ·Post, 1973, January 28.)
    Provides a journalist's account of the ambush of an elite
Tiger Force unit (42 men) of the 101st Airborne Division by a
company-sized force composed of Viet Cong and North Vietnamese
soldiers. In the firefight, which lasted several hours, 10 Americans
were killed and 20 wounded, including the author. (C)

Kelman, H. C. (1973). Violence without moral restraint: Reflections
on the dehumanization of victims and victimizers. Journal of Social
Issues, 29(4), 25-61.
    Explores the primary causes of "sanctioned massacres," as in
the instances of American soldiers killing Vietnamese civilians.
Kelman argues that such reduced restraint of violent action is
generated by a sanctioning authority, which allows for large
numbers of people to participate without legal or moral doubt or
any feeling of personal decision. Sanction may be granted overtly,
in the form of orders to kill, or covertly, through communication
that such actions will go unpunished. Imposing a justifying mission
that transcends customary moral considerations pertaining to violent behavior may accompany either form of communication. Other
institutional methods of reducing restraints against violence include routinization, which transforms the action into a business-
like, highly mechanical operation (e.g., Lt. Calley: "My Lai was no
big deal"), and dehumanization, which assists the process of victimization by robbing the potential victim first of his identity and
then of his community (e.g., "gook"). Kelman contends that the
latter also dehumanizes the victimizer by robbing him of the
capacity to care for the victim. To prevent future atrocities,
Kelman recommends overcoming the habit of unquestioning obedience by (1) decentralizing power back to smaller groups and individuals, (2) eliminating sanctioned victim categories, and (3)

reexamining our rigid male sex role stereotype, which tends to glorify violence. (M)

Lang, D. (1969). Casualties of War. New York: McGraw-Hill.
Provides a detailed, although disguised, account of events surrounding the kidnapping, rape, and murder of a Vietnamese girl by members of a reconnaissance patrol in November 1966. The story is told through the tortured recollections of one patrol member, Eriksson, who became the chief government witness, as well as through excerpts of official records of the various military tribunals and reviews. In this singular and subjective recounting, Lang seeks to show how often the code of conduct of the combat soldiers in Vietnam deteriorated to that of inflicting indiscriminate and gratuitous violence on the Vietnamese (typically justified by the wish to avenge similar behaviors by the enemy). In Eriksson's words, "From one day to the next, you could see for yourself changes coming over guys on our side--decent fellows, who wouldn't dream of calling an Oriental a 'gook' or a 'slopehead' back home. But they were halfway around the world now, in a strange country, where they couldn't tell who was their friend and who wasn't." (C)

Langner, H. P. (1971). The making of a murderer. American Journal of Psychiatry, 127, 950-953.
Contends that inadequately expressed anger and aggression are largely responsible for atrocities committed by our soldiers in Vietnam. Langner describes the case of a young man in late adolescence who attempted suicide after being involved in an incident like the My Lai massacre. He concludes that immaturity, basic personality problems, and the frustrating circumstances of combat in Vietnam all contribute to willful killing and the subsequent reactions to it. (MA)

Leventman, S., & Camacho, P. (1980). The "gook" syndrome: The Vietnam war as a racial encounter. In C. R. Figley & S. Leventman (Eds.), Strangers at home: Vietnam veterans since the war (pp. 55-70). New York: Praeger.
Examines race or racial consciousness as a variable affecting military as well as social facets of the Vietnam war. Race consciousness, which refers to a frame of reference by which one group ethnically defines another as everlastingly different and inherently inferior, is hypothesized to have shifted through the course of the Vietnam war. During the "good war" (1964-68), South Vietnamese troops and civilians were seen as being good "gooks" (possessing good qualities) whereas the Viet Cong and North Vietnamese were seen as being bad "gooks" (being weak and ineffective). Following the 1968 enemy Tet offensives, when the war

became "bad," the South Vietnamese troops and civilians were seen as inefficient, inferior, and untrustworthy while the Viet Cong and North Vietnamese became viewed as determined, gutsy fighters. All Vietnamese at one point or another were racially dehumanized, and this could and did lead to the killing of innocent civilians such as occurred at My Lai. (S)

Levy, C. J. (1971, October). ARVN as faggots: Inverted warfare in Vietnam. Trans-action, pp. 18-27.

Seeks to explain the U.S. Marine's high regard for the enemy (Viet Cong and North Vietnamese) and his equally low regard for his allies, the soldiers of the Army of the Republic of Vietnam (ARVNs). Levy uses material from his participant-observation with a large group of veterans in a working-class Irish neighborhood in Boston. He argues that this "inverted" phenomenon was the consequence of a mismatch between the Marine's intense "boot camp" indoctrination, with its repeated taunts of the recruits as feminine (designed to foster active aggression), and the guerrilla's "passive" tactics in Vietnam (i.e., the enemy controlled the pace of the fighting through such methods as hit and run, and booby traps). Thus the Marine, trained for aggressive warfare, was relegated to waiting passively for the enemy to stand and fight while his ranks were nonetheless gradually attrited. Levy believes it was in reaction to this dilemma that the Marine commonly scapegoated his allies, finding confirmation in their cultural characteristics and in the social patterns of his own disavowed fears of passivity. (C)

Lipsman, S., Doyle, E., & the editors of Boston Publishing Co. (1983). The Vietnam experience: Fighting for time. Boston: Boston Publishing Co.

Part of a multivolume series providing a historical account of America's war in Southeast Asia and liberally illustrated with photographs and detailed maps, this volume describes events in and surrounding the war (1969 to mid-1970) after the pivotal 1968 Tet enemy offensives and the consequent reversal in American attitudes toward further prosecution of the war. The volume's title refers to the precariousness of President Nixon's controversial plan to shift the fighting role to the South Vietnamese ("Vietnamization") and gingerly withdraw American troops while pursuing peace negotiations with the government of North Vietnam. The mounting impatience and opposition in the United States to the administration and the military negatively affected the morale of the replacement soldiers sent to Vietnam during this phase. This volume especially describes the impact on the soldiers in the field of having to fight battles of disengagement amid pressures from home to oppose their military leaders. (C)

Mahan, J. L., & Clum, G. A. (1971). Longitudinal prediction of
Marine combat effectiveness. Journal of Social Psychology, 83,
45-54.

Presents results of a study of 831 first-enlistment Marines,
most of whom served in Vietnam in 1964 and 1965. Each subject
received a single combat performance rating from his immediate
field supervisor, based on a 7-point scale (7 = highest). The group
achieved a mean rating of 4.99. One third of the sample had ratings of either 6 or 7, and only 3% had ratings of 1 or 2. Of the
original 70 individual predictor variables, 40 were significantly
correlated with combat effectiveness. Preservice background corre-
lations described the effective combat Marine as older, better educated, and Caucasian, with more siblings and fewer arrests. In
recruit processing, he had measurably higher intelligence and aptitude, especially in the areas of general information, mechanical
aptitude, and arithmetic reasoning. In recruit training, he showed
good drill instructor ratings. Similarly, 2nd-year ratings of performance, personal relations, and overall adjustment were predictive of later combat effectiveness. The authors note that these
findings, which indicate that "age, educational achievement, intelligence, obedience, and maturity seem important for military effectiveness," are consistent with findings from World War II and
Korea. (C)

Maitland, T., McInerney, P., & the editors of Boston Publishing
Co. (1983). The Vietnam experience: A contagion of war. Boston:
Boston Publishing Co.

Part of a multivolume series providing a historical account of
America's war in Southeast Asia and liberally illustrated with
photographs and detailed maps, this volume focuses on the early
years of the war (1965-67), describing the tactical situations as
well as the experiences of the soldiers who fought it, often using
their first-person accounts. Particular combat covered includes the
1st Air Cavalry's search-and-destroy Operation Masher/White Wing,
the 9-day siege of Con Thien by the men of the 9th Marines, the
enemy ambush of Task Force Black near Dak To, and activities
such as those of an artillery firebase in Tuy Hoa and a Marine
tactical air strike. This volume also describes the combat roles of
U.S. allies--South Vietnam, Australia, and Korea--as well as the
impact of the war on North Vietnam and its military units. (C)

Marshall, S. L. A. (1966). Battles in the monsoon: Campaigning in
the central highlands, South Vietnam, summer 1966. New York:
William Morrow.

Using the unique group method of battle debriefing he devised in 1943 during World War II, Marshall provides detailed
reconstruction of small unit combat activities by elements of the
1st Cavalry and the 101st Airborne divisions operating in the

central highlands during summer 1966. From his participant-observer vantage point, Marshall especially notes the stress of conducting irregular warfare in a dense jungle during the rainy season alongside an ally from a radically different culture. (M)

Marshall, S. L. A. (1968a). Bird. New York: Cowles Book Co.
    Presents participant-observer and historical data in an account of the events surrounding a 1966 battle in the province of Binh Dinh on the east coast of Vietnam. In this battle, one American rifle company and two undermanned artillery batteries (a total of 150 soldiers) successfully defend their position from an attack by three battalions of North Vietnamese troops. (C)

Marshall, S. L. A. (1968b). West to Cambodia. New York: Cowles Book Co.
    Provides a detailed recounting of small-unit combat activities among selected units of the 1st Cavalry and the 4th and 25th Infantry divisions operating in the rugged west central highlands of Vietnam near the Cambodian border in 1966. (C)

Marshall, S. L. A. (1969). Ambush. New York: Cowles Book Co.
    Presents participant-observer and historical data surrounding a Viet Cong ambush during the 1969 battle of Dau Tieng. (C)

Marshall, S. L. A. (1971). The Fields of Bamboo. New York: Dial Press.
    Provides detailed, day-to-day reconstruction of operations Nathan Hale and Thayer-Irving, two campaigns fought by elements of the 1st Cavalry Division in Vietnam in 1966. (C)

Moskos, C. C., Jr. (1969, November). Why men fight: American combat soldiers in Vietnam. Trans-action, pp. 13-23. (Reprinted in M. Oppenheimer (Ed.), (1971). The American military (pp. 16-36). Chicago: Aldine, Transition Books.)
    From a series of war correspondent experiences in 1965 and 1967, sociologist Moskos seeks to describe and understand the combat attitudes and behaviors of American soldiers in Vietnam. Included are references to the interdependencies between members of the combat group for the functional goal of survival. Typically during his year of intense stress, the soldier is narrowly focused on the safety of himself (especially because of the individualized 1-year rotation system) and his combat comrades, derives a fundamental motivation from his belief in the supremacy of the American way of life (while remaining profoundly apolitical), and feels no communion with peace demonstrators who articulate sentiments

contrary to his values (i.e., "the soldier is against the peace demonstrators rather than for the war"). (C)

Moskos, C. C., Jr. (1975). The American combat soldier in Vietnam. Journal of Social Issues, 31(4), 25-38.
    A sociological assessment of the attitudes and behavior of American combat soldiers over the course of the war in Vietnam suggests that primary-group interpretations of combat behavior must be modified, that combat groups were characterized by instrumental relationships and affected by latent ideological factors, and that the 12-month rotation cycle was the dominating feature of the Vietnam combat experience. Troop demoralization was accentuated by diverse sources of conflict, e.g., rank, generation, drug use, and racial strife. The analysis concludes with a discussion of troop reprisals ("fraggings") against superiors and the paradoxes of the antiwar movement within the military. (A)

Moskos, C. C., Jr. (1978). Military made scapegoat for Vietnam. In A. R. Millett (Ed.), A short history of the Vietnam war (pp. 67-72). Bloomington: Indiana University Press. (Originally published in the Washington Post, 1970, August 30.)
    A military sociologist who became familiar with the nature of combat and the attitudes of U.S. soldiers in Vietnam when he was a war correspondent there in 1965 and 1967, Moskos describes the rigors of the counterinsurgency warfare and the extremely inhospitable setting. He explains the episodes of brutality seen on both sides: "The misery of these conditions is so extreme that conventional moral standards are eclipsed in a way difficult for the noncombatant to appreciate." Moskos expresses his despair that "the justified opposition to the war (is) focused into a concerted attack on the armed forces per se." He notes that the typically working-class soldier in Vietnam reacts to peace demonstrators along class hostility lines and perceives them as "privileged anarchists" who mourn only the ennobled Vietnamese. Finally, he warns of a post-war situation with strained civil-military relations because the still massive military will be socially unrepresentative and "considered a pariah at elite cultural and intellectual levels." (C)

Nolan, K. W. (1983). Battle for Hue: Tet, 1968. Novato, CA: Presidio Press.
    Using interviews of participants, Nolan presents a mosaic description of the combat events and behaviors in the Marines' campaign to defend South Vietnam's ancient imperial capital. (C)

Norden, E. (1971). American atrocities in Vietnam. In R. A. Falk, G. Kolko, & R. J. Lifton (Eds.), Crimes of war (pp. 265-284). New

York: Random House. (Originally published in Liberation, 1966, February.)

Presents an elaborate eyewitness account of the excesses perpetrated by the American forces and their allies engaged in the fighting in Vietnam. Drawing on public sources, Norden argues that existing evidence clearly points toward the United States being guilty of war crimes as defined by the Nuremberg International Military Tribunal following World War II.   (C)

Oberdorfer, D. (1971). Tet! New York: Doubleday.

Reconstructs the crucial consequences, both military and political in the United States, of the broadscale enemy offensives that were staged coincident with the 1968 Vietnamese Tet celebration.   (C)

Pisor, R. (1982). The end of the line: The siege of Khe Sanh. New York: Norton.

Provides a detailed account, drawn from many sources, of the Vietnam war's most extensive and prolonged battle: the 1968 North Vietnam siege of the strategically located U.S. base at Khe Sanh. (C)

Roman, J., Older, H., & Jones, W. L., Jr. (1967). Flight research program: VII. Medical monitoring of Navy carrier pilots in combat. Aerospace Medicine, 38, 133-139.

Describes results of the first automated physiological monitoring of aviators in combat. This feasibility study was conducted aboard a Navy attack carrier off Vietnam in fall 1965 using 5 instrumented A4 jet pilots who each flew two 2-hour dive bombing missions per day. A recorder monitored heart rate and aircraft acceleration during the 18 hours of usable time. The moments of launch, bombing, and recovery were determined by visual examination of the acceleration trace. Results were noteworthy for the low average heart rate (87.6/min.) since these were opposed missions. Rates at launch and recovery were substantially higher than those during bombing, irrespective of acceleration similarities. Moreover, heart rates for the second mission of the day were lower than for the first. The authors consider their findings compatible with previous work that indicates that risk or danger are not major factors in determining heart rate in experienced pilots under moderate levels of nonphysical stress.   (C)

Rose, R. M., Bourne, P. G., Poe, R. O., Mougey, E. H., Collins, D. R., & Mason, J. W. (1969). Androgen responses to stress: II. Excretion of testosterone, epitestosterone, androsterone, and etiocholanolone during basic combat training and under threat of

attack. Psychosomatic Medicine, 31, 415-436. (This study is reviewed in R. M. Rose (1969). Androgen excretion in stress. In
P. G. Bourne (Ed.), The psychology and physiology of stress: With
reference to special studies of the Viet Nam war (pp. 117-147).
New York: Academic Press.)

Reports significant decreases in the excretion of testosterone,
epitestosterone, androsterone, and etiocholanolone in a group of
men undergoing basic combat training (n = 27), and in a group of
isolated Special Forces soldiers anticipating an imminent attack in
Vietnam in 1966 (n = 7). These levels were found to be low compared with those in a group of normal male controls (n = 12) and
with those reported in the literature. The decrease in excretion of
these testosterone metabolites occurred concomitantly with a rise
in 17-OHCS excretion. The authors speculate that there is a decrease in gonadal secretion while there is an increase in adreno-
cortical secretion, possibly reflecting a depression in LH while
ACTH increases, when the individual is under significant stress.
(C)

Rubin, R. T., Gunderson, E. K. E., & Arthur, R. J. (1972). Life
stress and illness patterns in the U.S. Navy: VI. Environmental,
demographic, and prior life change variables in relation to illness
onset in naval aviators during a combat cruise. Psychosomatic
Medicine, 34, 533-547.

Using demographic and symptom surveys, researchers examined patterns of illness occurrence in 121 naval aviators flying
combat missions from an aircraft carrier during a 6-month deployment to Vietnam in 1967. Mean illness rates varied with
operational conditions and personnel characteristics. Most illnesses
were concentrated in a small subgroup of the aviator sample.
Illness rates generally were elevated during the combat periods
and somewhat higher in those aviators who flew combat missions.
Higher illness rates occurred in younger age groups and among
those more preoccupied with their health. The aviator officers
differed from enlisted crew along several demographic dimensions.
The authors also note that the civilian scoring system for the
Schedule of Recent Experience (SRE), measuring recent life
change, was effective in discriminating future illness in this
officer sample. (C)

Schell, J. (1967). The village of Ben Suc. New York: Alfred A.
Knopf.

Presents Schell's account of the U.S. Army's struggle to
pacify a village in the central area of South Vietnam thought to
be loyal to the Viet Cong. Schell shows how the frustration
brought on by an unsuccessful program including provision of food
and medical care led to the total destruction of the village: "We
destroyed it in order to save it." (M)

Schell, J. (1968). The military half: An account of destruction in Quang Ngai and Quang Tin. New York: Alfred A. Knopf. (Reprinted in part (pp. 3-5, 14-16, 130-138, 142-145) as: Over Vietnam: An eyewitness report. In R. A. Falk, G. Kolko, & R. J. Lifton (Eds.), (1971). Crimes of war (pp. 345-356). New York: Random House.)

Provides a detailed firsthand report on the extensive damage caused by American military and government activities in two coastal provinces in South Vietnam in 1967. Paying special attention to the ground and air assaults by a collection of brigade-sized units (Task Force Oregon), the journalist notes the proportion of villages destroyed (70%) and the extent of indigenous population dislocated by the vigorous allied effort to eliminate the enemy's civilian sanctuaries. He concludes that, although functioning under legitimate authority, most of the American military forces are too casual and unspecific in pursuing their destructive goals: "These restraints (rules of engagement) were modified or twisted to such an extent that in practice the restraints evaporated entirely." Further, most civil-affairs officials and programs are inadequate to rectify the disintegration of Vietnamese society caused by the American and South Vietnamese military initiatives in Vietnam: "the overriding, fantastic fact (is) that we are destroying, seemingly by inadvertence, the very country we are supposedly protecting." (C)

Stanton, S. L. (1985). The rise and fall of an American Army: U.S. ground forces in Vietnam, 1965-1973. Novato, CA: Presidio Press.

Provides a detailed account of Army and Marine unit combat operations and their results throughout the war. Stanton, author of the official Vietnam Order of Battle (1981), draws particular attention to the undermining effect on combat effectiveness caused by the 12-month institutionalized inexperience and personnel turbulence in the U.S. forces in Vietnam that resulted from the individual replacement system. (C)

van Creveld, M. (1985). The helicopter and the computer. In M. van Creveld, Command in war (pp. 232-261). Cambridge: Harvard University Press.

Within the book's larger review of the challenges facing military command in war, this chapter focuses on the war in Vietnam as a case study. In particular, van Creveld examines data reflecting on the negative effects that apparently resulted from the explosion in technology of weapon systems, electronic communications and data processing, and helicopter transport. He argues that "the American command system was enormous, (involved) a heavy additional logistic burden and in the end collapsed under its own weight . . . and led to one of the least cost-effective wars known to history." Examining the limitations of the systems analysis approach in Vietnam for providing a rational basis for top-level decision making, he notes that "an approach whose favorite device is number-crunching may be tempted to exclude (all-important) moral and spiritual factors" and lead to an "information pathology" that fails to penetrate into the nature of things. He also highlights how ubiquitous helicopter mobility, undisciplined use of the tactical field radio, unrepresentative media coverage, and excessive and individualized replacement of personnel, especially commanders, all combined with the torrent of information that was collected to overwhelm the traditional triangular chain of command. He concludes that "to study command as it operated in Vietnam is, indeed, almost enough to make one despair of human reason; we have seen the future, and it does not work." (C)

Vietnam Veterans Against the War. (1972). The winter soldier investigation: An inquiry into American war crimes. Boston: Beacon Press.
    Presents without comment the abridged verbatim testimonies of 75 Vietnam veterans and 4 civilians regarding their witness of or participation in "war crimes" and related behaviors during the war. These firsthand accounts are representative of the testimony given at the Winter Soldier Investigation conducted by the Vietnam Veterans Against the War in Detroit in January 1971. Their goal was "to reflect the agonized experience shared by hundreds of thousands of Americans and Indochinese" as well as to "clearly show the consistency in the development and implementation of the (U.S. government's) criminal policy through the succession of administrations and top military commanders." (C)

Yager, J. (1975). Personal violence in infantry combat. Archives of General Psychiatry, 32, 257-261.
    Reports on psychiatric evaluations of 31 combat veterans, referred because of either symptoms or administrative reasons, who were interviewed while still on active duty, 2-18 months after returning from Vietnam. These soldiers served in Vietnam between 1966 and 1971, the majority in 1968 and 1969. They had a history of having at least one self-confirmed kill and were questioned about acts of "personal" violence in Vietnam (acts against persons at close range, which were judged to be unnecessary from a military point of view). Of the sample, 14 reported engaging in such personal violence ("participants"), while 9 others reported witnessing such behavior. All participants in acts of personal violence had volunteered for Vietnam service. Significantly more participants reported killing four or more persons in Vietnam than did nonparticipants, and they more frequently had a history of arrest prior to military service. As a group, participants could be distinguished from nonparticipants by the average number of posi-

tive items present in each of several groupings of precombat variables. Yager theorizes as to how such violence results from an interaction of individual, group, and situational dynamics. (C)

Zeller, A. F. (1973). Psychological aspects of aircrews involved in escape and evasion activities. Aerospace Medicine, 44, 956-960.
    Reviews the experiences of 200 Air Force aircrewmen who were forced to abandon the safety of their aircraft and survive until rescue in the Southeast Asia area. In general, these hazardous experiences were tolerated surprisingly well. With rare exceptions the crewmen retained their objectivity and precision of observation. The psychological difficulties experienced were mostly within normal limits, and even those that were extreme were not ultimately disabling. The study emphasizes the resilience of the healthy, trained individual. (C)

3   Psychiatric Conditions
and Military Psychiatry

Allerton, W. S. (1969). Army psychiatry in Vietnam. In P. G. Bourne (Ed.), The psychology and physiology of stress: With reference to special studies of the Viet Nam war (pp. 1-17). New York: Academic Press.

Reviews the configuration, programs, and results of Army psychiatry preventive and treatment efforts from 1962, when the first Army psychiatrist was assigned, to 1968, when 23 psychiatrists per year were assigned. Psychiatric statistics (hospitalization rate and evacuation rate) through that time were significantly lower than during any previous American armed conflict. Although some situational elements (brief periods of combat exposure, limited obligation through 1-year fixed tour, excellent training) contributed to minimal psychological adjustment problems, Allerton believes that the vigorous preventive psychiatry approach prescribed by Army psychiatry and implemented by the Army as a whole is the factor primarily responsible. (C)

Allerton, W. S., Forrest, D. V., Anderson, J. R., Tischler, G. L., Strange, R. E., Imahara, J. K., Talbott, J. A., Housman, W., & Bourne, P. G. (1970). Psychiatric casualties in Vietnam. Roche Medical Image and Commentary, 12, 27-29. (Reprinted in L. J. Sherman & E. M. Caffey, Jr. (Eds.), (1972). The Vietnam veteran in contemporary society: Collected materials pertaining to the young veterans (sec. III, pp. 54-59). Washington, DC: Veterans Administration.)

Military psychiatrists who served in Vietnam compare their experiences regarding psychological effects of combat there with the effects sustained by American soldiers in previous wars, and they conjecture regarding those differences. (C)

Anderson, J. R. (1968, January/February). Psychiatric support of III and IV Corps tactical zones. U.S. Army Vietnam Medical Bulletin, pp. 37-39.

Anderson, serving as the chief of the southern neuropsychiatric treatment team in Vietnam, contends that the expertise of the division psychiatrists in the southern half of Vietnam in 1967 would be better used if they were instead assigned to his team near Saigon. From his observation that the social engineering-unit consultation model has proved marginally successful, he postulates that, because of both the advent of rapid helicopter evacuation capability and the ability of battalion surgeons to use phenothiazines effectively, division-based psychiatrists are not necessary additions to the division's social worker, psychiatric technician, and battalion surgeon staff. He also notes that because these combat units are staffed with sophisticated professional officers, communications problems are rare and thus the incidence of psychiatric casualties is low. (C)

Anonymous. (1967). Help for war's bloodless casualties. Medical World News, 8, 54-56.
    Presents aspects of the experience of psychiatrist representatives of the Army, Navy, and Air Force serving in Vietnam. As of the first 7 months of 1966, the combined psychiatric casualty rate for U.S. troops was 15.1 per 1,000, far lower than for any previous conflict. Mitigating factors were believed to reside in both structural elements of the combat theatre (low intensity of combat situation, interspersed with respite periods; fixed 1-year tours) and elements of modern combat psychiatric treatment (treatment close to combat situation, expectancy of return for most, and use of phenothiazines). Noncoms and medical corpsmen seemed to be the most stressed and vulnerable groups, but the youth of all combatants and the ambiguities of counterinsurgency warfare were mentioned as compounding stressors. (C)

Arthur, R. J. (1978). Reflections on military psychiatry. American Journal of Psychiatry, 135 (supplement), 2-7.
    Reviews the contributions of psychiatry within the military in this century spanning four major armed conflicts. Arthur indicates that the lessons learned by military psychiatry have important applications for the rest of medicine, especially in the fields of stress, crisis therapy, and community psychiatry. (C)

Baker, S. L. (1980). Traumatic war disorders. In H. I. Kaplan, A. M. Freedman, & B. J. Sadock (Eds.), Comprehensive textbook of psychiatry III (pp. 1829-1842). Baltimore, MD: Williams and Wilkins.
    Presents a historical overview of traumatic war neurosis and outlines diagnosis and treatment procedures. Baker also discusses characteristics of the "post-Vietnam syndrome." (C)

Baker, W. L. (1967, November/December). Division psychiatry in the 9th Infantry Division. U.S. Army Vietnam Medical Bulletin, pp. 5-9.
    Describes a heterogenous group of psychological conditions seen among the combatant personnel of the 9th Infantry Division in Vietnam in early 1967. This report is unique in that the division went to Vietnam together; thus, the epidemiology of psychiatric reactions as force degradation reflects a time-stress continuum (incidence of classic combat fatigue went from rare to

4-12/month after the 5th month in Vietnam) as well as suggesting
an increased incidence of psychiatric reactions consequent to loss
of unit bonding (such as from heavy combat casualties and from
an administrative decision to transfer individuals to new units with
an intent to average individual rotation dates). Baker reports that
true psychosis rates remained about 1% of caseload and did not
apparently relate to external stress. He also discusses pathogenesis
and treatment of the "short-timers syndrome," sleep disorders, and
post-R&R (rest and recuperation) leave depression. (C)

Balser, B. H. (1969). Military psychiatry today. Military Medicine,
134, 1535-1536.
        Briefly summarizes Balser's observations from a visit to Viet-
nam in March 1969 as civilian psychiatrist consultant to the Army.
Balser visited all echelons of Army theatre psychiatric care, beginning with the first echelon medical care of four combat divisions.
There he noted how the basic "catharsis" care of the "emotionally
disturbed and upset soldier" was provided primarily by trained
mental health technicians under supervision of the battalion's
physician (who at times prescribed augmenting neuroleptic or
anxiolytic tranquilizer medications). He describes such care as
extremely effective, returning 80% of affected soldiers back to
their units and to combat duty. Intractable cases passed through
increasingly sophisticated treatment areas so that those who
reached the final theatre treatment center in Japan were, with
few exceptions, seriously ill. (C)

Bender, P. A. (1968, May/June). Social work specialists at the line
battalion. U.S. Army Vietnam Medical Bulletin, pp. 60-69.
        Describes unit (command) consultation and patient counseling
in the 11th Light Infantry Brigade (1967-68) from the enlisted
social work technician's point of view, both in a garrison setting
before departure and after arrival in Vietnam. The caseload in
Vietnam was divided among passive-aggressive (disciplinary) problems, anxious patients with secondary somatic symptomatology,
cases with functional somatic symptoms as primary symptoms, and
combat exhaustion cases. Bender highlights the special stresses and
encumbrances in providing clinical services in the combat setting,
and he emphasizes the challenge of countering the regressive lean-
ings in all categories of patients seen under those circumstances.
Clinical techniques and principles included reassurance (of normalcy), empathy, explanation (of mental mechanisms), reflection
(on how the patient may be contributing to his own problems by
defensive maneuvers such as isolation from peers), support for
adaptive behaviors (such as encouraging his return to his unit and
peer-support group), and, generally, the classic combat psychiatric
principle of expectancy (that the soldier will eventually overcome
his symptoms and return to duty). (C)

Bersoff, D. N. (1970). Rorschach correlates of traumatic neurosis of war. Journal of Projective Techniques and Personality Assessment, 34, 194-200.

Fifteen hundred soldiers with psychiatric diagnoses were evacuated to USAF Hospital, Clark AFB, Republic of the Philippines, over a 2-year period early in the Vietnam war. Only 2 of these cases produced Rorschach results unambiguously consistent with a diagnosis of traumatic neurosis (defined as a syndrome originating in an adequately functioning person and contracted acutely while the soldier was engaged in combat and in realistic danger of losing his life). This article presents Rorschach data on these 2 cases. Bersoff concludes that traumatic neuroses produce a different kind of anxiety than is usually associated with general anxiety neuroses. (C)

Bey, D. R. (1970). Division psychiatry in Viet Nam. American Journal of Psychiatry, 127, 228-232.

Describes primary, secondary, and tertiary preventive psychiatry within the combat division, based on Bey's experiences as the division psychiatrist for the 1st Infantry Division in 1968. Bey suggests that a knowledge of individual, group, hospital, community, and organizational dynamics may be necessary to effect interventions at these levels. Regarding prevention activities, he highlights special combat group stress points, such as a change in command or the infusion of new combat unit members, as well as factors adding to the stress of the individual soldier, such as his coming near the end of his tour (a "short-timer"), having less education, being foreign born, or having a language handicap. Considerations of treatment strategies include a description of the use of phenothiazines both for nonpsychotic combat exhaustion and for sleep therapy ("dauerschlaft") for more disorganized combat psychiatric casualties. Case examples are provided. (C)

Bey, D. R., & Smith, W. E. (1970). Mental health technicians in Vietnam. Bulletin of the Menninger Clinic, 34, 363-371.

Describes primary, secondary, and tertiary psychiatric activities with the 17,000 soldiers of the 1st Infantry Division conducted by the first author, the division psychiatrist, and his staff of one social work officer and eight 91G social work/ psychology-enlisted technicians (1969-70). The report focuses on the background, training, deployment, utilization, and supervision of these paraprofessionals who play a critical role dispersed among the organizationally, and often geographically, separate units of the division. The authors note how the technicians' medical/ psychiatric responsibilities and activities often exceed those performed in stateside settings because of the extremes of the combat situation. They provide case examples illustrating both case-oriented clinical approaches and organization-oriented consultative ones. (C)

Bey, D. R., & Smith, W. E. (1971). Organizational consultation in a combat unit. American Journal of Psychiatry, 128, 401-406.

Describes a method of unit consultation employing paramedical participant-observers that was developed and used successfully in a combat division in Vietnam. Consultation made the unit's problems legitimate ones for discussion, provided an opportunity to express frustrations, opened up communication between levels of command, and brought unit members together. The authors suggest that this approach may have wider application in both military and civilian community psychiatry. (MA)

Bloch, H. S. (1969). Army clinical psychiatry in the combat zone-- 1967-1968. American Journal of Psychiatry, 126, 289-298.

Outlines the present approach to treating U.S. Army psychiatric casualties in Vietnam, based on the principles of immediacy, proximity, and expectancy. Bloch, who served in Vietnam, also describes the Army psychiatric facilities, the principal resources being the two neuropsychiatric specialty teams. He cites statistics to show the effectiveness of the current treatment approach in returning men to active duty, and he includes some typical case examples. (MA)

Bloch, H. S. (1970a). Brief sleep treatment with chlorpromazine. Comprehensive Psychiatry, 11, 346-355.

Describes a technique using brief periods of chlorpromazine-induced narcosis (24-48 hours of sleep treatment) for severely disorganized and uncontrollable patients in an open, crisis-oriented milieu ward for combat troops in Vietnam. The apparent advantages from this uncontrolled experiment include that such treatment seems to be efficient and effective for a cross-section of severely disordered soldiers. It is most useful for acute and transient psychotic stress states and seems to have diagnostic value in differentiating (and treating) such conditions from the less responsive schizophrenias. Case examples are provided. (C)

Boman, B. (1982). The Vietnam veteran ten years on. Australian and New Zealand Journal of Psychiatry, 16, 107-127.

This comprehensive and elaborately referenced review synthesizes the relevant literature that highlights the particular nature of combat and environmental stress in Vietnam and its acute and long-term effects on the soldier. Expressing regret and wonder that so little study has been accomplished regarding the Australian veteran, Boman thus seeks to draw parallels from what has been published from among American forces. He reviews the psychiatric policies and practices of American military psychiatry and its results in Vietnam, and he makes comparisons with trends extracted from the psychiatric experience among Australian forces. He is frankly critical of the tendency in American military psychiatry to diagnose only limited categories of neurotic symptoms as psychiatric casualties and to classify behavioral and characterological manifestations as administrative problems. He posits that the ostensibly lower psychiatric casualty rate in Vietnam masked a much greater degree of psychiatric disability: "pushing the decompensated soldier back into battle without adequate assessment and treatment may not be beneficial either to him or to his fellows." Finally, he critically examines the published data that bear on the "melancholy legacy" of the veterans of the war.   (C)

Bostrom, J. A. (1967, July/August). Management of combat reactions. U.S. Army Vietnam Medical Bulletin, pp. 6-8.
    Describes three degrees of psychiatric reaction to combat (or anticipation of combat) seen in the 1st Cavalry Division in Vietnam in 1967: the "normal combat syndrome" with anxiety and its physiological concomitants, which nonetheless do not impair effectiveness; the "pre-combat syndrome," in which these symptoms do degrade effectiveness; and "combat exhaustion," which is a state of psychosis or near psychosis precipitated in a relatively stable individual by the stress of combat. Treatment derives from the traditional principles of combat psychiatry (decentralization, expectancy, and simple treatment). Bostrom recommends using a blend of limited indulgence (rest, empathy, food) combined with an emphatic expectation of combat performance, in addition to--in the more severe cases--sufficient chlorpromazine to induce arousable sleep for about 24 hours.   (C)

Bostrom, J. A. (1968, January/February). Psychiatric consultation in the First Cav. U.S. Army Vietnam Medical Bulletin, pp. 24-25.
    Through use of two hypothetical cases (one a soldier with psychosomatic back pain, and the other a "troublemaker"), Bostrom describes his recommended procedures for developing unit (command) consultation within the 1st Air Cavalry Division in Vietnam in 1967.   (C)

Bourne, P. G. (1969, May 15). Psychiatric casualties in Vietnam, lowest ever for combat zone troops (Interview). U.S. Medicine, pp. 10-11.
    Reviews findings related to the unprecedented low psychiatric casualty rate noted to date in Vietnam (12/1,000 troops/year). Bourne perceives that the hopefulness inherent in the fixed 1-year Vietnam tour and modern principles of preventive psychiatry adapted to the combat theatre have achieved this result. With only 57% of psychiatric admissions for combat breakdown and 40% for character disorders, clinical attention has been redirected to individual personality vulnerability. Predispositions in troops result in

findings such as "pseudocombat fatigue," as well as other non-combat categories of destabilization and dysfunction that are triggered by the stresses peculiar to each phase of the 1-year tour in Vietnam. Studies of urinary 17-OHCS levels have suggested that the average soldier is capable of maintaining psychological and physiological homeostasis in high-risk combat situations through a variety of psychological defenses serving to ignore the danger. Bourne adds, however, that the duration of the stress takes a toll, with psychological vulnerability increasing sharply after 80-100 days of exposure. (C)

Bourne, P. G., & San, N. D. (1967). A comparative of neuropsychiatric casualties in the U.S. Army and the Army of the Republic of Vietnam. Military Medicine, 132, 904-909. (This research is reported in more detail in P. G. Bourne, W. M. Coli, & N. D. San (September 1965-August 1966). U.S. Army Medical Research Team Vietnam: Annual progress report (pp. 51-58). Washington, DC: Walter Reed Army Institute of Research.)

Compares American and South Vietnamese theatre military neuropsychiatric incidence rates over a 6-month period in early 1966. Speculations on the key differences (psychoses = 20.9% versus 50.0%; character and behavior disorders = 38.5% versus 13.8%, respectively) include how social/cultural and policy features of each army may influence clinical presentations, especially regarding the "manipulative" goals of the various patient groups. (C)

Boydstun, J. A., & Perry, C. J. G. (1980). Military psychiatry. In H. I. Kaplan, A. M. Freedman, & B. J. Sadock (Eds.), Comprehensive textbook of psychiatry III (pp. 2888-2901). Baltimore, MD: Williams and Wilkins.

Reviews the fundamental elements of psychiatric care for military service members, their families, and especially those men and women who are required to function in high-stress circumstances. The authors highlight the historical forerunners of the contemporary military psychiatric approach and emphasize the similarities and differences between military psychiatry and civilian types of psychiatric practice. Throughout this review, they refer to the salient observations and research findings from the war in Vietnam and the Vietnam era. (C)

Braceland, F. J. (1967). Psychiatry, hospital ships, and Viet Nam (Editorial). American Journal of Psychiatry, 124, 377-379.

Comments on a paper by Strange and Arthur in the same issue. Besides underscoring how their report from Vietnam confirms hard-fought lessons of combat psychiatry from prior wars, Braceland also notes the novel and extensive use of phenothiazines in Vietnam as effective in treating acute combat syndromes: "(such conditions,) including agitated depressions, panic, and hysterical episodes were ameliorated within 48 hours by large doses of chlor-promazine coupled with nighttime sedation. Patients otherwise un-reachable were thus rendered amenable to a psychotherapeutic approach." (C)

Camp, N. M., & Carney, C. M. (1987a). U.S. Army psychiatry in Vietnam: Preliminary findings of a survey: I. Background and method. Bulletin of the Menninger Clinic, 51, 6-18.
    This two-part report provides preliminary results of a recent study of the U.S. Army's psychiatric activities in Vietnam. The ab-sence of detailed clinical records required contacting psychiatrists to obtain their perspectives on their Vietnam tours. An estimated 135 U.S. Army psychiatrists served in Vietnam between 1962 and 1973. The responses of 74% of the 115 locatable psychiatrists sug-gest patterns of their preparation, training, deployment, and clini-cal activities in Vietnam. This report also sets the emergent fea-tures of these psychiatrists within the context of the modern history of military psychiatry, and it considers preliminary impli-cations of these findings for military and general psychiatry. (C)

Camp, N. M., & Carney, C. M. (1987b). U.S. Army psychiatry in Vietnam: Preliminary findings of a survey: II. Results and dis-cussion. Bulletin of the Menninger Clinic, 51, 19-37. (A condensed version of Camp & Carney (1987a, 1987b) was published as: Viet-nam "dilemma" for psychiatrists. U.S. Medicine, 1987, August, pp. 41-43.)
    The second part of this report considers the findings and implications deriving from responses to a questionnaire completed by psychiatrists who served with the U.S. Army in Vietnam during the Vietnam war. The background, impetus, and methods for this study were considered in the first part of this report. (C)

Carden, N. L., & Schramel, D. J. (1966). Observations of conversion reactions in troops involved in the Vietnam conflict. American Journal of Psychiatry, 123, 21-31.
    Presents findings from 12 cases of classical conversion reac-tion sent to psychiatric evacuation hospitals in the Philippines in 1964-65. The most conspicuous psychologic features were secondary gain serving to decrease responsibility and death fears, conflicts in aggressive and erotic feelings, and a past identification with dis-ease or trauma to the site of somatization. No specific psycho-dynamic was felt to be common in these reactions. Emotional im-maturity and dependency were consistent premorbid findings, but parental characteristics and demographic variables were not. Pathogenesis revealed that symptoms followed closely the alleged

environmental stress--referred to as the face-saving event--but may have followed the actual underlying stress by a prolonged period. The authors discuss theories regarding the nature of conversion reactions, especially under the unique circumstances of war in Vietnam. Predictions of high vulnerability to recurrence and consequent unreliability lead them to recommend that such individuals not be returned to combat duty. Case histories are included. (C)

Clum, G. A., & Hoiberg, A. (1971). Diagnoses as moderators of the relationship between biographical variables and psychiatric decision in a combat zone. Journal of Consulting and Clinical Psychology, 37, 209-214.
     Presents a study of patterns of diagnosis and disposition among all Marine and Navy enlisted personnel admitted to two psychiatric facilities in Vietnam over a 1-year period ($\underline{N}$ = 1,005). Information was collected from patients regarding demographics and family and military history, as well as current attitudes toward the military (a total of 83 independent variables). Among the findings, 39% of all psychiatric patients from one hospital and 45% from the other were returned to full duty. The diagnostic groups of schizophrenia and depression were found to have a very high probability of evacuation from the combat zone. Using a multiple regression formula, a significant but low correlation was found between biographic variables and the likelihood of a soldier being returned to combat duty if diagnosis was not considered. However, when the interaction of diagnosis and biographic variables was tested, the prediction of return to combat duty using biographical variables was greatly increased for those patients receiving a character disorder or a neurotic diagnosis. There was little similarity between these two diagnostic groups as far as which biographical variables accounted for the prediction. (C)

Colbach, E. M., & Parrish, M. D. (1970). Army mental health activities in Vietnam: 1965-1970. Bulletin of the Menninger Clinic, 34, 333-342.
     Provides an overview of Army mental health activities in Vietnam from the military escalation of 1965 through mid-1970. Apparently due to several circumstantial factors (sporadic fighting, air and naval superiority, excellent supplies and communications) that led to high morale, as well as a network of mental health personnel trained to cultivate an attitude of high expectancy of return to duty and to use such psychoactive medications as phenothiazines effectively, psychiatric casualty rates remained exceptionally low up to the end of 1969. However, the authors express concern for the rise in the rate through June 1970 (37/1,000 troops/year); note an increase in racial tension and general decrement in feeling of purpose for the troops; and speculate that

the intent to disengage in Vietnam may result in a new and more challenging psychiatric phase. (C)

Conte, L. R. (1972). A neuropsychiatry team in Vietnam 1966-1967: An overview. In R. S. Parker (Ed.), The emotional stress of war, violence and peace (pp. 163-168). Pittsburgh, PA: Stanwix House.
     Describes the inception, structure, and function of one of the U.S. Army's two neuropsychiatry specialty teams. This unit, located on the central coast of South Vietnam, was comprised of the 8 officers (professionals) and 11 enlisted corpsmen (paraprofessionals) who traveled together to the combat zone aboard a troop ship. Once in place they provided inpatient and outpatient psychiatric care as well as related mental health consultation in performance of their mission "to evaluate, treat, return to duty and/or evacuate within thirty days." Conte notes that, consistent with other published reports from this early period of the war, the psychiatric casualty rate seen by his unit was low (300 inpatients over a 10-month period). Further, the kinds of problems presented did not appear to be different from those seen at stateside Army posts. (C)

Datel, W. E., & Johnson, A. W., Jr. (1981). Psychotropic prescription medication in Vietnam. Alexandria, VA: Defense Technical Information Center (Document AD No. A 097-610).
     Presents results of a survey of the psychotropic prescription patterns of 116 Army psychiatrists and general medical officers (GMOs) serving in Vietnam in 1967. Findings include that the annual prescription rate was 7.4% per year; that the most frequently treated condition was "anxiety" (treated with anxiolytic medications); that "combat fatigue," although undefined, was primarily treated with neuroleptic medication; and that 85% of the neuroleptic prescriptions written by GMOs were for 1 day only while 36% of those written by psychiatrists were on a "take as needed" basis. The investigators conclude, "across condition and across drug, then, the prescribing physicians were of the opinion that psychotropic drug treatment was by and large quite influential in reducing the problems presented." (C)

Davis, D. M. (1976, July/August). Special problems of psychiatric patients evacuated from Vietnam to a back up hospital. U.S. Army Vietnam Medical Bulletin, pp. 17-20.
     Enumerates patients evacuated to a hospital in Japan from Vietnam in 1966-67 as to final diagnosis following treatment there. Of 155 cases over a 15-month period, 66 received a schizophrenic diagnosis (73% of whom displayed prominent paranoid symptomatology). Only 5 of these individuals with schizophrenic reactions had a previous history of psychiatric hospitalizations, and the

onset of disabling symptomatology was not statistically related to any phase of the 1-year Vietnam tour. The average hospitalization was 46 days for the recovering 45% of schizophrenic patients, who were then returned to duty elsewhere in Asia. Davis speculates about a possible problem of excessive drowsiness in some individuals treated with phenothiazines in Vietnam who are also taking the weekly malaria prophylactic combination of chloroquine (500 mg) and primaquine (79 mg). (C)

Edmendson, S. W., & Platner, D. J. (1968, July/August). Psychiatric referrals from Khe Sanh during siege. U.S. Army Vietnam Medical Bulletin, pp. 25-30.
Reviews the psychiatric casualty rates for the 5,500 Marine defenders of the Marine base at Khe Sanh, Vietnam, during the 76-day siege in early 1968. Diagnoses rendered at either the 3rd Medical Battalion in Phu Bai or the hospital ship USS Repose were summed and compared with incidence figures from the same months the preceding year. The authors note that the incidence of psychiatric referrals did not increase significantly, and they conjecture that high moral and confidence may have protected these troops during this period of prolonged stress. (C)

Evans, O. N. (1968, May/June). Army aviation psychiatry in Vietnam. U.S. Army Vietnam Medical Bulletin, pp. 54-58.
Describes the qualifications, training, and demands on aviators sent to Vietnam based on Evans's service as a flight surgeon and psychiatrist there in 1967-68. He further argues for the regular posting to Vietnam of two psychiatrists with additional training as flight surgeons to provide specialized care to this highly stressed and vital element of the war effort. (C)

Fisher, H. W. (1972). Vietnam psychiatry: Portrait of anarchy. Minnesota Medicine, 55, 1165-1167.
Reviews background and service histories and diagnoses for 1,000 consecutive Marine and Navy psychiatric referrals to the division psychiatrist in the 1st Marine Division, Da Nang, Vietnam, between March 1970 and February 1971. Among the cases, 31 were designated as psychotic, 9 as neurotic, and 960 as personality disorders, usually antisocial. Drug abuse was a feature of the clinical presentation in 590 cases, and most of the psychotic episodes were felt to be drug related. Fisher posits that most referrals to military psychiatrists in the combat zone now represent antisocial characters in conflict with authority because of their attempts to avoid military and social obligations or punishment. He is critical of the military leadership for encouraging indiscipline by the tacit approval that seems to result from vacillations in enforcing regulations. Further, he believes these problems

are compounded by military leaders' expectation that psychiatry provide medevacuation out of Vietnam or recommend administrative separation from the service in lieu of punishment, thus serving as an accomplice in the deviant soldier's rebellion.   (C)

Gabriel, R. A. (1987). No more heroes: Madness and psychiatry in war. New York: Hill and Wang.
 Reviews the extensive proportions and variegated clinical presentations of soldiers who have suffered psychological trauma and breakdown in wars through the ages; the history of uncertainty within military psychiatry since the turn of the century as it has sought to manage or anticipate the epidemics of psychiatric attrition among battlefield soldiers; and the repeated tendency for combat leaders to overlook planning for these bloodless casualties despite the evidence from history. Gabriel refers periodically to the American military experience in Vietnam, and one chapter, "War and the Limits of Human Endurance" (pp. 70-96), compares the epidemiology of combat psychiatric conditions, "secondary" psychiatric symptoms such as behavioral disorders, and postcombat conditions such as PTSD among American troops deployed in wars of this century. In Gabriel's estimation, that the "Vietnam War was, by normal standards of combat intensity, not much of a war" is consistent with the observation that, with the exception of Vietnam (if one excludes the number of Vietnam veterans with PTSD), in every other war of this century the risks of becoming a combat stress psychiatric casualty have been greater than the chances of being killed by enemy fire.   (C)

Gordon, E. L. (1968, March/April). Division psychiatry: Documents of a tour. U.S. Army Vietnam Medical Bulletin, pp. 62-69.
 Describes, by way of Gordon's periodic official reports to the senior theatre Army psychiatrist, the evolution of problems in providing comprehensive mental hygiene services within the 1st Infantry Division in Vietnam in 1967-68.   (C)

Hayes, F. W. (1969). Military aeromedical evacuation and psychiatric patients during the Viet Nam war. American Journal of Psychiatry, 126, 658-666.
 Reports on a statistical study of all patients in the aeromedical system who entered Travis Air Force Base, CA, during a 6-month period (January-June 1967) that enumerates the percentage of patients with psychoses, neuroses, and character disorders. Hayes uses studies during World War II and the Korean war to assess the effectiveness of present-day preventive psychiatric practices in the military. He also discusses the effect of the Vietnam war on psychiatric patients at David Grant U.S.A.F. hospital.   (MA)

Hayes, F. W. (1970). Psychiatric aeromedical evacuation patients during the Tet and Tet II offensives, 1968. American Journal of Psychiatry, 127, 503-508.

Presents a statistical study of all patients in the Pacific aeromedical system who entered Travis Air Force Base, CA, between January 1 and June 30, 1968. Hayes compares these figures with those for the same period in 1967 to determine the effect of the 1968 Tet offensives. The considerable decrease in the percentage of psychiatric patients evacuated indicates that the principles of military psychiatry are being carried out effectively, particularly in the Army. (A)

Huffman, R. E. (1970). Which soldiers break down: A survey of 610 psychiatric patients in Vietnam. Bulletin of the Menninger Clinic, 34, 343-351.

Presents Huffman's professional and clinical experiences while he served as an Army psychiatrist in Vietnam in 1965-66. Huffman indicates he had little formal training in psychiatry before deployment and was dismayed to discover that for several months he was the only Army psychiatrist caring for Army troops in Vietnam. He describes the subsequent buildup of troops as well as of military psychiatrists and is frankly critical that Army-trained psychiatrists were not represented in greater numbers. Huffman enumerates various features noted among those in his American Army caseload for whom he could obtain sufficient records for review (N = 573): 11% were draftees; 97% were enlisted; 26% were referred by their officers prior to administrative or disciplinary processing; 28% had histories of previous legal difficulty; 15.6% had previous psychiatric consultation; 8% were diagnosed as having "combat fatigue"; 6.1% were associated with suicide attempts or gestures; 18.5% were diagnosed as having serious alcohol dependence; and less than 1% were seen for drug-induced reactions. Because 62% of his cases had not completed high school, Huffman concludes that this was a significant risk factor. (C)

Ingraham, L. H., & Manning, F. (1986). American military psychiatry. In R. A. Gabriel (Ed.), Military psychiatry: A comparative perspective. Westport, CT: Greenwood Press.

Traces the evolution of modern field psychiatric treatment principles and practices from the Civil War through the Vietnam conflict. In their analysis of data from the Vietnam period, the authors argue that the low published psychiatric casualty rate for the first half of the war was misleading and that the true (and rapidly rising) magnitude of psychosocial attrition was only belatedly recognized as the war extended: "'Search and avoid' missions were the responses of combat soldiers determined not to be the last to die in Vietnam, and resentful compliance with the letter of the law won bored, lonely, anxious, and angry support soldiers an uneasy stalemate with their leaders." They also review the various observations regarding the characteristics of the war, its participants, and public attitudes; and they speculate as to what these characteristics contributed to the deteriorating military in Vietnam as well as to the high psychosocial disability rate among its veterans. (C)

Johnson, A. W., Jr. (1967, January/February). Psychiatric treatment in the combat situation. U.S. Army Vietnam Medical Bulletin, pp. 38-45.

Having served in Vietnam as the senior Army psychiatrist in 1966-67, Johnson highlights the relatively low number of psychiatric casualties as a direct result of combat stress and summarizes the successes of military psychiatry in the Vietnam war during the buildup period. He describes the types of normal and abnormal reactions to combat, factors that erode group cohesion in battle, and the field principles of prevention and treatment of psychiatric disability as applied in Vietnam: decentralization of initial treatment; brief and simple treatment approaches; attitude of expectancy of recovery and return to duty; and centralization of triage for evacuation. He also reviews the evolution of these fundamentals, giving references from World War II and the Korean war to substantiate their effectiveness, both in the acute battle-field situation and regarding morbidity. (C)

Johnson, A. W., Jr. (1969a). Combat psychiatry: Part 1. A historical review. U.S. Army Europe Medical Bulletin, 26, 305-308.

Augments previously published material (Johnson, 1967, January/February). Johnson notes that for the Army, the incidence of psychiatric disorders in Vietnam in 1966-67 has represented 1%-2% of all admissions, and psychiatric out-of-theatre evacuations have been only 3/1,000 per year. These psychiatric rates are uncharacteristically low for a theatre of combat operations and have been echoed in similarly low figures for "deviant behaviors" (e.g., stockade confinement rates, disciplinary action rates, etc.). (C)

Johnson, A. W., Jr. (1969b). Combat psychiatry: Part 2. The U.S. Army in Vietnam. U.S. Army Europe Medical Bulletin, 26, 335-339. (Reprinted as: Psychiatry stresses activity in Vietnam. U.S. Medicine, 1970, June 1, pp. 8-13.)

Reviews Army policies and structures that determined deployment of psychiatric personnel during the buildup phase of the war in Vietnam. Johnson indicates that combat unit medical and psychiatric personnel linked with hospital-based personnel through evacuation networks and policies effectively implemented the combat psychiatry field treatment principles (outlined in Part 1 of this article) to minimize psychiatric attrition among deployed troops as well as symptom persistence in affected soldiers. Moreover, he underscores how effective leadership and training, limited tours, and conditions of combat in Vietnam have combined to raise troop morale and lower the incidence of emotional and psychosocial disturbance. (C)

Johnson, A. W., Jr., Bowman, J. A., Byrdy, H. S., & Blank, A. S., Jr. (1968). Panel discussion: Army psychiatry in Vietnam. In F. D. Jones (Ed.), Proceedings: Social and preventive psychiatry course, 1967 (pp. 41-76). Washington, DC: Government Printing Office. (See also Alexandria, VA: Defense Documentation Center (Document AD No. A 950-058), 1980.)
      Presents an overview of elements of Army medical and espe-cially psychiatric resource deployment during the buildup phase in Vietnam. Panel psychiatrists represent four separate echelons of treatment capability and thus reflect differently on types of casualties and patterns of treatment or evacuation as well as on speculations regarding prevalence and pathogenesis. (C)

Jones, F. D. (1967). Experiences of a division psychiatrist in Vietnam. Military Medicine, 132, 1003-1008.
      Recounts Jones's tour of duty with the 25th Infantry Division both before and after the division's deployment to South Vietnam in December 1965. Jones illustrates his predeployment mental health consultation role in assisting unit commanders to prepare their troops for combat, and he describes the subsequent evolution of emotional and behavioral problems among the deployed troops as they adjust to the combat environment. The psychiatric prob-lems encountered in Vietnam during his 7 months with the division were infrequent and more consistent with those seen in support units or garrisoned troops (e.g., psychiatric processing for disci-plinary action and alcohol-related problems, especially involving weapons). Although a few combat-related problems were seen, he failed to see a single case of "combat fatigue." However, he and his staff were frequently required to manage variations of "combat avoidance" symptoms (e.g., "helmet headaches," sleepwalking, and noise intolerance). Jones includes speculation as to why the psy-chiatric casualty rate in the Vietnam theatre remained especially low through 1965 and 1966. (C)

Jones, F. D., & Johnson, A. W., Jr. (1975). Medical and psychiatric treatment policy and practice in Vietnam. Journal of Social Issues, 31(4), 49-65.
      Initially contributing to the lowest incidence ever of United States combat psychiatric casualties (12/1000 per year), the pre-ventive and treatment policies of immediacy, expectancy, simplic-

ity, and centrality were established early in the Vietnam conflict. These policies are described, as well as a chronological view of the types of psychiatric problems encountered and a brief consideration of the "disorders of loneliness" (alcohol, drug abuse, venereal diseases). Combat versus support troop casualties are contrasted, especially in terms of the changing role of United States troops with the Vietnamization policy and withdrawal. The drug abuse epidemic revealed the inadequacy of traditional approaches and the need for developing new approaches, especially primary preventive methods.   (A)

Kenny, W. F. (1967, January/February). Psychiatric disorders among support personnel. U.S. Army Vietnam Medical Bulletin, pp. 34-37.
Enumerates the types of outpatients who sought psychiatric help or were referred to the 17th Field Hospital in Saigon in 1966. These were noncombatant American servicemen or civilians whose difficulties centered around heightened dependency needs. They most often presented as acute transient anxiety states, but many were diagnosed as depressions, chronic anxiety states, alcoholism, emotionally unstable personalities, and psychopathic personalities. Kenny discusses several psychotherapeutic strategies. He also presents results of his informal study of soldiers seeking official permission to marry Vietnamese women, a request he often found symptomatic of immature and conflicted character formation.   (C)

Kilpatrick, T. D., & Grater, H. A. (1971). Field report on Marine psychiatric casualties in Vietnam. Military Medicine, 136, 801-809.
Reports diagnostic, dispositional, and selective demographic data regarding 823 psychiatric admissions to the medical battalion of the 3rd Marine Division during 9 months of 1967. Overall, approximately two thirds of the casualties came from field units actively engaged in combat activities. It was the authors' impression that "the definite threat of combat seems to have been the basic precipitating factor for most of the psychiatric casualties." Predisposition, environmental stressors, and circumstances limiting therapeutic outcome (especially the high out-of-country evacuation rate of 42%) are discussed.   (C)

Kormos, H. R. (1978). The nature of combat stress. In C. R. Figley (Ed.), Stress disorders among Vietnam veterans: Theory, research and treatment (pp. 3-22). New York: Brunner/Mazel.
Reviews the literature regarding psychiatric observation, diagnosis, and treatment of combat-related casualties in American military involvements from World War I through the Vietnam war. Kormos argues that "refusal to fight" is the central operating dynamic explaining combat-related psychiatric conditions, which range from drug abuse to psychotic disorganization and assassina-

tion of superiors. He feels all such polymorphous symptoms or behaviors should be labeled acute combat reaction because they specifically meet the test of having the individual's combat reference
group (combat "buddies") accept his condition as legitimately representing an inability rather than an unwillingness to function. He
further speculates that military psychiatry's doctrine, which
emphasizes rapid return to duty and command's failure to plan for
the generation of combat casualties, reflects an assumption that
refusal to fight is at the root of the combat reaction. (C)

Menard, D. L. (1968, March/April). The social work specialist in a
combat division. U.S. Army Vietnam Medical Bulletin, pp. 48-57.
     Describes organization and process of front-line consultation
and casework treatment by enlisted social work medics (under
supervision of the division psychiatrist) with the 1st Infantry
Division in Vietnam in 1967. Menard presents individual as well as
unit (command) consultation case material. (C)

Morris, L. E. (1970). "Over the hump" in Vietnam: Adjustment patterns in a time-limited stress situation. Bulletin of the Menninger
Clinic, 34, 352-362.
     Reports a study of 225 noncombatant Air Force psychiatry
patients hospitalized at Cam Ranh Bay in 1966, with particular
attention paid to correlating the kinds of adjustment reactions
they manifested with phase-specific stresses inherent in the standard 1-year Vietnam tour. Study findings suggest that the psychiatric disabilities represented by these patients tend to array in a
diphasic pattern. Those with initial adjustment reactions (29%)
were hospitalized within the first 6 weeks of their tour; these
reactions were typically anxiety-based and occurred in those with
deeply entrenched dependent character styles who were overwhelmed by the separation from their families. Second-phase reactions (39%) were patients hospitalized between their 4th and 6th
months who exhibited various combinations of depression and irritability. These were otherwise capable individuals with rigid and
overly conscientious character styles, who became overwhelmed
due to depleted narcissistic supplies as a delayed reaction to
family absence and circumstantial stresses. Morris considers
treatment strategies and provides case examples. (C)

Motis, G. (1967, September/October). Freud in the boonies: A preliminary report on the psychiatric field program in the 4th Infantry Division. U.S. Army Vietnam Medical Bulletin, pp. 5-8.
     Describes establishment of a preventive psychiatry program
when Motis served as the division psychiatrist with the 4th Infantry Division in Pleiku in 1967. The primary organizational element
was the assignment of enlisted social work technicians to forward

medical clearing stations and medical companies so as to screen and treat combat stress casualties as close to their units as possible, and to serve as ready consultants to the battalion surgeons (the medical officers assigned to each battalion). Preliminary conclusions include that the technicians were invaluable in limiting the attrition of combat personnel due to treatable psychiatric conditions (only 25% of soldiers referred to these technicians were ultimately evacuated out of the division area for additional psychiatric care).   (C)

Motis, G. (1968, November/December). Psychiatry at the battle of Dak To. U.S. Army Vietnam Medical Bulletin, p. 57.
    Describes a 10-fold rise in combat reaction cases mirrored by an equivalent drop in psychiatric problems among base camp support troops during the 4th Infantry Division's participation in the battle of Dak To near Pleiku in November 1967. Motis speculates that the latter was secondary to the great increase in morale brought about by the division's concerted effort to win the battle. He reports that 75% of soldiers with combat reactions were treated by social work enlisted technicians and successfully returned to duty, and he posits that being seen personally by the psychiatrist at the front contributes to a soldier's reluctance to return to the field.   (C)

Motis, G., & Neal, R. D. (1968, January/February). Freud in the boonies: II. The 4th Infantry Division psychiatric field program at work in a sustained combat situation. U.S. Army Vietnam Medical Bulletin, pp. 27-30.
    Describes the use and effectiveness of "time-honored" forward treatment methods for acute psychiatric battle casualties applied by Neal, an enlisted social work technician, and the physicians of B Company, 4th Medical Battalion, in November 1967. This management plan was supervised during regular visits to the forward area by Motis, the division psychiatrist. The use of parenteral chlorpromazine to aid in rest and restraint proved invaluable. Typical counseling techniques used by the technician were ventilation, encouragement, and exhortation. The majority of soldiers were eager to rejoin their peers within 24 hours, and 78% (18 of 23) were returned to duty within 1-3 days. Only 13% required transfer to a noncombat assignment; none was evacuated beyond the division base camp. The authors also describe classic combat reaction types.   (C)

Motis, G., & West, H. E. (1968, March/April). The case of the dumbstruck soldier. U.S. Army Vietnam Medical Bulletin, pp. 70-73.
    Describes, through a case example, the effective use of a well-trained, well-supervised psychology-social work technician as

a primary therapist in the field treatment of a soldier who has become disabled by combat stress. (C)

Neel, S. (1973). Medical support of the U.S. Army in Vietnam, 1965-1970. Washington, DC: U.S. Government Printing Office.

Provides official review of the activities of the Army Medical Department in support of the U.S. Army in Vietnam through the early and middle years of the war (1965-70). Neel gives an overview of significant medical problems encountered, decisions made, achievements, mistakes, and lessons learned. He includes statistics on neuropsychiatric problems, which show rates rising in Vietnam beginning in 1968 similar to, but exceeding, the rise for the Army as a whole. Admission rates for neuropsychiatric conditions in Vietnam more than doubled between mid-1965 and mid-1970 (from 11.7 to 25.1/1,000 troops/year). In terms of estimated man-days lost, by 1970 neuropsychiatric conditions were the second-leading disease problems. In contrast to previous wars, in which there was a distinct correlation between neuropsychiatric rates and combat intensity, rates in Vietnam rose as combat activity diminished. Although publication before American withdrawal from Vietnam was concluded makes presentation of the scope of the heroin epidemic incomplete, this work portrays the Army's response to this mounting problem as flexible and nonpunitive, one that combined command and medical resources. (C)

Palinkas, L. A., & Coben, P. (1987). Psychiatric disorders among United States Marines wounded in action in Vietnam. Journal of Nervous and Mental Disease, 175, 291-300.

Explores the association between hospitalization rates for injury or wounding in action ($\underline{N}$ = 78,756) and those for psychiatric reasons ($\underline{N}$ = 8,835) among U.S. Marines deployed in Vietnam during the period of active combat there (1965-72). Among Marines who were wounded in action, 2,369 (3%) also had a record of hospitalization for psychiatric reasons. The sole demographic/service characteristic that distinguished this group from other wounded Marines was that a greater proportion of them came from the lowest military ranks. Overall, psychiatric hospitalization was significantly associated with an increased risk of becoming wounded. Further, the wounding incident most often followed the psychiatric hospitalization and tended to occur within the subsequent 4 months. A lower risk of becoming wounded noted with some psychiatric diagnoses (e.g., schizophrenia, anxiety neurosis, depressive neurosis) was explained as reflecting the practice of evacuating such patients to other treatment facilities. Patients with other diagnoses (e.g., social maladjustment, psychosomatic conditions, "nervousness and debility," transient situational disturbance, and acute situational maladjustment) were typically hospitalized, treated, and returned to combat duty, and they accounted for the higher wounded rate of the psychiatrically hospitalized. The 243 Marines listed as having combat fatigue were not shown to be at greater risk. The authors suggest that military psychiatrists weigh these findings against previous studies indicating a higher morbidity among combat soldiers who were not rapidly returned to duty following brief treatment. (C)

Parrish, M. D. (1968, May/June). The megahospital during the Tet offensive. U.S. Army Vietnam Medical Bulletin, pp. 81-82.
Presents an overview of the medical problems and solutions associated with the enemy's large-scale surprise Tet offensives in spring 1968. Parrish observes that under conditions of the extremely taxed medical system, psychiatric patients were by necessity evacuated over lower echelon psychiatric care facilities; in fact, they were evacuated out of Vietnam at three times the usual rate. He speculates that in many instances the psychiatric conditions of these patients became more intractable because treatment was applied too remote from the soldier's primary unit and comrades. (C)

Pettera, R. L. (1968, January/February). What is this thing called "field consultation" in psychiatry. U.S. Army Vietnam Medical Bulletin, pp. 31-36.
Describes Pettera's mode (as division psychiatrist) and perceived beneficial results in consultation-liaison activities within the Army's 9th Infantry Division in Vietnam in 1967. Pettera discusses various types of defensive resistance exhibited by commanders and recommends strategies to reduce obstacles to candid dialogue about unit problems. He argues that a psychiatrist is maximally useful when assigned directly within a division. (C)

Pettera, R. L., Johnson, B. M., & Zimmer, R. (1969). Psychiatric management of combat reactions with emphasis on a reaction unique to Vietnam. Military Medicine, 134, 673-678.
Reports the authors' clinical observations from serving as mental health components of the 9th Infantry Division in Vietnam in 1967-68. They speculate that the lack of sustained combat activities there resulted in few cases of the "combat fatigue" seen in previous American wars. Instead, their combat-related cases were either (1) "nebulous, ill-defined transient anxiety reactions with little or no specific etiology" and requiring only supportive therapy, or (2) the more incapacitating "Vietnam combat reaction." The latter was a common "psycho-physiological" condition that consistently presented with anorexia, nausea, and vomiting; insomnia and traumatic nightmares; survivor guilt and incomplete grieving; and severe anxiety with tremulousness. The authors refer to this condition as a normal combat-induced "neurotic somatic distress,"

which is caused by sustained psychic trauma and precipitated by the soldier approaching the end of his Vietnam tour. They contend it is not the product of neurotic psychodynamics and should be distinguished from other pathological states. Principles of treatment included management near the soldier's parent unit; brief removal from the combat environment; ventilation, reassurance, and limited use of anxiolytics and sedatives; and rapid return to combat duty, even when the soldier complains of residual symptoms. A case example is provided. (C)

Smith, J. R. (1981). A review of one hundred and twenty years of the psychological literature on reactions to combat from the Civil War through the Vietnam war: 1860-1980. Unpublished manuscript. Duke University, Dept. of Psychology, Durham, NC.
     Presents a historical review of the professional literature as well as of U.S. military policies regarding psychological breakdown in combat and its treatment, or compensation for combat veterans with psychological sequelae. Smith concludes that mental health professionals across time and varying wars have tended to over-emphasize static opposing conclusions regarding causality (i.e., pre-disposition vs. overwhelming stress), thus reinforcing society's moral judgments against such casualties and diverting scientific attention away from a more salient multifactorial process perspective. (C)

Stern, D. B. (1968, May/June). The social work/psychology specialist with the Mobile Riverine Force. U.S. Army Vietnam Medical Bulletin, pp. 70-74.
     Describes briefly the problems in and proposed solutions for providing technician-level psychiatric support to two combat battalions located on an inland floating base that is isolated from psychiatric supervision. (C)

Strange, R. E. (1968). Combat fatigue versus pseudo-combat fatigue in Vietnam. Military Medicine, 133, 823-826.
     Provides additional detail on combat stress casualties treated aboard the U.S. Navy hospital ship USS Repose stationed off the northern coast of South Vietnam in 1966 (see Strange, 1969; Strange & Arthur, 1967). These casualties represented evacuated patients who were unmanageable at the primary care level of the Marine medical units ashore. Roughly an equal number were successfully treated and returned to duty without resorting to evacuation to the offshore ship. Among all psychiatric patients admitted to the ship, 15% were considered "classical" combat fatigue ("situational reaction"), while 24% were felt to represent "pseudocombat" fatigue ("personality or psychoneurotic disorders"). Both types were associated with the stress of combat and produced similar symp-

toms of anxiety or depression with psychophysiological manifestations. In classical combat fatigue cases, the soldier typically had a
stable and responsible premorbid personality; apparently succumbed
to the combination of physical depletion and sustained combat
stress; and was quickly returned to function after physical resto-
ration, limited psychopharmacological support, and "supportive-
directive" psychotherapy. Pseudocombat fatigue cases were more
likely to occur in soldiers with characteristics of impulsivity, poor
stress tolerance, tenuous emotional control, and histories of previous psychiatric contacts and poor adjustment. Strange notes that
they showed inadequate motivation and poor identification with
their military group; and although they responded favorably at
first to the same treatment approach as combat fatigue cases, they
became more symptomatic when confronted with the prospect of
returning to duty in the combat environment. (C)

Strange, R. E. (1969). Effects of combat stress on hospital ship
psychiatric evacuees. In P. G. Bourne (Ed.), The psychology and
physiology of stress: With reference to special studies of the Viet
Nam war (pp. 75-93). New York: Academic Press.
      Reviews and expands on previously published diagnostic,
treatment, and dispositional data (Strange, 1968; Strange & Arthur,
1967) regarding Marine and Navy psychiatric casualties treated
aboard the U.S. Navy hospital ship USS Repose off the coast of
South Vietnam in 1966. (C)

Strange, R. E., & Arthur, R. J. (1967). Hospital ship psychiatry in
a war zone. American Journal of Psychiatry, 124, 281-286.
      Reports the psychiatric experience aboard the U.S. Navy hos-
pital ship USS Repose stationed off the northern coast of South
Vietnam. A review of the 143 cases admitted between February
and August 1966 revealed that 67% were categorized as character
and behavior disorders (52% were returned to duty), 20% were psy-
choneurotic (75% were returned to duty), and 13% were psychotic.
Similarities and differences on demographic variables were detailed,
and standard treatment approaches, including the use of chlorpromazine, were outlined. The authors note the low rate of psychiatric disability in Vietnam and speculate on the beneficial effect of
the "high sense of purpose and commitment on the part of the individuals facing combat." (C)

Talbott, J. A. (1968, March/April). The Saigon warriors during Tet.
U.S. Army Vietnam Medical Bulletin, pp. 60-61.
      Provides psychiatric prevalence figures for the Saigon area
during the intensified combat that was waged locally in conjunction with the enemy's 1968 Tet offensives. Talbott, who served as
a psychiatrist at the Army's 3rd Field Hospital in Saigon, notes

that reactions characterized by anxiety tripled in a short period compared with those of the previous 6 months, but he speculates that the support troops from whom these casualties derived, although living in the relative luxury of Saigon, suffered no higher incidence of combat reaction than would have been predicted from a battle-hardened infantry unit. (C)

Talbott, J. A. (1969). Community psychiatry in the Army: History, practice and applications to civilian psychiatry. Journal of the American Medical Association, 210, 1233-1237.
　　Using the pragmatically derived preventive principles of "proximity," "immediacy," and "expectancy," military psychiatrists have effectively treated conditions arising in combat and garrison. More recently, military psychiatry introduced the principle of "community," which holds that an individual's problems often reflect difficulties within the military unit. Talbott describes two consultation programs conducted by mental health workers in the Army community: one in a basic training post in the United States, the other in Vietnam. Both programs attempted to identify military units experiencing internal difficulties, to understand group factors contributing to individual pathology, and to reduce the incidence of both individual and unit problems. He contends that these community strategies can be effectively applied to the practice of civilian psychiatry. (C)

Tiffany, W. J., Jr. (1967). The mental health of Army troops in Vietnam. American Journal of Psychiatry, 123, 1585-1586.
　　Notes that the 1965-66 neuropsychiatric incidence rate of 12/1,000/year reported for Army troops in Vietnam was lower than that previously recorded for American combat troops (the Korean war figure was 73 and World War II combat area figures ranged from 28 to 101). Tiffany stresses the equally positive morale in Vietnam and speculates on combat theatre factors that apparently reduced the incidence of psychiatric problems: individualized 1-year tours, brief and sporadic combat, relative lack of indirect fire from the enemy, and high calibre medical care--especially preventive psychiatric care using the cardinal principals of combat psychiatry (i.e., providing "early treatment in forwardmost areas, de-emphasizing the hospital environment and instilling an attitude of expecting the man to return to duty"). (C)

Tiffany, W. J., Jr., & Allerton, W. S. (1967). Army psychiatry in the mid-60's. American Journal of Psychiatry, 123, 810-821.
　　Reviews use of psychiatric personnel, innovations in residency training, and current research programs as features of contemporary Army psychiatry. The authors note that the concepts of preventive and community psychiatry have long-established tenure in

military medicine. Statistics provided for January 1966 reinforce the impression that "psychiatric casualties of Army troops in Vietnam are few" (less than 3/1,000/year), especially in the category of "combat exhaustion." The authors enumerate those features of combat and military policies that appear to explain the low incidence rate. (C)

Tischler, G. L. (1969). Patterns of psychiatric attrition and of behavior in a combat zone. In P. G. Bourne (Ed.), The psychology and physiology of stress: With reference to special studies of the Viet Nam war (pp. 19-44). New York: Academic Press.
    Reviews the demographic and diagnostic features of 200 enlisted soldiers referred for evaluation to an evacuation hospital during the buildup period in Vietnam. Correlations of these data with the phase of the individual's 12-month tour, during which the disabling psychiatric condition arose, reveals a periodicity of attrition for Vietnam soldiers. Those presenting during the first 3 months of their tour (period of maximal attrition) had been relatively successful in mastering role tasks prior to combat duty and were now struggling with the psychosocial tasks of transition. Those presenting in the 4th through 9th month (period of decreased attrition) had functioned relatively adequately only in their roles prior to entering military service and were now struggling with the psychosocial tasks related to emotional depletion. The group evaluated during the last 3 months (period of minimal attrition) appeared to have experienced considerable difficulty in role functioning both prior to and within the military and were struggling with issues related to psychosocial disengagement. Tischler discusses the psychosocial milieu of the soldiers in Vietnam and explains the psychiatric attrition as reflecting variations in the balance of the individual's stress tolerance versus his specific resource requirements. Case examples are provided. (C)

Wallen, V. (1969). Background characteristics, attitudes, and self-concepts of Air Force psychiatric casualties from Southeast Asia. In P. G. Bourne (Ed.), The psychology and physiology of stress: With reference to special studies of the Viet Nam war (pp. 167-196). New York: Academic Press.
    Describes a study of self-satisfaction and self-concept among 30 Air Force psychiatric casualties from Vietnam evacuated to Japan in 1966-67. Each participant completed a background questionnaire, a standardized intelligence test, and a Q Sort instrument developed according to Carl Rogers' Self-Concept theory of personality. The average psychiatric subject was found either prior to his breakdown or as a result of his breakdown to have a high degree of self-dissatisfaction, limitations in personality adjustment, and limited inner personality strengths. Compared with other service personnel, he tended to view himself as dissatisfied, self-

rejecting, dependent, and experiencing poor control over his emotions. Wallen discusses the implications of these and other findings for personnel selection for deployment to a combat zone. (C)

4   Substance Abuse, Pre-heroin Epidemic

Bey, D. R., & Zecchinelli, V. A. (1971). Marijuana as a coping device in Vietnam. Military Medicine, 136, 448-450.
Presents demographic and clinical data collected in 1969 from 20 consecutive 1st Infantry Division soldiers who were treated by the division psychiatrist and his staff for acute psychotic reactions associated with the use of Cannabis sativa. The acute psychotic symptoms were successfully treated in 1-3 days using "dauerschlaft" (100 mg chlorpromazine taken orally every hour while awake to maintain sleep for 24 hours, with dosage being progressively decreased as the acute symptoms subside). Subsequent examination revealed all to have borderline personality features ("core problems of identity diffusion, ego weakness, low self-esteem, and inability to form close interpersonal relationships") and to be marginally adjusting to their Vietnam circumstance ("marijuana served directly and indirectly to assist the patients in achieving a costly homeostasis"). Besides the tranquilizing effects and oral gratification attained through use of the drug, additional defensive functions were accomplished through development of a "head" identity, and facilitation of "head" group affiliation centered around shared splitting and projection mechanisms. Treatment strategies stemming from these observations are suggested. (C)

Casper, E., Janacek, J., & Martinelli, H., Jr. (1968, September/October). Marijuana in Vietnam. U.S. Army Vietnam Medical Bulletin, pp. 60-72.
Reports results of a survey of marijuana use among soldiers of the Americal Division in Vietnam in 1968 ($N = 771$). Among the authors' findings was that at least 20% of all soldiers of the division had tried marijuana but only a few had become chronic users. Most of those surveyed had tried it on only a few occasions, typically reporting that they found it either unrewarding or unpleasant. Although a tour in Vietnam did seem to increase the number of soldiers who used marijuana, a considerable number, especially among chronic users, already were users prior to entering the military. The authors were puzzled to find that the departing soldiers reported less use than the entering group. One hypothesis was that this could reflect increased combat risk among users. The authors refer to the desperate need for more definitive research on questions stemming from their study. (C)

Colbach, E. M. (1971). Marijuana use by GIs in Viet Nam. American Journal of Psychiatry, 128, 204-207.
A Senate subcommittee has tried to implicate the use of marijuana in the My Lai episode. Stirred by this, the mass media has given sensational attention to the use of marijuana by U.S. servicemen in Vietnam. Reviewing the considerable professional literature on the subject, Colbach finds that marijuana smoking is a significant problem but not as serious as the mass media seems to imply. (MA)

Colbach, E. M., & Crowe, R. R. (1970). Marihuana associated psychosis in Vietnam. Military Medicine, 135, 571-573.
Reviews the literature on marijuana-associated psychosis, describes the organic psychosis with paranoid features seen in some Vietnam personnel at the 67th Evacuation Hospital (Qui Nhon) in 1969, and presents case examples. The authors theorize that the apparent increased incidence of such conditions in Vietnam compared with what is reported in the civilian literature is due to the availability of a much more potent drug, which is consumed by especially vulnerable servicemen with borderline personality organization. (C)

Colbach, E. M., & Willson, S. M. (1969, March/April). The binoctal craze. U.S. Army Vietnam Medical Bulletin, pp. 40-44.
Describes increasing barbiturate use among American troops in the area of the 67th Evacuation Hospital (Qui Nhon) in 1968. Typically, this use was of a French preparation, Binoctal, which consisted of amobarbital (50 mg) and secobarbital (70 mg) and was available to American troops over the counter from Vietnamese pharmacies throughout South Vietnam. In a study of all admissions treated at the hospital over a 3-month period, the authors discovered that 7% of nonpsychiatric patients reported use of Binoctal (2% acknowledged use more than five times). Among psychiatric patients, 16% were admitted for Binoctal use, and 15% of randomly selected outpatients were significant users. The authors review the diagnosis and management of barbiturate addiction, and describe the demographic and personality features of the typical user in their experience. (C)

Fidaleo, R. A. (1968, March/April). Marijuana: Social and clinical observations. U.S. Army Vietnam Medical Bulletin, pp. 58-59.
Describes local marijuana marketing, soldier use patterns, normal clinical reactions to marijuana use, and toxic variations in Vietnam. Fidaleo notes that 57% of the monthly admissions to the 935th psychiatric unit near Saigon in 1967-68 either were attributed to marijuana toxicity or were cases in which marijuana was a major contributor. (C)

Forrest, D. V. (1970). Marijuana to heroin . . . A missing link? (Letter). American Journal of Psychiatry, 127, 704-706.

In considering likely sequences in the development of an opiate addiction from a marijuana dependence, Forrest describes his observations as an Army psychiatrist in Vietnam in 1968-69. He recalls that the regular marijuana user almost always tended to use other psychoactive drugs, including opium- or heroin-dipped marijuana. An informal survey of 30 soldiers taking a college course in psychology in Vietnam revealed 13 abstentious individuals and 12 reporting use of marijuana. Two of these reported a continuing use of opium-dipped marijuana. (C)

Heiman, E. M. (1968, May/June). Marihuana precipitated psychoses in patients evacuated to CONUS. U.S. Army Vietnam Medical Bulletin, pp. 75-77.

Notes that psychiatric patients who were evacuated from Vietnam through Japan in 1967 frequently had their ultimate diagnosis changed from psychosis to character disorder after being reevaluated at the treatment center at Ft. Gordon, GA. Heiman reviews some psychoactive properties of marijuana and speculates that many acute psychoses seen in Vietnam and presumed to be functionally based may have chronic or excessive marijuana use as a critical and reversible etiologic factor. (C)

Master, F. D. (1971). Some clinical observations of drug abuse among G.I.'s in Vietnam. Journal of the Kentucky Medical Association, 69, 193-195.

Reports findings from Master's 1969-70 tour as an Army psychiatrist serving 45,000 troops in the Qui Nhon area (coastal Northern II Corps). These include clinical findings, observations of social factors associated with soldier drug use, and descriptions of the drugs available. Most unprescribed drug use was of a sporadic, recreational, and polydrug nature. From a survey of lower ranking soldiers, marijuana smoking was estimated to be at 70%. Of the 58 psychotic patients Master treated during his tour, 54 reported marijuana use (half reported combined use of other drugs; half reported exclusive use of marijuana). He reports that the available marijuana (Cannabis indica) had a much higher concentration of THC than that available in the United States and seemed to produce a predictable cognitive decrement in habitual users. Narcotic use, typically in the form of smoking raw opium mixed with marijuana, was not a serious clinical problem; however, Master notes that when he left Vietnam (October 1970), reports of heroin snorting were emerging. Barbiturate compounds (Binoctal, Iminoctal, and Ansional) were sold indiscriminately in Vietnamese pharmacies to American soldiers and occasionally accounted for addiction or accidental overdose. Equally available and popular were two amphetamine mixtures (Obesitol, Maxitron forte), which produced numerous cases of toxic psychoses. Master's treatment approach for such cases was to advise the soldier's unit to provide him 48-hour observation; then, if he failed to recover (as did 10% of cases), he would be hospitalized and treated with up to 800 mg of chlorpromazine per day. Follow-up of these patients revealed a consistent, relatively unremitting schizophrenic-like course. (C)

Mirin, S. M., & McKenna, G. J. (1975). Combat zone adjustment: The role of marijuana use. Military Medicine, 140, 482-485.
   Reports results of the consultative visits of two senior U.S. Air Force psychiatrists to a series of military installations in Southeast Asia in 1971. Prominent among the coping mechanisms used by most servicemen was the extensive use of marijuana. In the authors' opinion, periodic marijuana use generally provided self-medication to quell feelings of excessive anxiety and aggression. It also served as a peer group sacrament, binding comrades and defining group boundaries. Recent clinical and laboratory data regarding marijuana are also discussed. (C)

Postel, W. B. (1968, September/October). Marijuana use in Vietnam: A preliminary report. U.S. Army Vietnam Medical Bulletin, pp. 56-59.
   Reports on a study of the prevalence of marijuana use and the attitudes of soldiers about their use of marijuana. A questionnaire was administered in early 1968 to 50 psychiatry clinic patients and 76 surgical inpatients, all of whom were first-term enlisted soldiers of the 4th Infantry Division in Pleiku. An arbitrary distinction was made between experimenters (those having smoked less than five times) and habitual users (those having smoked five times or more). Results showed that 56% of psychiatry clinic patients and 46% of surgical inpatients acknowledged marijuana use overall, with 30% of the former and 21% of the latter qualifying as habituated. Psychiatry clinic patients who were habitual users tended to have started marijuana before entering the service and experimented more with other drugs than did the surgical habituated. All marijuana groups indicated that marijuana use tended to be a social group activity and was commonly used in the field, usually to calm down after a battle. In only one instance did someone acknowledge going into battle while under the influence. (C)

Roffman, R. A., & Sapol, E. (1970). Marijuana in Vietnam: A survey of use among Army enlisted men in the two Southern Corps. International Journal of the Addictions, 5, 1-42.
   Reports results of a survey regarding drug use patterns of 584 lower ranking enlisted soldiers departing Vietnam in 1967. Of the 32% who had ever smoked marijuana, 61% began in Vietnam,

and only one quarter of all users were considered heavy users. The heavy marijuana user was unique in being younger, of lower rank, and more likely to have marijuana-using friends. He also was more likely to have used marijuana before coming to Vietnam, used it earlier in his tour, used other drugs, and had a history of at least one minor disciplinary action. Alcohol use correlated positively across all marijuana-using groups. Generally, marijuana use tended to be a communal activity, with users overestimating prevalence among peers. The authors conclude that marijuana use in Vietnam, both in prevalence and incidence, is very similar to use among civilian peers. (See also Sapol & Roffman, 1969.) (C)

Sanders, C. R. (1973). Doper's wonderland: Functional drug use by military personnel in Vietnam. Journal of Drug Issues, 3, 65-78.
        Posits that although a sizable proportion of servicemen who used drugs in Vietnam (estimated at between 60%-90% of enlisted men below the rank of E-4) had not begun such use in Vietnam, their use while there was not the result of character disorders or simple "hedonism." Instead it was a realistic and rational attempt at self-medication to cope with the stresses of the Vietnam tour. Sanders draws on interviews with returning veterans between 1967-70 and on a review of the history of drug accessibility and official military policies and practices in Vietnam. Among his conclusions are that use of illegal drugs provided the soldier a means for counterauthority and antiwar group affiliation as well as a personal mechanism for "manipulating time" and withdrawing from the pressures and frustrations of Vietnam; that although few returnees reported use of drugs while on patrol, they habitually used them to "unwind" after the intense pressures of combat; and that the military's efforts at drug education, suppression, and rehabilitation in Vietnam have repeatedly been inadequate, perhaps because of the military's sense that drug use by servicemen reduced incidents of overt defiance. (C)

Stanton, M. D. (1972a). Drug use in Vietnam. Archives of General Psychiatry, 26, 279-286.
        Reports results of a study conducted in Vietnam in late 1969 regarding drug use patterns of 2,547 entering or departing Vietnam soldiers. Respondents were divided into several groups by age and rank and analyzed separately. When results were compared with a similar survey in 1967 (Roffman & Sapol, 1970), sizable increases were noted in the reported use of most drugs following a tour in Vietnam. Stanton speculates that marijuana and some other drugs may actually allow certain types of individuals to function under the stresses of a combat environment and separation from home. (C)

Steinbeck, J., IV. (1968, January). The importance of being stoned in Vietnam. Washingtonian Magazine, pp. 33-35, 56, 58, 60.

Comments on the social and political motivations underlying the war in Vietnam as well as on the attitudes and adaptations of the soldiers there. Steinbeck, an enlisted radio/television specialist stationed in the coastal region near Qui Nhon, makes passing allusion to the ease of interpenetration of GIs and civilian Vietnamese for mutual hedonistic exploitation. His primary attention, however, is on describing the central role of marijuana on both sides in the war. He speculates that 75% of young soldiers use it regularly, notes a relatively tolerant attitude within the command structure, and emphasizes its ubiquitous availability and extremely low cost. He also acknowledges his own regular use of marijuana in Vietnam and speculates that "everyone was taking the release from the war" by using marijuana to create "a calm, perceiving detachment . . . (during which) a wonderful change in war starts to occur. Instead of the grim order of terror, explosions modulate musically; death takes on a new approachable symbolism that is not so horrible." (C)

Talbott, J. A. (1968, January/February). Pot reactions. U.S. Army Vietnam Medical Bulletin, pp. 40-41.

Describes various levels of adverse reactions to marijuana use treated by the 935th psychiatry team in Vietnam in early 1967. Most reactions cleared in 12-72 hours with supportive management occasionally augmented by chlordiazepoxide or chlorpromazine. In the severest instances, patients were diagnosed as undergoing a transient acute paranoid psychosis with organic features. Talbott speculates that those who developed such adverse reactions have character defects, but he also considers contributing etiological factors to be relevant, such as the very high potency of the locally grown marijuana. (C)

Talbott, J. A., & Teague, J. W. (1969). Marihuana psychosis: Acute toxic psychosis associated with the use of cannabis derivatives. Journal of the American Medical Association, 210, 299-302.

Describe 12 cases of marijuana psychosis occurring in soldiers hospitalized at the southern Army psychiatric treatment center (935th) in Vietnam between late 1967 and early 1968. All 12 incidents consisted of self-limited (patients were successfully returned to duty within a week) acute attacks of disorganizing combinations of organicity and anxiety; 10 showed paranoid symptoms. Noteworthy was that the episodes followed the individual's first attempt to smoke marijuana. In only 2 cases was a premorbid personality disorder diagnosed. The authors speculate that in serving in a tertiary treatment setting, they are seeing only the tip of an iceberg of toxic reactions to marijuana that are successfully managed by other means. (C)

Treanor, J. J., & Skripol, J. N. (1970, July/August). Marijuana in a
tactical unit in Vietnam. U.S. Army Vietnam Medical Bulletin, pp.
29-37.

Presents results of a survey of drug use patterns among
soldiers (all ranks) of the 173rd Airborne Brigade in 1970
(N = 1,064). Findings include that 32% denied ever using an illegal
drug, and 37% acknowledged an isolated incidence of experimentation. The remaining 31%, the regular marijuana users, showed
lower rank, age, military experience, and formal education level;
higher incidents of civilian and military legal entanglements (including incidents suggestive of alienation to the military, such as
AWOL and insubordination); and increased field-type duty and job
dissatisfaction. Opium users were 6% of the overall population.
Nonusers of drugs, in contrast to users, perceived marijuana to be
more harmful than alcohol, addictive, and a prelude to use of
stronger drugs, while 48% of all subjects felt marijuana use should
be allowed on fire support bases. The authors include their clinical
impression that marijuana users are generally incapable, frustrated,
and poorly educated, and have passive-aggressive personalities.
(C)

5   Substance Abuse,
Heroin Epidemic

Baker, S. L. (1972). U.S. Army heroin abuse identification program in Vietnam: Implications for a methadone program. American Journal of Public Health, 62, 857-860.

Describes epidemiologic factors, U.S. government policy changes, and the development of the identification and management program. Baker emphasizes practical considerations regarding the technical aspects of user identification and discusses the liabilities of using methadone maintenance for active duty addicts. (C)

Bentel, D. J., Crim, D., & Smith, D. E. (1971). Drug abuse in combat: The crisis of drugs and addiction among American troops in Vietnam. Journal of Psychedelic Drugs, 4, 23-30.

Seeks to define the scope and nature of the drug abuse problem among U.S. troops in Vietnam primarily through interviews with returning soldiers as well as from information provided by medical personnel who treat veterans. Included are statistics from a survey of returning enlisted soldiers discharged from the Army at Oakland Army terminal in early 1971 (N = 1,000), which showed that nearly 25% acknowledged using heroin or other opiates while in Vietnam, and almost two thirds of these signified use greater than 10 times during their last month in Vietnam. The authors highlight not only how social bonding was facilitated among soldiers by the communal use of heroin, but also how many seemed to have sought "therapy" for their despair and frustration through the use of heroin. Other soldiers spoke of carefully titrating the use of marijuana or marijuana plus heroin while on combat patrols to calm down, enhance alertness, and increase suspicion of enemy activity. (C)

Black, F. W. (1975). Personality characteristics of Viet Nam veterans identified as heroin abusers. American Journal of Psychiatry, 132, 748-749.

MMPI testing of 100 Army enlisted soldiers confirmed as heroin users was performed shortly after their return from Vietnam in 1972. Of that sample, 71% were classified as psychiatrically abnormal and only 19% appeared relatively normal (10% were classified as invalid). A marked heterogeneity of MMPI profile types was found. Subjects showed neither more nor less psychopathology than previously reported samples of civilian addicts. (C)

Char, J. (1972). Drug abuse in Vietnam. American Journal of Psychiatry, 129, 463-465.

Having served as the division psychiatrist for the 101st Airborne Division located in the northernmost area of South Vietnam in 1970, Char presents results of a survey of drug use patterns among three groups of lower ranking enlisted soldiers in his division: those who were completing a year-long tour (n = 568), those who had been psychiatric outpatients (n = 467), and those who were new arrivals (n = 111). Of the first group--those departing Vietnam--41% admitted use of some drug during their tour (36% of these drug users acknowledged use of heroin or other "hard" drugs; 64% limited their drug use to marijuana). The drug use rate for these departing soldiers was roughly twice that for the soldiers arriving from the States (21%). Among the psychiatric patient group, 71% acknowledged a drug use history. Of the men using drugs in all three groups, 58% began as civilians. In Char's opinion, drug-using soldiers are being denied needed treatment because of the absence of "such treatment within the framework of a comprehensive plan that deals with the problem." (C)

Dehart, R. L., & Sorrentino, J. P. (1973). Experience with drug abuse. Military Medicine, 138, 294-297.

Describes a drug treatment and rehabilitation program and details the authors' experience with detoxification of nearly 100 users (mostly heroin) among Air Force personnel stationed at Da Nang Air Field in 1971. Of the 35 patients who were returned to duty and could be followed for at least 3 months, 26 (74%) were judged to be free from further drug use. This inpatient program constituted the medical portion of a much broader basewide program that was coordinated by a multidisciplinary staff council with the full support of the base commander. Case examples are provided. (C)

Fisher, A. H., Jr., Nelson, K. E., & Panzarella, J. (1972). Patterns of drug usage among Vietnam veterans. Alexandria, VA: Human Resources Research Organization.

Presents factor analysis results of drug use patterns reported by 1,010 enlisted Vietnam veterans who were separating from the Army in March 1973 upon completion of their service obligation. Respondents were asked to report the number of times they used each of seven categories of drugs both before going to Vietnam and during their tour. Of the four resultant factors, three indicate pre-Vietnam drug usage and imply that use of drugs does not necessarily originate in Vietnam. The fourth factor reflects only loadings for use of drugs (all types) in Vietnam and suggests a Vietnam drug experimentation phenomenon. The authors speculate on the need for separate rehabilitation approaches for the "before Vietnam" and "during Vietnam" narcotic users. (C)

Frenkel, S. I., Morgan, D. W., & Greden, J. F. (1977). Heroin use among soldiers in the United States and Vietnam: A comparison in retrospect. International Journal of the Addictions, 12, 1143-1154.

Provides results of a heroin use survey conducted in 1972 comparing 1,007 noncombat Army soldiers in Vietnam simultaneously with 856 counterparts assigned to a stateside post. The major finding was that 13.5% of the Vietnam soldiers and 14.5% of those in the States reported previous use of heroin. Not significant were demographic subgroup comparisons and those regarding past conflicts with authority (equally elevated in both heroin subgroups). The authors systematically compare their findings with previously published surveys, concluding that a heroin epidemic occurred in Vietnam earlier in the 1970s but that any conclusion that "such an epidemic was 'unique'. . . and 'infected' many average American soldiers appears inaccurate and misleading." (C)

Golosow, N., & Childs, A. (1973). The soldier addict: A new battlefield casualty. International Journal of the Addictions, 8, 1-11.

Discusses an examination of 36 heroin addicts who were currently or recently stationed in Vietnam. Collectively, the subjects resembled ghetto-raised civilian addicts in having histories of broken homes, disturbed family relationships, academic failures, and juvenile delinquency. Differences, however, included majority-group membership, middle-class origins, presence of paternal figures in the family, and absence of criminal activity. The authors suggest that these dissimilarities between military and civilian addicts may have favorable prognostic implications. Further, they feel that conditions peculiar to Vietnam were necessary for addiction to develop in most subjects, and that in their return to a more favorable environment, heroin usage may subside. (C)

Goodwin, D. W., Davis, D. H., & Robins, L. N. (1975). Drinking amid abundant illicit drugs: The Vietnam case. Archives of General Psychiatry, 32, 230-233.

Presents a study of reported drinking patterns and adjustment of 451 randomly selected Army enlisted soldiers 8-12 months after their return from Vietnam in September 1971. Before assignment to Vietnam, 50% were regular drinkers and 25% had drinking problems. Problem drinking declined in Vietnam while opiate use rose sharply; 50% tried opiates and 20% became opiate dependent. Upon the soldiers' return from Vietnam, opiate use decreased (less than 2% opiate dependent) and problem drinking again became ascendant. At the time of interviews, 17% reported alcoholic patterns at some period in their lives, and another 41% had had problems with drinking. (C)

Hampton, P. T., & Vogel, D. B. (1973). Personality characteristics of servicemen returned from Vietnam identified as heroin abusers. American Journal of Psychiatry, 130, 1031-1032.

Reports results of psychological testing of a sample of U.S. Army enlisted Vietnam returnees ($\underline{N}$ = 101) identified as heroin abusers in Vietnam between September 1971 and April 1972. The authors note marked heterogeneity of psychological test types. The four most common diagnostic classifications were normal, conduct disorder, abnormal but of indeterminate diagnosis, and psychosis. Compared with studies describing civilian addicts, this study suggests less pathology and a lower incidence of sociopathy in these military drug abusers. (C)

Helzer, J. E., Robins, L. N., & Davis, D. H. (1975). Antecedents of narcotic use and addiction: A study of 898 Vietnam veterans. Drug and Alcohol Dependence, 1, 183-190.

Reports on a study of 898 Vietnam veterans returning to the United States in September 1971 that gathered data on preservice variables including (1) socioeconomic background, (2) inner-city residence, (3) history of treatment for psychiatric difficulty, (4) broken home before age 16, (5) race, (6) employment history, (7) level of education, (8) history of antisocial behavior, and (9) current drug use. About half of these men were selected from a general sample of all returnees for this period, while the other half were selected from those whose urinalysis was drug positive just prior to returning to the States. The authors have selected this method to overcome problems of retrospective studies based on samples from legal and medical sources only. The strongest predictor of narcotic abuse was a history of antisocial behavior, followed by education level (e.g., high school dropouts were significantly overrepresented in the addict population). Socioeconomic background bore no relationship to drug involvement while the remaining antecedents were predictive of at least one level of involvement with drugs. (M)

Holloway, H. C. (1974). Epidemiology of heroin dependency among soldiers in Vietnam. Military Medicine, 139, 108-113.

Using data obtained in 1971 from interviews with 1,150 Vietnam servicemen, Holloway constructs an overview of heroin use among troops in Vietnam to include descriptions of drug availability, environmental and social settings of use, and the characteristics of the drug-using population. The profile of the typical Army heroin user revealed someone who was 18-23 years old, low ranking, and employed in a less skilled job; who might not have completed high school; and who had probably used marijuana, alcohol, or other drugs prior to heroin. Holloway also reviews the Army's

policies concerning drug abuse, its influence on the patterns of
drug use, and the types and effectiveness of the various treatment
programs implemented in Vietnam.   (C)

Holloway, H. C., Angel, C. R., Bardill, D. R., & the members of
work unit 032. (1972). Drug abuse in military personnel. In Annual
progress report (pp. 1185-1201). Washington, DC: Walter Reed Army
Institute of Research.
        Reports on research program developments directed at curb-
ing the mounting drug abuse problem of soldiers both in Vietnam
and in the States. The authors review the current technology
available for drug screening in Vietnam to accomplish "Phase I of
the presidentially directed drug abuse counteroffensive." They also
report findings from a survey of existent drug abuse treatment
and rehabilitation programs in Southeast Asia, which show that
drug abuse among U.S. military forces represents a "significant
threat to combat readiness." Included are interim findings from
physiological studies of 20 heroin users (with 5 controls) undergoing withdrawal in Vietnam: that withdrawal in short-term Vietnam addicts is less severe than clinically expected, especially
among those with nonparenteral routes of administration; that a
pattern of heavy intermittent use exists among some Army heroin
users in Vietnam in whom no overt evidence of abstinence syndrome occurs when use is curtailed; and that the heroin used is
relatively pure and administered primarily through insufflation. The
authors also refer to studies of drug use patterns in Army populations in the States, especially emphasizing the finding that previously heroin-using returnees from Vietnam "did not define themselves as addicts and emphatically denied both the need and desire
for further treatment." They conclude "that heroin use in Vietnam
is best viewed in terms of the social structure that encouraged
and maintained usage rather than in terms of personality, demographic, or pathological characteristics of individual users." (C)

Holloway, H. C., Collins, J. L., Bardill, D. R., & the members of
work unit 030. (1973). Interview study of 101 drug-using soldiers
and 44 mental hygiene controls. In Annual progress report (pp.
1049-1050). Washington, DC: Walter Reed Army Institute of
Research.
        Summarizes findings from a survey involving opiate-dependent
soldiers returned to stateside military duty. These findings were
compared with published findings regarding civilian addicts, which
highlight variables that serve to predict prognosis. The addicted
soldiers who were detected by urine screen as they departed Vietnam had a better prognosis than did soldiers who were not but
who sought medical attention after their return to the States;
both groups, however, more closely resembled successfully treated
rather than chronically addicted civilian addicts. Analysis of drug

use patterns failed to distinguish between addicted and polydrug non-addicts. Non-addicts actually exceeded the addicts on many drug usage variables. (C)

Holloway, H. C., Marlowe, D. H., Hollingshead, W. H., & the members of work unit 103. (1973). The socio-psychological aspects of heroin use in USARV (U.S. Army Vietnam). In Annual progress report (pp. 1261-1271). Washington, DC: Walter Reed Army Institute of Research.

Reports survey findings from 4,000 heroin-using soldiers in Vietnam. Those who became addicted in Vietnam possess characteristics that place them in the most prognostically favorable group of addicts. Comparisons of heroin users entering treatment before and after the introduction of urine screening reveal a shorter addiction history and less deviant characteristics in the soldiers referred as a result of a chemical detection. (C)

Holloway, H. C., Sodetz, F. J., Elsmore, T. F, & the members of work unit 102. (1973). Heroin dependence and withdrawal in the military heroin user in the U.S. Army, Vietnam. In Annual progress report (pp. 1244-1246). Washington, DC: Walter Reed Army Institute of Research.

Reports findings from a study of 31 heroin users (with 5 controls) in a controlled treatment environment in Vietnam. Heroin users in Vietnam differ from classic civilian addicts in their youth, good general health, and brief exposure--primarily through naso-pulmonary insufflation--of extremely pure heroin (92%-98%). Such "snorting" results in absorption of heroin of approximately the same magnitude as that associated with intravenous injection. Study subjects showed brief and benign withdrawal symptomatology, especially considering their tolerance to very large quantities of heroin. The authors make special note of the observation of morphine metabolite excretion as late as 14 days after the last dose of heroin. Pupil size remained abnormal well beyond other signs and symptoms of abstinence. The authors conclude: "These clinical findings support an uncoupling of tolerance and physiological dependence." (C)

Howe, R. C., Hegge, F. W., & Phillips, J. L. (1980a). Acute heroin abstinence in man: I. Changes in behavior and sleep. Drug and Alcohol Dependence, 5, 341-356.

Reports findings from a study of overt behavioral characteristics and sleep patterns during acute heroin abstinence in 20 heroin-dependent soldiers (compared with 5 nondrug-using controls) identified by the Army urine drug screening program in Vietnam. Both patients and control subjects were observed and monitored continuously for 5 to 7 days in a specialized research ward late in the course of the war. Data were analyzed for the frequency of occurrence of various behaviors, including signs and symptoms of withdrawal. The heroin-dependent subjects generally displayed a higher number of observations across all recording days. In addition, the signs and symptoms of withdrawal for these patients peaked on Day 1 or Day 2 and then declined over the remaining recording days. The EEG state data showed an increase in waking and decrease in both slow wave and REM sleep during acute heroin withdrawal. Total sleep was maximally suppressed on withdrawal Days 2 and 3 and was still below normal control values on withdrawal Days 5-7. REM sleep was more disrupted than slow wave sleep during withdrawal. The authors conclude that heroin withdrawal produces a differential action upon central nervous system structures responsible for the various states of sleep, waking, and related behaviors. (C)

Howe, R. C., Hegge, F. W., & Phillips, J. L. (1980b). Acute heroin abstinence in man: II. Alterations in rapid eye movement (REM) sleep. Drug and Alcohol Dependence, 6, 149-161.
    This report from a study of the behavioral and physiological correlates of acute heroin withdrawal in 20 heroin-dependent soldiers in Vietnam (Howe, Hegge, & Phillips, 1980a; Howe, Phillips, & Hegge, 1980) focuses on rapid eye movement (REM) sleep changes during the first week of withdrawal under continuous EEG telemetric monitoring. The results showed a marked reduction in total REM sleep, which was associated with a decrease in both duration and number of REM episodes. REM latencies were also prolonged and the number of REM shifts per 24-hour period were reduced. There was no observed difference in REM sleep interval between the drug users and controls. (C)

Howe, R. C., Phillips, J. L., & Hegge, F. W. (1980). Acute heroin abstinence in man: III. Effect upon waking and slow wave sleep. Drug and Alcohol Dependence, 6, 247-262.
    Reports further findings from a study evaluating the effects of acute heroin withdrawal in 20 heroin-dependent soldiers in Vietnam (see Howe, Hegge, & Phillips, 1980a, 1980b). The heroin-dependent patients showed approximately a 26% decrease in slow wave sleep and an 18% increase in waking behavior during withdrawal. The awake state in these patients also revealed an increase in number of both episodes and state shifts, and a decrease in duration and sleep onset latency. In addition, the slow wave sleep categories during withdrawal generally showed an increase in sleep onset latency and interstate interval, and a decrease in number of episodes. The authors conclude that heroin withdrawal is associated with marked disruptions of the central nervous system mechanisms responsible for maintaining the normal sleep-waking cycle. (C)

Ingraham, L. H. (1974). "The Nam" and "The World": Heroin use by U.S. Army enlisted men serving in Vietnam. Psychiatry, 37, 114-128.
    Presents findings of a sociological study of drug use patterns among Army enlisted soldiers in Vietnam. Findings were derived from unstructured small group interviews in the States using 78 soldiers identified as opiate positive at the conclusion of their Vietnam tours (late 1971). Demographic and other descriptors of the study respondents did not clearly identify risk factors. The men in this opiate-positive sample reported experience with illicit drugs before they went to Vietnam. Nearly three quarters had used at least one illegal substance weekly prior to entering the Army, and at least one fifth had tried heroin before Vietnam. Ingraham especially notes the fraternal social network described by his respondents (which existed within the larger but basically approving body of soldiers): the respondent group shared the perception that, as members of the "heads" (communal, drug-using lower ranking enlisted), they were distinct from and superior to the "juicers" (alcohol-consuming career military superiors). Within this "head" society, further status discriminations existed by drug choice and usage pattern (highest level for the exclusive marijuana users and lowest for those preferring barbiturates and amphetamines). The modal drug used among the study group was heroin, typically smoked or "snorted." Although acknowledging that they had become dependent upon heroin in Vietnam, they justified their use as adaptive to the unique stresses of the Vietnam theatre (not typically combat stress), considered their use as on a minor scale since they had not injected drugs, and denied any need for further treatment or rehabilitation. Most contended they were able to maintain their habits in Vietnam without loss of function or resort to theft. The jargon of the groups, exalting the enlisted "heads" and denigrating the "lifer/juicers," did not represent a "radical-left" political ideology or a rejection of conventional values but, Ingraham posits, was incidental to drug use per se (and, in fact, operated similarly around the use of marijuana before heroin became available). This argot instead reinforced the appreciation of an extended network of friends with whom a member could experience an immediate and intense sense of acceptance and belonging. Ingraham suggests that this is probably a variation of the enlisted coping styles that had been observed in prior armies in war: "Through their rhetoric, they presented themselves as being intensely anti-military, anti-army, and anti-war, but the content of their discourse could hardly be described as pacifist. They did not question the authority of their government to send them to Vietnam, nor did they question their obligation to serve." (C)

Johnson, A., Jr., & O'Rourke, K. (1974). Drug rehabilitation in the combat zone. Military Medicine, 139, 362-366.

Describes a drug rehabilitation program on the U.S. air base at Phan Rang in South Vietnam in 1971. The program, which achieved a 73% success rate, stressed prevention, isolation from the source, and rehabilitation of the heroin user. Evaluation and treatment procedures included weekly urine testing, psychological testing, and individual and group therapy. The patients were classified as "drug addicts" or "situational drug abusers." The addicts generally had pre-Vietnam histories of heroin involvement, and it was concluded that it was impossible to deal with these drug addicts within the scope of this program. In contrast, situational abusers were relatively open to therapy and were generally rehabilitated successfully. The authors discuss the physical withdrawal, psychological withdrawal, and reorientation portions of the program, as well as the role of both the medical staff and the office of the base commander. (C)

Joseph, B. S. (1974). Lessons on heroin abuse from treating users in Vietnam. Hospital and Community Psychiatry, 25, 742-744.
Joseph, a partially trained psychiatrist serving as a flight surgeon in Vietnam in 1971, describes his 3-week voluntary therapeutic community program for heroin users. This program was intended for users who were psychologically stable, yet Joseph concluded after 6 months of operation that it failed, largely because program participants were soldiers with character disorders who entered so as to evade disciplinary action. The more stable users apparently were able to continue to function and escape detection. Joseph stresses the need to constantly reevaluate assumptions about drug use. In his opinion, heroin use in Vietnam is primarily a social problem rather than one of individual pathology. (C)

Kojak, G., & Canby, J. P. (1975). Personality and behavior patterns of heroin-dependent American servicemen in Thailand. American Journal of Psychiatry, 132, 246-250.
Presents a study comparing a group of heroin-dependent American servicemen (N = 25) stationed in Thailand with a matched control group of men not dependent on heroin. The data gathered regarding social history, attitudes, work record, previous drug use, personality, and intelligence show significant differences between the two groups in four areas: intelligence, work record, number of years of schooling, and number of drugs used before using heroin. The data suggest that many of the heroin-dependent men had difficulties related to a distant or negative relationship with their fathers; however, in contrast to previous studies of heroin addicts, they do not confirm a relationship between heroin dependence and any particular personality pattern. (MA)

Kolb, D., Nail, R. L., & Gunderson, E. K. E. (1974). Differences in family characteristics of heroin injectors and inhalers. Journal of Nervous and Mental Disease, 158, 446-449.

Compares demographics of these two groups of heroin addicts serving with the Navy in Vietnam (N = 121). Although inhalers (those who smoked or snorted heroin) believed that by not inject-ing they would not become addicted, about two thirds had become addicted. Inhalers did not differ significantly on demographic characteristics from other nonheroin-using drug users in Vietnam or from a Navy control sample serving aboard combat ships. Injec-tors demonstrated lower socioeconomic status (based on father's educational level), decreased family stability, and greater reported tension between the service member and his family, especially as a result of harsh paternal discipline. (C)

Lloyd, S. J., Frates, R. C., & Domer, D. C. (1973). A clinical evaluation of 81 heroin addicts in Vietnam. Military Medicine, 138, 298-300.

Describes the authors' heroin treatment unit with the 101st Airborne Division in Vietnam in 1971. Over a 60-day period, 81 heroin addicts were voluntarily admitted for detoxication and rehabilitation (all were of lower enlisted ranks, and for 23%, it was not their first attempt at withdrawal under medical super-vision). Demographic comparisons with an equal number of controls revealed that the heroin users included a higher proportion of first-enlistment Regular Army soldiers and more often came from disrupted homes. The average daily consumption of heroin was six to eight "vials" (about 600-800 mg of 97% heroin). The majority either smoked or snorted the drug. Physical withdrawal symptoms were typically managed using low doses of chlorpromazine com-bined with diazepam. Detoxication success (67%) was strongly correlated with the soldier's intent to pass the Vietnam theatre exit urine screening test. In the authors' opinion, most of the patients appeared to begin using heroin as a transitory reaction to the distorted environmental and peer pressures in Vietnam. (C)

Murphy, M. (1971). When 30,000 GI's are using heroin, how can you fight a war? Drug Forum, 1, 87-98.

Summarizes a report by U.S. congressmen following a drug abuse investigation tour in Vietnam in April 1971. By their esti-mate 30,000-40,000 troops (10%-15% of soldiers) were addicted to various drugs, especially heroin. They also reported that the open drug market was likely the result of high-level Vietnamese official corruption. Among possible causative factors considered for soldier drug use, most important is his dilemma of being sent to risk death or injury when the government has elected not to seek to win. Other perceived contributing factors were boredom, group pressure, and experimentation. Murphy includes quotes from the press providing a chronology of public reactions and government policy changes after the extent of the drug problem in Vietnam surfaced. (C)

Nace, E. P., Meyers, A. L., & Rothberg, J. M. (1973). Addicted Viet Nam veterans: A comparison of self-referred and system-referred samples. American Journal of Psychiatry, 130, 1242-1245.
Reports that addicts who volunteered for an Army heroin treatment program differed from those who were detected by urine screening in that they had shown a greater degree of antisocial behavior in civilian life and had more frequent psychiatric contacts in the service as well as a more extensive history of drug use. All subjects in the study had become addicted while serving in Vietnam. The finding that drug use is less frequent during the earliest months of military training than during both the preceding civilian months and the later phases of military duty suggests that recognition and intervention during the early months of military training may be the chief means of primary prevention. (MA)

Nail, R. L., Gunderson, E. K. E., & Kolb, D. (1974). Family characteristics associated with heroin dependence among Navy men in Vietnam. Military Medicine, 139, 967-970.
Compares 121 heroin-dependent Navy enlisted men with 119 nonheroin, drug-using controls. All participants were admitted under conditions of exemption to a Navy drug rehabilitation program in the States, and all had served at least one tour in Vietnam. Survey and interview data showed only small differences in family characteristics and generally in the opposite direction from those predicted. Items that did discriminate tended to reflect closer and more positive family relationships among the heroin-using subjects, especially for those who were not intravenous users. The 28% of the heroin users who injected the drug revealed family characteristics more like addicts of civilian studies. (C)

Ratner, R. A. (1972). Drugs and despair in Vietnam. University of Chicago Magazine, 64, 15-23.
Summarizes Ratner's observations regarding the predispositions, patterns of use, clinical presentations, and responses to treatment of over 1,000 drug-dependent soldiers who were voluntary residents in the Army Amnesty Center between January and July 1971. As a psychiatrist serving with the Army in Vietnam, Ratner considers that this caseload is only a fraction of the estimated 30% of all younger, lower ranking soldiers who use heroin regularly; and that they in turn only partially reflect the pervasive despair within the larger military population of the lower ranks in Vietnam. Although alluding to likely individual premorbidity factors in the drug-dependent soldier, Ratner per-

ceives their universal "despair" as due more to a combination of societal factors (e.g., America's motivation for waging war in Southeast Asia represents a displacement of its internal "racial hostilities") and the "inhumane" Army conditions that the soldiers are now unwilling to bear because they perceive that society is trying to destroy them. Ratner conveys his sense of clinical impotence in working with these soldiers and their frustrations ("there seems to be no place for a psychiatrist to begin") and admittedly shares some of their cynicism: "The Army (is) our institution of the impulse to destroy." (C)

Robins, L. N. (1976). Estimating addiction rates and locating target populations: How decomposition into stages helps. Report of the Task Force on the Epidemiology of Heroin and Other Narcotics, National Institute on Drug Abuse.

   Uses previously published data regarding drug use by U.S. enlisted men in Vietnam (Robins, Davis, & Goodwin, 1974) to address the methodological problems inherent in measuring present and predicting future addiction rates. Such problems include defining what constitutes a heroin addict and estimating those so defined, given the difficulty of detecting them in general population surveys. The four addiction predictors were initially subjected to a Multiple Classification Analysis, which explained only 6% of the variance using all four scales. Having failed to find adequate predictors of heroin addiction, the researchers next postulated a set of necessary stages between drug naivety and drug addiction, and then reanalyzed the data with the objective of predicting progression from one stage to the next. This process was more successful and increased the percentage of explained variance to 25%. (M)

Robins, L. N. (1978). The interaction of setting and predisposition in explaining novel behavior: Drug initiations before, in, and after Vietnam. In D. Kandel (Ed.), Longitudinal research in drug use: Empirical findings and methodological issues (pp. 179-196). Washington, DC: Hemisphere and Wiley.

   Uses previously published longitudinal data on reported drug use by U.S. enlisted men in Vietnam (Robins, Davis, & Goodwin, 1974; Robins, Helzer, & Davis, 1975) compared with nonveteran controls to demonstrate how individual characteristics interact with the influence of the immediate situation to affect readiness to use drugs (predisposition). Some methodological problems in this type of study were that individuals often chose the setting, thus confounding its influence on behavior, and that factors such as age and historical period changed during the course of the study. Vietnam offered greater availability of heroin, which Robins believes increased the impact of a prior predisposition to abuse narcotics. She deemphasizes either setting or predisposition as singly causing narcotic abuse, however, stressing instead the interaction of these factors. Men with histories of preservice deviant behavior who did not use heroin prior to Vietnam may simply have lacked opportunity, while those "who had the opportunity before service and chose not to use narcotics then might be expected to be especially invulnerable to their use, perhaps because they were satisfied with alcohol." (M)

Robins, L. N., Davis, D. H., & Goodwin, D. W. (1974). Drug use by U.S. enlisted men in Vietnam: A follow-up on their return home. American Journal of Epidemiology, 99, 235-249.
    Provides details of a previously summarized study (Robins, 1974). The authors note that, compared with soldiers who used no drugs or only marijuana in Vietnam, drug users tended to be younger, single, less well educated, from larger cities, and more often reared in broken homes. They also were more likely to come to Vietnam with a history of deviant behavior (crime, drug use, or high school dropout). Race was not significantly related to drug use although blacks were more likely to be detected as positive at the point of their return to the States. The strongest preservice factor that predicted continuing use after Vietnam was preservice narcotic use. The only pre-Vietnam military indicator was a history of disciplinary action. Among substance abuse patterns in Vietnam, a preference for heroin sniffing or injecting (versus smoking), combined with frequent use of amphetamines or barbiturates and little use of alcohol, was strongly predictive of continued narcotic use. The authors underscore that although almost half the Army enlisted men who left Vietnam in September 1971 had tried one or more narcotic drugs, most of the men who used narcotics heavily in Vietnam stopped when they left and had not begun again 8-12 months later. (C)

Robins, L. N., Helzer, J. E., & Davis, D. H. (1975). Narcotic use in Southeast Asia and afterward. Archives of General Psychiatry, 32, 955-961.
    Extends findings from a previously described 1972 survey (Robins, 1974; Robins, Davis, & Goodwin, 1974; Robins, Davis, & Nurco, 1974). Results indicate that pre-Vietnam hard drug use was largely casual and that less than 1% had ever been addicted to narcotics. In Vietnam, almost half the general sample had tried narcotics, and 20% reported opiate addiction. After return, usage and addiction decreased to pre-Vietnam levels. No correlation was found between drug use in Vietnam and assignments, danger, or death of friends. Besides the wish to achieve euphoria, the most common explanations for heroin use included improved tolerance of Army regulations and reduction of homesickness, boredom, depression, and fear. One fifth of all users began within the first week of arrival and three fifths within the first 2 months. Use of non-narcotic drugs, predictors and correlates of drug use in the sam-

ples, and the relationship of drugs to post-Vietnam social adjustment are discussed.   (C)

Robinson, M. G. (1974). Biochemical and behavioral findings during
acute heroin abstinence in Vietnam. Clinical Toxicology, 7, 314.
     This symposium abstract highlights findings from a field
study of 10 addicts (and 5 controls) undergoing heroin abstinence
and withdrawal in Vietnam. Robinson notes major differences in
demographics and use patterns distinguishing these military addicts
from typical civilian addicts (i.e., they were young, healthy, and
relatively free of other illicit drug use; they typically used pure
heroin through nasal insufflation or smoking modes; and they had
relatively mild withdrawal symptoms). Their withdrawal symptoms
peaked at approximately 36 hours and waned over the next 72-96
hours. The pupillary miosis present on admission was soon replaced
by mydriasis, which persisted for 5 days. During the final 9 days
of the 14-day study, morphine equivalents excretion persisted at
lower and fluctuating but still significant levels, suggesting that
overt clinical withdrawal symptoms represent only the initial phase
of a far more prolonged total abstinence process. (See also
Holloway, Sodetz, Elsmore, & the members of work unit 102, 1973;
Robinson, Howe, Varni, Ream, & Hegge, 1974.)   (C)

Robinson, M. G., Howe, R. C., Varni, J. G., Ream, N. W., & Hegge,
F. W. (1974). Assessment of pupil size during acute heroin withdrawal in Vietnam. Neurology, 24, 729-732.
     Photographic pupillometry was used to evaluate 10 heroin
users and 5 controls three times daily for 6 days after the patients' last heroin dose (Robinson, 1974). Stimulation with intense
light further constricted the miotic pupils of heroin-intoxicated
patients. Heroin users' initially constricted pupils dilated as
withdrawal progressed and remained mydriatic thereafter. Results
confirm pupil diameter as an excellent differential indicator of
heroin intoxication and withdrawal. The authors highlight that
since the abstinence syndrome in Vietnam heroin users was clinically mild, it was possible to conduct these studies without
pharmacologic intervention.   (C)

Siegel, A. J. (1973). The heroin crisis among US forces in Southeast Asia: An overview. Journal of the American Medical Association, 223, 1258-1261.
     Describes environmental, psychological, and medical observa-
tions made while Siegel treated 200 drug abuse cases among U.S.
Army support troops stationed in Bangkok, Thailand, in 1971 and
1972. Isolation from home, service in a foreign environment, lack
of identification with the military and its mission, and lack of
military supervision, as well as prominent pro-drug use peer influ-

ence and pre-Vietnam drug use experience (70%), characterized the
circumstances for the population at risk. Readily available and
extremely inexpensive pure heroin served as a uniquely appealing
offending agent. Most users preferred the oral-respiratory route in
that it removed the fear of needles, hepatitis, and overdose, and
sidestepped the stigma of the stateside junkie. Many users continued to function in their jobs while under its influence. Most abstinence syndromes were mild (insomnia, mild agitation, and transient muscle cramps) and were readily controlled by reassurance or
antianxiety compounds. Although 5% of abstainers demonstrated a
more severe flulike illness, narcotic replacement medications were
rarely needed. Most heroin users in this study appeared to have
major underlying personality deficiencies and histories of adaptive
failure. A high rate of recidivism was common. (C)

Solomon, R. (1979). The rise and fall of the Laotian and Vietnamese opiate trades. Journal of Psychedelic Drugs, 11, 159-171.
     Summarizes the political and geographical features of narcotic
trafficking in and around Vietnam from the French colonial rule in
Indochina through the communist military victory in South Vietnam
in 1975. It has been charged that the wide-scale, inexpensive
availability of narcotics late in the war was the result of the
communists' intent to demoralize American troops and promote
opposition to the war within the United States. The available data,
however, suggest that the motivating factors were opportunity,
widespread corruption among South Vietnamese officials, and effective criminal syndicates. As the large number of U.S. troops
stationed in Vietnam became an expanded market, a consequent
expansion occurred in the Golden Triangle's heroin-refining facilities, almost all of which were owned and protected by pro-
American Thai and Laotian forces. Thai, Laotian, and South Vietnamese air forces and the paramilitary charter airline companies,
such as Air America and Continental Air, soon dominated the
opiate transportation business. (C)

Stanton, M. D. (1976). Drugs, Vietnam, and the Vietnam veteran:
An overview. American Journal of Drug and Alcohol Abuse, 3, 557-
570. (Reprinted as: The hooked serviceman: Drug use in and after
Vietnam. In C. R. Figley & S. Leventman (Eds.), (1980a). Strangers
at home: Vietnam veterans since the war (pp. 279-292). New York:
Praeger.)
     Reviews previous drug use prevalence studies conducted with
Vietnam soldiers, and integrates this data with political and social
events and military policy changes to define the shifting scope of
the drug problem. Stanton notes two stages of Vietnam drug use: a
period of increasing marijuana use, followed by the 1970 influx of
highly potent heroin to which one fifth of enlisted troops became
addicted at some time during their tour. When drug use is exam-

ined in general, the most impressive rise is in use prior to service in Vietnam rather than in that which began in Vietnam between 1966 and 1970. The meteoric rise in heroin use beginning in 1970, however, does not coincide with increasing pre-Vietnam heroin use but instead with the sudden availability in Vietnam of very inexpensive, almost pure heroin. Stanton considers epidemiological factors as well as physical and social consequences. Given a remission rate of 95% for heroin-using soldiers once they returned to the States and the lack of data indicating that heroin use in Vietnam degraded individual or group performance, he questions if heroin use was more deleterious than the alcohol use of previous wars. (C)

Sullivan, M. B. (1975). A study of psychological and sociological correlates of Vietnam drug abusers. Dissertation Abstracts International, 35 (12-A), 7665.
    Reports results of a survey of 101 Navy servicemen referred to the Naval Drug Rehabilitation Center in San Diego, CA, between June 1971 and August 1972. Sullivan used the Tennessee Self Concept Scale (TSCS) and the Community History Form to compare Vietnam (n = 42) and non-Vietnam (n = 59) subjects, and heroin (n = 42) and nonheroin (n = 59) users. The Vietnam and non-Vietnam groups both exhibited high scores on the TSCS general maladjustment and personality disorder scales. Sullivan concludes that the Vietnam drug abuse population reflects an inadequate self-concept stemming from a difficult developmental background and insufficient psychological coping skills. (C)

Zinberg, N. E. (1972a). Heroin use in Vietnam and the United States: A contrast and critique. Archives of General Psychiatry, 26, 486-488.
    Reports on Zinberg's 1971 3-week survey in Vietnam of heroin use patterns and efforts at physiological and psychological rehabilitation of users. In contrast to stateside patterns, use in Vietnam is a broadscale social group phenomenon by young soldiers who are self-administering extremely inexpensive and available heroin to achieve relief from stresses of low morale, mistrust of military authority, insignificant jobs, jail-like restriction to military bases, and the perception that Americans at home have discredited them. Further, soldiers consider the military's heroin education programs neither credible nor effective. The 16 Army rehabilitation and treatment programs Zinberg visited assumed one of three types: (1) psychologically oriented programs outside of either medical or penal authority, managed by ex-addicts and minimizing the physical symptoms of withdrawal; (2) medically oriented programs with reversed priorities; and (3) involuntary programs emphasizing detoxification enforced through urine testing. Zinberg suggests that the marginal results of these programs are due to

the emphasis on group treatment, which allows for the persistence of low motivation and strong countermores. He believes it is vital to distinguish the genuinely drug-dependent soldier in need of medical/psychiatric attention from the larger segment of socially habituated soldiers who need other rehabilitative or administrative steps. (C)

Zinberg, N. E. (1972b). Rehabilitation of heroin users in Vietnam. Contemporary Drug Problems, 1, 263-294.

Expands on observations gleaned from his 1971 visit to Vietnam (Zinberg, 1972a). According to Zinberg, heroin users in Vietnam belong to three groups: (1) an urban type with a criminal record, (2) a middle-class individual with a record of trouble in school, and (3) a small-town dweller in good physical condition and representing all ethnic groups. Special aspects of the Vietnam drug problem include low troop morale, the social use of heroin, and the overriding tendency there to do all things in excess. Five rehabilitation programs are described: (1) one employing a counter-culture against heroin, (2) one in which the troops merely go through the motions of rehabilitation, (3) a medical program, (4) an outpatient program, and (5) a penal approach. Zinberg deduces that occasional and moderate users recover, but heavy, committed users do not benefit from the programs. Most importantly, across all programs it is primarily the soldier nearing his scheduled date of return to the States who manifests the motivation to discontinue heroin use. (C)

6   Special Groups

Anderson, C. R. (1985). Black and white. In M. H. Greenberg & A. R. Norton (Eds.), Touring Nam: The Vietnam war reader (pp. 287- 300). New York: William Morrow.

Describes the evolution and patterns of racial tension that developed within the military in Vietnam as the war progressed. (C)

Berry, J. S. (1984). Those gallant men: On trial in Vietnam. Novato, CA: Presidio Press.

From his personal records and official trial transcripts, Berry reconstructs and narrates the story of his tour of duty in Vietnam (1968-69) as a defense counsel in the Army Judge Advocate General Corps. In seeking to describe the peculiar nature of military law as applied in the Vietnam combat theatre, he writes, "We did not know where we were, and we represented GIs, none of whom knew where they were. So we tried to work the approximate magic of the law in utter blindness, during a firestorm." (C)

Binkin, M., & Eitelberg, M. J. (1982). From Bunker Hill to Vietnam. In M. Binkin & M. J. Eitelberg, Blacks and the military (pp. 11-38). Washington, DC: Brookings Institution.

Within the larger context of black participation in America's military services, this chapter provides a historical account of the various roles and achievements of blacks in combat situations. Generally, the trend was one of gradual reduction in government and service policies that limited black combat roles. During Vietnam the previously prevailing "fight for the right to fight" by blacks was replaced by growing concern that selective service policies favored recruitment of blacks over whites. Although across the full scope of the war blacks suffered a rate for combat deaths (13% of all combat deaths) roughly equivalent to their proportion in the population, the rates for 1965-66 were approximately 20% and led the Pentagon to order a cutback "in frontline participation by Negroes." Ultimately, studies of draft and casualty data for the war have disputed existence of institutional racism and have instead pointed toward overrepresentation in the draft among the low-income strata. Although anecdotal reports of racial conflict in the theatre abound, systematic studies of interracial relations were not undertaken as they were in previous wars. Incidents with racial overtones plagued the Vietnam theatre beginning in 1968. Also discussed is "Project 100,000," an experimental program between October 1966 and June 1969 in which 246,000 men (40% black) were inducted who would ordinarily have been rejected because of limited education. Over half of these who entered the Army and Marines were sent to Vietnam--primarily for combat duty. (C)

Boyle, R. (1972). The flower of the dragon: The breakdown of the U.S. Army in Vietnam. San Francisco: Ramparts Press.
     Presents a journalist's personal account of his travels and observations among combat units of the U.S. Army and the Army of the Republic of Vietnam. Although Boyle provides a backdrop by initially describing his experiences in Vietnam in 1965 during the opening phase of America's combat activities, his emphasis is on his later travels throughout South Vietnam in 1969 and 1971, when America's military presence was withdrawing and demoralization and dissent within the ranks were reaching unprecedented levels. His antiwar sentiments are undisguised, and he ultimately encourages and even leads protest demonstrations by U.S. servicemen. (C)

Crowe, R. R., & Colbach, E. M. (1971). A psychiatric experience with project 100,000. Military Medicine, 136, 271-273.
     Reports referral rates to the 67th Evacuation Hospital (Qui Nhon) in 1969 of soldiers inducted into the Army with less than induction-standard educational achievement, compared with controls. "Project" soldiers were referred 10 times as frequently, but diagnosis and severity were not different. The authors posit that more vigorous consultative efforts with command may reduce the noneffectiveness rate for these soldiers. (C)

Dunn, J. (1983). The POW chronicles: A bibliographic review. Armed Forces and Society, 9, 495-514.
     Reviews the scope and merits of the publications of and, in most cases, by various prisoners of the Vietnam war. (C)

Falabella, J. R. (1971). Vietnam memoirs: A passage to sorrow. New York: Pageant Press.
     A personal narrative of Falabella's 1968 tour in Vietnam as an Army chaplain who chose to live in the field with his troops and to accompany them on combat missions. (C)

Fallaci, O. (1972). Nothing, and so be it. Garden City, NY: Doubleday.

Presents Fallaci's diary written during her year's tour as a combat correspondent in Vietnam in 1967-68. (C)

Fiman, B. G., Borus, J. F., & Stanton, M. D. (1975). Black-white American-Vietnamese relations among soldiers in Vietnam. Journal of Social Issues, 31(4), 39-48.

Presents results of an anonymous questionnaire administered to assess the attitudes and perceptions of 126 black and 359 white enlisted soldiers who served in Vietnam between 1968 and 1971 as to black-white and American-Vietnamese relations there. Factor scores developed for each of these two areas served as the dependent variables. Blacks, and especially younger blacks, held a more negative view of the race relations than did whites. However, black-white relationships were reportedly better in Vietnam than in the United States, especially among soldiers who served in combat. Blacks reported less negative attitudes toward the Vietnamese than did whites, and soldiers who served in combat units perceived the American-Vietnamese relationship more negatively. (MA)

Flood, C. B. (1970). The war of the innocents. New York: McGraw-Hill.

Presents a journalist's observations from a year in Vietnam (1967). Flood's account is unique in his inclusion of participant-observation reportage as an attached member of a dive-bomber unit. He also spent 3 months near the Cambodian border with an infantry battalion and another 4 months with American civilian and military advisers to the South Vietnamese. (C)

Freedman, D., & Rhoads, J. (Eds.). (1987). Nurses in Vietnam: The forgotten veterans. Austin, TX: Texas Monthly Press.

Presents the oral histories and impressions from nine nurses, including Rhoads, who served tours with the Army in Vietnam. Their collective service there spanned from 1965 through 1971 and ranged over a variety of assignments and locations. The work is dedicated by name to the eight nurses who died in Vietnam and includes an introduction that traces the history of combat nurses in American military history as well as reflects on the experiential similarities and differences between female veterans and their male counterparts. (C)

Hart, G. (1973). Psychological aspects of venereal disease in a war environment. Social Science and Medicine, 7, 455-467.

Presents results of a study of Australian soldiers who were treated at a venereal disease clinic in Vietnam. The participants (400 consecutive patients and 206 randomly selected controls) completed an Eysenck Personality Inventory and a questionnaire

tapping attitudes and demographics. Generally, the findings confirmed the study hypothesis that a more liberal attitude toward
sexual expression prevails in the war environment and that what
constitutes normalcy among the patients studied (e.g., the relatively normal personality measures among soldiers who acknowledged performing cunnilingus on Vietnamese prostitutes) contrasts
markedly from that found among noncombat zone clinic populations. Extroversion was found among VD patients in Vietnam, but
it was less prominent than it would be in homeland studies. In-
troversion and neuroticism were elevated in those expressing a
desire to marry Vietnamese or experiencing emotional rapport with
their prostitute partners. Neuroticism scores also correlated closely
with indicators of "venereoneurosis" (preoccupation with bodily
processes and worries about the persistence of VD following
treatment). (M)

Hart, G. (1975). Sexual behavior in a war environment. Journal of
Sex Research, 11, 218-226.
     Questionnaires were administered to 488 consecutive venereal
disease patients and 230 randomly selected soldiers of similar rank
from among Australian troops in Vietnam. Overall, masturbation,
intercourse, and fellatio were the most frequently reported sexual
behaviors, whereas cunnilingus, anal intercourse, and homosexual
behaviors were the least. Hart posits that environmental stress and
relative peer acceptance may have had a marked effect on sexual
behavior, and that the sexual output of an individual was markedly
influenced by his sociological background. (C)

Herr, M. (1968). Dispatches. New York: Alfred A. Knopf.
     Presents a personal journal of the war. Herr uses his vantage
point as a war correspondent to capture the fundamental experience of the U.S. military in Vietnam and its manifest horrors. He
pays particular attention to the Marines in their battle at Khe
Sanh. (M)

Holm, J. (1982). Women in the military: An unfinished revolution.
Novato, CA: Presidio Press.
     This comprehensive review of the policies and events related
to the role of women in America's military organizations includes
two chapters--"Vietnam" (pp. 205-229) and "Tet Offensive: The
Test" (pp. 230-243)--that summarize the female military contri-
bution to the war effort in Vietnam. (C)

Hubbell, J. G. (1977). P.O.W.: A definitive history of the American
prisoner-of-war experience in Vietnam, 1964-1973. New York:
Readers Digest Press.

Drawing on government and other documentation and extensive interviews with almost 200 individuals, Hubbell and his col-
laborators from the Readers Digest staff provide a collective
narrative history of American prisoners-of-war in Southeast Asia
from the first capture on August 5, 1964, until the negotiated
POW release in February 1973.   (C)

Knightley, P. (1975). The first casualty: From the Crimea to
Vietnam: The war correspondent as hero, propagandist, and myth
maker. New York: Harcourt Brace Jovanovich.
     Included in this review of how the role of war correspon-
dents and their influences developed over the past 120 years are
two chapters--"Vietnam, 1954-1975" (pp. 373-400) and "War Is Fun,
1954-1975" (pp. 401-425)--that chronicle the experiences of these
journalists in the conflict in Southeast Asia. Knightly notes that it
was not until Vietnam that war correspondents began to perceive
an obligation for truthful and compassionate reporting, and he illustrates not only that the task in Vietnam was harrowing and bewildering, but also that ethical conflicts were constantly present,
especially because of the introduction of television coverage. (C)

Kroll, J. (1976). Racial patterns of military crimes in Vietnam.
Psychiatry, 39, 51-64.
     Presents data and case examples from examination of the
Vietnam returnees who were confined to the U.S. Disciplinary Barracks (Ft. Leavenworth, KS) between February 1968 and November
1969 (N = 293) for crimes committed in Vietnam. White soldiers
were statistically more prone to have been incarcerated for being
AWOL (absent without leave) or for committing violent crimes
against Vietnamese civilians. Blacks were more likely to have been
convicted for combat refusal or for a violent crime against another American soldier. Overall, rates for incarceration of blacks
greatly exceeded those for whites. Explanations for these racial
differences include that white soldiers acted on racial prejudices,
which were displaced to the Vietnamese, whereas black soldiers
felt allied with the Vietnamese and acted upon perceptions that
whites were the enemy. Kroll reviews the regression-inducing
nature of combat exposure in Vietnam, the ambivalent nature of
buddy relationships under those circumstances (most of the murder
victims were buddies or friends), and the causal connection between forced passivity in the face of the "crushing terror" of
combat and racially oriented violence.   (C)

Marshall, K. (1987). In the combat zone: An oral history of American women in Vietnam, 1966-1975. Boston: Little, Brown.
     Provides a series of interviews with 20 American women who
served in Vietnam at various times during the war. These women

are presented as examples of the "invisible veterans"--Marshall's reference to the 33,000 to 55,000 women there on active military duty or as civilians--who include military nurses; those serving in the Women's Army Corps; Army Special Services and Red Cross workers; those employed in civilian jobs; and religious mission volunteers. Marshall also describes the various jobs and challenges women encountered in Vietnam and highlights the common themes revealed through her interviews. (C)

Odom, J. D. (1986). The Vietnam nurses can't forget: Letters home chronicle long hours of surgery and gunfire. American Journal of Nursing, 86, 1035-1037.
    Provides excerpts from Odom's letters to his fiancée (November 1967 to March 1968) during his tour in Vietnam as an Army nurse assigned to the 18th Surgical Hospital (MUST). This portable hospital--the acronym is for Medial Unit, Self-contained, Transportable--was the first such facility deployed by the Army. (C)

Page, T. (1983). Tim Page's Nam. New York: Alfred A. Knopf.
    Presents a collection of photographs accompanied by narrative reflection by a photographer who achieved distinction in his close coverage of the war in Vietnam and who was himself wounded numerous times throughout its course. (C)

San, N. D. (1969). Psychiatry in the Army of the Republic of Vietnam. In P. G. Bourne (Ed.), The psychology and physiology of stress: With reference to special studies of the Viet Nam war (pp. 45-73). New York: Academic Press.
    Presents the history of various sociocultural features of the Vietnamese, particularly those factors influencing the epidemiology and patterns of mental illness and treatment. San also describes the psychiatric organization for identifying and treating psychiatric conditions among members of the army of South Vietnam, and provides incidence figures for the major categories of psychiatric conditions that affected military manpower during 1963-67. (C)

Saywell, S. (1985). Women in war: First-hand accounts from World War II to El Salvador. New York: Viking.
    In a chapter entitled "Twilight Zone: Vietnam, 1965-72" (pp. 225-258), Saywell presents the narratives of 6 women nurses who served in Vietnam at various periods throughout the war, all of whom reportedly developed PTSD symptoms after their tours. (C)

Spelts, D. (1986). Nurses who served--and did not return. American Journal of Nursing, 86, 1037-1038.

Provides brief biographic sketches of the 10 military nurses (2 male) who died during their service in Vietnam. Seven of the group died in aircraft crashes, 2 from illness, and 1 as a consequence of an enemy attack. (C)

Spragg, G. S. (1972). Psychiatry in the Australian military forces. Medical Journal of Australia, 1, 745-751.
    Describes the clinical features and management of 100 psychiatric patients among the Australian Forces in Vietnam between February and June 1970. Spragg indicates that adequate personality assessment of soldiers and rapid removal of those who are emotionally disturbed are important to maintaining the stability of the deployed force. (C)

Terry, W. (1971). The angry blacks in the army. In D. Horowitz & the editors of Ramparts (Eds.), Two, three . . . many Vietnams: A radical reader on the wars in Southeast Asia and the conflicts at home (pp. 222-231). San Francisco: Canfield Press.
    Reports results of a 1970 survey of soldiers in Vietnam regarding racial perceptions and attitudes, and compares the "frightening" results with the much more harmoniously integrated period of 3 years earlier. Terry emphasizes the "very deep layer of bitterness" he found among black soldiers and notes that (1) they are adverse to fighting in a war they consider to be the white man's folly; (2) they have directed their anger primarily toward racism in America; (3) they contend that their fight is in the United States against repression and racism; (4) "schooled in the violent art of guerrilla warfare," most say they would join riots and take up arms in the States to achieve rights and opportunities previously denied them; and (5) many declare their intention to join radical groups upon return home. (C)

Terry, W. (1984). Bloods: An oral history of the Vietnam war by black veterans. New York: Random House.
    Presents the personal accounts of 20 black veterans who served in Vietnam against the backdrop of the evolving civil rights and black nationalist movements in the States, the racial tensions and racist expressions among the military in Vietnam, and the mounting political pressures on black soldiers not to fight other people of color. (C)

Vance, S. (1970). The courageous and the proud: A black man in the white man's Army. New York: Norton.
    An infantry sergeant's personal account of his combat tour in Vietnam in 1965. Twice wounded, he also earned the Silver Star while serving as a platoon sergeant. His acknowledged purpose for

writing his story was to achieve public recognition for the accomplishments of black soldiers under fire in Southeast Asia. (C)

Van Devanter, L. M. (1983). Home before morning: The story of an Army nurse in Vietnam. New York: Beaufort Books.

Presents an autobiographical account of an operating room nurse before, during, and after a year's tour with the Army in Vietnam in 1969-70. Besides vividly recounting the grim experiences of caring for seriously wounded soldiers in Vietnam, Van Devanter describes the hostility she encountered upon reentry to the United States, the disabling psychological symptoms that affected her for many years afterward, and ultimately her emergence as the leader for the Vietnam Veterans of America Women's Project. (C)

Walker, K. (1985). A piece of my heart. Novato, CA: Presidio Press.

Provides a collection of oral histories from 26 American women who served during the war. In Vietnam they held positions within the military as nurses and WACs (Women Army Corps), as well as civilian jobs such as airline flight attendants, American Red Cross workers, and an Armed Forces Radio announcer. (C)

Bloch, H. S. (1970b). Dr. Bloch replies (Letter). American Journal of Psychiatry, 126, 1039-1040.
    Replying to a letter to the editor (see Maier, 1970), Bloch notes that in his clinical experience in the field in Vietnam he did not see soldiers beset with normal doubt about war and killing. Instead, most "doubt" was symptomatic of underlying aggressive impulses, castration anxiety, or exaggerated separation anxiety. He contends that dispositional decisions were based solely on the soldier's psychological state, with diagnostic labeling of secondary importance. In defense of military psychiatry in Vietnam he concludes, "If reality is that America's youth are now fighting, then they deserve the best psychiatric care that can be afforded them. Such care neither oversimplifies issues nor encumbers and compromises the evaluation or treatment setting by intrusion of the psychiatrists' moral judgments and emotions." (C)

Bloch, S., & Chodoff, P. (Eds.). (1981). Psychiatric ethics. Oxford: Oxford University Press.
    Presents a more general review of ethical aspects of psychiatric labeling and treatment, including occasional references to potential ethical dilemmas confronting military psychiatrists serving in Vietnam and related issues in the treatment of Vietnam veterans. Most of these remarks are extrapolated from writings of R. J. Lifton. (C)

Brass, A. (1970). Medicine over there. Journal of the American Medical Association, 213, 1473-1475.
    Reviews two books, one of which is P. G. Bourne's Men, Stress, and Vietnam (1970). Regarding Bourne's description of the practices of military psychiatrists in Vietnam, Brass asks: "If the soldier is seriously enough disturbed to require hospitalization or evacuation, is it good medicine to treat only his symptoms and then reexpose him to the cause of his breakdown? Just how well does a GI on tranquilizers (a) fight, (b) look after his own skin. . . . One would like to know the comparative casualty figures of soldiers on tranquilizers against those not taking prescribed drugs." (C)

Colbach, E. M. (1985). Ethical issues in combat psychiatry. Military Medicine, 150, 256-265.

Presents a highly subjective retrospective of Colbach's service as an Army psychiatrist in Vietnam in 1968 and as the assistant psychiatric consultant to the Army Surgeon General the year after. Through these recollections, particularly those of especially challenging cases, Colbach details a personally and professionally wrenching experience, which he believes affected him both while serving in Vietnam and since his return. He sums up his ethical position 16 years later: "Whether the Vietnam conflict fits these criteria (of a just war) or not is really beyond me to say. I did accept it as a just war when I agreed to serve in it. . . . I then had to accept that my obligation to my individual patient was far superseded by my obligation to the military and, eventually, to my country." (C)

Lifton, R. J. (1975a). Advocacy and corruption in the healing professions. Connecticut Medicine, 39, 803-813. (Republished in N. L. Goldman & D. R. Segal (Eds.), (1976). The social psychology of military service (pp. 45-64). Beverly Hills, CA: Sage Publications; and in C. R. Figley (Ed.), (1978a). Stress disorders among Vietnam veterans: Theory, research and treatment (pp. 209-230). New York: Brunner/Mazel.)
      Holds up the military psychiatrist facing the ethical dilemma in Vietnam as an example of a professional who adopted an unquestioning "technicist" collusion with an "absurd and evil organization." Lifton primarily draws on his experiences with Vietnam veteran "rap groups" (Lifton, 1972a) and on published works of psychiatrists who served with the Army (Bey & Smith, 1971; H. S. Bloch, 1969; Gault, 1971). (C)

Livingston, G. S. (1969, September 20). Letter from a Vietnam veteran. Saturday Review, pp. 22-23. (Republished as: Healing in Vietnam. In R. A. Falk, G. Kolko, & R. J. Lifton (Eds.), (1971). Crimes of war (pp. 430-440). New York: Random House.)
      Livingston, an ex-military physician and a graduate of West Point, describes the development of his moral and ethical conflict while he served with a combat regiment in Vietnam in late 1968. Among his perceptions were that broadscale racism was one of the basic motivations of American combat activities, and that the self-interest of the American participants lay in the direction of "more war, more death" to the exclusion of the ostensible goal of promoting the "search for pride and identity" of the Vietnamese. He describes how his assignment in Vietnam was ultimately curtailed and he was discharged prematurely from the Army because of an incident in which he disseminated a satirical prowar prayer at a high-level military ceremony. (C)

Livingston, G. S. (1972). Medicine in the military: Some ethical problems. In M. Visscher (Ed.), Humanistic perspectives in medical ethics (pp. 266-274). Buffalo, NY: Prometheus Books.

Livingston, who served in Vietnam as a military physician, argues that although as an abstraction, medical activities have been ethically defined as neutral, humanitarian, and noncombatant, a latent conflict of interest exists for the physician functioning within the military. This conflict can most simply be considered as a divided loyalty between serving the needs of the group ("conserve the fighting strength") and those of the individual patient. Livingston describes his distress regarding incidents he witnessed or participated in--some involving psychiatric treatment and disposition--that led him to conclude that America's participation in Vietnam was "one of the most antilife enterprises of our time"; that physicians serving with the military in this war were being used as political instruments, rendering the medical care they provided a "parody" and a "charade"; and finally, that physicians should organizationally "take positions on sociopolitical issues which are not generally considered to be within their field of expertise." (C)

Maier, T. (1970). The Army psychiatrist: An adjunct to the system of social control (Letter). American Journal of Psychiatry, 126, 1039.

Reacting to Bloch (1969), Maier comments on the ethics and practices of military psychiatrists from his vantage point of having served as an Army psychiatrist who served in Japan in 1965-67. He suggests that the soldier-patient is someone who does not seek treatment but struggles with "his confrontation with the tragic absurdity of risking his life or of killing other human beings in this meaningless military exercise and whose entire being is devoted to extricating himself from the situation." He notes that "recipients of the character disorder diagnosis are returned forthwith to the coercive province of command," and concludes that "by acting to 'conserve the fighting strength' in their war of boundless immorality, (the military psychiatrist) partakes of the passive complicity that is the mark of guilt in our time. . . . Whatever else Army psychiatry may be, I see neither moral nor scientific justification for the dignity of its definition as clinical psychiatry." (See H. S. Bloch, 1970b, for his reply.) (C)

Meshad, S. (1982). Captain for dark mornings: A true story. Playa Del Rey, CA: Creative Image Associates.

Provides a fictionalized description of Meshad's Army assignment in Vietnam as a social work officer ("psych officer") in 1970. Meshad elaborates his intensely frustrating experience of attempting to provide psychosocial assistance to soldiers and commanders in a war he believes is wrong. As the narrative unfolds, he comes to acknowledge his role-linked guilt and subsequent identification with the confused, frightened, and often traumatized soldiers: "It could have been me. I'd watch them and I'd have to ask myself, 'do I have the balls to do what they're doing?' Meanwhile, I'd be sitting there counseling them about their problems--the main problem being the same thoughts I was grappling with." In time he decides the chief problem is that the soldiers, as well as himself, are victims of military authority: "We were on a tight wire balanced between the chaos of war and the madness of military regulations. . . . I began to think my biggest service to them was to help them manipulate the system." Ultimately, he seeks to martyr himself by becoming embroiled with and court martialed by military authorities because of the length he kept his mustache. (C)

Parrish, M. D. (1972). A veteran of three wars looks at psychiatry in the military. Psychiatric Opinion, 9, 6-11.
    Drawing upon his professional experiences as a participant in World War II, Korea, and Vietnam, Parrish summarizes the principles of providing social and psychiatric support for the combat forces and combat veterans. He devotes special attention to refuting contemporary criticisms of the goals and practices of military psychiatry. (C)

Veatch, R. M. (1977a). The psychiatrist's role in war. In R. M. Veatch (Ed.), Case studies in medical ethics (pp. 245-251). Cambridge: Harvard University Press.
    Presents commentaries of a panel (R. G. Newman, E. T. Englehardt, & P. London) providing contrasting perspectives on ethical issues inherent in practicing combat psychiatry in wartime. For illustrative purposes, the panelists focus on a clinical case that described the treatment and eventual "successful" return to combat flying of an Air Force gunner who initially presented with a "frank admission of fear of flying" after 7 months and more than 100 flying missions over Vietnam. (C)

Adler, B. (Ed.). (1967). Letters from Vietnam. New York: Dutton.
    Presents a collection of letters written during the early period of American involvement in the war by individuals representing the various armed forces as well as by nurses, Red Cross workers, U.S. civilian personnel, and Vietnamese citizens. Adler pays special attention to the viewpoint of the American soldier, who he feels had gone substantially unheard from until this time. The result is a broad and vivid portrayal of the horrors of combat, the customs of the Vietnamese people, and the controversy at home. (M)

Baker, M. (1981). Nam. New York: William Morrow.
    Presents an oral history of the participants in the Vietnam conflict through a collection of narrative segments. (C)

Broughton, J. (1985). Thud Ridge. New York: Bantam Books.
    Augmenting his memory for events with actual in-action cockpit recordings, Broughton presents a narrative account of his combat activities over North Vietnam flying the F-105 ("the Air Force workhorse, the 'thud'"). (C)

Caputo, P. (1977). A rumor of war. New York: Holt, Rinehart & Winston.
    Describes Caputo's experiences and observations both as a young infantry officer with the Marines in Vietnam in 1965-66 and upon his return to Vietnam in 1975 as a newspaper correspondent covering the communist offensives that culminated in the fall of Saigon. (C)

Donovan, D. (1985). Once a warrior king: Memories of an officer in Vietnam. New York: McGraw-Hill.
    A partially disguised personal narrative of a 1st lieutenant's tour (1969-70) in a remote region of the South Vietnam delta serving as team leader of a five-man Army Mobile Advisory Team that provided combat training and support for local militia forces. (C)

Downs, F. (1978). The killing zone: My life in the Vietnamese war. New York: Norton.

Presents an autobiographical account of Downs's experiences as a leader of an infantry platoon of the Fourth Division in Vietnam. The narrative covers the period of September 1967 through January 1968, at which time Downs was disabled by shrapnel from an enemy booby trap. (See Downs, 1984.) (M)

Duncan, D. (1971). "I quit": Memoirs of a special forces hero. In D. Horowitz & the editors of Ramparts (Eds.), Two, three . . . many Vietnams: A radical reader on the wars in Southeast Asia and the conflicts at home (pp. 222-231). San Francisco: Canfield Press.
      Duncan, a highly decorated senior noncommissioned officer who served 18 months (1964-65) in Vietnam during the advisory period of the war, describes his cumulative experiences that led to a reversal in his motivation for service there and a belief that the American intervention in Vietnam was "corrupting the very word democracy." He progressively became convinced that the Viet Cong elements were becoming stronger and receiving more support from the Vietnamese, and he felt the real question was "whether communism was spreading in spite of our involvement--or because of it?" (C)

Edelman, B. (Ed.). (1985). Dear America: Letters home from Vietnam. New York: Norton.
      Presents a series of letters written home throughout the war in Vietnam by the soldiers who served there and, in some cases, died there. Appended to many letters are the editor's notations as to the soldiers' subsequent fate. (C)

Ehrhart, W. D. (1983). Vietnam-Perkasie: A combat Marine memoir. New York: Kensington Publishing.
      Provides a personal narrative of Ehrhart's year-long tour with a Marine infantry battalion in 1967. (C)

Esper, G., & Associated Press. (1983). The eyewitness history of the Vietnam war: 1961-1975. New York: Ballantine Books.
      Presents a chronological review of the war using Associated Press photographs and the personal accounts of military personnel who fought there. (C)

Goff, S. (1985). The big battle. In M. H. Greenberg & A. R. Norton (Eds.), Touring Nam: The Vietnam war reader (pp. 68-77). New York: William Morrow.
      Goff, winner of the Distinguished Service Cross, offers his personal account ("a grunt's-eye view") of a firefight with a

battalion-sized force of North Vietnamese. (See also Goff & Sanders, with Smith, 1982.) (C)

Goff, S., & Sanders, R., with Smith, C. (1982). Brothers: Black soldiers in the Nam. Novato, CA: Presidio Press.
      Presents an oral history of simultaneous combat tours in Vietnam (1968-69) of two black soldiers who had become close friends during their predeployment training. Goff served with the 196th Light Infantry Brigade (I Corps) and received the Distinguished Service Cross for his bravery under fire (see Goff, 1985). Sanders served with the 173rd Airborne (Southern II Corps) and earned the Air Medal for over 25 combat assaults. Smith notes, "(This book seeks) to give the black Vietnam veteran a voice in the history of the Vietnam war. Too often it is forgotten that the military executors of American foreign policy had to base their success or failure in Vietnam ultimately on the man in the field with the weapon. And, as often as not, that man was black." (C)

Goldman, P., & Fuller, T. (1983). Charlie Company: What Vietnam did to us. New York: William Morrow.
      Presented by the staff of Newsweek, this is a "collective memoir" of the experiences in Vietnam and afterward of 65 soldiers who served with a company of the 1st Infantry Division in 1968-69. The members of this unit were selected for study as representative of a "grunt company" that had sustained heavy combat and had served in the "crucible years" surrounding the enemy Tet offensives in spring 1968. (C)

Herbert, A. B. (1973). Soldier. New York: Holt, Rinehart & Winston.
      Contains the memoirs of a career soldier who served as an enlisted man in Korea and later as an officer in Vietnam. Included is a discussion of war crimes in Vietnam that Herbert witnessed or had personal knowledge of and his efforts to end a coverup of those events by the Army. (M)

Huggett, W. T. (1973). Body count. New York: Putnam Books.
      Presents the individual combat experiences of members of a Marine infantry platoon. (M)

Ketwig, J. (1985). . . . And a hard rain fell: A G.I.'s true story of the war in Vietnam. New York: Macmillan.
      The personal narrative of a drafted soldier's year (1966-67) in and around Pleiku in the central highlands of South Vietnam,

his 2nd year assigned in Thailand, and his subsequent return to stateside life. (C)

Klein, J. (1984). Payback: Five Marines and Vietnam. New York: Ballantine Books.
Presents the narrative accounts of 5 Marines who served together with 3rd Marine Regiment in Vietnam in 1967. (C)

Lanning, M. L. (1987). The only war we had: A platoon leader's journal of Vietnam. New York: Ivy Books.
A personal narrative of Lanning's tour (1969) as a junior commissioned officer with the 199th Light Infantry Brigade. He served variously as an infantry platoon leader, a reconnaissance platoon leader, and a company commander. (C)

Lowry, T. S. (1985). And brave men, too. New York: Crown.
Presents the personal accounts of 14 surviving Congressional Medal of Honor recipients from the Vietnam war (a total of 238 were awarded). Lowry, himself a veteran of two tours with the Marine Corps in Vietnam, obtained much of his material from interviews with these men since they returned. These unusually courageous men were considered representative of the commitment of the troops in the first half of the war, before the enemy's Tet offensives changed America's strategy from "escalation" to "extrication." Descriptions of the recipients' exploits and their reactions since are interwoven with a recounting of the unfolding contextual events of the times, both in Vietnam and in the States. (C)

Mason, R. (1983). Chickenhawk. New York: Viking.
A personal narrative of Mason's experiences in Vietnam, where he flew over 1,000 helicopter combat missions before being discharged from the military in 1968. (C)

McDonough, J. R. (1985). Platoon leader. Novato, CA: Presidio Press.
McDonough, a West Point graduate, provides an account of his 6-month experience in heavy combat as a platoon leader with the 173rd Airborne Brigade in the coastal province of Binh Dinh in 1970. Among his reflections on the war he remarks, "Like the entire American system in Vietnam, we had fought a limited military war with constrained objectives; the enemy had fought a total political war with no preordained restrictions. We were doomed from the outset." (C)

O'Brien, T. (1973). If I die in a combat zone: Box me up and ship me home. New York: Delacorte Press.

A personal narrative of O'Brien's 1969 tour in Vietnam as a drafted infantryman with the Army's Americal Division. (C)

Santoli, A. (1981). Everything we had: An oral history of the Vietnam war by thirty-three American soldiers who fought it. New York: Ballantine Books.

Presents a composite history of the Vietnam conflict through a collection of narrative segments by 33 veterans whose service there (1962-75) spanned the entire period of U.S. military involvement. (C)

West, F. J., Jr. (1972). The village. New York: Harper & Row.

West, who served as a Marine officer in Vietnam, provides an account of a 12-man Marine unit that fought for several months in conjunction with South Vietnamese militiamen in an attempt to dislodge Viet Cong guerrillas from a strategic village in Quang Ngai province. (C)

Yezzo, D. (1974). A G.I.'s Vietnam Diary, 1968-1969. New York: Franklin Watts.

Using entries from his personal diary, Yezzo chronicles his tour in Vietnam as an enlisted soldier assigned to an Army Civil Affairs and Psychological Operations section of the 1st Cavalry Division. (C)

II   VETERAN ADAPTATION

Within a relatively short period of time--roughly from 1965, when large numbers of infantry troops were deployed to Vietnam, to the spring of 1968, when the American people became disheartened with the war following the enemy's "Tet" offensives-- public reaction toward the returning veterans reversed from acceptance to scorn. Further, 5 more years of U.S. combat activities and associated public protest followed that turning point in the war before a negotiated withdrawal could be completed and all the troops were returned home.

References in this section describe and explain the adaptational stress associated with the veteran's reentry into the increasingly disapproving American society following service, particularly combat service, in Vietnam; the interacting causes for the various forms of adaptive failure and psychiatric symptoms that emerged among unprecedented numbers of returned veterans; and the evolving clinical and institutional strategies that sought to relieve suffering and promote the veteran's successful resumption of his civilian life.

1   Reentry Stress and Adaptation: Nonclinical Populations

Anonymous. (1972). A study of the problems facing Vietnam-era veterans on their readjustment to civilian life. Report of the Senate Committee on Veterans Affairs. Washington, DC: U.S. Government Printing Office.
    Contains the full report of a survey conducted for the VA by Louis Harris & Assoc., Inc. The first professional research survey the VA made among veterans of the Vietnam war, it also measures attitudes of the general public and employers toward veterans. Between August 15 and August 30 of 1971, the survey team interviewed 2,003 veterans recently separated from the service, 1,498 households representing a cross-section of the American public, and 786 employers. They concentrated on four areas: (1) the reception the veteran receives upon returning home, (2) the problem the returning veteran has in finding employment, (3) the problem of drug use and abuse among servicemen and its treatment, and (4) the role of the VA in facilitating the veteran's readjustment after separation from the armed forces. (MA)

Anonymous. (1978). President's commission on mental health: Mental health problems of Vietnam-era veterans (Report No. PCMH/P-78/18). Washington, DC: U.S. Government Printing Office.
    Includes official statistics that help define the scope of the problem: the Vietnam war era is defined as 1963-73; the number of era veterans from all service branches is 8.5 million; the number of those who served in the Vietnam theatre is 2.8 million; the number of those in the military who faced combat or otherwise hazardous circumstances is estimated at 1 million; and the number wounded in the theatre is 304,000. The principle five types of readjustment problems identified as affecting Vietnam-era veterans are (1) psychiatric disorders, (2) drug abuse and alcoholism, (3) social stigma, (4) failure of social integration, and (5) family breakdown. Although the high prevalence rates for drug abuse in Vietnam reverted back to pre-Vietnam levels upon return to the States, the commission highlights VA statistics indicating current high levels of alcoholism in Vietnam veterans. The stigma on Vietnam veterans, as they are reflected in the media, renders them "losers, misfits, poor soldiers physically or mentally unfit to fight; and as drug addicts, homicidal maniacs, and individuals who cannot be relied upon to act in an emotionally controlled and rational manner." The commission refers to VA studies that "indicate (that) serious and prolonged readjustment problems exist in approximately one out of five veterans but, to a lesser degree, are experienced by all." The report concludes with a discussion of action proposals

that include a call for the VA to provide comprehensive mental health, psychosocial readjustment assistance, counseling, and other services as may be necessary to assist Vietnam and other veterans and their dependents. Another suggestion is to execute a national media program to correct public misperception of Vietnam veterans, but they acknowledge that this may fail to achieve results because social blame may be the root cause of the distortion. (C)

Baker, J. E. (1984). Monitoring of suicidal behavior among patients in the VA health care system. Psychiatric Annals, 14, 272-275.

Reviews suicide behavior patterns within the VA system since 1950. Regarding veterans of Southeast Asia, data has neither confirmed or refuted reports of 50,000-70,000 suicides, in part because the veteran status of suicide victims is often unknown. However, the VA has determined that between October 1978 and September 1980, Vietnam-era veterans, who represented only 14% of all VA patients, constituted 29% of suicides among that population, thereby overcontributing by 15%. In comparison, for the same period World War II veterans undercontributed by 20% and Korean war veterans by 4%. Baker concludes that Vietnam-era veterans require the most attention for suicide prevention. (S)

Bey, D. R. (1972c). The returning veteran syndrome. Medical Insight, 4, 42-49.

Suggests that the symptoms shown by many Vietnam veterans, such as sleeplessness, depression, hyperirritability, and lack of energy, may be part of a specific syndrome caused not only by the problems of readjustment to their home environments but also by the loss of the close relationships formed in Vietnam. Bey describes the group process of becoming initiated into the soldier's unit in Vietnam after undergoing the sadness of saying goodbye to loved ones, as well as the ways in which the veteran must later disengage from his unit when he is close to finishing his tour of duty. He notes that it is often not apparent to either the veteran or his family that he suffered an emotional loss in separating from the intense relationships formed in Vietnam. Bey feels this loss is basic to the depressive symptoms often observed in the returning veteran. What the veteran is experiencing is akin to a period of mourning before he can fully invest in his stateside relationships and interests. Bey considers that the process of reintegration can be hastened by enabling the veteran to discuss his experiences and work through his feelings with other veterans who have completed their readjustment. (S)

Borchard, D. C. (1977). Self-actualization in Vietnam veteran and non-veteran male college students. Dissertation Abstracts International, 37 (8-A), 4975. (University Microfilms No. 77-02944)

The Personality Orientation Inventory (POI), a research instrument for measuring "self-actualization," was given to 183 male students between ages 21 and 36 who were enrolled in mathematics and English classes at a large suburban Maryland community college. Of these subjects, 85 were Vietnam-era veterans who served in localities other than Vietnam; 15 were veterans who served in noncombat capacities in Vietnam; 30 were combat veterans of Vietnam; and 53 were a nonveteran control group. The general hypothesis was that military service during the Vietnam era has significantly affected the subsequent psychological well-being of the veteran, rendering him less "self-actualizing" than the nonveteran, and that the closer the veteran's exposure to combat, the greater his resulting psychological dysfunctionality. Overall, the nonveterans showed the lowest self-actualization scores, but Borchard cautions that this may be more correlated to younger age. Among his interpretations is that the veteran population is significantly more able than the nonveteran population to accept themselves despite their weaknesses and to accept their ordinary feelings of anger or aggression. (M)

Borus, J. F. (1973a). Reentry: I. Adjustment issues facing the Vietnam returnee. Archives of General Psychiatry, 28, 501-506.
     Provides results of interviews and military records reviews of 64 veterans who had served a year's tour in Vietnam between June 1969 and December 1970. Their success in functioning over the 6-month period following their arrival at their stateside garrison unit was considered along military, family, social, and emotional lines. Study participants were divided into three groups: adjusting (n = 22), legally maladjusting (n = 22), and emotional maladjusting (n = 20). Borus discusses the Vietnam veteran adjustment issues illuminated by this study. (S)

Borus, J. F. (1973b). Reentry: II. "Making it" back in the states. American Journal of Psychiatry, 130, 850-854.
     Presents further analysis of a study of 64 veterans (Borus, 1973a), in which Borus examines the coping methods of the adjusters and maladjusters (both legal and emotional) to stateside military life. Adjusters could best tolerate the frustrations of garrison life because they were more adept at getting the institution to meet their needs. Legal maladjusters were quite disappointed with the low status accorded them as combat veterans and missed the intense combat unit relationships that had supported them in Vietnam. They replaced these mission-syntonic relationships with relationships based on a shared hatred of the Army. Emotional maladjusters saw the frustrations of garrison life as personally directed against them and were least successful in forming supportive relationships. This group felt the most guilt about their

activities in Vietnam and saw themselves as damaged, as evidenced by "shot nerves," short tempers, and belligerent or isolated inter-personal relationships. They also were most haunted by recurrent nightmares and intrusive thoughts, and had the highest frequency of regular use of drugs in Vietnam and on return. Borus argues for the establishment of intervention programs within the military to foster healthy coping upon reentry. (S)

Borus, J. F. (1973c). Reentry: III. Facilitating healthy readjustment in Vietnam veterans. Psychiatry, 36, 428-439.
       Integrates results from his previous reports of Vietnam vet-eran studies (Borus, 1973a, 1973b) with data from World War II veteran studies, principles of military psychiatry, and civilian studies of coping with stressful transitions. Borus suggests the following outline for a preventive intervention program to facili-tate healthy readjustment in returning combat veterans: (1) the general atmosphere of the program should acknowledge both the normality of stress in the transition period of reentry and the need for gradual accommodation to the changes of the new milieu, and it should also provide advance information about expectable stresses and group support from other combat veteran peers to fa-cilitate successful coping; (2) there should be an opportunity to anticipate and rehearse with a peer group the possible stressful situations that may await the veteran; (3) when the soldier reports to his new garrison assignment, his first week should be spent in "rap sessions" led by paraprofessional combat veteran readjustment counselors; (4) ongoing sources of support should be made avail-able by having such counselors hold weekly discussions during the first 6 months of return in each company-sized unit; (5) mental hygiene consultation service professionals should supervise and coordinate the paraprofessional veteran counseling effort, serve as backup resources to help returnees with more difficulties, and consult commanders about recognizing and dealing with expectable transition stresses in their men; and (6) both professionals and paraprofessionals should share with policymakers the information gleaned from this readjustment effort to decrease some of the un-necessarily stressful aspects of return. (S)

Borus, J. F. (1974). Incidence of maladjustment in Vietnam re-turnees. Archives of General Psychiatry, 30, 554-557.
       Tabulates and compares indexes of disciplinary/legal and emotional maladjustment for 577 Vietnam veterans and 172 non-veterans entering garrison duty in 1970. Borus reports that only 23% of veterans showed indexes of either type of maladjustment and that incidence of veteran maladjustment was not significantly different from that of nonveterans. (S)

Borus, J. F. (1975). The reentry transition of the Vietnam veteran. Armed Forces and Society, 2, 97-114. (Reprinted in N. L. Goldman & D. R. Segal (Eds.), (1976). The social psychology of military service (pp. 27-43). Beverly Hills, CA: Sage Publications.)
      Synthesizes Borus's four previous publications (1973a, 1973b, 1973c, 1974) regarding the common adjustment issues faced by veterans as well as proposed intervention programs for alleviating the severity of these difficulties.   (S)

Boulanger, G. (1986b). Violence and Vietnam veterans. In G. Boulanger & C. Kadushin (Eds.), The Vietnam veteran redefined: Fact and fiction (pp. 79-90). Hillsdale, NJ: Lawrence Erlbaum Associates.
      Reviews the literature regarding violent behaviors among Vietnam veterans and explores correlations with background and predisposition, combat experience, and PTSD. In general, the data indicate that combat veterans are significantly more violent than controls. This violence is not attributable to precombat basic training, an influence that has been thought to release the soldier from society's prohibitions against violence. Boulanger profiles the violent veteran as a younger man with a background of antisocial behaviors before entering the military and a history of disciplinary problems while in it. But independent of these factors, combat experience and having PTSD alone are sufficiently predictive of veteran violence: veterans with PTSD are three times more likely to be violent than those with no stress symptoms.   (S)

Boulanger, G., & Kadushin, C. (Eds.) (1986). The Vietnam veteran redefined: Fact and fiction. Hillsdale, NJ: Lawrence Erlbaum Associates.
      Seeks to understand the meanings and effects of the various myths that surround the veterans of the war in Southeast Asia. Contributors also explore the realities of those who served there, the validity of the PTSD diagnosis, and the etiologic importance of predisposition, as well as how substance abuse, violent expression, and political alienation relate to Vietnam combat experience and reentry social support. (See also Boulanger, 1986a, 1986b; Boulanger, Kadushin, Rindskopf, & Carey, 1986; Canter, 1986; Dermatis & Kadushin, 1986; Kadushin, 1986; Lerer & Kadushin, 1986; J. L. Martin, 1986; R. Martin, 1986; Roth, 1986.)   (S)

Bourne, P. G. (1972a). The Vietnam veteran. In L. J. Sherman & E. M. Caffey, Jr. (Eds.), The Vietnam veteran in contemporary society: Collected materials pertaining to the young veterans (sec. IV, pp. 83-86). Washington, DC: Veterans Administration.
      Summarizes the various stresses associated with veteran maladjustment among Vietnam returnees. These range from features associated with service in the theatre, such as the social discon-

tinuities resulting from the 1-year tours or the drug usage there, to those facing the veterans upon their return, such as the blaming attitude of American society and the extra burden carried by black veterans. (C)

Bourne, P. G. (1972b). The Vietnam veteran: Psychosocial casualties. Psychiatric Medicine, 3, 23-27.
    Seeks to describe and explain the increasing prevalence of Vietnam veteran maladjustment. Regarding the experience of serving in Vietnam, Bourne speculates that features that protected the soldier may ironically have left him more vulnerable upon his return. He especially emphasizes the identity-distorting influence of an alienated American society that maligns the veteran of the war in Vietnam. (C)

Brady, D., & Rappoport, L. (1974). Violence and Vietnam: A comparison between attitudes of civilians and veterans. Human Relations, 26, 735-752.
    Presents results of a survey of attitudes toward violence among middle-aged males and females, college males and females, enlisted Vietnam veterans, and active duty officers above the grade of Major, using a multidimensional concept of violence. Overall, the civilian middle-aged males expressed the highest positive attitude and the college females the lowest. Among the military/veteran groups, those with the most combat experience achieved the highest scores. Using factor analysis, the authors found that the attitude patterns among the different groups varied with the conditions of violence, with violence in the service of law and order being the chief dimension of response variance. (C)

Brende, J. O., & Parson, E. R. (1985). Vietnam veterans: The road to recovery. New York: Plenum Press.
    Provides a condensed history of American political and military commitment in Southeast Asia. The authors review the especially stressful characteristics of the war and the consequences for the troops (i.e., guerrilla warfare and the U.S. "body count" strategy, combat atrocities, soldiers "fragging" military leaders, racial conflicts, etc.); reflect on how returning veterans were affected by the indifferent or hostile homecoming they received; and elaborate on the variations, consequences, and clinical management of readjustment failures seen among large numbers of veterans. PTSD is distinguished from diagnoses noted in past wars, such as "shell shock" and "battle fatigue." The authors outline various treatment strategies and a five-stage recovery process model. Using a systems theory approach, they also describe how service in Vietnam affected the veteran's family, and they devote special attention to the additional problems of female and minority group veterans. Fi-

nally, they review the readjustment services that are available to Vietnam veterans to include a list of VA readjustment outreach centers and inpatient specialized treatment units. (S)

Brett, E. A., & Mangine, W. (1985). Imagery and combat stress in Vietnam veterans. Journal of Nervous and Mental Disease, 173, 309-311.
Provides a preliminary report on a study of recurrence of Vietnam-linked imagery in Vietnam veterans ($\underline{N}$ = 50). Equal numbers of subjects from a VA readjustment center and a medical outpatient clinic completed a combat exposure instrument and three measures of imagery (an experimental task, an Impact of Event Scale, and a measure of imagery experienced since return from Vietnam). Results supported previous studies of civilian and military populations and verify the relationship between degree of stress and intrusive imagery. (C)

Briggs, R. A. (1984). Combat level and family support: Correlates of post-Vietnam adjustment. Dissertations Abstracts International, 45 (3-B), 1005.
Reports results of a survey study of Vietnam-era veterans ($\underline{N}$ = 68) identified by levels of combat exposure and family support, as well as by measures of stress, the nature and severity of problems experienced since leaving the military, mood, and self-reported alcohol use. Findings include that stress levels were higher for combat compared with noncombat veterans, for heavy-combat compared with light-combat veterans, and for those reporting low levels compared with high levels of family support. Reported alcohol problems as well as current mood disturbance were more common in the combat as compared with the noncombat veterans. (C)

Bupp, C. S. (1984). An examination of shame and guilt among the American veterans of the Vietnam conflict. Dissertation Abstracts International, 45 (2-B), 633.
Reports results of a survey study of guilt and shame dimensions among 176 Vietnam-era veterans, in which their strong guilt scores and moderately strong shame scores were shown not to be correlated with service experience variables (i.e., nonpresence in Vietnam, presence in Vietnam in support assignment, presence in Vietnam as combatant, wounded in action in Vietnam). Analysis of the more extreme scores suggests a significant relationship between high guilt and receipt of psychiatric care, and low guilt and receipt of drug dependency treatment. High shame scores were correlated with low education levels and low life satisfaction, findings consistent with previous research with other clinical populations. (C)

Camacho, P. (1980). From war hero to criminal: The negative priv-
ilege of the Vietnam veteran. In C. R. Figley & S. Leventman
(Eds.), Strangers at home: Vietnam veterans since the war (pp.
267-277). New York: Praeger.
    Discusses the Vietnam war and posits that growing awareness
of military corruption and inefficiency, as well as the public's
frustration in fighting a no-win guerrilla war, led to scapegoating
of veterans by American society. These factors also led to a series
of buck-passing tactics, such as Congress absolving itself by re-
pealing the Tonkin Gulf Resolution and the administration defer-
ring to the military; thus, again, the blame eventually filtered to
the lowest level--the enlisted veteran. Camacho argues that Vietnam veterans as a group have undergone de-statusing by society,
in which discrimination and stigma become collective--for example,
the media's portrayal of Vietnam veterans as crazed killers or
psychotic drug addicts. This has led many Vietnam veterans to try
to maintain a low public profile, seeking not to reveal themselves
as members of a discredited status group. Camacho also suggests
that Vietnam veterans are beginning to represent a new hetero-
genous minority status group, which qualifies--along with more
homogenous minorities such as blacks, Hispanics, and the elderly--
as members of an ever-developing welfare quasi-caste. (S)

Caplan, G. (1972). Testimony before U.S. Senate subcommittee on
veterans affairs, November 25, 1970. In L. J. Sherman & E. M.
Caffey, Jr. (Eds.), The Vietnam veteran in contemporary society:
Collected materials pertaining to the young veterans (sec. IV, pp.
18-28). Washington, DC: Veterans Administration.
    Reviews the adjustment problems facing veterans of the war
in Southeast Asia and highlights four causal factors: (1) estrangement from home values and behavior due to remote assignment; (2)
closing ranks at home during the veteran's absence; (3) brutalizing
of the soldier by combat experience, especially in guerrilla warfare; and (4) ambivalent welcome home by a society in unstable
equilibrium, with precarious control over its own violence. Caplan
also offers policy suggestions for providing preventive assistance
to veterans. (C)

Caputo, P. (1982, January). The unreturning army. Playboy, pp. 29,
107-108, 118, 260-274.
    Summarizes the especially harrowing and stressful nature of
combat duty in Vietnam as well as the pathogenic nature of America's treatment of Vietnam veterans. Using case examples, Caputo
particularly highlights the extreme youthfulness of the soldiers
who went, the prolonged extent of each soldier's time in the field,
the arduous environmental conditions, the unpredictable and
treacherous nature of guerrilla warfare, the "morally corrupting"
quality of the tactical objective of the "body count," the elusive-

ness of victory, and the neglect and contempt by Americans at home. He also reviews the various forms--in some instances, dramatic and compelling, and in others, latent and insidious--of maladjustment exhibited by unprecedented numbers of returning veterans, and he explores the roots of their "triple burden of guilt" (for having broken the taboo against killing; for having fought in actions that resulted in the deaths of civilians; and, in response to society's attitude of blame, for feeling personally a moral responsible for the war). Caputo offers suggestions for societally based restitution (offering veterans "genuine compassion, dignity and respect" in addition to appropriate programs) and cautions those veterans who accept society's pity: "Having been denied the laurels due victorious heroes, they are clutching at the sprigs of sympathy offered the victim." (C)

Card, J. J. (1983). Lives after Vietnam. Lexington, MA: Lexington Books.
    Presents the results of a prospective study (Project TALENT) regarding career potentials and achievements of high school Americans. The 1963 graduating class cohort was studied using three data collection points for 1,500 men (in ninth grade, at 11 years, and at 18 years after high school). The third survey sought information on background characteristics, family, career, health, quality of life, and military service. Three groups of roughly 500 men each were identified: nonveterans, non-Vietnam veterans, and Vietnam veterans. Case weights were applied to the nonveteran and non-Vietnam veteran groups to match them with the Vietnam group on 51 measures. Among the many findings of this study was that the two veterans groups--even at age 15 and especially among those who ultimately served in Vietnam--appeared different from nonveterans in reflecting lower self-confidence, interest levels, and activity levels. Card suggests that "the groups' early differences in behavioral and attitudinal indicators of control and efficacy may have spelled out the difference between service and escape from service." Further, this lower "sense of efficacy" was interpreted as differentiating between those who did or did not benefit from their military service when measuring the postservice schooling patterns. In general, the Vietnam-era veterans consistently appeared to suffer sustained, career-related deficits compared with nonveterans in terms of unemployment, job prestige, and income (especially for those who served in Vietnam). Given the DSM-III definition of PTSD, the study found a prevalence of 19% among Vietnam veterans (heavy combat exposure appeared to double the risk) and 12% among non-Vietnam veterans and nonveterans. Social support (e.g., being married or a churchgoer) does appear to attenuate the risk; and minority status, low socioeconomic status, or low educational or occupational attainment does not increase vulnerability. The only early correlate of midlife PTSD was lack of self-confidence at age 15. (C)

Card, J. J. (1987). Epidemiology of PTSD in a national cohort of Vietnam veterans. Journal of Clinical Psychology, 43, 6-17.

Reviews and expands on a previously reported (Card, 1983) prospective study of approximately 1,500 males, which was begun in 1960 when the cohort was in ninth grade. In a recent survey, the Vietnam veterans in the cohort reported significantly more nightmares, loss of control over behavior, emotional numbing, withdrawal from the external environment, hyperalertness, and anxiety and depression, as well as other associated features of PTSD, than did classmates matched with them on high school characteristics. Having a wife or being active in one's religion reduced PTSD symptom levels. The implications of these findings are discussed. (C)

Centers for Disease Control Vietnam Experience Study. (1988). Health status of Vietnam veterans: I. Psychosocial characteristics. Journal of the American Medical Association, 259, 2701-2707.

Reports findings from a multidimensional assessment of the health of Vietnam veterans. From a random sample of enlisted men who entered the U.S. Army from 1965 to 1971, 7,924 Vietnam and 7,364 non-Vietnam veterans participated in a telephone interview; a random subsample of 2,490 Vietnam and 1,972 non-Vietnam veterans also underwent a comprehensive health examination, including a psychological evaluation. At the time of the study, the two groups of veterans were similar in terms of level of education, employment, income, marital status, and satisfaction with personal relationships. Certain psychological problems, however, were significantly more prevalent among Vietnam veterans than among non-Vietnam veterans. These included depression (4.5% vs. 2.3%), anxiety (4.9% vs. 3.2%), and alcohol abuse or dependence (13.7% vs. 9.2%). About 15% of Vietnam veterans experienced combat-related PTSD at some time during or after military service, and 2.2% had the disorder during the month before the examination. (MA)

Centers for Disease Control Vietnam Experience Study. (1988). Health status of Vietnam veterans: II. Physical health. Journal of the American Medical Association, 259, 2708-2714.

Reports additional findings from a multidimensional assessment of the health of Vietnam veterans (see CDC Vietnam Experience Study, Part I, 1988). Vietnam veterans reported current and past health problems more frequently than did controls (non-Vietnam veterans), although medical examinations showed few objective differences between the groups. The Vietnam veterans did show more hearing loss, and among a subsample of 571 participants, they had lower sperm concentrations and a lower proportion of normal sperm cells. (Reproductive rates did not differ, however.) (MA)

DeFazio, V. J. (1975). The Vietnam era veteran: Psychological problems. Journal of Contemporary Psychotherapy, 7, 9-15.
Notes that many Vietnam veterans seem to be troubled with problems such as jumpiness, irritability, mistrust, nightmares, feelings of alienation and estrangement, various psychosomatic ailments, depression, and an inability to form or sustain intimate relationships. DeFazio considers these problems apparently greater in the veterans of the Vietnam war and caused by the psychological climate of the combat (i.e., a clandestine and personally brutal war against an indigenous revolutionary army in an alien culture), the public's hostile response to their homecoming, the fact that most veterans had been adolescents when they entered the military, their moral doubt as to the justifiability of the war, and the survival experience and its effects. (S)

DeFazio, V. J., Rustin, S., & Diamond, A. (1975). Symptom development in Vietnam era veterans. American Journal of Orthopsychiatry, 45, 158-163.
Two hundred seven Vietnam-era veterans attending a community college responded to a questionnaire and symptom checklist based on selected items from the MMPI and the Mooney Problem Check-List. Subjects were asked to indicate the presence or absence of symptoms before entering the service, upon leaving active duty, and at present. Of the participants, 144 had some combat experience and 63 had none. For the analysis, 46 subjects who had been in a combat zone for 6 months or more and had fired a weapon in combat constituted the combat group. From the non-combat group a like number was chosen at random. Significant differences in the mean number of symptoms were found between the two groups as well as among the three time scales. (S)

Dermatis, H., & Kadushin, C. (1986). Is the Vietnam generation politically alienated? In G. Boulanger & C. Kadushin (Eds.), The Vietnam veteran redefined: Fact and fiction (pp. 91-114). Hillsdale, NJ: Lawrence Erlbaum Associates.
Reviews previous research on the effects of war on the political attitudes of former soldiers and predicts the effects on Vietnam veterans of participation in a war surrounded by such extreme political and social turmoil. The authors present results of a study of functional adjustment and political attitudes and behaviors in Vietnam veterans, Vietnam-era veterans, and nonveterans. The findings suggest that, except for their greater desire for government aid, Vietnam veterans are no different in their political beliefs from other men of their generation. However, they have been psychologically affected by a sense that government has neglected them, and feeling unwelcome and alienated upon return from Vietnam has also been found to have a modest effect on current levels of PTSD. (S)

Egendorf, A. (1975). Vietnam veteran rap groups and themes of postwar life. Journal of Social Issues, 31(4), 111-124.

From late 1970 through late 1974 New York City veterans held rap sessions which over 200 attended. Assisted by volunteer therapists the groups met weekly and offered a unique opportunity to explore the meaning of the veteran experience in a therapeutic context. Therapists reported becoming more involved emotionally in these than in groups they actually lead. While much of the work covered standard therapeutic issues, all of it was colored by the special nature of the military experience during the Indochina war and the prominence of the historical dimension in the traumas suffered by veterans. (A)

Egendorf, A. (1982). The postwar healing of Vietnam veterans: Recent research. Hospital and Community Psychiatry, 33, 901-908.

Discusses the literature on readjustment of Vietnam veterans in terms of unique characteristics of the war, postwar malaise and clinical syndromes, varying response patterns to combat experiences, and unique aspects of psychological recovery and healing. Egendorf warns therapists and researchers of the diversity in experiences and response patterns of veterans. He argues that many veterans do not warrant a diagnosis of PTSD, yet most Vietnam veterans do show signs of troubling, unresolved war experiences and could benefit from some form of intervention. He concludes with both professional and societal suggestions to advance postwar healing. (S)

Egendorf, A., Kadushin, C., Laufer, R. S., Rothbart, G., & Sloan, L. (Eds.). (1981a). Legacies of Vietnam: Comparative adjustment of veterans and their peers (Vols. 2-5). New York: Center for Policy Research.

Reports results of a comprehensive random interview study of 714 Vietnam veterans and 626 nonveterans conducted from December 1976 to June 1977 and from December 1978 to October 1979. Site sampling was done in New York City; Atlanta; Chicago; Los Angeles (metropolitan areas); parts of Los Angeles county urban cities near the metropolitan areas); Bridgeport, CT; South Bend, IN; Columbus, GA; and rural zones surrounding these latter cities. Twenty-five percent of respondents were black. Adjustment patterns of veterans and nonveteran peers were examined in the following areas: (1) educational careers and benefit utilization, (2) occupational careers, (3) mental health, (4) capacities to deal with stress, (5) drug and alcohol use, (6) arrests and convictions, (7) marital status and satisfaction, (8) peer integration and the nature of friendship networks, and (9) working through of war experiences. Major findings reveal that Vietnam veterans have not achieved as high a level of education as their peers and hold jobs that are generally of lower level than those held by nonveterans and by veterans who served outside the war zone; that exposure to combat bears a direct and significant relation to current alcohol and drug use, arrests, medical problems, and stress-related symptoms; that varying levels of stability in the family of origin interact with the amount and intensity of combat to produce different degrees of stress reactions; that naturally occurring relations with others can substantially reduce the incidence of stress reactions, even among veterans of heavy combat; and that successful adjustment among Vietnam veterans is related to the degree to which they engage in "working through" their experience as opposed to either forgetting it or clinging to it steadfastly as an experience that must be avoided at all costs in the future. The authors make the following recommendations: (1) extend the period of eligibility for G.I. educational and training benefits; (2) target manpower training programs to reach the chronically unemployed veteran; (3) enlist employers and other private sector organizations in efforts to assist Vietnam veterans; (4) continue to provide for outreach by well-trained veteran peer counselors; and (5) develop expertise in the area of PTSD through focusing research, training, and treatment innovations. (See Egendorf, Kadushin, Laufer, Rothbart, & Sloan, 1981b; Egendorf, Remez, & Farley, 1981; Kadushin, Boulanger, & Martin, 1981; Laufer, Yager, Frey-Wouters, & Donnellan, 1981; Rothbart & Sloan, 1981.) (S)

Egendorf, A., Kadushin, C., Laufer, R. S., Rothbart, G., & Sloan, L. (1981b). Legacies of Vietnam: Comparative adjustment of veterans and their peers: Vol. 1. Summary of findings. New York: Center for Policy Research.
    Summarizes the study findings as well as the history and organization of this comprehensive random multisite interview study of 714 Vietnam veterans and 626 nonveterans conducted from December 1976 to June 1977 and from December 1978 to October 1979. (See Egendorf, Kadushin, Laufer, Rothbart, & Sloan, 1981a.) (S)

Egendorf, A., Remez, A., & Farley, J. (1981). Legacies of Vietnam: Comparative adjustment of veterans and their peers: Vol. 5. Dealing with the war: A view based on the individual lives of Vietnam veterans. New York: Center for Policy Research.
    Presents an intensive study of 403 Vietnam and Vietnam-era veterans selected randomly from a larger sample of 1,380 veterans and nonveterans nationwide. These case reviews reveal that Vietnam veterans differ markedly in the extent to which they have worked through their war experiences. About half are still troubled by unresolved experiences. Emotional avoidance has been used by about one fifth to ward off inner conflict. The authors suggest it may be difficult to help these troubled veterans in that those most likely to respond to offers of help frequently have problems

that are more severe than many counselors and therapists can handle. They present several ways of helping these veterans, ranging from recognition of the social basis for their troubles to establishment of service delivery and retraining programs. (See Egendorf, Kadushin, Laufer, Rothbart, & Sloan, 1981a.) (S)

Enzie, R. F., Sawyer, R. N., & Montgomery, F. A. (1973). Manifest anxiety of Vietnam returnees and undergraduates. Psychological Reports, 33, 446.
    Presents data from a study designed to determine whether the level of manifest anxiety in a sample of Vietnam veterans differed significantly from that in a control group of randomly selected undergraduate students without military experience. The study group consisted of 73 males who had recently returned from duty in Vietnam in 1970. Although the study apparently did not measure the extent of the veterans' combat exposure in Vietnam, it was noted that one third of them were wounded there. Data indicated that the sample of Vietnam returnees did not have higher levels of anxiety on the Taylor Anxiety Scale. (S)

Ewalt, J. R. (1981). What about the Vietnam veteran? Military Medicine, 146, 165–167.
    Summarizes preliminary results of VA-contracted studies on Vietnam veterans and their patterns and problems of readjustment. These studies include the first phase of the Legacies of Vietnam project (Egendorf, Kadushin, Laufer, Rothbart, & Sloan, 1981a) and the recently completed Louis Harris survey (Fischer, Boyle, Bucuvalas, & Schulman, 1980) of attitudes of the public and employers toward Vietnam-era veterans. Ewalt also describes the VA's Vietnam Veteran Outreach Program. (S)

Faulkner, R. R., & McGaw, D. B. (1977). Uneasy homecoming: Stages in the reentry transition of Vietnam veterans. Urban Life, 6, 303–328.
    Shows how change, occurring in both the Vietnam veteran and the homeland he left, created alienation between the two. The authors see the reintegration process as one of "unlearning the war's moral order and relearning the home's moral order." They list three stages in homecoming: (1) disengagement from the war, (2) reentry into "the World," and (3) movement toward reintegration; and they recommend an interactionist approach that emphasizes how the interpersonal relationships between veterans and significant others, along with the subjective meaning they attach to the homecoming, affect the reentry process. (M)

Figley, C. R. (1978, April). American Legion study of the psycho-social adjustment among Legion veterans. Final report submitted to the American Legion.

Reports results of a 1977 survey of American Legion members ($\underline{N}$ = 681) regarding military experience, combat experience, current functioning, and demographics. Of the study population, 196 were Vietnam-era veterans. Major findings reveal that nearly one third of the Vietnam veterans found combat in Vietnam stressful or highly stressful; that a significant percentage of veterans from all wars still have dreams and nightmares related to their military experiences; that combat experiences appear to be the focal point of most of the nightmares; and that when the sample of Vietnam-era veterans is separated by combat experience, there are significant differences in almost every category of postmilitary psychosocial adjustment.   (S)

Figley, C. R. (Ed.). (1978a). Stress disorders among Vietnam veterans: Theory, research and treatment. New York: Brunner/Mazel.

Presents a collection of papers devoted to understanding the social dynamics and psychodynamics of combat stress and reentry stress among Vietnam veterans, as well as to providing rationales for treatment strategies. (See also Bourne, 1978; DeFazio, 1978; Egendorf, 1978; Figley, 1978a; Haley, 1978; Horowitz & Solomon, 1975; Kormos, 1978; Leventman, 1978; Lifton, 1975a; Nace, O'Brien, Mintz, Ream, & Meyers, 1978; Panzarella, Mantell, & Bridenbaugh, 1978; Shatan, 1978; Spilka, Friedman, & Rosenberg, 1978; Stanton & Figley, 1978; Worthington, 1978.)   (C)

Figley, C. R. (1978b). Psychosocial adjustment among Vietnam veterans: An overview of the research. In C. R. Figley (Ed.), Stress disorders among Vietnam veterans: Theory, research and treatment (pp. 57-70). New York: Brunner/Mazel.

Presents a comprehensive review of research on postmilitary service adjustment of Vietnam veterans with particular attention to the broad area of psychosocial adjustment. Figley concludes that (1) very little attention has been focused on the family readjustment problems of Vietnam veterans; (2) preservice factors including personality, family life, and psychosocial variables appear to be related to in-service and postservice adjustment among Vietnam veterans; (3) Vietnam-era veterans in general do not appear to differ significantly from nonveterans in most areas of interpersonal and intrapsychic adjustment when either service in Vietnam or combat experiences are not controlled; (4) there is considerable evidence to suggest that service in Vietnam is a significant factor in psychological readjustment; and (5) there have been few published reports of attempts to systematically investigate the psychological readjustment process of the Vietnam veteran.   (C)

Figley, C. R. (1978c). Symptoms of delayed combat stress among a college sample of Vietnam veterans. Military Medicine, 143, 107-110.

Reports on a survey study of 101 Vietnam-era veterans selected at random from a list of all veterans receiving VA educational assistance at a large midwestern university and a large 2-year community college on the West Coast during spring 1975. The instrument included demographic questions and 26 scales covering, for example, experiences of violence, family relationships, coping in social and isolated settings, substance abuse, accidents, intimate relationships, general morale, political attitudes of self and family members toward the Vietnam war, military experiences, combat experience, etc. Results indicated that interpersonal adjustment (IPA)--defined as a state of general emotional well-being, satisfaction, and relative comfort with others in general and with family and intimate friends in particular--varied as a function of military service experiences during the four adult life periods measured (year before military service, period of military service, year after service, present year) among combatants but not among noncombatants, and that, except for the premilitary period, the noncombatants had significantly higher IPAs than did combatants. (C)

Figley, C. R. (1979, April). Confusing the warrior with the war. APA Monitor, p. 2.

Recalls the intense debate among psychologists 10 years ago over the merits of the Vietnam war and speculates that it persists and has become transformed into a debate over the mental health status of Vietnam veterans. Figley suggests the veteran is caught in the middle of opposing factions: one argues that the Vietnam war has had little or no long-lasting effect; the other contends that Vietnam veterans are having serious adjustment problems resulting from the war but primarily uses this perception to highlight the evils of the Vietnam war. Both groups seem to be using the Vietnam veteran as a political symbol. Figley further suggests that, as a social science discipline, psychology should include the study of the manifestations, antecedents, and consequences of combat-related stress reactions as it is beginning to do with the study of disaster reactions. (S)

Figley, C. R., & Leventman, S. (Eds.). (1980a). Strangers at home: Vietnam veterans since the war. New York: Praeger.

Presents an interdisciplinary collection of papers seeking to place the Vietnam war and the Vietnam veteran in sociohistorical perspective. (See also Bitzer, 1980; Camacho, 1980; Figley & Leventman, 1980b; Figley & Southerly, 1980; L. Johnson, 1980; Leventman & Camacho, 1980; Milano, 1980; Moskos, 1980; C. Smith, 1980; M. D. Stanton, 1976; Wikler, 1980; J. P. Wilson, 1978.) (C)

Figley, C. R., & Leventman, S. (1980b). Introduction: Estrangement and victimization. In C. R. Figley & S. Leventman (Eds.), Strangers at home: Vietnam veterans since the war (pp. xxi-xxxi). New York: Praeger.

Focuses on the processes by which American society made strangers of the men who fought in the Vietnam war. The discussion centers on the nature of the war itself, the overrepresentation of working-class and minority men as combatants, the negative consequences of the individualized 12-month rotation system, the erroneous assertions for low psychiatric casualty rates during the war, the veterans' too rapid return to American society--an often hostile populace--with no preparation for reassimilation, the stigmatization of veterans for participating in the unpopular war (blaming the victim), the negative labeling of Vietnam veterans by the media and mental health experts, and the institutional neglect by the VA. (C)

Figley, C. R., & Southerly, W. T. (1980). Psychosocial adjustment of recently returned veterans. In C. R. Figley & S. Leventman (Eds.), Strangers at home: Vietnam veterans since the war (pp. 167-180). New York: Praeger.

Vietnam-era veterans (N = 906) were interviewed in spring 1974. Data were collected for the periods before military service, during service, and after service for a large number of demographic, social, and military variables. The sample was selected from a list of 12,000 veterans living in the East St. Louis area of Illinois, who had been discharged since 1964. Results revealed that most veterans had achieved a relatively high degree of personal adjustment when viewed as a group. However, sleep difficulties continued to affect combat veterans in contrast to noncombatants. Combatants reported significantly more nightmares that (1) were related to military service in general, (2) were recurring, (3) woke them up, (4) made them fear or fight sleep, and (5) are still occurring. (S)

Fischer, V., Boyle, J. M., Bucuvalas, M., & Schulman, M. A. (1980). Myths and realities: A study of attitudes toward Vietnam era veterans. New York: Louis Harris & Associates.

Provides results and analysis of a comprehensive survey study of the attitudes of Vietnam-era veterans (VEV) contrasted with the attitude trends of the general public toward them and the war. The study was sponsored by the VA, and the data were collected between November 1979 and March 1980 using four separate national interview samples: general public (N = 2,604), the VEV (N = 2,464), educators (N = 510), and employers (N = 1,000). This study provides evidence that most VEV were not drafted but instead enlisted; that minority veterans were not overrepresented in the military, and that while they were slightly more likely than white veterans to serve in Vietnam and to be involved in heavy combat, this difference is no larger than might occur by chance alone; that almost half of all veterans who served during the Vietnam era served in the Vietnam theatre; that most veterans who served in Vietnam experienced moderate or heavy combat; and that the "poor and the young" were those who bore the brunt of combat, regardless of race. Further, "Pride rather than shame is the most common characteristic of the VEV. Most are glad they served their country, and would serve again if asked to. Nevertheless, a significant minority--particularly younger veterans and those exposed to heavy combat--reject their military experience and would not serve again." The study notes that the VEV feel negatively about the reentry reception they experienced. The authors state, "Nearly three-quarters of the veterans of (previous) wars feel that people their own age gave them a very friendly reception, compared to less than half of the VEV." Finally, although the public (and the VEV) is disillusioned with political leaders and governmental institutions as a legacy of the Vietnam war and feels that the war itself was a mistake, it does not hold "the warrior" responsible. (C)

Fleming, R. H. (1984). The flotsam of war and peace: A study of the Vietnam veteran in American society. Dissertation Abstracts International, 45 (3-A), 952-953.
    Reports results of interviews with 5 Army Vietnam veterans conducted in 1978-79. Two had served as junior officers and 3 as enlisted soldiers; 3 had served in combatant roles, 1 in a support assignment, and 1 in both types. Although Fleming considers these veterans to reflect the American post-Vietnam social "neurosis," he sees the differences in their readjustment as resulting from the interaction of the individual's childhood training and character development, his particular Vietnam experience, disparities between anticipated and actual reception upon his return home, the extent of support systems available to him, and his experience of societal attitudes concerning the Vietnam veteran. (C)

Fleming, R. H. (1985). Post Vietnam syndrome: Neurosis or sociosis. Psychiatry, 48, 122-139.
    Examines the impact of social, political, and historical forces on the adjustment of Vietnam veterans. Fleming advocates the judicious use of three categories for prolonged problems in veteran adjustment: (1) "post-Vietnam syndrome"--a subclinical "existential malaise" affecting large numbers of veterans as a consequence of the stresses of Vietnam service and reentry to civilian life; (2) PTSD--a dysfunctional neurotic condition affecting a small number as a consequence of the trauma of their wartime experience, which created a condition of unconsummated grief; (3) Vietnam veteran syndrome--a condition analogous to a personality disorder in which

individuals with premorbid dependent character features cling to their Vietnam experience and dwell on helplessness, opposition- alism, and insatiability. Fleming further emphasizes that these distinctions have critical treatment implications. Case examples are provided. (C)

Fox, R. P. (1972). Post-combat adaptational problems. Comprehen- sive Psychiatry, 13, 435-443.

Presents results of a survey and a review of the clinical records of 106 Marines referred for psychiatric evaluation over an 18-month period (1967-68) after service in Vietnam. This number represented approximately 1% of the combat veterans in the division-sized catchment population. (Of those surveyed, only 18 gave a history of previous psychiatric evaluation; 13 had been seen in Vietnam, and of these, 8 had been returned to the States for psychiatric reasons.) The majority of patients received a diagnosis of Adjustment Reaction of Adult Life, and the following difficul- ties emerged as influential in their maladaptation: (1) persistence of the ego modifications that had been adaptive in the combat situation, (2) problems dealing with unresolved feelings, and (3) inability to respond to new or complex situations. Fox provides suggestions for therapeutic intervention, concluding that some modifications of the policy of individualized troop replacement could lower the incidence of postcombat disorders. (C)

Fraas, L. A., & Mathes, E. W. (1970). Aspirations and concerns of hospitalized psychiatric and medical casualties evacuated from the Republic of Vietnam. Journal of Psychology, 76, 149-156.

Through a structured interview, the aspirations and concerns of soldiers hospitalized at the 249th General Hospital in Japan were reviewed and compared with those revealed in an earlier study involving ninth graders in Georgia. All 121 subjects were single, white, under 22 years of age, and high school graduates. None had sustained permanently handicapping wounds in Vietnam; 30% were psychiatric patients. Comparisons were also made be- tween responses of the psychiatric patients and the other patients. Psychiatric patients were more concerned about their present life and future business or financial success than were medical pa- tients. Medical patients expected to marry earlier and make more money than psychiatric patients. The ninth graders were more aware of home and school influences in their lives. (C)

Glover, H. (1984a). Survival guilt and the Vietnam veteran. Journal of Nervous and Mental Disease, 172, 393-397.

Discusses the concept of survival guilt among Vietnam veter- ans. The syndrome is characterized by frequent dreams of friends dying in battle, along with the avoidance of interpersonal intimacy due to fear that the other party may abandon them or die. Glover refers to four conditions that can predispose a combat soldier to survival guilt: (1) a person in a leadership position who felt strongly protective of his men, (2) a person who lost a close friend in battle, (3) a person who emerged from the war unscathed while others around him were killed or maimed, and (4) a person who had fantasies and expectations of personal heroism. Glover recommends that psychotherapists continuously confront the veteran's self-destructive patterns of behavior and address those false beliefs he may have regarding the nature of his survival.   (S)

Hartke, V. (1975, February). Vietnam veterans bibliography. Congressional Record, E556-560.
    Reviews references from behavioral and social sciences literature that focus on the Vietnam veterans' experience. Of special importance are manuscripts that deal with (1) the development and maintenance of intimate relationships during and after military service, (2) the relationship between combat experience and interpersonal competence, and (3) the relationship between the American family system and interpersonal violence. The primary purpose of this bibliography is to stimulate and facilitate research in the area of interpersonal adjustment and family life among Vietnam veterans.   (C)

Hearst, N., Newman, T. B., & Hulley, S. B. (1986). Delayed effects of the military draft on mortality: A randomized natural experiment. New England Journal of Medicine, 314, 620-624.
    Presents a study of mortality rates among men whose birth date numbers were selected by national lottery for Vietnam war draft eligibility in 1970-72. The study compared the 10-year mortality rates among selectees in California and Pennsylvania with those of their exempt cohorts. Findings revealed a small but significant rise, with total deaths among draft-eligible men 4% higher than expected. The excess mortality was primarily due to suicide (13% excess) or motor vehicle accidents (8% excess), and this increase is assumed to be entirely due to the excess risk among those who actually served (25.6% of draft-eligible men entered the military, and 9.3% of draft-exempt men volunteered to serve).   (C)

Helzer, J. E., Robins, L. N., & Davis, D. H. (1976). Depressive disorders in Vietnam returnees. Journal of Nervous and Mental Disease, 163, 177-185.
    Presents results of interviews conducted between May and September 1972 with a random sample of Army enlisted men (N = 470) who returned from Vietnam in September 1971. Additional information was obtained from their military records (for 99% of the sample) and from VA files (for 22%). Depressive dis-

orders appeared to be a significant problem in these returnees: 26% of the total sample reported at least some symptoms of depression and 7% reported a full affective syndrome. A third of those with depressive syndromes had received psychiatric care since their return. The authors discuss the association of depression with combat, use of illicit drugs, and other pre- and post-Vietnam variables. (S)

Helzer, J. E., Robins, L. N., Wish, E. D., & Hesselbrock, M. (1979). Depression in Viet Nam veterans and civilian controls. American Journal of Psychiatry, 136, 526-529.
    Reports results of interviews with 571 randomly selected Vietnam veterans (and 284 matched civilian controls) 3 years after their return from Vietnam in September 1971. The authors found a weak association between combat and subsequent depressive symptoms, but this association disappeared after controlling for preservice factors. The incidence of depressive symptoms and syndromes was similar when veterans were compared with non-veterans. (C)

Jay, J. A. (1978, July). After Vietnam: I. In pursuit of scapegoats--the veteran as pariah. Harper's, pp. 14-23.
    Argues that the veteran's conflicts are not his alone but are bound to the trauma and guilt of the nation. Failure to deal with this national guilt renders the veteran the symptom-carrier for society (i.e., "foolish for going to war, wrong for participating . . . , and inadequate for losing it") and increases his moral and emotional burden. This burden then isolates him in an attitude of perpetual combat until the issues of the war are confronted in the national conscience. Jay suggests the nation address its responsibilities for Vietnam in the following ways: (1) political leaders and policymakers can publicly acknowledge their once-active support for the war, pointing out what they have learned and justifying their current attitudes; (2) conferences similar to the teach-ins of the '60s can be organized to review and evaluate America's participation; (3) churches can direct attention to the unresolved moral dilemmas of the war; (4) legal investigations of leaders regarding soldiers' acts of atrocity can be undertaken; (5) reparations can be offered to the people of Vietnam; and (6) new and more humane immigration policies can be generated, which would benefit the many postwar refugees scattered throughout Southeast Asia. (S)

Jennings, M. K., & Markus, G. B. (1976). Political participation and Vietnam war veterans: A longitudinal study. In N. L. Goldman & D. R. Segal (Eds.), The social psychology of military service (pp. 175-200). Beverly Hills, CA: Sage Publications.

Presents results of a longitudinal study of active political participation among American youth. The sample consisted of 611 male high school seniors, who were interviewed in 1965 and again in 1973. A little more than half (n = 328) served on active duty during the 8-year period between interviews. Measures of political resources and use of the media found no discrete differences between veterans and nonveterans. Experiential differences between veterans who served early in the period and those who served later account for the variable impact of participation in the military among these subcohorts. The authors point out that the incomplete development of this sample's political makeup made it difficult to generalize about the effect of military service on political participation. (M)

Jones, T. (1972, August). The invisible Army. Harper's, pp. 10-18.
Explores the psychological and social myths and realities affecting the Vietnam veteran. The title refers to America's indifference toward the veteran, to which the veteran responds with (typically unacknowledged) confusion, pain, anger, and despair. Jones highlights how the soldier in Vietnam was stressed in fighting on the distant edge of an attenuated national resolve while being regularly confronted with contradictory images ("both the logical and absurd, the banal and heroic, and the human and inhuman"). He believes society's inability to establish "bridges for reintegration" with the veterans will be an incredibly costly mistake. This is even more the case regarding this war because of society's probable waste of the veterans' enhanced capacity for generating creative change that they developed as a result of serving during that tumultuous era. (C)

Jury, D. (1979, July). The forgotten warriors: New concern for the Vietnam vet. Behavioral Medicine, pp. 38-41.
Using statistics and brief descriptions, Jury delineates the unique and persistent readjustment problems of the Vietnam veteran. He also describes a pilot outreach program, sponsored by the Disabled American Veterans organization, that seeks to provide adjustment counseling for affected veterans. (C)

Kadushin, C. (1985). Social networks, helping networks, and Viet Nam veterans. In S. M. Sonnenberg, A. S. Blank, Jr., & J. A. Talbott (Eds.), The trauma of war: Stress and recovery in Viet Nam veterans (pp. 57-68). Washington, DC: American Psychiatric Press.
Presents data on the effects of social support and "networking" among a sample of 274 male Vietnam veterans and 275 male Vietnam-era veterans. Social density was found to have a significant effect (lower levels of PTSD symptoms) in smaller cities but

no effect in larger ones. Further, cohesive communities, particularly in small cities, were found to be helpful to veterans. Spousal support was found to be particularly helpful. From his study results, Kadushin speculates that in some instances, mental health professionals may not be helpful to veterans with PTSD symptoms. (S)

Kadushin, C. (1986). The interpersonal environment and Vietnam veterans. In G. Boulanger & C. Kadushin (Eds.), The Vietnam veteran redefined: Fact and fiction (pp. 121-131). Hillsdale, NJ: Lawrence Erlbaum Associates.

Contrasts the influence of two opposite types of community settings ("traditional village" and "metropolis") on the adjustment of Vietnam veterans. Kadushin interprets the data to indicate that working-class veterans who returned to the former--an integrated interpersonal environment where everyone knows everyone else-- have fewer PTSD symptoms. This buffering effect was not found for veterans with professional occupations. Regarding veterans residing in big cities, the data indicate that talking with a fellow Vietnam veteran was found to be especially useful in lowering the incidence of PTSD symptoms. Kadushin concludes that friends and relatives are helpful only under selected circumstances. (S)

Kadushin, C., Boulanger, G., & Martin, J. L. (1981). Legacies of Vietnam: Comparative adjustment of veterans and their peers: Vol. 4. Long term stress reactions: Some causes, consequences, and naturally occurring support systems. New York: Center for Policy Research.

Based on 1,380 interviews, this volume reveals that Vietnam veterans, particularly those who experienced heavy combat, exhibit more current symptoms of psychological distress than do other Vietnam-era veterans or nonveterans. These symptoms are more intense and more persistent among minority groups, the unemployed, the poor, or men with varying levels of family instability during childhood. Married veterans, especially Vietnam veterans, were found to be better off than unmarried men, but positive social support rather than the mere fact of being married was key. Having Vietnam veteran friends was found to help reduce current levels of stress among veterans in large cities; for those in smaller cities and towns, close-knit groups of friends, including nonveterans, were found to provide a buffer against stress reactions. (See Egendorf, Kadushin, Laufer, Rothbart, & Sloan, 1981a.) (S)

Kolb, L. C. (1986a). Post-traumatic stress disorders in Vietnam veterans (Editorial). New England Journal of Medicine, 314, 641-642.

Comments on the published epidemiological findings revealing increased mortality, primarily from suicide or motor vehicle accidents, among men chosen by lottery for the Vietnam war draft (Hearst, Newman, & Hulley, 1986). Kolb reviews the nature and symptoms of chronic PTSD, highlights modes of medical presentation that nonpsychiatric physicians may encounter, and provides approaches to treatment or referral. (C)

LaGuardia, R. L., Smith, G., Francois, R., & Bachman, L. (1983). Incidence of delayed stress response disorder among Vietnam era veterans: The effect of priming on response set. American Journal of Orthopsychiatry, 53, 18-26.

Presents results of a study to determine whether prior research reports indicating a high incidence of delayed stress syndrome among Vietnam veterans may be the result of priming (i.e., the biasing of the response set of an individual to favor one direction of responding over another). The study design included 38 volunteer Vietnam-era veterans (nonpatient) representing both combat and noncombat experience and three types of prime: negative (maladjustment expectancy), neutral, and positive (well-adjustment expectancy). Responses to items that were related to the veteran's opinions of himself, how others view him, and his overall judgment of whether his military experiences left him better or worse off were found to be affected by priming. Items that were not affected related to feelings of being forgotten, the ability to cope with societal pressures resulting from military service, a perception of ability to control present and future life events, government efficiency ratings, and estimates of alcohol and drug use by servicemen during the war era. Interaction effects indicated that combat veterans were affected more by positive prime while noncombat veterans were affected more by negative prime. The authors recommend that subsequent veteran adjustment research include more measures of their positive adaptations. (S)

Laufer, R. S. (1985). War trauma and human development: The Viet Nam experience. In S. M. Sonnenberg, A. S. Blank, Jr., & J. A. Talbott (Eds.), The trauma of war: Stress and recovery in Viet Nam veterans (pp. 31-56). Washington, DC: American Psychiatric Press.

Reviews past research on Vietnam veterans in terms of the difficulties they have experienced in readjusting to civilian life, the differences between Vietnam veterans and veterans of other wars, the relationship of predispositional factors to adjustment problems of Vietnam veterans, and the effects of combat or other war experiences in producing the veterans' postwar adjustment problems. (S)

Laufer, R. S., Brett, E. A., & Gallops, M. S. (1985). Dimensions of posttraumatic stress disorder among Vietnam veterans. Journal of Nervous and Mental Disease, 173, 538-545.

Presents a study derived from the larger national probability sample Legacies of Vietnam study (Egendorf, Kadushin, Laufer, Rothbart, & Sloan, 1981a). The authors studied 251 Vietnam veterans in seven sites using a 21-item Stress Scale (self-reported symptoms) and a 10-item Combat Scale (exposure/participation), as well as interviews, to determine if war trauma differentially affects four separate dimensions in posttraumatic stress: (1) intrusive imagery, (2) hyperarousal (believed linked to "reexperiencing" the traumatic experience), (3) numbing, and (4) cognitive disruption (believed to represent "defenses against reexperiencing"). Significant differences were found among these four dimensions depending on the veteran's race, the type of war trauma sustained, and the extent of time elapsed since the traumatic events. Over time the combat veteran most likely complains of intrusive imagery, secondly of hyperarousal, and thirdly of numbing, whereas participation in abusive combat violence is associated most strongly with cognitive disruption, secondly with hyperarousal, and thirdly with numbing. The authors discuss the implications for findings relating specific dimensions of stress to life course development.   (C)

Laufer, R. S., Frey-Wouters, E., & Gallops, M. S. (1985). Traumatic stressors in the Vietnam war and post-traumatic stress disorder. In C. R. Figley (Ed.), Trauma and its wake: Vol. 1. The study and treatment of post-traumatic stress disorder (pp. 73-89). New York: Brunner/Mazel.

Presents results of a study of the relationship between experiential and subjective indicators of war stress among 326 Vietnam veterans (226 whites, 100 blacks) who were interviewed as part of a nationwide study of Vietnam and Vietnam-era veterans (see Egendorf, Kadushin, Laufer, Rothbart, & Sloan, 1981a). The results show that experiential indicators of war stress (combat, participation in and witnessing of abusive violence, killing the enemy) are more consistent predictors of PTSD symptomatology. They also show that several subjective indicators of war stress (denial, intrusive imagery, numbing) are significantly related to PTSD symptoms and disorder. The authors feel that both traumatic experience and the types of psychological reaction to it directly affect the presence and level of stress symptoms, and that conceptualizing the dimensions of the traumatic experience is central to understanding the relationship between stressors and stress symptoms.   (S)

Laufer, R. S., Gallops, M. S., & Frey-Wouters, E. (1984). War stress and trauma: The Vietnam veteran experience. Journal of Health and Social Behavior, 25, 65-85.

Presents results of interviews with 350 Vietnam veterans taken from a larger stratified probability sample ($\underline{N}$ = 1,342) of the noninstitutionalized civilian population (see Egendorf, Kadushin, Laufer, Rothbart, & Sloan, 1981a). The authors present a test model of war trauma that contains three elements: (1) combat experience, (2) witnessing abusive violence, and (3) participating in abusive violence. Results of a hierarchical regression analysis of scales of psychiatric symptomatology confirm that each element of war trauma affects postservice psychological states of veterans in significant and different ways. Exposure to abusive violence was found to have significantly different effects for black and white veterans. (S)

Laufer, R. S., Yager, T., Frey-Wouters, E., & Donnellan, J. (1981). Legacies of Vietnam: Comparative adjustment of veterans and their peers: Vol 3. Post-war trauma: Social and psychological problems of Vietnam veterans in the aftermath of the Vietnam war. New York: Center for Policy Research.

Deals with the effects of the Vietnam war experience on the social and psychological adjustment of over 1,300 randomly selected Vietnam and Vietnam-era veterans. Among the significant findings is that the incidence of stress symptoms during and immediately after military service increases with combat exposure primarily for veterans who served in the latter half of the war (1968-74). The correlation between symptoms and exposure to combat, however, diminished among veterans who returned to smaller cities. The major readjustment problems reported by veterans relate to the traumatic nature of combat and to the perception of loss of support by the military. Complaints include lack of interest in normal activities, explosive anger, confusion, loss of confidence, and recurrent war-related nightmares. The incidence of medical problems during and immediately after military service was found to increase with combat exposure. Overall, combat veterans were found to have significantly more psychological and behavioral problems than Vietnam-era veterans, noncombat Vietnam veterans, or nonveterans. (See Egendorf, Kadushin, Laufer, Rothbart, & Sloan, 1981a.) (S)

Lawrence, C. E., Reilly, A. A., Quickenton, P., Greenwald, P., Page, W. F., & Kuntz, A. J. (1985). Mortality patterns of New York State Vietnam veterans. American Journal of Public Health, 75, 277-279.

Presents a study comparing mortality odds ratios (MORs) of deceased Vietnam veterans ($\underline{n}$ = 555) and of Vietnam-era veterans without service in Vietnam ($\underline{n}$ = 941) who died in New York State (excluding New York City) between 1965 and 1981. The most elevated MORs were for nonmotor vehicular accidents, other accidents and burns, homicides, and suicides. Liver disease, primarily cirrhosis caused by alcoholism, was the most highly elevated disease category distinguishing the Vietnam veterans. Overall, the study shows no remarkable disease differences between the two groups, and the authors cautiously suggest that herbicide exposure in Vietnam is not a cause of subsequent death. (C)

Lerer, N., & Kadushin, C. (1986). Effects of group cohesion on posttraumatic stress disorder. In G. Boulanger & C. Kadushin (Eds.), The Vietnam veteran redefined: Fact and fiction (pp. 51-59). Hillsdale, NJ: Lawrence Erlbaum Associates.
     Presents quantitative data that defines the group cohesion formed within combat units in Vietnam and its effects on the participants' psychological functioning. Contrary to contemporary opinion, the authors report little evidence to indicate a reduction in combat group cohesiveness following the 1968 Tet offensives, nor was any evidence found among Vietnam veterans for the positive effects of group cohesion on psychological functioning during or after combat. The authors present suggestions for additional research on cohesion. (S)

Levenberg, S. B. (1983). Vietnam combat veterans: From perpetrator to victim. Family and Community Health, 5, 69-76.
     Reviews the unique aspects of the war in Vietnam and speculates on their epidemiological importance in the large-scale readjustment problems among returning veterans. Levenberg concludes by describing the VA Vet Center Program and how it seeks to help the veteran readjust by using the peer therapy "rap group" approach. (S)

Leventman, S. (1978). Epilogue: Social and historical perspectives on the Vietnam veteran. In C. R. Figley (Ed.), Stress disorders among Vietnam veterans: Theory, research and treatment (pp. 291-296). New York: Brunner/Mazel.
     The stresses caused by war have been buffered in wars previous to Vietnam by "sufficient social support to render it meaningful and relevant for goals understood to be constructive." The unpopular and controversial nature of the Vietnam war, however, evoked public reactions of fear, suspicion, and even hostility toward returning veterans, often exacerbating problems within the veteran that originated in combat. Official discharge codes that are routinely made available to prospective employers have been used to screen out veterans who were perceived as "troublemakers" while in the service. Highlighting the contextual features of the period, Leventman conjectures that American society itself has undergone a "stress reaction," and he suggests that the problems of the Vietnam veteran may reflect a projection of society's problems. (M)

Levy, C. J. (1974). Spoils of war. Boston: Houghton Mifflin.
    Presents a study of the combat experiences and subsequent
readjustment of 60 Marine veterans from the Boston area. The
diary of one Marine's combat experience is included. Levy underscores the high rate of violent crime among the study population
after their return to the States (e.g., 2 were charged with murder
and 4 with attempted murder within 1 year). He speculates on the
government's tendency to emphasize characterological over psychotic diagnoses in psychiatric conditions so as to avoid focusing
attention on combat stress as a source of mental disorders.   (M)

Lewis, C. N. (1975). Memories and alienation in the Vietnam combat veteran. Bulletin of the Menninger Clinic, 39, 363-369.
    Speculates that although the Vietnam combat veteran often
returns to civilian life with traumatic war memories, perhaps more
importantly, through combat and reentry, he may be faced with
revived "autobiographical" memories from before his military service, which then unconsciously but powerfully subvert his postwar
adaptation. Lewis posits that "psychic numbing" (alienation and
withdrawal) may not be the result of traumatic war experiences
alone but, rather, may represent a defense against combat-aroused,
emotionally charged memories (i.e., the soldier/veteran's defense
against further revival of inadequately sublimated and previously
disavowed archaic drives). A case example is provided.   (C)

Lifton, R. J. (1969, October). Vietnam: Betrayal and self-betrayal.
Trans-action, pp. 6-7.
    Posits that contemporary youth are suffering from feelings of
disaffection from conventional American institutions and values because they perceive themselves as having been betrayed by the society and its leaders, and from equally disturbing feelings as a
result of self-disapproval for having sought deferment from military service through advanced schooling. In those youths who enter the service and are sent to Vietnam, Lifton sees compounding
factors that serve to distort their development and adaptation.
This process begins in basic training with the rearrangement of
their identity toward reliance on skills of self-defense and killing.
Next, in the combat activities and environment of Vietnam, they
become anxious about death while also experiencing a residual love
of the death encounter and an attraction to related forms of violence. Lifton notes that guilt associated with having participated
in evil is a predictable consequence of war but is especially unresolvable when the war cannot be inwardly justified.   (C)

Lifton, R. J. (1972b). Testimony before U.S. Senate subcommittee
on veterans affairs, January 27, 1970. In L. J. Sherman & E. M.
Caffey, Jr. (Eds.), The Vietnam veteran in contemporary society:

Collected materials pertaining to the young veterans (sec. IV, pp. 29-43). Washington, DC: Veterans Administration.

Provides a record of Lifton's testimony regarding his perspective on the adjustment problems affecting veterans of the war in Vietnam. Lifton reviews the stresses faced by veterans of previous wars and those unique to the extremes in Vietnam. He also refers to the aggravating effect on the veteran of the reciprocal difficulties within the American society as it struggles to reconcile its feelings about the war and its attitudes toward the returning soldiers.   (C)

Lifton, R. J. (1973). Home from the war: Vietnam veterans neither victims nor executioners. New York: Simon and Schuster.

As a "psychohistorian," Lifton elaborates his unapologetically antiwar perspective regarding the individual and collective consequences of America's war in Vietnam. He describes the "malignant bind into which American GIs were helplessly thrust" as resulting from the contextual clash of post-World War II American anticommunist militarism with a 50-year-old Vietnamese anticolonial revolution, the American preoccupation with technicist methodologies, and the soldier's human potential for guilt as well as for connection and continuity. Lifton feels that the extent of psychological and moral "inversions" experienced by those associated with the war, especially the veterans, was extreme, and he sees many parallels with wars through time, such as World War I, with its combination of slaughter and meaninglessness.   (C)

Lifton, R. J. (1974). "Death imprints" on youth in Vietnam. Journal of Clinical Child Psychology, 3, 47-49.

As a psychiatrist experienced with military populations, veterans, and survivors of extreme military and civilian stress, Lifton comments on the "psychological predicament" of the Vietnam veteran. In considering the combat veteran of war in general, he highlights how the psychological reentry task of attenuating indelible images of death, dying, and suffering must come about through finding meaning and justification in having fought, killed, and survived. This adjustment task is "greatly influenced by the extent to which the veteran becomes inwardly convinced that his war and his participation in that war had purpose and significance." Reflecting on the combat veterans of Vietnam, Lifton notes the prominence of their dehumanization of all Vietnamese, the reports of indiscriminate destruction there, and their tendency toward "psychic numbing," apparently in reaction to the stresses of guerrilla war in an alien environment. He believes that the veteran was left with unusual and extreme guilt as a consequence of having survived such a "filthy ambiguous war" and that his psychological burden has been worsened by his feeling blamed for the war by his society.   (C)

Lifton, R. J. (1975b). The postwar war. Journal of Social Issues, 31(4), 181-195.

Contending expressions of survival are examined in terms of their implications for the American post-Vietnam experience. The author draws on his work with rap groups of antiwar veterans to describe the struggles of these men with their personal and the country's socio-political survivor's mission. He contrasts the responses and strategies of the antiwar enlisted personnel to those of the POW returnees (mainly military elite), considers that most of the American people find themselves somewhere in the middle of these two polar response groups, and speculates on the insight that possible survivor formulations may provide about war in general.   (A)

Milano, F. (1980). The politicization of the "Deer Hunters": Power and authority perspectives of the Vietnam veterans. In C. R. Figley & S. Leventman (Eds.), Strangers at home: Vietnam veterans since the war (pp. 229-247). New York: Praeger.

Presents results of an interview and participant-observer study of 15 Vietnam-era veterans and 15 nonveterans in an Italian-American community of a small Pennsylvania steel town in 1976. Milano believes the acclaimed movie The Deer Hunter accurately reflects how individual lives can be shaped by larger socio-political systems such as the military and were shaped by "the unmeasurable psychological pain and confusion experienced by the American combatant in Vietnam." In his study, he sought to determine how much the veteran had been politicized as a result of military service during the controversial Vietnam period. In general, members of both groups showed a relatively low involvement in formal electoral politics, preferring to exercise their individual influence within smaller-scale organizations such as union locals or fraternal-type associations. However, study findings demonstrated that veterans expressed more interest in politics than did nonveterans. Not only were they more politicized, but they were also more critical toward society's political system and leadership. Milano believes these findings confirm his hypothesis that military service generally had a powerful and negative influence on this generation of young men.   (S)

Musser, M. J., & Stenger, C. A. (1972). A medical and social perception of the Vietnam veteran. Bulletin of the New York Academy of Medicine, 48, 859-869.

Presents characteristics, needs, and problems of Vietnam veterans as they affect the VA, with its mandate to provide assistance to this "new breed" of veterans. Vietnam veterans are distinct from other veterans in that they are younger, better educated, and of a higher calibre by virtue of having been selected by a more stringent selective service procedure. The nature of the combat in Vietnam and of improvements in medical care delivery there led to different types of wounds and to a greater survivability of soldiers with more severe and multiple wounds. Moreover, there was a higher incidence of multiple amputations (18.1%) as compared with those resulting from the Korean war (9.3%) or World War II (5.8%). In addition, Vietnam produced a larger incidence of paraplegia and quadriplegia from spinal cord injuries. Drug abuse is considered a problem but only to a limited extent. Given a lack of data, the best guess is that there are about 50,000-75,000 hard drug users among Vietnam veterans, with most being from the so-called alienated segment of society (60%-70% were black, 90% had a high school education or less, 60% had been arrested, 30% had used drugs prior to service, and 40% became addicted in Vietnam). The authors cite findings from a Louis Harris poll of public opinions about Vietnam veterans ("A Study of the Problems Facing Vietnam Era Veterans on Their Readjustment to Civilian Life," 1972), which indicate that, among other things, the Vietnam veteran is different because he has been treated by society with indifference, disapproval, and scorn. Finally, of the Vietnam-era veterans interviewed for the Harris poll, generally 15% were unemployed. However, when nonwhites and those who had not completed high school are considered separately, the unemployment figures are much higher (21% and 31%, respectively). (S)

Nace, E. P., Meyers, A. L., O'Brien, C. P., Ream, N. W., & Mintz, J. (1977). Depression in veterans two years after Viet Nam. American Journal of Psychiatry, 134, 167-170.
    Evaluates the incidence of depression in a sample of 202 Vietnam veterans an average of 28 months after their return from Vietnam (see Nace, O'Brien, Mintz, Ream, & Meyers, 1977). Approximately one third of the sample fell within the clinically depressed range of the Beck Depression Inventory. Comparison of the depressed and nondepressed groups indicated that the former had higher frequencies of drug abuse (particularly while in Vietnam), more marital difficulties, higher unemployment, and more current legal problems. This high incidence of depression, coupled with the finding that few of these men were being treated for the illness, indicates the need for an outreach approach to this population. (MA)

Pardeck, J. T., & Nolden, W. L. (1983). Aggression levels in college students after exposure or non-exposure to an aggressive life experience. Adolescence, 18, 845-850.
    Describes results of a study of assaultiveness reported by 14 Vietnam veteran college students compared with 66 non-Vietnam veteran and nonveteran students. The finding of higher rates among the Vietnam veteran sample suggests that assault is a type

of aggressive activity strongly influenced by previous aggressive
life experience. (C)

Pilisuk, M. (1975). The legacy of the Vietnam veteran. Journal of
Social Issues, 31(4), 3-12.
    Presents an overview of the demographics and social climate
of Vietnam veterans. Pilisuk points out that the predominantly
poor and working-class composition of the force during the Vietnam era resulted from the unprecedented mass deferment of college students from the draft. Racial friction is also a key element
in the veteran's legacy. Pilisuk notes how racism contributed to
the dehumanization of the Vietnamese and eroded the relationships
between black and white soldiers. He also shows how sentiment at
home over many years socialized youth into antiwar attitudes;
many of these young men joined the GI antimilitary movement
after entering the military. Thousands of veterans have returned
home after either being held as prisoners of war, becoming addicted to drugs, or suffering from the emotional consequences of
their war experience. Pilisuk reviews the veterans' current low
status in society and questions their further progress. (M)

Pollock, J. C., White, D., & Gold, F. (1975). When soldiers return:
Combat and political alienation among white Vietnam veterans. In
D. Schwartz & S. Schwartz (Eds.), New directions in political
socialization (pp. 317-333). New York: Free Press.
    In a 1972 survey of 163 college-enrolled Vietnam veterans,
the authors found that combat veterans (n = 54) differed significantly from noncombat veterans in that (1) they displayed markedly different political attitudes; (2) they were more likely to
exhibit alienation from the activities of the U.S. military forces in
Vietnam; (3) they showed little confidence in their ability to control their own destiny; and (4) they were more likely to view violence as necessary for disadvantaged groups in America to improve
their circumstance. The authors conclude, "For the soldier engaged
in combat in the Vietnam war, a war fraught with controversy,
the trauma of high risk and killing do not diminish with the
passing months. Time does not heal the combat soldier's psychic
wounds. Nor does success." (C)

Rothbart, G., & Sloan, L. (1981). Legacies of Vietnam: Comparative
adjustment of veterans and their peers: Vol. 2. Educational and
work careers: Men in the Vietnam generation. New York: Center
for Policy Research.
    Addresses the employment adjustment and satisfaction of over
1,300 randomly selected Vietnam and Vietnam-era veterans. The
study found that 5-10 years after release from the military,
Vietnam-era veterans have less education and hold lower-level jobs

than do nonveterans. This is particularly true for those veterans
who actually served in Vietnam. Nonveterans were found to be
better educated than the Vietnam-era veterans, who were better
educated than the Vietnam veterans. Black veterans, however,
were slightly better educated than black nonveterans. Few differences were found in the unemployment rates of veterans and
nonveterans. Overall, the authors conclude that the military has a
negative impact on the educational and occupational achievement
of Vietnam and Vietnam-era veterans. (See Egendorf, Kadushin,
Laufer, Rothbart, & Sloan, 1981a.) (S)

Scruggs, J. C., Berman, A. L., & Hoage, C. (1980). The Vietnam
veteran: A preliminary analysis of psychosocial status. Military
Medicine, 145, 267-269.
    Reports survey results from 233 combat, noncombat, and
Vietnam-era veterans attending college in the Washington, DC,
area. Veteran's combat status was established by extent of unit
casualties reported. Combat veterans reported (1) less trust in
people, (2) greater rate of divorce, (3) greater approval of violence, (4) greater belief in residual psychological impairment
related to their experiences, (5) increased frequency of combat
dreams, and (6) distrust of VA mental health services. Of the
sample, 38% believed their participation in the Vietnam conflict
caused them psychological problems. (C)

Shapiro, R. B. (1978). Working through the war with Vietnam vets.
Group, 2, 156-183.
    Describes the evolution of and group processes in a series of
loosely structured "rap groups" that brought together members of
Vietnam Veterans Against the War (VVAW) and antiwar civilian
mental health professionals. The experiment lasted over 3 years
and involved several hundred veterans and 20 therapists. Shapiro
provides case vignettes and discusses the themes that repeatedly
emerged in these groups: control of rage and violent impulses,
guilt, mistrust of those in authority, loss and separation, dehumanization, and incapacity for tenderness. He also explores the implications of the finding that therapeutic use of the transference was
consistently not employed, apparently because of the therapists'
political sympathies. Noting that "the necessity of dealing simultaneously with social and internal factors became clear in our work
with anti-war veterans," Shapiro concludes with a set of principles
for therapeutic work with "socially oppressed and politically alienated minority group members" gleaned from the group experience
with VVAW members. (C)

Shatan, C. F. (1972). Soldiers in mourning. American Journal of
Orthopsychiatry, 42, 300-301.

Presents observations and theory regarding emotionally troubled combat veterans of Vietnam from the veterans' own revela-
tions in self-help group "rap sessions." Basic components of the
"post-Vietnam syndrome" are (1) guilt feelings and self-punitive
behaviors, (2) feelings of being scapegoated by American society,
(3) consequent rage and aggressive impulses, (4) combat brutaliza-
tion, (5) alienation from feelings and people, and (6) anguished
doubt about one's ability to love and trust other human beings
again. (C)

Shatan, C. F. (1973a). The grief of soldiers: Vietnam combat veterans' self-help movement. American Journal of Orthopsychiatry,
43, 640-653.
    Seeks to refute published military claims of there being few
psychiatric casualties among Vietnam war soldiers. Shatan asserts
that extensive numbers of veterans suffer from symptoms that are
delayed in onset due to emotional anesthesia brought on by a
combination of combat trauma and the military's counterguerrilla
training, both of which discourage grief and intimacy ("impacted
grief"). He describes symptoms reported by veterans, their self-
help movement of group sessions, and steps for therapist involvement. The goals of treatment include those promoting reintegration
and "rehumanization." (See also Shatan, 1972, 1973b, 1974, 1978.)
(C)

Shatan, C. F. (1973b). "How do we turn off the guilt?" Human Behavior, 2, 56-61.
    Summarizes Shatan's observations of Vietnam combat veterans
who participated in support groups ("rap groups") sponsored by
Vietnam Veterans Against the War (VVAW) and proffers a system
of causality as well as recommendations for treating those with
delayed "post-Vietnam syndrome." Pathogenesis begins in basic
training, with its intense and brutalizing indoctrination and the
teaching of basic survival skills of guerrilla warfare. Then, in the
"corrupt reality of Vietnam" follow dehumanization of the enemy,
"psychic numbing," and survival guilt. Some soldiers respond by
learning destruction and death, and some develop physiological
equivalents of depression that go unrecognized by military psychiatrists. Most develop a defensive "shoot first and investigate
afterwards" attitude and become emotionally disoriented yet unable
to forget or to endow their combat experience with meaning. Reentry adjustment becomes equally problematic because of feelings
of being scapegoated by society and inadequately provided for by
government programs. The consequences, although often delayed in
onset, are powerful feelings of guilt and rage combined with suspiciousness, social isolation, and an inability to form bonds of
intimacy. Treatment recommendations focus on a goal of "rehumanization," with mental health professionals being urged to become

emotionally connected with the veterans as if they too were war survivors. More generally, such professionals are advised to move beyond therapy to public advocacy. (C)

Shatan, C. F. (1974). Through the membrane of reality: "Impacted grief" and perceptual dissonance in Vietnam combat veterans. Psychiatric Opinion, 11, 6-15.
     Summarizes impressions gained by a panel of volunteer psychotherapists working with veterans' self-help programs (Shatan, 1972, 1973a, 1973b, 1977, 1978). Strong similarities were noted among the emotional difficulties apparently consequent to extensive Vietnam combat experience, the homecoming syndrome of POWs, and the survivor syndrome of living concentration camp inmates. Common themes reiterated by the 165 veterans in the program included guilt and remorse, violent impulses against indiscriminate targets, combat brutalization and emotional anesthesia, and alienation and detachment. (C)

Shatan, C. F. (1978). Stress disorders among Vietnam veterans: The emotional context of combat continues. In C. R. Figley (Ed.), Stress disorders among Vietnam veterans: Theory, research and treatment (pp. 43-52). New York: Brunner/Mazel.
     Elaborates on Shatan's six basic symptom components common to Vietnam veterans suffering from the "post-Vietnam syndrome" (Shatan, 1972) and reviews the unique features of combat service in Vietnam (e.g., counterguerrilla combat experience, random individualized assignment through the combat theatre, neglect by military psychiatrists in Vietnam, and the ambivalent or blaming attitude of society on return) that generated such symptoms. Shatan asserts that these and related stressors force the returned combatant into a conflict between competing reality-perception systems--that is, the civilian peacetime state requiring a capacity for empathy and trust versus the survival-oriented paranoid posture of the combatant. (C)

Shatan, C. F. (1985). Have you hugged a Vietnam veteran today? In W. E. Kelly (Ed.), Post-traumatic stress disorder and the war veteran patient (pp. 12-28). New York: Brunner/Mazel.
     Discusses the impact of overwhelming man-made stress on Vietnam veterans, using the experience of the survivors of the Holocaust as a model. Shatan emphasizes natural posttraumatic adaptation to combat and other traumas. He also discusses the value of psychotherapy in promoting the healing process. (S)

Silver, S. M. (1985). Post-traumatic stress and the death imprint: The search for a new mythos. In W. E. Kelly (Ed.), Post-

traumatic stress disorder and the war Veteran patient (pp. 43-53).
New York: Brunner/Mazel.

Examines the soldier mythoi in America and posits that the
socially approved "warrior" mythos, which ordinarily provides a
soldier with a satisfying rationale for submerging his concern for
himself in his new military identity and combat goals, changed
during the Vietnam war to one in which the soldier (and later the
veteran) became a social pariah and outlaw. This "outlaw" mythos
came to include characteristics such as participation in war atrocities, drug abuse, poor discipline, potential for uncontrollable
violence, insanity, and having lost the war. Silver argues that this
new mythos is now changing to one in which society can partially
identify with the veteran and share the experience of the war.
(S)

Smith, J. R. (1986). Sealing over and integration: Modes of resolution in the post-traumatic stress recovery process. In C. R. Figley
(Ed.), Trauma and its wake: Vol. 2. Traumatic stress theory, research, and intervention (pp. 20-38). New York: Brunner/Mazel.

Describes the normal posttraumatic stress recovery sequence
of sealing over, integration, and atonement, which allows one to
feel at peace with society. "Sealing over" refers to a psychological
process of binding the loose ends of traumatic experience and is
fostered through social rituals, rites, and sanctions. Smith contends that, unlike veterans of previous wars, most Vietnam veterans have been deprived of the necessary social support and must
therefore resort to integration alone. This is more difficult
because the veteran must accept personal responsibility for his
war actions and seek personal meaning for each aspect of his
military experience or remain psychologically disordered.   (S)

Smith, J. R., Parson, E. R., & Haley, S. A. (1983). On health and
disorder in Vietnam veterans: An invited commentary. American
Journal of Orthopsychiatry, 53, 27-33.

Interprets findings from various studies of combat-related
stress reactions among Vietnam veterans as showing that veterans
exhibit healthy adaptation, stability, and traumatic stress-related
symptoms all at the same time. The authors contend that the presence of stress reaction symptoms does not represent psychological
illness but instead is evidence of normal stress recovery. Rather
than argue for or against predisposing factors as a cause of stress
reactions, they maintain that adverse reactions to catastrophes
such as combat stem from a combination of the experience of the
catastrophic events themselves, the individual's actions in that
context, and the meaning those events have for the individual.
Moreover, the individual's personality and the nature of the environmental support to which survivors return play as great a role.
The authors conclude with a call for careful consideration and

documentation of the normal stress recovery process and for precise attention to the cognitive, affective, and real-life behavior of all survivors of catastrophe. (S)

Spilka, B., Friedman, L., & Rosenberg, D. (1978). Death and Vietnam: Some combat veteran experiences and perspectives. In C. R. Figley (Ed.), Stress disorders among Vietnam veterans: Theory, research and treatment (pp. 129-147). New York: Brunner/Mazel.
   Traces the development of a psychology of death, which began with Kubler-Ross's work in 1969, and reports results of a survey of 104 Vietnam combat veterans that explored their death-related experiences. Questions included (1) background demographic information; (2) early contact and feelings toward death; (3) experiences and perspectives relative to the threat of death while in Vietnam; (4) current death perspectives, concerns, and expectations; and (5) the degree and nature of any military-related disabilities. Experiencing both the death of friends or family and the threat of being killed in combat was clearly found to have a profound impact on those who fought in Vietnam. A veteran's reactions to death were shown to be affected by his early home religious atmosphere, his investment in education, and his investment in his own family. Of the respondents, 66% had some contact with death prior to military service. Those with college educations were more likely to have a strong response of either survivor guilt or anger after someone they knew died in combat. (M)

Stenger, C. A. (1974). The Vietnam veteran. Psychiatric Opinion, 11, 33-74.
   Reviews recent studies reflecting on the characteristics of Vietnam veterans. One questionnaire study of 4,155 VA patients using the Interpersonal Style Inventory indicated Vietnam veterans to be more open, nonconforming, and impulsive than veterans of previous wars. When disciplinary/legal incidents and mental health clinic visits were studied among 577 combat and 172 noncombat Army veterans, 20% showed readjustment problems that were more difficult than those experienced after previous wars. Stenger describes features of the war in Vietnam and reentry to the States that were unique stressors on those who served--for example, the type of war, the surrounding controversy, and the drastic changes occurring in the United States during their absence. (C)

Strayer, R., & Ellenhorn, L. (1975). Vietnam veterans: A study exploring adjustment patterns and attitudes. Journal of Social Issues, 31(4), 81-94.
   The veterans interviewed in this study indicate that the adjustment processes they face upon return to civilian life are unusually difficult and complex. Severe depression, hostility, and

guilt characterize many of them. The veteran's perception of the extent and intensity of his combat involvement as well as his participation in atrocities is closely related to his overall adjustment to civilian life. Intraception (i.e., "critical self-insightfulness") versus authoritarianism on the part of these veterans tends to differentiate between those who withdraw and are apathetic upon return and those who find employment or schooling and are in favor of the war effort. Race is also a discriminating factor, with black and Mexican-American veterans being far more often unemployed, opposed to the war, and perceiving themselves as less able to control their own personal world. (A)

Stretch, R. H. (1986b). Post-traumatic stress disorder among Vietnam and Vietnam-era veterans. In C. R. Figley (Ed.), Trauma and its wake: Vol. 2. Traumatic stress theory, research, and intervention (pp. 156-192). New York: Brunner/Mazel.

Reviews results from a four-phase research project on the prevalence and etiology of PTSD among Vietnam veterans (see Stretch, 1985, 1986a; Stretch, Vail, & Maloney, 1985). Questionnaire data were collected from more than 2,700 Vietnam and Vietnam-era veterans representing active duty Army personnel, active duty Army nurses, U.S. Army reservists, and prior-service civilians. Results show the highest rates of PTSD among the civilians sampled, followed by the reservists and both active duty Army samples. Combat/war zone experiences and reentry social support were found to have the greatest impact on the development and attenuation of PTSD symptomatology. Additional data highlight the relationship between physical and psychological health. (S)

Tanay, E. (1985). The Vietnam veteran: Victim of war. In W. E. Kelly (Ed.), Post-traumatic stress disorder and the war veteran patient (pp. 29-42). New York: Brunner/Mazel.

Contends that the Vietnam veteran is primarily a victim. Tanay argues that the soldier's basic military training and indoctrination predisposed him to participate in guilt-provoking combat activities in Vietnam. Thus, his training to "dehumanize" the enemy contributed to the incidence of atrocities. Moreover, military service in Vietnam was experienced more as a prison term than as a military expedition. Soldiers who served there returned burdened with both individual and collective guilt. A case example is provided. (S)

Wikler, N. (1980). Hidden injuries of war. In C. R. Figley & S. Leventman (Eds.), Strangers at home: Vietnam veterans since the war (pp. 87-106). New York: Praeger.

Presents excerpts from interviews with Vietnam veterans conducted between 1970 and 1972 in the San Francisco area that reflect on what Wikler calls the "hidden injuries of the Vietnam war": the anguish of losing buddies; the intense fear of death and injury; the self-discovery resulting from a forced maturity; the adjustment to violence and to one's own violent capacities; and the moral readjustment to one's own killing acts, both legal and illegal. Wikler briefly discusses the many readjustment problems veterans faced upon returning home and encountering the lack of adequate resources to help them cope. (S)

Wilson, J. P. (1978). Identity, ideology, and crisis: The Vietnam veteran in transition (Pt. 2). A final report submitted to the Disabled Veterans Association, Forgotten Warrior Project, Cleveland State University. (Presented in abbreviated form as: Conflict, stress, and growth: The effects of war on psychosocial development among Vietnam veterans. In C. R. Figley & S. Leventman (Eds.), (1980a). Strangers at home: Vietnam veterans since the war (pp. 123-165). New York: Praeger.)
Presents findings and interpretations of an interview study of 356 Vietnam veterans in the Cleveland, OH, area. The sample, designed to reflect a statistical profile of the military population that served in Vietnam, was divided on the basis of race and combat experience and included a matching control group of Vietnam-era veterans who did not serve in Vietnam. Interviews focused on areas related to identity integration and emotional adjustment: (1) personality characteristics and personal attributes, (2) interpersonal relationships and adjustment, (3) moral reasoning and ethical beliefs, (4) military experience, (5) political attitudes and ideology, and (6) perception of society. Results identified changes in ego-identity, ideology, and subjects' attitudes owing to their involvement in the war. More specifically, the strength of an individual's self-esteem did not change greatly during military duty; however, there were more individuals with higher and lower degrees of self-esteem after military service than before it, suggesting a polarization effect. Other findings included a left-wing shift away from more conventional ideological beliefs, with white combat veterans tending to have more conservative and stronger ideological beliefs than their black counterparts. As a group, veterans tended to feel society greeted them with apathy, which eroded their faith in the system. Approximately half of them, particularly the combat veterans, felt they had been exploited for their service, stated they would refuse to participate in a similar war, and indicated they would also encourage their sons not to fight. (S)

Worthington, E. R. (1976). The Vietnam era veteran anomie and adjustment. Military Medicine, 141, 169-170.

Summarizes findings of studies comparing Vietnam veterans with non-Vietnam veterans to discern whether the Vietnam participants suffered more feelings of meaninglessness, valuelessness, hopelessness, or aloneness (Worthington, 1977, 1978). Subjects were 147 veterans released from active duty in 1972-73 in the Salt Lake City area. Worthington concludes that the veterans of that era and in that area did not manifest serious readjustment problems, and that there was no clear evidence of a relationship between service in Vietnam and civilian readjustment. (C)

Worthington, E. R. (1977). Post-service adjustment and Vietnam era veterans. Military Medicine, 142, 865-866.
    Analyzes data from 147 Vietnam-era veteran males collected in 1973-74 (within one year from their release from active service) to identify factors associated with postservice adjustment as measured by the Tennessee Self Concept Scale, the Socialization Scale of the California Psychological Inventory, and the general anomie factor of meaninglessness from the Elmore Scale of Anomie (Worthington, 1978). Results indicated correlation between positive postservice adjustment and (1) viable marriage, (2) continuing religious affiliation, (3) high school completion or better, (4) postservice employment, (5) service history as officer, (6) service history in higher ranks, (7) negative service history for disciplinary action, (8) preservice history of active employment or schooling, (9) age greater than 21 years on entry to service, (10) absence of legal/school authority problems, and (11) time away from home prior to service. Worthington concludes these data suggest that postservice adjustment is more closely linked to maladaptive behavior problems than to military service. (S)

Worthington, E. R. (1978). Demographic and pre-service variables as predictors of post-military service adjustment. In C. R. Figley (Ed.), Stress disorders among Vietnam veterans: Theory, research and treatment (pp. 173-187). New York: Brunner/Mazel.
    Presents results of a study conducted in 1973-74 of 147 male Army veterans living in Salt Lake County, UT (Worthington, 1977). Worthington sought to correlate postservice psychosocial adjustment with two independent variables: whether the veteran liked his service tour and whether he served in Vietnam. The findings of the study did not support the thesis that the veteran's postservice adjustment was related to his having served in Vietnam. Differences existed in measures of adjustment between veteran groups on their like or dislike of their service tours, regardless of where they served. A second phase of the study found that postservice adjustment problems could be attributed to social, educational, or vocational problems not connected with military service, as well as to problems that might relate to military experiences. Worthington also presents results from a 1976 study of a group of

75 Army trainees having trouble adjusting to both basic combat training and advanced individual training. Noteworthy among the findings was that both the preservice background of the unsuccessful soldier and his family of origin were highly reflective of poor coping resources. Worthington argues that preservice adapting behaviors may be the best predictors of service success. (S)

Yager, J. (1976). Postcombat violent behavior in psychiatrically maladjusting soldiers. Archives of General Psychiatry, 33, 1332-1335.

Reports results of psychiatric examinations of 31 maladjusting combat veterans referred for psychiatric evaluation for either administrative reasons or specific psychiatric symptoms. The soldiers were interviewed while still on active duty 2-18 months after returning from Vietnam (see Yager, 1975). Of the sample, 13 reported at least one act of violence against another person since their return. These soldiers more often reported fighting in childhood or adolescence, volunteering for Vietnam, having killed four or more persons, and reenlisting for additional tours of duty in Vietnam than had the nonviolent soldiers. Yager notes that maladjusting soldiers who are violent following combat may as a group be more violence prone both before and during combat than soldiers who are not violent following combat, but definitive studies are lacking. (MA)

Yager, T., Laufer, R. S., & Gallops, M. S. (1984). Some problems associated with war experience in men of the Vietnam generation. Archives of General Psychiatry, 41, 327-333.

Summarizes impressions from interviews with 1,342 Vietnam/Vietnam-era veterans (see Egendorf, Kadushin, Laufer, Rothbart, & Sloan, 1981a). Findings indicate that violent war experiences were associated with various postcombat behavioral and emotional problems. After controlling for preservice background factors, combat exposure was found to be associated with arrests and convictions (primarily for nonviolent offenses), excessive drinking, and symptoms of PTSD. Participants in combat atrocities reported more stress symptoms and greater use of heroin and marijuana than did other veterans. Not all men who experienced combat or took part in atrocities reported personal difficulties, however. Responses from 10 blacks and 18 whites who took part in atrocities suggest that soldiers' emotional responses may have been determined by their tendency to dehumanize their victims. Black participants in atrocities reported more personal difficulties than did whites. (S)

Arnold, A. L. (1985a). Diagnosis of post-traumatic stress disorder in Viet Nam veterans. In S. M. Sonnenberg, A. S. Blank, Jr., & J. A. Talbott (Eds.), The trauma of war: Stress and recovery in Viet Nam veterans (pp. 99-123). Washington, DC: American Psychiatric Press.

Presents guidelines to aid in the diagnosis of PTSD in Vietnam veterans. Arnold addresses issues of clinical attitude, critical information needed for proper diagnosis, the technique of examination, and the diagnostic elements. To make an accurate assessment, three key factors should be examined: a detailed description of the traumatic events, the form of reexperiences and their content, and patterns of avoidance of reexperiencing. (S)

Arnold, A. L. (1986). Selected bibliography: II. Post-traumatic stress disorder with special attention to Vietnam veterans (25th rev.). Phoenix AZ: VA Medical Center. Reproduced by Springfield, VA: National Technical Information Service (Document No. 86-216595).

Includes over 900 references, mostly clinically oriented publications, most of which focus on combat-associated psychiatric conditions. Some were published as far back as before World War I, but the majority concern the clinical observations of Vietnam soldiers and veterans. About one eighth are clinically relevant accounts of the Vietnam experience by those who served there. (C)

Atkinson, R. M., Sparr, L. F., Sheff, A. G., White, R. A. F., & Fitzsimmons, J. T. (1984). Diagnosis of posttraumatic stress disorder in Viet Nam veterans: Preliminary findings. American Journal of Psychiatry, 141, 694-696.

Presents preliminary data from a systematic survey of VA disability evaluations for PTSD in Vietnam veterans during a 13-month period in 1981-82. The purpose of the study was to determine the validity of DSM-III criteria for PTSD. The authors state that their findings confirm the notion that PTSD is a specific disorder discrete from other disorders and from nonspecific adjustment problems. (S)

Baskett, S. J., & Henager, J. (1983). Differentiating between post-Vietnam syndrome and preexisting psychiatric disorders. Southern Medical Journal, 76, 988-990.

Presents a case history of a Vietnam veteran to show how considerations of complex, interacting issues of personality traits and combat experience are necessary in diagnosing PTSD. The authors call for a large-scale study of Vietnam veterans to identify the risk factors involved in postwar psychiatric disorders. (S)

Blank, A. S., Jr. (1985b). The unconscious flashback to the war in Viet Nam veterans: Clinical mystery, legal defense, and community problem. In S. M. Sonnenberg, A. S. Blank, Jr., & J. A. Talbott (Eds.), The trauma of war: Stress and recovery in Viet Nam veterans (pp. 293-308). Washington, DC: American Psychiatric Press.

Presents a series of case examples of "flashbacks" in Vietnam veterans to demonstrate that such phenomena, which often lead to explosive behavior such as hostage taking or demands for treatment, have gone largely undetected in clinical and forensic cases during the past 10 years. Blank believes this has occurred because clinicians as well as the veterans themselves have failed to link these symptoms with combat experiences. Further, this oversight has led to both clinical and legal mismanagement. (S)

Blum, M. D., Kelly, E. M., Meyer, M., Carlson, C. R., & Hodson, W. L. (1984). An assessment of the treatment needs of Vietnam-era veterans. Hospital and Community Psychiatry, 35, 691-696.

Presents the results of a needs assessment study of 210 Vietnam-era veterans and 244 veterans of World War II and Korea by the Northport VA Medical Center. Questionnaire data were gathered on general adjustment, occurrence of PTSD, and attitudes toward the VA among veterans in the Nassau and Suffolk counties of New York. The results indicated that, compared with World War II and Korean war veterans, a greater percentage of Vietnam-era veterans reported experiencing symptoms of PTSD as well as more overall adjustment problems. A greater number of Vietnam-era veterans expressed a need for psychotherapy and anger-control therapy, and they generally preferred to be treated with other Vietnam-era veterans who have had combat experiences. (S)

Boman, B. (1986). Combat stress, post-traumatic stress disorder, and associated psychiatric disturbance. Psychosomatics, 27, 567-573.

Reports the prevalence of associated features of PTSD (depression, anxiety, irritability with unpredictable explosions of aggression, impulsivity, suicidal behaviors, and substance abuse) among Australian enlisted Vietnam veterans studied between January 1981 and December 1984. Results showed equal prevalence among Vietnam veterans with PTSD (n = 23), Vietnam veterans without PTSD (n = 27), and active duty controls with no overseas experience (n = 25). Boman concludes that clinicians should not assume wartime service to be a primary etiologic factor in the development of these symptoms, which can be associated with PTSD. (S)

Boulanger, G. (1985). Post-traumatic stress disorder: An old problem with a new name. In S. M. Sonnenberg, A. S. Blank, Jr., & J. A. Talbott (Eds.), The trauma of war: Stress and recovery in Viet Nam veterans (pp. 13-30). Washington, DC: American Psychiatric Press.

Using a historical review of various conceptions regarding psychic trauma, Boulanger contends that psychiatry has been reluctant to accept the fact that sustained impairment can arise in psychologically traumatized adults who have no history of childhood problems. He presents results from a recent multisite probability sample of 274 male Vietnam veterans and 275 male Vietnam-era veterans. Latent class analysis was used to determine that symptoms of PTSD do indeed form a specific syndrome. Stability of family background was found to be strongly correlated with greater posttraumatic stress tolerance. (S)

Boulanger, G. (1986a). Predisposition to post-traumatic stress disorder. In G. Boulanger & C. Kadushin (Eds.), The Vietnam veteran redefined: Fact and fiction (pp. 37-50). Hillsdale, NJ: Lawrence Erlbaum Associates.

Uses data from a nationwide sample of 1,001 Vietnam veterans and nonveterans to refute the hypothesis that men from the most stable families are the least likely to experience traumatic stress reactions from exposure to combat. In this sample, predisposition appears to have no influence on the development of traumatic stress reactions in veterans who experienced high levels of combat exposure. At low levels of exposure, men from the more stable families remain relatively free of stress reactions, but men from average families (one or two predisposing factors) are more likely to develop them. Boulanger found that stress symptoms can exist independently of a traumatic stressor among men from the least stable families. (S)

Boulanger, G., Kadushin, C., Rindskopf, D. M., & Carey, M. A. (1986). Posttraumatic stress disorder: A valid diagnosis? In G. Boulanger & C. Kadushin (Eds.), The Vietnam veteran redefined: Fact and fiction (pp. 25-36). Hillsdale, NJ: Lawrence Erlbaum Associates.

Notes a continued disagreement within American mental health as to the validity of the PTSD diagnosis despite its official recognition in the DSM-III. The authors describe the use of a rigorous statistical procedure, Latent Class Analysis (LCA), to test the coherence of the symptoms included in PTSD to determine whether they form characteristic patterns and whether their empirically observed patterning can be accounted for by postulating a specific underlying construct. LCA was used on data from 1,001 respondents representing a nationwide probability sample of Vietnam-era veterans. These data consisted of seven composite symptoms that have face validity with DSM-III criteria for PTSD. Overall results indicate that traumatic experiences in adult life can produce long-lasting psychological consequences in a significant minority of exposed persons, that these reactions are similar in that the form they take does not appear to depend on prior pathology, and that the symptoms of PTSD presented in the DSM-III are necessary for the diagnosis of PTSD. (S)

Bourne, P. G. (1978). Foreword. In C. R. Figley (Ed.), Stress disorders among Vietnam veterans: Theory, research and treatment (pp. vii-ix). New York: Brunner/Mazel.
    Reviews the unique features of the Vietnam war as it affected the participant both during assignment in Vietnam and as a Vietnam veteran. Emphasized is the delayed nature of the maladaptation consequent to the stress of that war, the unconventional nature of the symptoms, and the special obstacles encountered in trying to provide help to such affected veterans. (C)

Braatz, G. A., & Lumry, G. K. (1969). The young veteran as a psychiatric patient. Military Medicine, 134, 1434-1439.
    Presents the results of a review of the records of all patients under age 26 who were admitted to the psychiatry service of the Minneapolis VA hospital between 1963 and 1968 (N = 273). The survey was undertaken to ensure that treatment modalities were effectively directed toward the actual needs of these increasing numbers of younger patients. Compared with others sampled, the Vietnam veterans had a very low frequency of admission to the psychiatric service (21 out of the 750 Vietnam vets admitted to the hospital in the previous 12 months). Only 1 of the 33 Vietnam veterans in the sample was determined to have a psychiatric problem directly related to his war experiences. The authors recommend use of adolescent-type treatment programs for the younger veteran because of the high frequency of acute psychotic episodes, drug and alcohol addiction, and suicidal/homicidal tendencies. (S)

Braatz, G. A., Lumry, G. K., & Wright, M. S. (1971). The young veteran as a psychiatric patient in three eras of conflict. Military Medicine, 136, 455-457.
    Reviews the records at the Minneapolis VA hospital of psychiatric patients from World War II (n = 81), the Korean war (n = 235), and the war in Vietnam (n = 458), particularly previous MMPI records. The Vietnam sample differed from the other two as

well as from normal controls in having a sharp decline in diagnoses of psychoneurosis and psychophysiologic reactions, a significant trend toward more character disorder symptoms and outward
expression of feelings, and the tendency toward greater discontent
with their life situation, greater proneness to delinquent behavior,
less respect for others, less trust, and diminished feelings of
social responsibility.   (C)

Breen, H. J. (1982). Post Viet Nam syndrome: A critique. Arizona
Medicine, 39, 791-793.
        Criticizes the notion of a unique psychiatric syndrome asso-
ciated with service in Vietnam. Breen argues that there is not a
1:1 correlation between level of combat and stress, and he also
discounts results of research that may be based on weak anecdotal
material. He states that cultural factors are of major importance
in the incidence of acute or delayed stress reactions and in compensation neurosis.   (S)

Brende, J. O. (1983). A psychodynamic view of character pathology
in Vietnam combat veterans. Bulletin of the Menninger Clinic, 47,
193-216.
        Seeks to explain the apparently higher incidence of postwar
psychopathology in U.S. combat veterans by highlighting certain
unusual circumstantial and environmental features of the war (e.g.,
functioning in a "uniquely inhumane guerrilla war," feeling aban-
doned by "mother country," and perceiving betrayal of "ideological
expectations" by military leaders). In the Vietnam combat setting,
buddy attachments often achieved symbiotic-like proportions secondary to identifications reflecting both aggressive and protective
needs as well as mutual survival purposes. Combat loss of such a
relationship could be experienced as a devastating narcissistic
wound and contribute to sadistic combat aggression and pyramiding
atrocities. Brende uses Kohut's intrapsychic model of Self Psychology and presents brief clinical observations to support a pathogenesis of PTSD as the consequence of fragmentation of the veteran's
identity occurring in three phases: (1) loss of self-identity, (2)
development of "splits" in the self-system, and (3) pathological
killer-victim identifications.   (C)

Brende, J. O., & McCann, I. L. (1984). Regressive experiences in
Vietnam veterans: Their relationship to war, post-traumatic symptoms and recovery. Journal of Contemporary Psychotherapy, 14,
57-75.
        Highlights the conceptual importance of regression in under-
standing the psychological alterations inherent in military training,
combat experience (especially problematic in the Vietnam war), and
PTSD, and in the treatment and recovery of veterans with PTSD.

The ordinary soldier regresses when he conforms to his country's demands to surrender some of his individual autonomy and function as part of a combat team. He further regresses in training and then in combat because he directly expresses primitive aggression (and sexuality). Soldiers in Vietnam apparently became victimized by the especially dehumanizing character of the war experiences there (e.g., patriotic justification had been replaced with "killing for the sake of killing"), and regression became more pathological and included "identification with aggressor." Brende notes that regression in the service of treatment seems especially threatening for these veterans who anticipate the dissolution of their unstable ego boundaries. However, sustained initial support to them in managing disturbing regressive symptoms can be followed by the productive use of specific regressive techniques ("integrative regression"). (C)

Breslau, N., & Davis, G. C. (1987). Posttraumatic stress disorder: The etiologic specificity of wartime stressors. American Journal of Psychiatry, 144, 578-583.
     Examines effects of wartime stressors in a sample of 69 Vietnam veterans who were psychiatric inpatients in a VA hospital. Participation in atrocities and the cumulative exposure to combat stressors, each independently of the other, conferred a significant risk for PTSD. In contrast, the effect of these war experiences on the onset of panic, major depression, and mania was not significant. The results indicate that extreme stressors are uniquely linked with PTSD's characteristic cluster of symptoms, but the authors challenge DSM-III's implicit assumption that the reexperienced trauma is the stressor responsible for PTSD. (MA)

Brett, E. A., & Ostroff, R. (1985). Imagery and posttraumatic stress disorder: An overview. American Journal of Psychiatry, 142, 417-424.
     A review of theories of traumatic neurosis or PTSD reveals a relative neglect of the role of posttraumatic imagery. The broad range of imagery has not been recognized, nor has its role in the disorder been adequately formulated. A two-dimensional framework for understanding PTSD based on (1) repetitions of trauma-related images, affects, somatic states, and actions, and (2) defensive functioning puts into perspective the centrality of traumatic imagery, implies a reorganization of DSM-III criteria, points to new directions for research, and clarifies diagnostic and clinical confusion. (MA)

Buck, O. D., & Walker, J. I. (1982). Posttraumatic stress disorder in Vietnam veterans: A review. Southern Medical Journal, 75, 704-706.

Reviews the general as well as the special etiologic factors that apparently led to psychiatric difficulties among the veterans of Vietnam. The authors review the symptoms seen in PTSD and differential diagnosis considerations, and they recommend either specialized psychiatric treatment or referral of less severe cases to one of the VA veterans outreach centers. In their opinion, the best approach is group therapy in that it provides the missing elements of group sanction and identity. (C)

Burke, H. R., & Mayer, S. (1985). The MMPI and the post-traumatic stress syndrome in Vietnam era veterans. Journal of Clinical Psychology, 41, 152-156.
Presents results of MMPI profiles from 30 Vietnam veterans diagnosed with PTSD compared with 30 randomly chosen veterans who were new admissions to a psychiatric inpatient service. Results revealed few differences. Overall the profiles were consistent with the diagnosis of schizophrenia. The authors underscore this evidence of the extensive psychiatric disability found among veterans of Vietnam. (C)

Carroll, E. M. (1983). Stress disorder symptoms in Vietnam and Korean war veterans: A commentary on Thienes-Hontos, Watson, and Kucala. Journal of Consulting and Clinical Psychology, 51, 616-618.
Questions the published results of the Thienes-Hontos, Watson, and Kucala study (1982), in which PTSD was not found to be particularly characteristic of Vietnam veterans when compared with Korean veterans. Carroll argues that the Vietnam veterans sampled were atypical in that PTSD was probably underrepresented in the sample. A second difficulty noted is the lack of comparison data for the two groups in that it is unclear whether the subjects were actual combat veterans. Carroll also suggests that changes in diagnostic criteria over time may account for some of the differences in war-related symptoms (22 of 29 Korean veterans were diagnosed schizophrenic). Finally, he questions the distinction between stress disorder and "control" symptoms, and notes that 8 of the 15 control symptoms are also strongly associated with PTSD. (S)

Cavenar, J. O., Jr., & Nash, J. L. (1976). The effects of combat on the normal personality: War neurosis in Vietnam returnees. Comprehensive Psychiatry, 17, 647-653.
Seeks to alert clinicians to pathogenesis, symptoms, and treatment principles of delayed war neurosis in previously normal men through review of psychiatric observations from other American wars as well as presentation of five case histories from Vietnam. These men demonstrated either psychotic-like syndromes of a

brief nature, depressive reactions with marked survivor guilt, or a psychophysiologic gastrointestinal reaction with marked regression to an infantile and oral level. Onset of psychiatric disabilities ranged from 1-1/2 to 7 years after traumatic combat events. The authors note that such syndromes are often misdiagnosed but do not appear to be different from those described by Grinker in his classic studies from World War II. They also describe use of narcosynthesis as an economic treatment approach. (C)

Clark, A., & Friedman, M. J. (1983). Factor structure and discriminant validity of the SCL-90 in a veteran psychiatric population. Journal of Personality Assessment, 47, 396-404.
    Reports on a validity study of the symptom dimension subscales for the Symptom Checklist-90 (SCL-90) using 442 veteran psychiatric outpatients. Factor analysis yielded a factor structure that was different from those previously reported for other populations. The first factor, depression, accounted for 37% of the variance for the instrument. Only 5 of the 9 reported SCL-90 symptom subscales emerged, and the authors note that in this population, the instrument seems instead to measure a single global distress factor. (C)

Crumpton, E., & Mutalipassi, L. R. (1972). The veteran NP patient: Past and present. Journal of Clinical Psychology, 28, 94-101.
    Presents a review of neuropsychiatric patients admitted to a VA hospital in Los Angeles. The authors compared psychological test results (MMPI and Shipley-Hartford) obtained from patients admitted in 1948 (n = 381), 1958 (n = 528), and 1968 (n = 780); additional comparisons were made between two randomly selected subpopulation groups of patients, 17-25 years of age (n = 100) and 40-45 years of age (n = 100), all admitted in 1968. The 1968 patient showed minor but significant differences from patients of earlier decades, especially in being less psychotic but more paranoid; he experienced considerable emotional distress and was vocal about it. The 17- to 25-year-old patient admitted in 1968 showed definite psychotic symptoms, anxiety, and emotional confusion; he was somewhat rebellious though far from simply representing a character disorder. The 40- to 45-year-old patient showed anxiety but not bizarre or floridly psychotic symptoms. Implications for treatment are discussed. (C)

Davidson, J., Swartz, M., Storck, M., Krishnan, R. R., & Hammett, E. (1985). A diagnostic and family study of posttraumatic stress disorder. American Journal of Psychiatry, 142, 90-93.
    Reports on a family history study of 36 World War II and Vietnam veterans with chronic PTSD, which revealed a positive history of familial psychopathology in 66% of the patients. Alco-

holism, depression, and anxiety disorders were the conditions most commonly found. The patients also had a higher prevalence of alcoholic siblings than did a retrospectively derived control group of depressed and anxious male patients. Regarding the proportion of familial anxiety to familial depression, the probands with PTSD more closely resembled probands with generalized anxiety than probands with depression. Every patient had experienced at least one significant psychiatric illness during his lifetime, most commonly alcohol abuse or depression. (MA)

DeFazio, V. J. (1978). Dynamic perspectives on the nature and effects of combat stress. In C. R. Figley (Ed.), Stress disorders among Vietnam veterans: Theory, research and treatment (pp. 23-42). New York: Brunner/Mazel.

Through a review of psychiatric literature regarding effects of being psychologically overwhelmed by circumstantial events, whether in civilian settings or in those of combat, and from his own experiences counseling Vietnam veterans, DeFazio highlights features common to all such psychic trauma cases (psychological instability, propensity to regression, delayed onset, guilt, and traumatic nightmares) and describes three general maladaptation categories: (1) traumatic war neurosis, (2) exaggerated character pathology, and (3) disassociated symptom pictures. Case examples are provided. (C)

DeFazio, V. J. (1984). Psychoanalytic psychotherapy and the Vietnam veteran. In H. J. Schwartz (Ed.), Psychotherapy of the combat veteran (pp. 23-46). Jamaica, NY: Spectrum Publications.

Reviews (1) the scope, nature, and special pathogenic features of the war, (2) the clinical dilemma faced by mental health workers there ("healing the injured . . . (while) charged with a partial responsibility for manpower"), (3) the history of psychopathologic sequelae among combat veterans, and (4) the psychoanalytic concepts of psychic trauma. From these considerations DeFazio views the veteran's condition as representing a regression that results from the interaction of the severity of combat stress he sustained and the extent of his pretrauma dependency. He posits a continuum of posttraumatic personality disturbances (e.g., attitudinal change only (mildest), qualitatively unaltered character disorder, delayed regressed character disorder, and chronic regressed character disorder), which can provide a foundation for psychoanalytically oriented treatment recommendations for the veteran. Case material is provided. (C)

Domash, M. D., & Sparr, L. F. (1982). Post-traumatic stress disorder masquerading as paranoid schizophrenia: Case report. Military Medicine, 147, 772-774.

Briefly reviews unique traumatic aspects of the Vietnam war and their implications for producing pathology that closely resembles schizophrenia but is more a product of extreme coping strategies. The authors present a case report in which a Vietnam veteran originally classified as a paranoid schizophrenic was later reclassified as suffering from delayed PTSD, and they discuss treatment implications, especially in avoiding the use of neuroleptic medications. (S)

Evans, R. L., & Mobberly, B. D. (1973). Post military adjustment as a function of environmental and social change. Newsletter for Research in Mental Health and Behavioral Science, 15, 7-9.
    Reports results of a survey consisting of demographic questions and a stress inventory administered to 309 Vietnam and Vietnam-era veterans who requested VA outpatient mental health services. The purpose of the assessment was to facilitate identification of veteran needs; alert service delivery personnel to "social information syndromes," which predict success or failure in civilian living; and define areas in which interventions would be most effective. Veterans in this study typically were seen for services within 24 months after discharge, their residences were transient in nature (73% had lived at their current address for less than 1 year), and over half met the stress inventory criteria predictive of serious physical or psychological ailments. The authors recommend the collection of this data during screening interviews to facilitate service delivery. (M)

Fairbank, J. A., Keane, T. M., & Malloy, P. F. (1983). Some preliminary data on the psychological characteristics of Vietnam veterans with posttraumatic stress disorders. Journal of Consulting and Clinical Psychology, 51, 912-919.
    Presents data supporting the use of traditional psychological inventories for assessing PTSD. The MMPI, Beck Depression Inventory, Zung Depression Scale, State-Trait Anxiety Inventories, and the Fear Survey Schedule II were given to 36 Vietnam-era veterans at the Jackson VA Medical Center, who were put into three groups: (1) 12 Vietnam combat veterans in a program designed for treating PTSD, (2) 12 Vietnam combat veteran controls without PTSD or other psychological disorders, recruited from the medical center staff, and (3) 12 noncombat Vietnam-era psychiatric inpatients with other disorders. Univariate and multivariate statistical analyses indicated that the assessment battery could discriminate Vietnam combat veterans with PTSD from the other groups. (S)

Fairbank, J. A., Langley, M. K., Jarvie, G. J., & Keane, T. M. (1981). A selected bibliography on posttraumatic stress disorders in Vietnam veterans. Professional Psychology, 12, 578-586.

Lists 171 references to publications regarding the etiology, symptomatology, and the treatment of PTSD. These sources include veterans' accounts of their combat experiences as well as observations and research from wars preceding Vietnam. (C)

Foy, D. W., Sipprelle, R. C., Rueger, D. B., & Carroll, E. M. (1984). Etiology of posttraumatic stress disorder in Vietnam veterans: Analysis of premilitary, military and combat exposure influences. Journal of Consulting and Clinical Psychology, 52, 79-87.
At the Los Angeles VA Medical Center, 21 Vietnam-era veterans evaluated for PTSD symptoms and 22 Vietnam-era veterans seeking psychiatric treatment for non-PTSD disorders were administered a problem checklist, the MMPI, and an extensive structured interview designed to obtain a premilitary, military, and post-military history. Results of multiple regression analyses demonstrated that combat exposure and, to a lesser degree, military adjustment were significantly related to PTSD symptomatology, whereas premilitary adjustment was not. The MMPI was found to have moderate ability to correctly classify subjects on the basis of PTSD diagnosis. Problem checklist items indicative of anxiety-based disorders were able to correctly classify more than 90% of study subjects. (S)

Friedman, M. J. (1981). Post-Vietnam syndrome: Recognition and management. Psychosomatics, 22, 931-943.
Provides an overview of the signs, symptoms, and psychodynamics of PTSD, as well as of the relevant literature, and offers case vignettes to illustrate characteristics of a special form of PTSD, the "post-Vietnam syndrome" (intrusive, combat-related thoughts, "flashbacks," and nightmares; numbed interpersonal responsiveness; drug dependence; guilt, depression, and anxiety; exaggerated startle response; and rage episodes). Friedman explains his multifaceted treatment approach, which includes pharmacotherapy (especially regarding sleep disturbances), group or individual therapy, and behavioral techniques. (S)

Friedman, M. J., Schneiderman, C. K., West, A. N., & Corson, J. A. (1986). Measurement of combat exposure, posttraumatic stress disorder, and life stress among Vietnam combat veterans. American Journal of Psychiatry, 143, 537-539.
Two scales developed to assess combat exposure and PTSD symptomatology in Vietnam veterans displayed very high reliability. High levels of PTSD were associated with more current life stresses and other standardized indexes of dysphoria. (A)

Frye, J. S., & Stockton, R. A. (1982). Discriminant analysis of post traumatic stress disorder among a group of Viet Nam veterans. American Journal of Psychiatry, 139, 52-56.

Describes the authors' study designed to identify those independent variables that would statistically discriminate between a group of Vietnam veterans who were experiencing PTSD. The 88 subjects were graduates of Army Officers Candidate School who served in Vietnam in 1969 or later. Through a self-report format and a retrospective design, 43.2% met the criteria indicating moderate to strong symptoms of the disorder. Five variables distinguished between those affected and those not affected. Veterans with the disorder reported a negative perception of their family's reception on their return home, a higher level of combat, a more rapid discharge from the service after the war, more of an external locus of control, and a more supportive attitude toward the war before they entered the service. The authors discuss the implications and limitations of these findings. (S)

Glover, H. (1984b). Themes of mistrust and the posttraumatic stress disorder in Vietnam veterans. American Journal of Psychotherapy, 37, 445-451.

Explores three types of interacting influences that contribute to extremes of mistrust and cynicism in many Vietnam veterans with the diagnosis of PTSD. Glover notes that mistrust is common among survivors of man-made and accidental traumas, and he posits that many soldiers who served in Vietnam developed a profound sense of disappointment and betrayal because (1) they were so young when they went (the identities of adolescent soldiers were less stable because they over-idealized mentors, institutions, and themselves); (2) they encountered a uniquely traumatizing combat environment (the stress of guerrilla warfare was aggravated by the ambiguous U.S. strategy and the constraining rules of engagement); and (3) they suffered a disillusioning negative or hostile reception upon return to the States. Glover considers treatment strategies--especially those of group therapy, which derive from an understanding of sources of veteran suspiciousness and hostility--and provides two case examples. (C)

Goldsmith, W., & Cretekos, C. (1969). Unhappy odysseys: Psychiatric hospitalizations among Vietnam returnees. Archives of General Psychiatry, 20, 78-83.

Presents conclusions from a pilot study of 10 Vietnam returnees who were psychiatric admissions to a stateside Army hospital between February and March, 1968. Reviewed were case summaries, data from open-ended interviews, and family histories. Among the trends noted were that (1) all subjects had experienced combat, (2) 4 had passive-aggressive personality disorders with depression, and (3) 7 had prominent depressive features. All subjects displayed mixed attitudes toward the war. Three had been volunteers to escape an unhappy social life. The sole draftee was also the only psychotic in the group. (C)

Goodwin, J. (1980). The etiology of combat-related post-traumatic stress disorders. In T. Williams (Ed.), Post-traumatic stress disorders of the Vietnam veteran (pp. 1-24). Cincinnati, OH: Disabled American Veterans.

Presents a history of stress disorders in combat and catalogs the special features of the Vietnam war that contributed to the formation of PTSD among its veterans. Goodwin highlights as especially stressful the individual replacement system, the exaggerated use of administrative discharges that subsequently created problems in obtaining VA benefits, and the depressed economy to which veterans returned in the early 1970s. (M)

Hendin, H. (1984). Combat never ends: The paranoid adaptation to posttraumatic stress. American Journal of Psychotherapy, 38, 121-131.

Presents a case example of the "paranoid" adaptation seen among some Vietnam veterans with PTSD. This is characterized by mistrust, proneness to take offense, and restricted affectivity. Rage and readiness to counterattack, both in combat and in postwar civilian lives, serve to repress the veterans' fear and vulnerability and to deflect their guilt. They commonly describe similar adaptation in their precombat lives: a history of parental frustration or deprivation but without rage or anger expressed directly toward their parents; more than usual fighting; and a strong tendency to have experienced a pleasurable excitement in combat. (S)

Hendin, H., & Haas, A. P. (1984b). Wounds of war: The psychological aftermath of combat in Vietnam. New York: Basic Books.

Using case history examples from semistructured interviews with more than 100 Vietnam veterans, the authors explore the interactive elements of developmental background, preservice character and adjustment, combat-related traumatic events and conditions in Vietnam, and postservice experience and adjustment as a means of understanding the psychosocial relevance for the individual (his "meaning of combat") as generating, or protecting against, chronic PTSD. They argue for the general application of individual "stress-oriented psychotherapy" as a sensitive and focused approach to fostering the successful psychological integration and mastery of the combat-related psychic trauma in affected veterans. Of special note is a section devoted to examining data from 10 combat veterans who seemed psychologically "inoculated" against developing PTSD. (C)

Hendin, H., Haas, A. P., Singer, P., Gold, F. S., & Trigos, G. (1983). The influence of precombat personality on posttraumatic stress disorder. Comprehensive Psychiatry, 24, 530-534.

Summarizes and interprets findings from the authors' evaluation of more than 100 Vietnam combat veterans with PTSD (Hendin & Haas, 1984b). Emphasizing the interplay of personality and combat stress variables in the genesis, consequent shape, and treatment of the veteran's PTSD, they highlight the need to explore the veteran's precombat personality: "Character is more apt to play a role in posttraumatic stress disorders emanating from the experience in combat (because the soldier is an active participant in the stress) than is the case with most other forms of trauma." Finally, they note that veterans who functioned effectively in combat develop a qualitatively different stress syndrome than those who did not. (MA)

Hendin, H., Haas, A. P., Singer, P., Gold, F. S., Trigos, G., & Ulman, R. B. (1983). Evaluation of posttraumatic stress in Vietnam veterans. Journal of Psychiatric Treatment and Evaluation, 5, 303-307.

Describes a clinical assessment procedure for evaluating PTSD among Vietnam veterans. The procedure involves a self-administered questionnaire and five semistructured interviews, and includes an emphasis on the veteran's precombat, combat, and postcombat experiences. A case summary is provided to illustrate the use of this method. (S)

Hendin, H., Haas, A. P., Singer, P., Houghton, W., Schwartz, M. F., & Wallen, V. (1984). The reliving experience in Vietnam veterans with posttraumatic stress disorder. Comprehensive Psychiatry, 25, 165-173. (Reprinted in W. E. Kelly (Ed.), (1985). Post-traumatic stress disorder and the war veteran patient (pp. 71-84). New York: Brunner/Mazel.)

Presents case histories of 3 Vietnam veterans suffering from "reliving experiences"--that is, the postwar emergence of dissociative episodes in which the individual appears conscious and often has subsequent amnesia for what has taken place. In these incidents, the individual "relives" certain aspects of his previous combat-generated traumatic situations. The authors discuss the adaptive value of reexperiencing traumatic events in a waking state and consider treatment implications. (S)

Hendin, H., Pollinger, A., Singer, P., & Ulman, R. B. (1981). Meanings of combat and the development of posttraumatic stress disorder. American Journal of Psychiatry, 138, 1490-1493.

Presents four case examples to illustrate some unique responses to combat stress and the individual dynamic differences

that contribute to the formation of stress disorders affecting the
soldiers before, during, and after combat. (C)

Holloway, H. C., & Ursano, R. J. (1984). The Vietnam veteran:
Memory, social context, and metaphor. Psychiatry, 47, 103-108.
    Provides case studies to illustrate the active generative role
of memory and the importance of social context and metaphor in
affecting combat memories of Vietnam veterans diagnosed as having PTSD. The authors emphasize that the recall of traumatic
combat events is subject to symbolic reorganization--that is, as
with the dream, the memories become modified by issues past,
present, and future. Thus, the psychological meaning of combat
trauma must be also understood in terms of present context and
association. (S)

Horowitz, M. J., & Solomon, G. F. (1975). A prediction of delayed
stress response syndromes in Vietnam veterans. Journal of Social
Issues, 31(4), 67-80. (Reprinted in C. R. Figley (Ed.), (1978a).
Stress disorders among Vietnam veterans: Theory, research and
treatment (pp. 268-280). New York: Brunner/Mazel.)
    It is posited that over the next years civilian mental health
professionals will encounter stress response syndromes in Vietnam
veterans, will misread etiological factors, and will be unable to
treat such persons effectively. This paper attempts to describe the
types of problems which may be expected and suggests special approaches (e.g., conceptual labeling) which will be required and may
assist the treatment process. (A)

Huppenbauer, S. L. (1982). PTSD: A portrait of the problem. American Journal of Nursing, 11, 1699-1703.
    Discusses how Vietnam differed from past wars and how
these differences contributed to the development of psychiatric
difficulties such as PTSD. Huppenbauer describes the major symptoms associated with PTSD as well as some ways therapeutic intervention can help the veteran cope with his problems. (S)

Hyer, L., O'Leary, W. C., Saucer, R. T., Blount, J., Harrison, W. R.,
& Boudewyns, P. A. (1986). Inpatient diagnosis of posttraumatic
stress disorder. Journal of Consulting and Clinical Psychology, 54,
698-702.
    Reports a study of randomly selected Vietnam-era veterans
admitted for psychiatric hospitalization in 1983. Vietnam combat
veterans with PTSD (n = 26) and without PTSD (n = 24), and noncombat veterans (n = 25) were identified using a test battery that
included background; preservice, service, and current adjustment
variables; and psychometrics. The groups did not differ on demo-

graphics or premorbid variables; however, PTSD veterans indicated more psychopathology on psychometric and adjustment variables. The PTSD subscale of the MMPI subscale was cross-validated and the amount of combat exposure correlated with PTSD variables. (C)

Jackson, H. C. (1982). Moral nihilism: Developmental arrest as a sequela to combat stress. Adolescent Psychiatry, 10, 228-242.

Using clinical material from 4 Vietnam veterans in outpatient psychiatric treatment, Jackson posits that the collection of symptoms (e.g., defensive passivity, outbursts of rage, and inability to effect satisfying relationships) that arose in these premorbidly unaffected men represents arrested superego development consequent to their combat experience and subsequent rejection upon their return home. In particular, she alludes to how "the disparity between the adolescent's inner life and the reality of the chaotic and irrational combat world in which he found himself was so great that he was unable to integrate the experience either cognitively or morally." Further, in the case of chronically affected veterans, they became arrested in an adolescent phase of moral development "strikingly similar to nihilism." Jackson discusses treatment implications, especially the value of group therapy. (C)

Keane, T. M., Malloy, P. F., & Fairbank, J. A. (1984). Empirical development of an MMPI subscale for the assessment of combat-related posttraumatic stress disorder. Journal of Consulting and Clinical Psychology, 52, 888-891.

Using data from veteran patients with PTSD symptoms, the authors established MMPI criteria to aid in the diagnosis of such conditions. The empirically derived decision rule correctly diagnosed 74% of the patients in each group. (C)

Keane, T. M., Scott, W. O., Chavoya, G. A., Lamparski, D. M., & Fairbank, J. A. (1985). Social support in Vietnam veterans with posttraumatic stress disorder: A comparative analysis. Journal of Consulting and Clinical Psychology, 53, 95-102.

Compares social support measures for a sample of Vietnam-era veterans ($\underline{N}$ = 45) divided equally into three groups: VA patients with combat-related symptoms of PTSD, VA medical inpatients with no PTSD symptoms, and well-adjusted individuals. Indexes of social support were obtained for the present as well as for the periods of 1-3 months before entering the service and 1-3 months following discharge from the service. Although the three groups reported comparable levels of support across all dimensions, only the PTSD patients showed a consistent decline to current low levels. (C)

Kelly, W. E. (Ed.). (1985). Post-traumatic stress disorder and the war veteran patient. New York: Brunner/Mazel.

Presents a collection of research studies, case reports, and therapeutic approaches reflecting on the etiology, diagnosis, and treatment of PTSD and related adjustment disorders among Vietnam veterans. Appendixes include a suggested reading list on Vietnam veterans and PTSD as well as a guide to self-history taking. (See also Brende, 1985; R. B. Fuller, 1985; Haley, 1985; Hendin, Haas, Singer, Houghton, Schwartz, & Wallen, 1984; Marrs, 1985; Parson, 1985a; Racek, 1985; Sax, 1985; Shatan, 1985; Silver, 1985; Silver & Kelly, 1985; Tanay, 1985; Van Devanter, 1985; Wilson & Krauss, 1985; Woods, Sherwood, & Thompson, 1985.) (S)

Langley, M. K. (1982). Post-traumatic stress disorders among Vietnam combat veterans. Social Casework, 63, 593-598.

Reviews the characteristics of the Vietnam war as they affect the development of PTSD among combat veterans. One-year individualized tours of duty tended to increase already high stress levels by emphasizing the soldier's interest in his personal survival, especially as his tour's end approached. Numerous other factors contributed to the cluster of PTSD symptoms, including a public antiwar attitude, ineffective leadership, and the culture shock of fighting in a distant country in which soldiers could not grasp the culture of or communicate effectively with the people. Symptoms include some combination of guilt, depression, social alienation, irritability, nightmares and related sleep disturbances, aggression or fear of aggression, "flashbacks," and exaggerated startle response. (M)

Laufer, R. S., Brett, E. A., & Gallops, M. S. (1984). Post-traumatic stress disorder (PTSD) reconsidered: PTSD among Vietnam veterans. In B. A. van der Kolk (Ed.), Post-traumatic stress disorder: Psychological and biologic sequelae (pp. 59-79). Washington, DC: American Psychiatric Press.

Seeks to rectify--through a review of research and clinical observations previous to, and generating out of, the experience with Vietnam veterans--a deficiency in the literature on PTSD by providing a systematic conceptualization of the nature of war stress and its sequelae. The authors note that research on combatants or survivors of war is unique in that it is concerned with both "traumatic stress" (as in most civilian disasters) and "chronic stress" (as in life events stress). Thus, a triad of influences must be measured together to understand war stress: war stress itself, length of stress exposure, and subjective reactions to stress (reflecting ego mechanisms and emotional responses). Further, "war stress" is thought to be composed of at least five classes of stress: (1) combat intensity (i.e., the degree to which the soldier's life was threatened), (2) exposure to abusive violence, (3) the

death or wounding of friends, (4) social isolation from peers, and
(5) exposure to death and dying apart from combat roles (as with
graves registration or medical personnel).   (C)

Lindy, J. D., Grace, M. C., & Green, B. L. (1984). Building a conceptual bridge between civilian trauma and war trauma: Preliminary
psychological findings from a clinical sample of Vietnam veterans.
In B. A. van der Kolk (Ed.), Post-traumatic stress disorder: Psychological and biologic sequelae (pp. 43-57). Washington, DC:
American Psychiatric Press.
    Reviews 10 years of research on the psychological effects of
disaster on survivors, and presents a working model for the genesis and natural history of posttraumatic states. This model suggests that the traumatic stressor, personality features, and social
and environmental reaction interact in complex ways over time in
the development and course of PTSD. The authors use research on
combatant survivors of the Vietnam war to compare the effects of
civilian disasters with those following war trauma. They also discuss the implications of their point of view for the goals of psychotherapy with such survivors.   (S)

Lipkin, J. O., Blank, A. S., Jr., Parson, E. R., & Smith, J. R.
(1982). Vietnam veterans and posttraumatic stress disorder. Hospital and Community Psychiatry, 33, 908-912.
    Discusses reasons why many Vietnam veterans have developed
PTSD, problems in diagnosing and treating PTSD, and a theoretical
basis for the behavior of veterans with PTSD using an ego psychology model. The authors also outline some clinical considerations for therapists treating Vietnam veterans.   (S)

Lorr, M., Peck, C. P., & Stenger, C. A. (1975). Interpersonal styles
of Vietnam era veterans. Journal of Personality Assessment, 39,
507-510.
    Presents results of a study designed to distinguish the inter-
personal style characteristics of Vietnam-era veterans from those
of World War II veterans using the Interpersonal Style Inventory.
The sample included 3,075 veterans, categorized as either medical-
surgical, psychiatric, or drug-addicted patients, in treatment in 47
VA health care facilities. They were distinguished by age as being
either 24 or less, or 45-55. Group differences on 17 scores were
tested by discriminant function analyses. The Vietnam-era veterans
were found to be more rebellious, mistrustful, adventure-seeking,
and self-centered than the older veterans.   (C)

Lumry, G. K., & Braatz, G. A. (1972). The Vietnam era veteran and
psychiatric implications. In L. J. Sherman & E. M. Caffey, Jr.

(Eds.), The Vietnam veteran in contemporary society: Collected
materials pertaining to the young veterans (sec. IV, pp. 97-106).
Washington, DC: Veterans Administration.

Reviews, synthesizes, and expands on published studies
(Braatz & Lumry, 1969; Braatz, Lumry, & Wright, 1971) of Vietnam
veteran adjustment patterns. The authors also comment on findings
from a recent national study of youth attitudes, which describes
their estrangement from the history, traditions, and values (indi-
vidualistic, competitive, economic) of the American society of their
parents to embrace instead the values of social justice and equal-
ity. The young veterans share the cynical, confrontational, antiestablishment sentiments of today's youth. (C)

Lumry, G. K., Cedarleaf, C. B., Wright, M. S., & Braatz, G. A.
(1972). Psychiatric disabilities of the Vietnam veteran. Minnesota
Medicine, 55, 1055-1057.

Reviews the records of 458 psychiatric and 48 medical patient
controls who were under 26 years of age and who were admitted
to the psychiatric service of the Minneapolis VA hospital from
1963 to 1969. Demographically, the only difference between the
two groups was that about one third of the psychiatric patients
were still on active duty at the time of admission while none of
the 48 medical controls was. The findings suggest that the psychiatric disabilities of Vietnam veterans follow a continuous pattern
similar to those seen in civilian practice. Almost all the psychiatrically disabled veterans had educational, vocational, or social
problems of a serious nature prior to entering active duty. Sexual
adjustment had not been adequate, and general interpersonal adjustment and family relationships could be characterized as either
unsatisfactory or insufficient. From the data it appeared that
active military service may exacerbate symptoms but is not a sufficient cause in itself to explain the veterans' disabilities and
psychiatric illnesses. The authors note that the variable of combat
exposure in Vietnam cannot alone account for their psychiatric
disabilities since most of the psychiatrically disabled veterans had
not served in combat. (S)

Lund, M., Foy, D. W., Sipprelle, R. C., & Strachan, A. (1985). The
combat exposure scale: A systematic assessment of trauma in the
Vietnam war. Journal of Clinical Psychology, 40, 1323-1328.

Reports results of an interview study of 43 Vietnam veteran
patients exploring the nature of their combat experiences and the
extent of residual psychiatric symptoms. Findings correlated seven
experience areas with the development of PTSD and the intensity
of symptoms: serving in Vietnam, witnessing the injury or death of
an American soldier, firing a weapon or being fired upon, killing
an enemy combatant, becoming wounded, killing an enemy civilian,
and serving a third tour in Vietnam. Using the Guttman scaling

technique allowed an ordering of clinical information in understanding the pathogenic influence of combat experiences. (C)

Morrier, E. J. (1984). Passivity as a sequel to combat trauma. Journal of Contemporary Psychotherapy, 14, 99-113.
Presents a psychodynamic explanation for the passivity seen among many Vietnam veterans with posttraumatic symptomatology. Morrier considers these veterans to manifest a fixation of regressed defenses that thereby perpetuates repetition-compulsion and prohibits mastery over ego-passivity. This extensive regression resulted when the veteran's insufficiently developed ego encountered both the extremely traumatic conditions in Vietnam and the subsequent lack of societal supports, leading to the dissolution of his ego-ideal. These veterans are consequently unable to integrate nonaggressive activity and intimacy, and so they resort to their ego-passive stance. (C)

Mueser, K. T., & Butler, R. W. (1987). Auditory hallucinations in combat-related chronic posttraumatic stress disorder. American Journal of Psychiatry, 144, 299-302.
Compares 5 veterans with PTSD (2 of whom served in Vietnam) who report auditory hallucinations with 31 nonhallucinating veterans on demographic, military, postmilitary, and symptom variables. Veterans reporting hallucinations had higher combat exposure and more intense PTSD symptoms than the other veterans and also tended to be more refractory to treatment. The implications for this subgroup of chronic PTSD veterans are discussed. (C)

Mullis, M. R. (1984). Vietnam: The human fallout. Journal of Psychosocial Nursing, 22, 27-31.
Describes traumatic responses of many survivors of the Vietnam war in terms of three overlapping phases: impact, or the Vietnam war zone experiences; recoil, in which denial and numbing blunt the impact of the trauma; and posttrauma, in which the defensive functions of the denial-numbing response are no longer adequate to ward off intolerable thoughts or emotions related to Vietnam. Mullis concludes by urging the nursing profession to provide proper assessment and treatment of Vietnam veterans with PTSD. (S)

Norman, E. M. (1982). PTSD. The victims who survived. American Journal of Nursing, 11, 1696-1698.
Discusses the symptoms of PTSD among Vietnam veterans and reviews various theories regarding its causation. Among these is the survivor theory, which is based on the psychoanalytic observation that denial, repression, and emotional avoidance--typical PTSD

symptoms--are often associated with surviving a traumatic event. Others argue that PTSD is the result of emotional difficulties that predate military service in Vietnam. Further, some believe it is often a misdiagnosis and not nearly as pervasive as reported. (S)

Pearce, K. A., Schauer, A. H., Garfield, N. J., Ohlde, C. O., & Patterson, T. W. (1985). A study of post-traumatic stress disorder in Vietnam veterans. Journal of Clinical Psychology, 41, 9-14.
    Compares the frequency of self-reports of PTSD symptoms among three groups of Vietnam-era veterans: 30 individuals who sustained a combat-related traumatic event; 30 individuals who sustained a noncombat-related traumatic event; and 30 individuals with neither. Both groups with traumatic experiences reported significantly more PTSD symptoms. Further, symptoms among the combat-related group exceeded those of the noncombat-related group. The authors interpret the latter finding to suggest that human-generated events are potentially more traumatic than accidental ones. Taken together, all these findings add support for the validity of the PTSD diagnostic entity. (C)

Resing, M. (1982). Mental health problems of Vietnam veterans. Journal of Psychosocial Nursing and Mental Health Service, 20, 40-43.
    Discusses ways in which the Vietnam war differed from past wars, especially with regard to the features of PTSD. Resing highlights the need for the nursing profession to help identify and differentiate delayed stress reactions from psychosis or character disorders, and to establish a plan of care for veterans. (S)

Robert, J. A., Ryan, J. J., McEntyre, W. L., McFarland, R. S., Lips, O. J., & Rosenberg, S. J. (1985). MCMI characteristics of DSM-III posttraumatic stress disorder in Vietnam veterans. Journal of Personality Assessment, 49, 226-230.
    Compares Millon Clinical Multiaxial Inventory (MCMI) profiles of 25 veterans with PTSD diagnoses with 25 veterans diagnosed as other psychiatric disorders having features overlapping with those of PTSD. In 9 of the 20 MCMI scales, the PTSD veterans had significantly higher scores. The profiles also differed in shape and scatter. A discriminant analysis accounted for 100% of the variance and correctly distinguished 88% of the patients. (C)

Rosenheck, R. (1985). Malignant post-Vietnam stress syndrome. American Journal of Orthopsychiatry, 55, 166-176.
    Describes an extreme and disabling form of PTSD seen among Vietnam veterans, in which there is an escalating mutual interaction of (1) explosive and violent behavior, (2) social isolation

and ostracism, (3) an extremely negative identity, and (4) pervasive reexperiencing of traumatic war memories. These veterans appear to have participated in extraordinarily violent combat in Vietnam, come from backgrounds in which intense feelings were often acted out, and been burdened with intense overstimulation when they returned to the States. Rosenheck offers treatment suggestions derived from an understanding of these etiological considerations. (C)

Rosoff, E. (1985). Variations in response to high stress in humans: An exploration among Vietnam veterans of some antecedent variables. Dissertation Abstracts International, 45 (B-9), 3082.
    Reports results of a study exploring the relationship between symptom "choice" (medical, psychiatric, substance abuse) and antecedent variables among 72 veterans who reported traumatic combat stress in Vietnam. The participants, most of whom were selected from veteran outreach centers, completed questionnaires for three time frames: before Vietnam, during Vietnam, and current. Premorbid variables included socioeconomic status (SES), religiosity, religious importance, church attendance, religious activity, parental attitudes toward childhood illness, family medical symptoms, family psychiatric symptoms, and social support. Results showed that SES, family patterns of medical and of psychiatric problems, and parental attitudes toward childhood illness predicted types of later medical and psychiatric problems. High combat exposure in combination with being wounded in Vietnam correlated strongly with later symptomatology. Substance use patterns, however, were not affected by Vietnam service. (C)

Salley, R. D., & Teiling, P. A. (1984). Dissociated rage attacks in a Vietnam veteran: A Rorschach study. Journal of Personality Assessment, 48, 98-104.
    Presents a case report of a Vietnam combat veteran with episodic rage attacks. Rorschach data suggest a near neurotic level of ego organization with massive repression in the form of dissociated violent impulses precipitated by Vietnam combat trauma. Developmental differences between preoedipal splitting and higher-level dissociation are discussed. Dissociative states are posited to represent a development level of ego organization midway between borderline and neurotic. (S)

Schwartz, H. J. (1984b). Introduction: An overview of the psychoanalytic approach to the war neuroses. In H. J. Schwartz (Ed.), Psychotherapy of the combat veteran (pp. xi-xxviii). Jamaica, NY: Spectrum Publications.
    Recommends a "bifocal" approach to understanding the etiology of traumatic reactions to combat, in which one takes into ac-

count both the traumatizing sensory overload and the evoked and overwhelming "specific long-repressed drive derivatives." This dual explanatory model serves also to recommend treatment modalities that allow both for the catharsis of the helplessness and regression associated with terror-filled combat memories and for the reworking, through the transference relationship, of character-distorting drive-defense compromise formations with long-repressed infantile roots. Case material is provided.   (C)

Schwartz, H. J. (1984c). Unconscious guilt: Its origin, manifestations, and treatment in the combat veteran. In H. J. Schwartz (Ed.), Psychotherapy of the combat veteran (pp. 47-84). Jamaica, NY: Spectrum Publications.
    Posits that persistent postcombat psychological and adaptational problems reflect a critical intrapsychic conflict surrounding unconscious guilt. This often overlooked primary dynamic is the result of the combat veterans having undergone a psychic trauma as the predictable consequence of participating in unrestrained violence. Schwartz alludes to environmental conditions of the Vietnam war (i.e., jungle war, violence against civilians, and the absence of admired, limit-setting military superiors), which exacerbated "individual tendencies" to regress. He primarily emphasizes the inevitable attachment of conflicted infantile impulses to the pervasive acting out of violence in susceptible soldiers (i.e., by actually experiencing "the most generic fantasies of incorporation, annihilation and mutilation," they regressed to oral-sadistic levels, which aroused their unrelenting primitive superego). Schwartz recommends a "therapeutic-analytic" treatment for veterans in whom the necessary mourning process has been blocked by this retaliatory superego (evidence for which is often in the form of defenses against the guilt, as in aggressivity, paranoia, masochism, or psychosomatic illness). Through two case examples, he shows the challenges inherent in providing such analytically oriented treatment. The therapist must provide "an unambivalent and consistent emotional attitude (which) allows for the interpretation of layers of resistance and the unfolding of the transference regression with its safe reexperiencing of infantile wishes and distortions. This secure frame permits interpretations of unconscious guilt and aggression to be perceivable." Thus the therapist becomes available for use by the patient as a "new auxiliary superego."   (C)

Scurfield, R. M., & Blank, A. S., Jr. (1985). A guide to obtaining a military history from Viet Nam veterans. In S. M. Sonnenberg, A. S. Blank, Jr., & J. A. Talbott (Eds.), The trauma of war: Stress and recovery in Viet Nam veterans (pp. 263-292). Washington, DC: Psychiatric Press.
    Presents a comprehensive catalog of questions that mental health professionals can use to obtain information from Vietnam

veterans experiencing postwar readjustment problems. This information is critical in establishing diagnostic and therapeutic precision. Major areas of concern in the interview guide surround immediate premilitary experiences, entry into military service, military training, Vietnam history, military discharge, and post-Vietnam readjustment. (S)

Shipko, S., Alvarez, W. A., & Noviello, N. (1983). Towards a teleological model of alexithymia: Alexithymia and post-traumatic stress disorder. Psychotherapy and Psychosomatics, 39, 122-126.
Presents data from a study assessing the presence of alexithymia (diminished capacity to articulate emotions) among 22 Vietnam combat veterans who met DSM-III criteria for PTSD. Although approximately 8% of males in the general population are alexithymic, within the group studied, 9 veterans (41%) were diagnosed as such. The authors posit that alexithymia should be considered a secondary symptom of PTSD. They acknowledge that the "emotional numbing" characteristic of PTSD may have caused veterans to develop social values similar to those of chronic civilian alexithymics, but they point out that clinical interviews with subjects elicited other alexithymic traits, such as vague physical complaints and concrete operational thinking. They conclude that treatment planning for veterans with PTSD must take into account the possibility of alexithymia since such individuals are poor candidates for insight-oriented psychotherapy. (S)

Sierles, F. S., Chen, J. J., McFarland, R. E., & Taylor, M. A. (1983). Posttraumatic stress disorder and concurrent psychiatric illness: A preliminary report. American Journal of Psychiatry, 140, 1177-1179.
Presents results of interviews with 25 combat veterans (24 Vietnam, 1 Korea) hospitalized for PTSD at the North Chicago VA Medical Center. In 4 cases (16%), PTSD was the sole diagnosis; 14 patients (56%) had one additional diagnosis; 5 (20%) had two additional diagnoses; and 2 (8%) had three additional diagnoses. These diagnoses included alcohol abuse (64%), drug abuse (20%), antisocial personalties (12%), endogenous depression (8%), and organic mental syndrome (4%). In addition, 18 patients (72%) gave a history suggestive of some form of depression that was not currently active; 16 (64%) had had episodes of severe anxiety; and 15 (60%) had taken two or more categories of illicit drugs. The authors suggest that routinely assuming PTSD to be the underlying cause of all symptoms may deprive some patients manifesting PTSD symptoms of specific treatments of known efficacy for other disorders. (S)

Sierles, F. S., Chen, J. J., Messing, M. L., Besyner, J. K., & Taylor, M. A. (1986). Concurrent psychiatric illness in non-

Hispanic outpatients diagnosed as having posttraumatic stress disorder. Journal of Nervous and Mental Disease, 174, 171-173.

Of 25 veterans who fit DSM-III criteria for PTSD and who were referred for outpatient group therapy, 84% were found to have coexisting psychiatric conditions (e.g., alcoholism, antisocial personality, drug abuse, depression, and anxiety). The authors note that, with one exception, the prevalence of these conditions was not significantly different from that of those they reported among an inpatient sample of combat veterans (Sierles, Chen, McFarland, & Taylor, 1983). (C)

Silsby, H. D., & Jones, F. D. (1985). The etiologies of Vietnam post-traumatic stress syndrome. Military Medicine, 150, 6-7.

Posits that conditions diagnosed as PTSD in many Vietnam veterans are not generally the result of severe combat trauma but of predisposing, unresolved conflicts within the soldiers that were exacerbated by the environmental stress of the war. Case material is provided. (C)

Silver, S. M. (1982). Posttraumatic stress disorders in Vietnam veterans: An addendum to Fairbank et al. Professional Psychology, 13, 522-525.

Provides selected references centering on the topics of PTSD generally and on Vietnam veterans specifically to augment a previously published listing (Fairbank, Langley, Jarvie, & Keane, 1981). (C)

Silver, S. M., & Iacono, C. U. (1984). Factor-analytic support for DSM-III's post-traumatic stress disorder for Vietnam veterans. Journal of Clinical Psychology, 40, 5-14.

Presents results of two studies designed to verify the diagnostic criteria of PTSD and to determine whether Vietnam veterans with PTSD are distinct from non-Vietnam veterans with similar symptoms. Vietnam veterans from Disabled American Veterans' (DAV) Vietnam veteran outreach centers seeking treatment for personal problems ($\underline{N}$ = 405) completed a symptom checklist devised from clinical observations and research studies of Vietnam veterans. Factor analysis produced four factors that supported the DSM-III criteria for the diagnosis of PTSD. The major exception involved the relevance given to depressive symptoms. In the DSM-III, depression is an "associated feature" whereas the authors found it to be a major part of the overall factor structure. They also found anger and hostility to be of more importance than does the DSM-III. They conclude that their findings support a separate diagnostic category of "Post-Traumatic Stress Disorder for Vietnam Veterans." In the second study, comparisons were made between Vietnam and non-Vietnam veterans. The latter group consisted of

63 veterans who also sought counseling from the DAV for personal problems. Five variables specific to service in Vietnam were dropped from the questionnaire for these veterans. Data were then combined with that from the 405 Vietnam veterans from the first study and were again factor analyzed. The results indicate that Vietnam and non-Vietnam veterans are quite different with respect to evaluating their service-related experiences. Vietnam veterans appear to have experienced greater intensity of aggressive feelings and detachment, as well as to have reexperienced service-related traumatic events more intensely. (S)

Smith, J. R. (1982). Personal responsibility in traumatic stress reactions. Psychiatric Annals, 12, 1021-1030.
    Explores the interaction of circumstance and personal meaning in the generation of PTSD using a series of clinical vignettes, many from Vietnam veterans. Smith's focus is especially on the insidious effect of unconscious guilt, which often leads patients to distort their recollection of the traumatic incident so as to explain their sense of culpability. It also often motivates them to seek displacement activities that are unconsciously designed to serve as a penance. Smith recalls his own participation in establishing the PTSD diagnostic criteria in the DSM-III and notes how intensified interest in the long-term reactions of the Vietnam veterans played a major role in determining the concepts used to define that disorder. (C)

Solkoff, N., Gray, P., & Keill, S. (1986). Which Vietnam veterans develop posttraumatic stress disorders? Journal of Clinical Psychology, 42, 687-698.
    Reviews the literature supporting opposing viewpoints (stress vs. predisposition) about the pathogenesis of PTSD among combat veterans, and presents results of a retrospective study of 50 Vietnam combat veterans with PTSD compared with 50 Vietnam veteran controls. A structured interview was used to determine how childhood and immediate preservice, combat, and postservice experiences contribute to the generation of PTSD. The only measures distinguishing PTSD patients from the controls were heightened combat traumatization ("PTSD patients more frequently sustained injuries and reported being closer, not only to their own death, but to the deaths of others") and greater indifference or hostility to their homecoming from families or others. (C)

Solomon, G. F., Zarcone, V. P., Jr., Yoerg, R., Scott, N. R., & Maurer, R. G. (1971). Three psychiatric casualties from Vietnam. Archives of General Psychiatry, 25, 522-524.
    Describes 3 veterans whose psychiatric illnesses were precipitated by events experienced in the Vietnam conflict. Two cases

have features relatively unique to that war: the first involved a
corporal who ordered the murder of an innocent civilian, and the
second involved the use of drugs that contributed to a tragic combat error. The third case is that of a "classical" war neurosis. In
all cases interviews were conducted under the influence of sodium
amobarbital and methamphetamine to elicit suppressed memories
and affects. (MA)

Sonnenberg, S. M. (1982). A transcultural observation of post-
traumatic stress disorder. Hospital and Community Psychiatry, 33,
58-59.
    Uses Shakespeare's Hamlet to dramatize how features of
PTSD among Vietnam veterans can best be explained in terms of
intrapsychic conflict: "Like the most tragic of our untreated and
scorned Vietnam veterans, our subject committed an act symbolic
of survivor guilt, destructive to others, and ultimately suicidal."
(C)

Sonnenberg, S. M. (1985). Introduction: The trauma of war. In
S. M. Sonnenberg, A. S. Blank, Jr., & J. A. Talbott (Eds.), The
trauma of war: Stress and recovery in Viet Nam veterans (pp. 3-
12). Washington, DC: American Psychiatric Press.
    Presents several case histories of Vietnam veterans to illus-
trate problems of PTSD and other psychological difficulties experienced by many Vietnam veterans. (S)

Sonnenberg, S. M., Blank, A. S., Jr., & Talbott, J. A. (Eds.). (1985).
The trauma of war: Stress and recovery in Viet Nam veterans.
Washington, DC: American Psychiatric Press.
    Presents data-based and clinical reports on the nature of the
war trauma and subsequent readjustment difficulties sustained by
returning Vietnam veterans. Topics include the concept of PTSD
and stress reactions; the diagnosis of PTSD; the role of social
supports and networks on the pathogenesis of PTSD; VA-sponsored
outreach programs; and various treatment modalities such as psychotherapy, group therapy, "rap group" approaches, family therapy,
and narcosynthesis. The contributors also discuss readjustment
problems in the context of various subgroups, such as active duty
veterans, Air Force former POWs, female veterans, black veterans,
Hispanic veterans, and incarcerated veterans. (See also Arnold,
1985a, 1985b; Blank, 1985a, 1985b, 1985c; Boulanger, 1985; Holloway
& Ursano, 1985; Kadushin, 1985; L. C. Kolb, 1985; Laufer, 1985;
Lipkin, Scurfield, & Blank, 1983; Ott, 1985; Parson, 1985b; Pentland
& Dwyer, 1985; Pina, 1985; Scurfield & Blank, 1985; J. R. Smith,
1985a, 1985b; Sonnenberg, 1985; Ursano, 1985; C. M. Williams &
T. Williams, 1985.) (S)

Strange, R. E. (1974). Psychiatric perspectives of the Vietnam veteran. Military Medicine, 139, 96-98.

Reviews findings of a 1969 study of Navy and Marine Vietnam returnee psychiatric admissions in a VA hospital compared with non-Vietnam service veteran psychiatric patients (Strange & Brown, 1970). Results suggest that Vietnam returnees tend to be more depressed, to have more disciplinary and alcohol problems, and to be somewhat more threatening in word, but not in deed. However, duty in Vietnam did not correlate with veteran drug abuse. Strange discounts studies that suggest the Vietnam-era veteran is more self-centered, more irresponsible, more impulsive, and more prone to psychiatric illness by recounting studies that reveal such tendencies in nonveteran cohorts of that age.   (C)

Strange, R. E., & Brown, D. E., Jr. (1970). Home from the war: A study of psychiatric problems in Viet Nam returnees. American Journal of Psychiatry, 127, 488-492.

Reports on a study comparing 50 patients who developed psychiatric problems after they returned from combat duty in Vietnam with a group of patients who had not had such duty. The Vietnam returnees reported more conflicts in intimate relationships and had a higher incidence of depression and somatization than did the noncombat group. Although they also manifested more aggressive and suicidal threats, they did not evidence more direct aggressive or suicidal behavior. The authors suggest that while Vietnam returnees face significant readjustment stress, their reactions are generally internalized and their potential for violence is no greater than that in those without Vietnam experience. (MA)

Stretch, R. H., & Figley, C. R. (1984). Combat and the Vietnam veteran: Assessment of psychosocial adjustment. Armed Forces & Society, 10, 311-319.

Reports on the development of the Vietnam Veterans Questionnaire (VVQ), a research and diagnostic instrument developed for use with Vietnam veterans, which assesses extent of combat experience and psychosocial adjustment. The instrument was validated in fall 1979 using a sample of 34 veterans currently receiving psychiatric help and 48 nonclinical veterans obtained through VA medical centers and university VA student affairs offices across the country. Results supported the validity of the instrument to discriminate between clinical and nonclinical veterans and also demonstrated that combat is largely associated with the presence of psychosocial adjustment problems. Combat veterans exhibited a greater number of adjustment problems than did noncombat veterans, with those veterans who experienced "heavy" combat revealing more problems than those who experienced "light" combat. The authors speculate that a great many Vietnam combat veterans suffering from problems of psychosocial adjustment are not receiving or even seeking any type of treatment for their problems. (S)

Stuen, M. R., & Solberg, K. B. (1972). The Vietnam veteran: Characteristics and needs. In L. J. Sherman & E. M. Caffey, Jr. (Eds.), The Vietnam veteran in contemporary society: Collected materials pertaining to the young veterans (sec. IV, pp. 115-126). Washington, DC: Veterans Administration.

Compares a group of psychiatric patients at a VA hospital (N = 50) with a matched-by-age comparison group (N = 54) at a nearby Army post. Along with diagnosis, the authors investigated the subjects' relationship with parents, family mental health, mobility during childhood, dependency needs, sexual identification, socioeconomic status, drug use, ability to cope with transition to civilian life, and conflicts with wife/family. Although both groups were experiencing some degree of problems in most areas, the veterans group differed significantly from controls in that the veterans (1) had lower coping abilities (2) reported more parental--particularly paternal--rejection, and (3) had a greater incidence of drug and alcohol abuse. In terms of illness, 76% were considered disturbed enough to be diagnosed as schizophrenic. Regarding their course of hospitalization, these young veterans were noted to suffer deep feelings of failure; used "attack as a defense"; lacked educational, vocational, and social skills; and were unable to identify with older staff and patients or with peers. (C)

Sudak, H. S., Martin, R. S., Corradi, R. B., & Gold, F. S. (1984). Antecedent personality factors and the post-Vietnam syndrome: Case reports. Military Medicine, 149, 550-554.

Reviews the preservice histories of all Vietnam veteran admissions between March 1979 and November 1981 who satisfied DSM-III criteria for PTSD (N = 10). The authors found extensive premorbid character vulnerability consequent to severely disturbed backgrounds in all subjects. They interpret the findings as contradicting the prevalent assumption that antecedent personality factors are incidental in the pathogenesis of PTSD, and they posit that such childhood traumas and deprivations reduce the soldier's capacity for tolerating the subsequent war trauma: "The Vietnam experiences appeared to tax already rather tenuous ego function; stress became trauma due to its psychologic specificity. Combat experiences appeared to activate unresolved childhood conflict and issues; combat precipitants usually involve object loss or uncontrolled aggression, with unconscious affective displacements from parents to parental symbols." Case material is provided. (C)

Theines-Hontos, P. (1983). Stress-disorder symptoms in Vietnam and Korean war veterans: Still no difference. Journal of Consulting and Clinical Psychology, 51, 619-620.
     Rebuts objections raised over the author's previous study publication (Thienes-Hontos, Watson, & Kucala, 1982), which found no difference in prevalence of stress disorder and nonstress disorder symptoms as reflected in the hospitalization records of Vietnam veterans compared with veterans of the Korean war. Carroll (1983) criticized the study for its use of hospitalized veterans as subjects, its failure to distinguish levels of combat exposure, its use of medical records for analysis, the validity of its diagnoses, and its choice of control symptoms.   (S)

Thienes-Hontos, P., Watson, C. G., & Kucala, T. (1982). Stress-disorder symptoms in Vietnam and Korean war veterans. Journal of Consulting and Clinical Psychology, 50, 558-561.
     Compares files of 29 combat veterans from Korea and 29 combat veterans from Vietnam who had been psychiatrically hospitalized at the St. Cloud VA Medical Center between 9 and 36 months after returning from the war zone. Files are also compared for nonstress disorder "control" symptoms in both groups. Results suggest that stress disorder symptoms are not unique to Vietnam veterans: 42.2% of Korean veterans' and 42.3% of Vietnam veterans' reported symptoms were in the stress disorder category. (S)

van der Kolk, B. A. (Ed.). (1984). Post-traumatic stress disorder: Psychological and biologic sequelae. Washington, DC: American Psychiatric Press.
     Presents a collection of interrelated perspectives on the nature, etiology, assessment, and treatment of PTSD among Vietnam veterans. The work includes chapters on the effects of stressors in war, including neurophysiological correlates; parallels between psychic trauma in civilian and military circumstances; implications of the Rorschach findings, dream disturbances, and other clinical observations in affected veterans; and specialized treatment strategies, including those of psychopharmacology. (See also de la Pena, 1984; Kolb, Burris, & Griffiths, 1984; Kramer, Schoen, & Kinney, 1984; Laufer, Brett, & Gallops, 1984; Lindy, Grace, & Green, 1984; van der Kolk, Boyd, Krystal, & Greenberg, 1984; van der Kolk & Ducey, 1984.)   (S)

van der Kolk, B. A., & Ducey, C. (1984). Clinical implications of the Rorschach in post-traumatic stress disorder. In B. A. van der Kolk (Ed.), Post-traumatic stress disorder: Psychological and biologic sequelae (pp. 29-42). Washington, DC: American Psychiatric Press.

Presents Rorschach results from 15 Vietnam veterans who report weekly traumatic nightmares in conjunction with their PTSD. The data are interpreted as representing a lack of integration of affective experience and a failure to cognitively structure the traumatic experience. The authors speculate that the veteran's lack of affect tolerance interferes with his ability to not only grieve his Vietnam losses but also resolve contemporary conflicts. Instead, he reacts with a fight or flight reaction to new emotional stimuli as if it were a recurrence of the traumatizing situation. The learning of affect tolerance is viewed as critical in his psychotherapy and may need to be temporarily supplemented by medication that reduces the level of autonomic activation. Case examples are provided. (S)

Van Putten, T., & Emory, W. H. (1973). Traumatic neuroses in Vietnam returnees: A forgotten diagnosis? Archives of General Psychiatry, 29, 695-698.
Discusses how traumatic neuroses of war in Vietnam returnees are frequently overlooked. Vietnam returnees, because they reject authority and mistrust institutions, come to the VA only out of desperation. Often they come years after discharge from the service and after ineffective trials of psychotherapy in the community. Explosive aggressivity, "flashbacks" of combat scenes, and phobic elaborations about the world as an unbearably hostile place have led to such misdiagnoses as psychomotor epilepsy, LSD abuse, or schizophrenia. The misdiagnosis of schizophrenia may lead to long-term phenothiazine treatment rather than to appropriate psychotherapy. Case examples are provided. (MA)

Van Putten, T., & Yager, J. (1984). Posttraumatic stress disorder: Emerging from the rhetoric. Archives of General Psychiatry, 41, 411-413.
Seeks to refute certain conclusions deriving from the Center for Policy Research study of 1,342 Vietnam and Vietnam-era veterans regarding postservice adjustment (see Egendorf, Kadushin, Laufer, Rothbart, & Sloan, 1981a). The authors argue that the data provide only weak support for the conclusion that veterans who were exposed to combat and those who took part in atrocities manifest more subsequent behavioral and emotional problems than those from comparable social backgrounds without such experiences. They contend that checklist endorsement of haunting memories of the war, occasional startle reactions or nightmares, and one or two mild, nonspecific symptoms should not qualify veterans for a diagnosis of PTSD unless that diagnosis is confirmed with a clinical interview. They also take exception to the finding that combat was strongly associated with subsequent behavioral problems (e.g., veterans with heavy combat experience had a 23% higher arrest rate and a 12% higher conviction rate), arguing that

most arrests were for "disorderly behavior" and raising the possibility that these were alcohol related or associated with antiwar demonstrations. They state that most veterans with PTSD have coexisting psychiatric disorders and point to the need to determine whether these disorders were triggered by the unusual stress of combat service or whether a predisposition to such disorders rendered veterans more susceptible to PTSD. (S)

Walker, J. I. (1981a). Psychological problems of Vietnam veterans. Journal of the American Medical Association, 246, 781-782.
Discusses some of the problems facing Vietnam veterans, given that as many as 1.5 million Vietnam-era veterans may eventually need psychiatric help. Relevant statistics include a suicide rate 23% higher for veterans younger than 34 compared with non-veterans of the same age; a rise in the proportion of Vietnam-era veterans hospitalized for alcohol-related problems from 13% in 1970 to 31% in 1977; and approximately 29,000 Vietnam-era veterans incarcerated in state or federal prisons, 37,500 veterans on parole, 25,000 under probation supervision, and 87,000 awaiting trial. Walker presents an overview of the symptoms of PTSD and suggests that although no well-controlled studies have been done on treatment of Vietnam-related PTSD, findings of a study conducted at the VA in Durham, NC, suggest that group therapy is the treatment of choice for these patients. Walker includes a description of the nationwide VA storefront counseling centers. (S)

Wilson, J. P., & Krauss, G. E. (1985). Predicting post-traumatic stress disorders among Vietnam veterans. In W. E. Kelly (Ed.), Post-traumatic stress disorder and the war veteran patient (pp. 102-147). New York: Brunner/Mazel.
Five major classes of variables are hypothesized to affect post-Vietnam adaptation and psychosocial functioning: pretrauma personality characteristics, combat role, nature of stressors in combat in Vietnam, "short-timers syndrome," and the homecoming experience (social support versus isolation). The results of questionnaire data from 114 combat veteran volunteers attending the VA's Operation Outreach program reveal that the best predictors of PTSD are knowledge of combat role factors (including the veteran's subjective assessment of combat stress); exposure to physically traumatic situations, particularly injury and death; and degree to which the veteran felt psychologically isolated upon returning home. The authors present a framework for understanding the pathogenesis of PTSD, which proposes that until the individual successfully assimilates a past trauma, he cannot understand its nature, intensity, and meaning in terms of his existing conceptual schemata of current reality. (S)

Wolff, B. M. (1985). The relationship between perceived social support and posttraumatic stress disorder in Vietnam veterans. Dissertation Abstracts International, 46 (1-B), 320.
    Presents survey data regarding the relationship between combat intensity, reentry social support, and PTSD symptomatology among 90 Vietnam veterans (mixed, patient and nonpatients). Besides answering demographic questions, the veteran participants completed the Combat Index questionnaire; the Traumatic Stress Reaction Scale; Scales of Perceived Social Support; the Social Network Questionnaire; the Life Experience Survey; and the Marlowe-Crowne Scale of Social Desirability. Overall, comparison of the veterans grouped into three levels of combat intensity sustained in Vietnam demonstrated no significant differences. Further analysis revealed that self-reports of PTSD symptomatology correlated positively with extent of combat exposure and negatively with amount of perceived social support from family and friends. However, the "buffering hypothesis" of social support was unconfirmed. PTSD levels at the time of discharge from the service was the best predictor of current PTSD.   (C)

Yesavage, J. A. (1983a). Dangerous behavior by Viet Nam veterans with schizophrenia. American Journal of Psychiatry, 140, 1180-1183.
    Reports on a study of the military histories of 80 Vietnam-era veterans (30 had served in Vietnam, 20 had been in combat) in the psychiatric intensive care unit of the Palo Alto VA Medical Center. All patients were being treated for schizophrenia. A stepwise multiple regression analysis revealed that high scores on several inpatient and outpatient measures of violence and dangerousness were significantly correlated with combat experience in Vietnam and particularly with killing or witnessing the killing of the enemy. Apparently the schizophrenic combat veterans have carried their anger and frustration from the war into their current lives. Yesavage suggests that future research should measure violence outside the treatment context as it affects the family context.   (S)

Yesavage, J. A. (1983b). Differential effects of Vietnam combat experiences vs. criminality and dangerous behavior by Vietnam veterans with schizophrenia. Journal of Nervous and Mental Disease, 171, 382-384.
    Reports results of a study correlating combat experiences and criminality before and during military service with postservice violent behavior among 70 schizophrenic Vietnam-era veterans (including 27 Vietnam veterans and 19 combat veterans) hospitalized for schizophrenia at the Palo Alto VA Medical Center. The effects of these variables on assaultive behavior on the wards were assessed through stepwise multiple regression analyses. Results indicate that certain violent tendencies in schizophrenic

Vietnam veterans are better explained by war experiences than by premorbid criminal behavior. (S)

Zarcone, V. P., Jr., Scott, N. R., & Kauvar, K. B. (1977). Psychiatric problems of Vietnam veterans: Clinical study of hospital patients. Comprehensive Psychiatry, 18, 41-53.

Presents results of a clinical study of 50 Vietnam veterans who were psychiatrically hospitalized in the Palo Alto VA hospital. Of the sample, 31 patients demonstrated a psychotic condition, often masked by character and behavior disorder symptoms. But although 19 of the 31 had become seriously disabled in Vietnam, only 7 had been treated as psychotic while there. The authors emphasize that none of these patients had a history of classical combat exhaustion. Seven were diagnosed as psychotic as soon as 1 month after their return to the States. Many of the patients had significant drug and alcohol abuse problems. The authors discuss some methods and problems of both military psychiatry and the VA, and they provide case examples. (C)

Zimering, R. T. (1984). Post-traumatic stress disorder in Vietnam veterans: An empirical evaluation of the diagnostic criteria. Dissertation Abstracts International, 45 (5-B), 1599.

Reports results of a study of six criterion symptoms among 16 Vietnam combat veterans diagnosed as having PTSD and an equal number without the diagnosis. Each symptom was measured following exposure to combat auditory stimuli. Five of the six measures successfully distinguished the PTSD subjects (i.e., elevated levels of intrusive thoughts; decreased interpersonal contact; anxiety; impaired concentration; and symptom intensification). Measures of short-term memory were not significantly different. (C)

3 Etiology and Diagnosis of Psychiatric Conditions: Biologic and Behavioral Approaches

Blanchard, E. B., Kolb, L. C., Pallmeyer, T. P., & Gerardi, R. J. (1983). A psychophysiological study of post-traumatic stress disorder in Vietnam veterans. Psychiatric Quarterly, 54, 220-229.

Describes a study of psychophysiological responses to combat sounds presented to 11 Vietnam veterans suffering from PTSD compared with an age- and sex-matched group who had not served in the armed forces during the Vietnam era. Measured were heart rate, blood pressure, forehead EMG, skin resistance level, and peripheral temperature. Response differences were seen in heart rate, systolic blood pressure, and forehead EMG. Elevated heart rate was found to correctly classify 95.5% of the combined sample. The one participant who had been incorrectly classified was a veteran who was on neuroleptic medication. The authors caution that this approach is not without risk. One veteran reported aftereffects such as nightmares and panic attacks. These findings support the notion of PTSD as a persistent conditioned emotional response to traumatic events of combat. (S)

Brende, J. O. (1982). Electrodermal responses in post-traumatic syndromes: A pilot study of cerebral hemisphere functioning in Vietnam veterans. Journal of Nervous and Mental Disease, 170, 352-361.

Presents findings from 6 subjects with PTSD symptoms, 5 of whom were Vietnam combat veterans. Continuous visual displays of bilateral extremity electrodermal responses (EDRs) were monitored while subjects were supportively interviewed regarding past traumatic experiences. Part of each interview consisted of a hypnotic trance. Findings include that hypnotically induced imagery of past traumatic events was associated with left-sided EDR increases (representing increased contralateral right cerebral hemispheric activity); that "psychic numbing" was associated with left-sided EDR decreases or bilateral EDR unresponsiveness; and that revivifications of hypervigilant states were associated with right-sided EDR lateralization. In several cases, control of the experience of fear was associated with left-sided or bilaterally decreased EDR. Brende interprets the data to indicate that PTSD symptoms are associated with poorly integrated cerebral hemisphere functioning, with psychic numbing and intrusive imagery associated with abnormal right hemisphere function or integration, and with excessive aggression, hypervigilance, and character pathology associated with dysfunction of the left one. (C) de la Pena, A. (1984). Post-traumatic stress disorder in the Vietnam veteran: A brain-modulated, compensatory information-augmenting response to information underload in the central nervous system? In B. A. van der Kolk (Ed.), Post-traumatic stress disorder: Psychological and biologic sequelae (pp. 108-122). Washington, DC: American Psychiatric Press.

Presents data from a study of various psychophysiological parameters in 12 drug-free Vietnam veterans suffering with PTSD. Data from this study are interpreted as contradicting the prevalent theory that PTSD represents hyperarousal induced by the uncertain Vietnam combat environment (i.e., generating an exacerbated state of stress characterized by autonomic hyperarousal and subsequent defensive perceptual and behavioral strategies). De la Pena suggests instead that, in certain individuals--especially those parasympathetic-dominant individuals who may have adapted best in the high-intensity Vietnam combat environment--once out of the combat situation, "CNS activation levels and/or information-processing rates reached some critical lower limit, thereby calling into play brain-controlled, homeostatic information-augmenting mechanisms to help rectify the brain's own information underload state." Thus, these veterans are at a greater risk for subsequent development of PTSD than those veterans who are constitutionally more autonomically balanced (sympathetic-dominant). (S)

Greenberg, R., Pearlman, C. A., & Gampel, D. (1972). War neuroses and the adaptive function of REM sleep. British Journal of Medical Psychology, 45, 27-33.

Presents findings from a sleep lab study of 7 Vietnam veterans with persistent postcombat trauma symptoms, including repetitive war nightmares. Besides REM cycle data, the investigators obtained clinical information bearing on individual psychodynamics and dream content, and quantitatively rated pre- and postsleep interview material along three axes (measuring "defensive strain"). Strong correlation was noted between lengthening REM latencies and reductions in defensive strain. The correlation between lengthening REM duration and lowered defensive strain (predicted by the authors as demonstrating how dreaming serves adaptive and mastery functions of the ego) was statistically weaker; however, the authors feel that methodological improvements in this type of approach will demonstrate a clearer correlation between dream activity and specific psychodynamics. (C)

Keane, T. M., Zimering, R. T., & Caddell, J. M. (1985). A behavioral formulation of posttraumatic stress disorder in Vietnam veterans. Behavior Therapist, 8, 9-12.

Reports on the authors' studies of Vietnam veterans with PTSD. The cardinal symptoms of PTSD are intrusive thoughts regarding the traumatic events and vivid recollections or dreams of those events, which feel as if they are recurring. The authors posit that PTSD represents high-order conditioning with stimulus generalization. Generally, when exposed to cues resembling the original traumatizing, veterans with PTSD showed exaggerated physiological arousal, motor agitation, and intrusive combat-related thoughts. When comparing Vietnam combat veterans with PTSD with a well-adjusted group of combat veterans using cognitive performance tests and questionnaires, the authors found the performance on five of the six tasks effective in distinguishing the PTSD veterans.   (C)

Kolb, L. C. (1983). Return of the repressed: Delayed stress reaction to war. Journal of the American Academy of Psychoanalysis, 11, 531-545.
     Discusses and interprets data generated from Kolb's use of modified narcosynthetic interviews (including presentation of combat sounds and physiological monitoring) with 14 Vietnam veterans with chronic PTSD symptomatology. Kolb discusses PTSD in these veterans as "a primitively fixed psychobiological conditioning to fear with its accompanying fight-flight-freeze action components intertwined with and driving the individual's developmentally determined defensive structure as well as the secondary reflective cognitive consequences of the catastrophic experiences" (such as avoidance behaviors, survival guilt, or shame). He states that preexistence of a childhood neurosis renders the individual vulnerable to less intense catastrophic threats. Kolb also discusses treatment strategies derived from these perspectives and provides a transcript from one case example. (See also Kolb & Mutalipassi, 1982.)   (C)

Kolb, L. C. (1984). The post-traumatic stress disorders of combat: A subgroup with a conditioned emotional response. Military Medicine, 149, 237-243.
     Discusses research on veterans with chronic and delayed forms of PTSD, and posits that there is a subgroup of veterans who have physiologically measurable and persisting conditioned emotional responses to external stimuli that are reminiscent of battle sounds. These responses reinforce memory traces of combat experiences, which evoke reflections of acts, committed or uncommitted, as well as drives for revenge, which in turn generate secondary affects of anxiety, guilt, and shame. Attempts are then made to defend against these primary and secondary affects through avoidance behaviors such as social withdrawal, withdrawal from external stimulation, or self-medication through alcohol or drug abuse. Kolb contends that most interventions such as group and individual psychotherapy, standard psychopharmacotherapy, hypnosis, biofeedback, and relaxation do not generally eliminate the symptoms of PTSD in these patients. Methods must also be

found to eliminate the conditioned emotional response and its subjectively perceived physiologic concomitants. Kolb reports that his attempts at deconditioning such patients through desensitization to combat sounds have been unsuccessful, but he also reports use of propranolol and clonidine as promoting recovery. (S)

Kolb, L. C. (1986b). Treatment of chronic post-traumatic stress disorders. Current Psychiatric Therapies, 23, 119-127.
    Synthesizes Kolb's clinical experiences with victims of physical and psychological trauma (World War II combatants, civilian casualties, and military veterans) and the results of his research on Vietnam veterans (Blanchard, Kolb, Pallmeyer, & Gerardi, 1983; Kolb & Mutalipassi, 1982). Kolb postulates that the PTSD patient suffers with a neurohumoral abnormality, which results when a sufficiently intense stimulus causes both functional and structural changes (which may be reversible or permanent) in the inhibitory cerebral cortical structures. Lack of cortical inhibition results in increased activation of agonistic subcortical systems, which are concerned with the behavioral effects of threatening but nonpainful external stimulus and dreaming sleep. Thus, PTSD symptoms fall into classes that represent (1) defect (expressive of impaired inhibition such as irritability, aggressive reactions, startle responses, and episodic dissociations); (2) neuronal release (repetitive memories carried in intrusive thinking and dissociative states, dreams, nightmares, and "flashbacks"); and (3) attempts at restitution of social function. Kolb discusses treatment implications of these and other observations. (C)

Kolb, L. C. (1987). A neuropsychological hypothesis explaining posttraumatic stress disorders. American Journal of Psychiatry, 144, 989-995.
    Reports findings from recent psychophysiological and biochemical research on Vietnam combat veterans with chronic PTSD. Applying these data and the analogy of the known functional and structural defects that can occur in the peripheral (cranial) sensory system following high-intensity stimulation, Kolb hypothesizes that cortical neuronal and synaptic changes occur in PTSD because of excessive and prolonged sensitizing stimulation, which leads to depression of habituating learning. He postulates that the "constant" symptoms of the disorder are due to changes in the agonistic neuronal system, which impair cortical control of hindbrain structures concerned with aggressive expression and the sleep-dream cycle. (MA)

Kolb, L. C., & Mutalipassi, L. R. (1982). The conditioned emotional response: A sub-class of the chronic and delayed post-traumatic stress disorder. Psychiatric Annals, 12, 979-987.

Summarizes results of a narcosynthesis study of a subgroup (n = 18) of 94 Vietnam combat veterans with PTSD symptomatology whose clinical examination indicated the presence of intensely repressed affect unaltered by psychotherapeutic approaches. When exposed to recorded combat sounds while under light barbiturate narcosis, 14 immediately responded by emotionally abreacting a traumatic war memory. The authors argue that such veterans have a "perceptual-motor abnormality with regressive impairment of perceptual discrimination and fixation through emotional conditioning to a primitive startle-arousal pattern," which is mediated through central adrenergic pathways. Consequently, in situations resembling past traumatic events, they undergo the pathophysiological arousal of self-preservative emotion as well as secondary anxiety, guilt, and shame, or defenses against these affects. Effective treatment must focus on attenuating or suppressing the conditioned emotional response through imaginal desensitization or prescription of adrenergic blocking agents. (C)

Kramer, M., Schoen, L. S., & Kinney, L. (1984). The dream experience in dream-disturbed Vietnam veterans. In B. A. van der Kolk (Ed.), Post-traumatic stress disorder: Psychological and biologic sequelae (pp. 81-95). Washington, DC: American Psychiatric Press.
        Presents findings of a sleep and dream study of 7 Vietnam combat veterans who complained of disturbing dreams, compared with a "control" group of 8 otherwise symptomatic Vietnam combat veterans without disturbing dreams. Both groups awakened frequently and tended to recall their dreams at the same rate. About half the time the dreams of the study group were of military themes while almost none of the control group's were. The controls tended to have a lower rate of dream recall from REM awakenings, suggesting that they may be avoiding potentially disturbing memories in their dreams. The authors believe the intensity (recallability), content, and distribution of the dream experience may lie at the heart of PTSD and continually reinforce the traumatic neurosis. (S)

Malloy, P. F., Fairbank, J. A., & Keane, T. M. (1983). Validation of a multimethod assessment of posttraumatic stress disorders in Vietnam veterans. Journal of Consulting and Clinical Psychology, 51, 488-494.
        Presents a multimethod assessment approach to the diagnosis of PTSD. Subjects consisted of 10 veterans under treatment for PTSD at the Jackson VA Medical Center, 10 psychiatric inpatients with other psychological disorders, and 10 normal combat veteran controls from the staff. All subjects were presented with mild combat stimuli, consisting of sounds and photographs of an assault, with the hypothesis that these stimuli would be uniquely arousing for combat veterans diagnosed as having PTSD. Dependent mea-

sures consisted of self-reports of anxiety and physiologic data such as heart rate and skin resistance. The results indicate that the approach could discriminate veterans with PTSD from veterans with other psychological disorders and from well-adjusted combat veterans. (S)

Pitman, R. K., Orr, S. P., Forgue, D. F., de Jong, J. B., & Claiborn, J. M. (1987). Psychophysiologic assessment of post-traumatic stress disorder imagery in Vietnam combat veterans. Archives of General Psychiatry, 44, 970-975.

This study used psychophysiologic techniques to test for exaggerated emotional arousal during imagery of psychologically traumatic experiences among Vietnam veterans with PTSD. All subjects were medication-free Vietnam combat veterans, classified on the basis of DSM-III-R criteria into those with PTSD (n = 18) and controls with no mental disorder (n = 15). The controls did not differ from the veterans classified as having PTSD in extent of combat experienced in Vietnam. "Scripts" describing each subject's combat experiences, as well as other experiences, were read to them in the laboratory, and they were instructed to imagine the events the scripts portrayed while heart rate, skin conductance, and electromyogram (frontalis muscle) changes were recorded. The PTSD subjects' physiologic responses were markedly higher than those of the controls. The combined physiologic variables identified PTSD subjects with a specificity of 100% and a sensitivity of 61%. (MA)

Stutman, R. K., & Bliss, E. L. (1985). Posttraumatic stress disorder, hypnotizability, and imagery. American Journal of Psychiatry, 142, 741-743.

Reports results of a study of hypnotizability among a sample of 26 Vietnam veterans with a diagnosis of PTSD. The intensity of PTSD symptoms was measured through self-reports. Hypnotizability scores, vividness of imagery scores, and symptomatic profiles were also ascertained. Veterans with low or no PTSD scores had normal hypnotizability and imagery scores, whereas those with high PTSD scores had high hypnotizability and imagery scores. The authors conclude that either combat traumas enhanced hypnotic potential in some veterans or veterans with excellent premilitary hypnotic potential were more susceptible to PTSD. (MA)

van der Kolk, B. A., Blitz, R., Burr, W., Sherry, S., & Hartmann, E. (1984). Nightmares and trauma: A comparison of nightmares after combat with lifelong nightmares in veterans. American Journal of Psychiatry, 141, 187-190.

Presents results of a study comparing 15 Vietnam veterans with PTSD, including chronic frequent nightmares, with 10 lifelong nightmare sufferers without any combat experience, using a 3-5 hour semistructured psychiatric interview. The results indicate that the traumatic nightmares of combat veterans tend to occur earlier in the sleep cycle, are more likely to be perceived as replicas of historical events, and are more commonly accompanied by gross body movements. The noncombat cohort showed evidence of a thought disorder in the Rorschach. The authors suggest that the veterans with PTSD had failed to integrate their combat experiences psychologically and used dissociation to deal with the resultant strong affects. (S)

van der Kolk, B. A., Boyd, H., Krystal, J., & Greenberg, M. (1984). Post-traumatic stress disorder as a biologically based disorder: Implications of the animal model of inescapable shock. In B. A. van der Kolk (Ed.), Post-traumatic stress disorder: Psychological and biologic sequelae (pp. 123-134). Washington, DC: American Psychiatric Press.

Noting the many similarities between the behavioral sequelae to inescapable shock in animals and the constricted affect, decreased motivation, and functional decline in people following extreme psychic traumatization, the authors speculate on etiologic changes in catecholamine and endorphin neurochemical systems in humans with PTSD. Treatment strategies following these hypotheses are also considered. (S)

4 Treatment of Psychiatric Conditions: General Approaches

Arnold, A. L. (1985b). Inpatient treatment of Vietnam veterans with post-traumatic stress disorder. In S. M. Sonnenberg, A. S. Blank, Jr., & J. A. Talbott (Eds.), The trauma of war: Stress and recovery in Viet Nam veterans (pp. 239-261). Washington, DC: American Psychiatric Press.

Discusses both inpatient and outpatient treatment of Vietnam veterans suffering from PTSD. Issues considered include indications for admission, specificity of treatment, crisis resolution, initial risk assessment, staff authority, medications, patient education, substance abuse, psychotherapy, follow-up, and specialized inpatient units, as well as the basic rationale of treatment. Arnold concludes by addressing such related aspects as the impact of variations in staff workload, approaches in risk management, and factors surrounding disability compensation. (S)

Berkowitz, M. (1980). Themes in treatment of Vietnam veterans. In T. Williams (Ed.), Post-traumatic stress disorders of the Vietnam veteran (pp. 133-135). Cincinnati, OH: Disabled American Veterans.

Berkowitz, a nonveteran therapist, observes that the issues of trust, guilt, hostility, self-confidence, and mortality, and the experience of nondirected anger, were prominent in groups of Vietnam veterans he led or in which he participated. He also shows how the group can be used to provide the affirmation that was withheld by other Americans when veterans returned from Vietnam. (M)

Berman, S., Price, S., & Gusman, F. (1982). An inpatient program for Vietnam combat veterans in a Veterans Administration hospital. Hospital and Community Psychiatry, 33, 919-922.

Describes the VA's first inpatient program for Vietnam veterans at Palo Alto, CA, which opened in January 1978. The three main goals of the program are to relieve acute psychological distress, restore the Vietnam veteran to a maximum level of functioning within the shortest period of time, and reintegrate the veteran into the community and its support systems. The program minimizes medication and reflects the assumptions that a "debriefing" of military experience is essential and that the clinical regimen should enable veterans to restore their transition to adulthood, which was interrupted by the war. (S)

Blank, A. S., Jr. (1982a). Apocalypse terminable and interminable: Operation outreach for Vietnam veterans. Hospital and Community Psychiatry, 33, 913-918.
    Describes the history of the VA Vietnam Veteran Outreach Program as well as the theoretical and clinical aspects of this unconventional program, and discusses some factors related to stress disorders in Vietnam veterans and various treatment methods that have proven to be effective or noneffective. (C)

Blitz, R., & Greenberg, R. (1984). Nightmares of the traumatic neuroses: Implications for theory and treatment. In H. J. Schwartz (Ed.), Psychotherapy of the combat veteran (pp. 103-123). New York: Spectrum Publications.
    Reviews the literature on personality theories as used to explain the traumatic war neurosis and the traumatic nightmare; discusses the implications of recent research on the theory of dreaming; and uses Kohut's theory about the development of "the self" to provide a comprehensive orientation for understanding and treating traumatic neuroses. The authors consider the nightmare a "failed dream"--that is, one that does not complete the process of integrating present and past experience. Thus, the traumatic events depicted in the dream "can be interpreted as mental representations of an imperiled self." The treatment implication is that the therapist should focus on "the patient and his (self-state) rather than on the possible symbolic meaning of the dream." (C)

Brende, J. O. (1981). Combined individual and group therapy for Vietnam veterans. International Journal of Group Psychotherapy, 31, 367-378.
    Discusses the advantages of combining individual and group psychotherapy in treating Vietnam veterans. In the example discussed, Brende notes that the development of group cohesiveness is the primary prerequisite for a therapeutic revivification of the loss of buddies during combat. Further, it is the individual therapeutic process that seems to enhance the development of trust, partly because the therapist is perceived as an important consultant to the group, and hence, an indirect group leader. Brende concludes that, since Vietnam veterans have difficulty developing trust as a group, either group or individual therapy alone may be inadequate for that purpose. (S)

Crump, L. D. (1984). Gestalt therapy in the treatment of Vietnam veterans experiencing PTSD symptomatology. Journal of Contemporary Psychotherapy, 14, 90-98.
    Describes the rationale, indications, techniques, and beneficial results using gestalt therapy approaches in the treatment of persisting combat-related PTSD symptoms in Vietnam veterans. Exam-

ples include the guided reenactment of emotionally traumatic combat situations. Crump underscores the requirement that such a treatment approach be prescribed and applied judiciously by those with a solid background in general psychotherapy as well as in gestalt therapy. (C)

Egendorf, A. (1978). Psychotherapy with Vietnam veterans: Observations and suggestions. In C. R. Figley (Ed.), Stress disorders among Vietnam veterans: Theory, research and treatment (pp. 231-253). New York: Brunner/Mazel.

Provides an orientation for psychotherapists regarding the Vietnam veteran's war experience and offers suggestions regarding the therapeutic issues they may present. War experiences are posited as being extraordinary life events that "absolutize" all experience into a life-or-death frame of mind and make the veteran more like a survivor of a catastrophic event. This may make him reluctant to communicate with nonveterans, decrease his sensitivity to his own feelings ("psychic numbing"), or increase his nostalgic attachment to military ways. Egendorf suggests that therapists encourage but not insist on the veteran discussing his war experience and offer him the opportunity to see how his past military experience affects his current life and relationships. He recommends a perspective on pathogenesis that goes beyond a standard clinical consideration to one that integrates history, sociology, and philosophy (i.e., one that leads to "apprehending fully the question of a healing antidote to war"). (M)

Eisenhart, R. W. (1977). Flower of the dragon: An example of applied humanistic psychology. Journal of Humanistic Psychology, 17, 3-24.

Describes the "Flower of the Dragon" (Sonoma County, CA, Vietnam Veterans Service Project) as being a program to treat veterans through "awareness, psychological wholeness, more effective communication, finding one's center and rebuilding a sense of community among them." Eisenhart discusses applications of humanistic psychology to understand the veterans' problems and to design the most effective treatment approaches. According to him, brutal methods were used in basic training to achieve psychological control of recruits and to equate masculine identity with performance of the military mission. After arrival in Vietnam, soldiers had to cope with a vastly different war from that for which they were trained. Among their frustrations, the enemy often refused to engage. Also, the troops suffered extensive stress from the lack of meaning in their involvement in the war. Following their service in Vietnam, reentry and reintegration into society were made difficult by lack of ritual acceptance and cathartic outlets. These experiences often culminated in a "psychic numbing": social alienation and an almost paranoid attitude toward any kind of authority.

Eisenhart states that resistance to breakdown of this defensive psychic numbing is responsible for the typically long delay between combat trauma and the onset of symptoms. (M)

Frick, R., & Bogart, L. (1982). Transference and countertransference in group therapy with Vietnam veterans. Bulletin of the Menninger Clinic, 46, 429-444.
    Describes the progressive transference-countertransference shifts observed in the authors' 15-month group treatment of 8 Vietnam combat veterans who suffered with varieties of delayed stress syndrome. The authors emphasize the use of psychoanalytic principles, including that of (relative) therapist neutrality. They describe the emergence of an important group transference theme in which the patients functioned as if they were members of a combat squad and the cotherapists were their military officers. The five treatment phases identified were (1) development of group cohesion, (2) catharsis of Vietnam combat memories, (3) rage toward the therapists, (4) facing of current life realities, and (5) termination. The group therapy process facilitated the revivification and working through of traumatic combat memories and provided a supportive culture for the veterans as they reintegrated into the larger society. (C)

Haley, S. A. (1985). Some of my best friends are dead: Treatment of the PTSD patient and his family. In W. E. Kelly (Ed.), Posttraumatic stress disorder and the war veteran patient (pp. 54-70). New York: Brunner/Mazel.
    Catastrophic stress for many Vietnam veterans resulted from the combat loss of a buddy. Moreover, in numerous cases this loss led to the surviving soldier reactively committing atrocities. Haley uses veteran case reports to demonstrate combat's traumatic effect on the fluid adolescent psychic structures. (S)

Harrington, D. S., & Jay, J. A. (1982). Beyond the family: Value issues in the treatment of Vietnam veterans. Family Therapy Networker, 6, 13-15, 44-45.
    Describes a 12-week group treatment program called "Back in the World" for Vietnam veterans suffering from PTSD. The program is designed to enhance communication with peers so as to heighten trust and respect as well as to foster greater appreciation of (1) the events that led to their involvement in the war, (2) the circumstances directing their actions in the war (thus helping them formulate a new view of their roles during this period in history), (3) how their experiences since the war are also related .to their personal history and makeup, and (4) how they have remained isolated from their family and friends since Vietnam. The last part of the program involves bringing in signifi-

cant others (wives, relatives, friends, lovers) to foster their understanding of the forces that served to perpetuate the emotional numbing and isolation in the veteran. (C)

Hendin, H. (1983). Psychotherapy for Vietnam veterans with posttraumatic stress disorders. American Journal of Psychotherapy, 37, 86-99.

Discusses the merits of individual psychotherapy in treating PTSD among Vietnam combat veterans. Hendin comments, "Often a variety of traumatic combat events experienced by the veteran will be organized around certain themes that are unique to his particular perception. Understanding the common meanings of such experiences is central to the treatment of posttraumatic stress in the many veterans for whom the disorder is not centered on one overwhelming event." Hendin underscores the delayed presentation of symptomatology as well as the common clinical failure to understand how current life symptoms represent generalization from the earlier traumatizing combat events. He presents three case summaries that show various ways in which the disorder may be manifested and the effectiveness of specific therapeutic strategies. (C)

Lifton, R. J. (1972a). Experiments in advocacy research. In J. H. Masserman (Ed.), Science and psychoanalysis: Vol. 21. Research and relevance (pp. 259-271). New York: Grune and Stratton.

Presents Lifton's theories, goals, and design for conducting "advocacy psychiatry" with psychologically impaired Vietnam veterans through the formation of nontraditional "store-front rap groups." Among his observations of such groups was that these veterans manifested complex patterns of guilt and rage stemming from their experiences of being survivors of a form of "absurd evil." Lifton posits that the only effective approach to such men is by the group leaders' expressing their subjective reactions, and he contrasts this approach to that of traditional caregivers such as psychiatrists and ministers, who are mistrusted by veterans because they were perceived in Vietnam as loyal to the military mission and neglectful of the needs of the soldiers. Recognized phases in the therapeutic transformation of these veterans included their (1) discovering the humanity of the Vietnamese, (2) rejecting the idealized male warrior role, (3) adopting a protesting counterculture stance and joining that political group, and (4) allowing trust and intimacy with others. (C)

Marin, P. (1981, November). Living in moral pain. Psychology Today, pp. 68-80.

From interviews with numerous Vietnam veterans, Marin hypothesizes that there are two ignored but crucial aspects of the Vietnam veteran's suffering: his deep moral distress resulting from a realization that he has committed acts with real and terrible consequences; and the inadequacy of the prevailing, culturally shaped modes of therapy typically offered him. Marin posits that, as a society, we have few useful ways to approach moral pain or guilt, and that therapists tend not to deal with problems of guilt but rather to treat the veterans' difficulties as problems in adjustment. For example, some VA therapists are referring to the need to "deresponsibilize" their patients: to encourage them to attribute their actions in Vietnam to external causes rather than to moral choice. Marin feels the major reason why most psychological thinking about Vietnam has avoided the issue of judgment is that psychological language is inadequate to describe the nature and pain of human conscience. The therapeutic future for the Vietnam veteran lies in his seeing life once again in a context that includes a valid moral experience and assigns a moral significance to human action. (C)

McKinnon, J. A. (1984). Brief psychotherapy of the Vietnam combat neurosis. In H. J. Schwartz (Ed.), Psychotherapy of the combat veteran (pp. 125-151). Jamaica, NY: Spectrum Publications.
     Discusses the nature of "war neurosis" from the standpoint of pre-Vietnam clinical reports as well as of the contemporary literature that has led to the DSM-III diagnostic criteria for PTSD. McKinnon considers that the delayed stress response syndrome (i.e., PTSD) represents an eruption of the "numbed" chronic stress response syndrome, which in itself represents incompleted grief stemming from combat losses. He acknowledges that characterologically related predispositions (i.e., lowered "resilience") contribute to the development of traumatic combat reactions as well as to the "enormity of the bolus of trauma" sustained by the individual. Through use of clinical material, McKinnon provides a rationale for a brief, focused psychotherapeutic approach to selected symptomatic combat veterans "to foster a measured associative remembering, and to reach a point of completion (bereavement)." (C)

Miller, M. J. (1983). Empathy and the Vietnam veteran: Touching the forgotten warrior. Personnel and Guidance Journal, 62, 149-154.
     Reviews the use of empathy and its therapeutic implications in counseling the Vietnam veteran with adjustment difficulties. Miller highlights how the nonveteran counselor can develop this critical dimension of care only by seeking a thorough understanding of the special features of the war in Southeast Asia. (C)

Parson, E. R. (1984a). The reparation of the self: Clinical and theoretical dimensions in the treatment of Vietnam combat veterans. Journal of Contemporary Psychotherapy, 14, 4-56.

Reviews the psychologically traumatizing features surrounding combat activities in Vietnam and reentry to the States, and presents Parson's model for the pathogenesis of PTSD and related identity distortions in Vietnam veterans. Using self-psychology and ego-psychology constructs, he proposes a four-phase clinical "self-reparative" intervention designed to promote resolution of narcissistic rage, reestablishment of a cohesive self, and enhancement of psychological control. The intervention begins with a more active behavioral-cognitive approach and concludes in a phase that uses a less active psychodynamic methodology. Case material is provided. (C)

Parson, E. R. (1984b). The role of psychodynamic group therapy in the treatment of the combat veteran. In H. J. Schwartz (Ed.), Psychotherapy of the combat veteran (pp. 153-220). Jamaica, NY: Spectrum Publications.

Discusses the use of groups in the psychodynamic treatment of combat veterans, and presents Parson's multiple group developmental treatment model designed to address the progressive and changing needs of the veteran. In the first phase, a homogenous group of combat veterans is encouraged to share similar experiences to strengthen each member's ego capacity to regulate intrusive ideas and affects. In Phase 2, the group is expanded to include appropriate noncombat veterans, allowing the members to focus on emotions and motivational life more generally. In Phase 3, more diversity of membership is created in an attempt to resemble the outside world. The aim of this group experience is to change character features that are still interfering with successful adaptation. Case material is provided. (S)

Racek, W. D. (1985). An approach to treatment of post-traumatic stress disorder. In W. E. Kelly (Ed.), Post-traumatic stress disorder and the war veteran patient (pp. 276-291). New York: Brunner/Mazel.

Describes a series of interventions that have often been proven necessary in the successful treatment of PTSD in Vietnam veterans. These include proper diagnosis; occupational and rehabilitation therapy; physical exercise; anxiety reduction through biofeedback and deep muscle relaxation; and family, vocational, and spiritual counseling. (S)

Sax, W. P. (1985). Establishing a post-traumatic stress disorder inpatient program. In W. E. Kelly (Ed.), Post-traumatic stress disorder and the war veteran patient (pp. 234-248). New York: Brunner/Mazel.

Provides an account of the development of an inpatient PTSD treatment program at the Coatsville VA Medical Center. Sax describes the organization, structure, and goals of the program as well as the various treatment modalities offered (e.g., peer support groups, group and individual therapy, and pharmacotherapy). (S)

Schwartz, H. J. (Ed.). (1984a). Psychotherapy of the combat veteran. Jamaica, NY: Spectrum Publications.
    Provides a collection of papers, most of which deal specifically with the form, pathogenesis, and psychotherapeutic treatment of residual symptoms in psychologically affected veterans of the Vietnam war. (See also Blitz & Greenberg, 1984; DeFazio, 1984; McKinnon, 1984; Parson, 1984b; Schwartz, 1984b, 1984c; Shapiro, 1984.) (C)

Shapiro, R. B. (1984). Transference, countertransference and the Vietnam veteran. In H. J. Schwartz (Ed.), Psychotherapy of the combat veteran (pp. 85-102). Jamaica, NY: Spectrum Publications.
    Elaborates on general principles for approaching the complex problems in psychotherapy with veterans. Shapiro suggests initially deflecting the early negative transference, focusing on extratherapeutic relationships, and accepting the patient's early identification with the therapist. He outlines an approach that carefully titrates the patient's ability to tolerate the frustration that accompanies direct work on the transference, and he notes that a therapist's inadvertent intrusive sympathy and self-protective displacements can serve to further traumatize the struggling patient. The therapist must be able to accept and contain his own disturbing affects and be prepared to face a view of humanity at its worst. (C)

Silver, S. M. (1986). An inpatient program for post-traumatic stress disorder: Context as treatment. In C. R. Figley (Ed.), Trauma and its wake: Vol. 2. Traumatic stress theory, research, and intervention (pp. 213-231). New York: Brunner/Mazel.
    Describes an inpatient treatment program for veterans, which lasted for 4 months and combined individual, group, family, and milieu therapies. Approximately 85% of veterans with PTSD completed the program. Of the 62 Vietnam veterans with PTSD who completed the program and were followed, only 4 returned to a psychiatric inpatient setting. Of the 16 who failed to complete the program, 7 were readmitted. (S)

Smith, C. (1980). Oral history as "therapy": Combatants' accounts of the Vietnam war. In C. R. Figley & S. Leventman (Eds.), Strangers at home: Vietnam veterans since the war (pp. 9-34). New York: Praeger.
    Describes the use of oral history as a means of providing therapeutic aid to Vietnam veterans. Smith points out some of the

unique stresses the veteran faced, which created the need for him to unburden himself while paradoxically leading him to be suspicious of traditional psychiatric care. These stresses include characteristics of the war such as counterinsurgency tactics, which made survival an individual preoccupation and combat paranoia endemic. The soldier who accepts an invitation to an oral history interview believes the focus to be informational rather than personal (i.e., toward "the political, social, (and) institutional features of the military experience in Vietnam"). He is told he will receive a copy of the transcript and may withdraw any portion of it at a later date. This allows him to circumvent any initial reluctance to share his experiences for fear of being viewed as "disturbed" or "defective." Most relish the opportunity to tell their whole story, often for the first time. Smith notes, "Oral history helps bring (one's) identity into a clearer and more positive focus. In so doing, it releases pent-up emotions; this catharsis is added to the positive assurance that if the Vietnam war was morally wrong, the experience in the war was a lesser evil." Case examples are provided. (M)

Smith, J. R. (1985a). Individual psychotherapy with Viet Nam veterans. In S. M. Sonnenberg, A. S. Blank, Jr., & J. A. Talbott (Eds.), The trauma of war: Stress and recovery in Viet Nam veterans (pp. 125-164). Washington, DC: American Psychiatric Press.

Using a case study approach, Smith elaborates on the cognitive/affective perspective needed to understand and treat PTSD among Vietnam veterans. Four major issues that emerge in early encounters with veterans suffering from PTSD include control, ambiguity, integrity, and personal accountability. Smith views the subsequent psychotherapy as a process in which the survivor integrates and masters the conscious and unconscious effects of traumatic experiences. He describes nine major themes encountered by the veteran and therapist during the course of therapy: trust and rapport; control; anger, rage, and blame; uncovering; transformation; relationship to other life experiences; repetition and falsification; affective articulation; and animation of action and the survivor mission. (S)

Smith, J. R. (1985b). Rap groups and group therapy for Viet Nam veterans. In S. M. Sonnenberg, A. S. Blank, Jr., & J. A. Talbott (Eds.), The trauma of war: Stress and recovery in Viet Nam veterans (pp. 165-192). Washington, DC: American Psychiatric Press.

Describes the evolution of the "rap group" as a therapeutic tool in the treatment of PTSD among Vietnam veterans. Smith discusses rap groups in relation to the stress recovery process, the ways in which they differ from other therapy groups, the group process in rap groups and modified rap groups, and the structures that determine their effectiveness. (S)

Walker, J. I., & Cavenar, J. O., Jr. (1982). Vietnam veterans: Their problems continue. Journal of Nervous and Mental Disease, 170, 174-180.

Discusses some unique characteristics of the Vietnam war that have contributed to emotional problems of returning veterans, and also explores the diagnosis, etiology, treatment, and prognosis of PTSD among Vietnam veterans. (C)

Walker, J. I., & Nash, J. L. (1981a). Group therapy in the treatment of Vietnam combat veterans. International Journal of Group Psychotherapy, 31, 379-389.

Presents findings and recommendations based on the authors' 2-year experience of treating 19 Vietnam combat veterans in a group therapy model. Among their observations, the authors note that such groups function best with 5 to 8 members, preferably of mixed racial composition; that a common problem is that combat veterans tend to exclude veterans without combat experience; and that use of cotherapists is critical in reducing countertransference distortion. The therapeutic work often revolves around issues of mistrust, fear of losing control, defenses erected to avoid intimacy, and guilt. Methods for resolving these problems are presented. (S)

Walker, J. I., & Nash, J. L. (1981b). Post-traumatic stress disorders in combat veterans: Diagnosis of treatment. Journal of Psychiatric Treatment and Evaluation, 3, 247-250.

Posits that veteran patients with PTSD are often misdiagnosed and consequently mistreated. Using reports of 4 cases in which sodium amytal interviews were used as a diagnostic aid, the authors demonstrate how, even after proper diagnosis, these patients failed to do well until they were placed in group therapy with other Vietnam veterans suffering from PTSD and were allowed to work through and master the trauma. (C)

Wilbur, M. P. (1984). Vietnam: Completing the emotional sequence. Personnel and Guidance Journal, 62, 280-284.

Presents a therapeutic approach to Vietnam veterans with emotional and adjustment difficulties. Wilbur's paradigm, a further application of the termination and loss therapy approach, considers that in these veterans "the greatest emotional conflict results from 'unfinished business' and unexpressed resentments." Thus, the therapeutic intent is to "address and complete the expression of underlying fear, hurt and anger." The expression and resolution of these emotions are "necessary to move on to new relationships." Wilbur includes specific advice as to how to get beyond the psychological defenses veterans use to distance themselves from those seeking to assist. (C)

Williams, C. C. (1983). The mental foxhole: The Vietnam veteran's search for meaning. American Journal of Orthopsychiatry, 53, 4-17.
    Reviews the literature on PTSD, including the DSM-III criteria for diagnosis. Williams takes exception to the idea that intrusive recollections of Vietnam necessarily indicate dysfunction and sees them instead as a healthy coping strategy the veteran can use to search for the personal meaning of his experiences in Vietnam. Williams argues for therapists to confront their own beliefs about the war; become more aware of the dilemmas faced by Vietnam vets; select treatment modalities that will best enhance the veteran's search for new meaning; and provide an approach that incorporates a nonjudgmental view of the veteran's situation, including that of his family, community, and country. (S)

Williams, T. (Ed.). (1980a). Post-traumatic stress disorders of the Vietnam veteran. Cincinnati, OH: Disabled American Veterans.
    Represents observations and recommendations gathered from clinical experience in the psychological treatment of the veteran and his family. Williams also includes a selected annotated bibliography. (See also Berkowitz, 1980; J. Goodwin, 1980; Marafiote, 1980; C. M. Williams, 1980; T. Williams, 1980b, 1980c; Yost, 1980.) (M)

Williams, T. (1980b). A preferred model for development of interventions for psychological readjustment of Vietnam veterans: Group treatment. In T. Williams (Ed.), Post-traumatic stress disorders of the Vietnam veteran (pp. 37-48). Cincinnati, OH: Disabled American Veterans.
    Outlines strategies for forming, maintaining, and terminating a therapy group for Vietnam veterans. Williams emphasizes the parallels between the bonds formed in a therapeutic group and those that develop in the small combat unit as a means of receiving support from "buddies" to solve a difficult problem. A typical therapy group might be time-limited (10 to 20 sessions) and combine a process-oriented, less structured approach with specific behavioral interventions aimed at curbing intrusive imagery and sleep disturbances. Termination has been noted to be a particularly sensitive issue that needs to be planned several sessions ahead to avoid the reexperience of the "separation anxiety" many veterans felt upon leaving their buddies in Vietnam. Formation of a leaderless support group after termination can help this group of survivors continue their reintegration into society. (M)

Williams, T. (1980c). Therapeutic alliance and goal setting in the treatment of Vietnam veterans. In T. Williams (Ed.), Post-traumatic stress disorders of the Vietnam veteran (pp. 25-36). Cincinnati, OH: Disabled American Veterans.

Williams, a former Marine infantry officer who later became a psychologist, suggests how to overcome the veteran's mistrust and cynicism, which often blocks the formation of a therapeutic relationship. He also suggests goals of controlling anger, diminishing guilt, expressing emotions, and becoming resocialized into the mainstream of society as appropriate for most veterans in treatment. Case examples are provided. (M)

Wilmer, H. A. (1982). Vietnam and madness: Dreams of schizophrenic veterans. Journal of the American Academy of Psychoanalysis, 10, 47-65.
Discusses a special group therapy technique called a Dream Seminar for Vietnam veterans suffering from PTSD. Wilmer presents three case reports in which the dreams and nightmares of Vietnam veterans are understood in conjunction with individual psychotherapy. (S)

Woods, G. C., Sherwood, T. A., & Thompson, R. M. (1985). Management and implementation of nursing care for the post-traumatic stress disorder patient. In W. E. Kelly (Ed.), Post-traumatic stress disorder and the war veteran patient (pp. 249-275). New York: Brunner/Mazel.
Uses the authors' experiences in working within an inpatient PTSD program in a VA psychiatric center as the basis for identifying factors affecting the nurse-patient relationship. Guidelines for providing care for these patients are also presented. (S)

5 Treatment of Psychiatric Conditions: Biologic and Behavioral Approaches

Balson, P. M., & Dempster, C. R. (1980). Treatment of war neuroses from Vietnam. Comprehensive Psychiatry, 21, 167-175.

Describes evaluation, treatment, and follow-up care for 15 combat veterans. The authors demonstrate that psychotherapy with adjunctive hypnotherapy, carried out in a psychodynamic model, may be effective in controlling both acute and chronic forms of war neuroses. The hypnotherapy, consisting of abreaction and interpretation, was sufficient to produce marked symptomatic improvement. However, some residual symptoms always persisted, and the hypnotherapeutic experience remained somewhat unreal to the patient until transition was made to full consciousness for final working through. As demonstrated in 3 of the 6 chronic cases (officers or senior enlisted with more rigid personality types), failure to experience the recommended 3-6 monthly booster sessions resulted in some return of symptomatology. The authors discuss implications regarding a psychodynamic etiology of combat neurosis (i.e., the conjunction of a chance traumatic reality stress with an internal affectual experience), symptom selection (i.e., direct symbolic expression of a disordered self-perception), and factors leading to chronicity (especially in individuals whose more rigid superegos demand higher levels of performance as well as forbid outward expressions of shame). Case examples are provided. (C)

Birkhimer, L. J., DeVane, C. L., & Muniz, C. E. (1985). Post-traumatic stress disorder: Characteristics and pharmacological response in the veteran population. Comprehensive Psychiatry, 26, 304-310.

Presents results of a review of the clinical records of all patients with the primary diagnosis of PTSD admitted to a VA medical center over a 1-year period (N = 15). Fourteen had served in Vietnam and 1 in World War II. All patients attributed their symptoms to combat-related experiences, but only 11 (73%) identified a single recognizable stressor. An average of 4.3 diagnoses had been applied to the group during an average of 3.2 hospital admissions before the DSM-III was introduced in 1980. The patients averaged 2.5 hospital admissions after their redesignation to PTSD. Symptoms clustered around depression, anxiety, and poor social functioning in addition to the DSM-III criteria for PTSD. "Self-medication" with alcohol was present for 80% of the sample. Although the group had received an average of nearly 12 different psychopharmacologic agents in conjunction with other treatments, none of the agents was judged completely effective in symptom

remission. Phenelzine, alprazolam, and lithium showed some benefits over the more commonly prescribed agents. (C)

Bowen, G. R., & Lambert, J. A. (1986). Systematic desensitization
therapy with post-traumatic stress disorder cases. In C. R. Figley
(Ed.), Trauma and its wake: Vol. 2. Traumatic stress theory, research, and intervention (pp. 280-291). New York: Brunner/Mazel.
    Reviews recent behavioral approaches for assessing and treat-
ing anxiety arousal associated with PTSD and presents results of a
study of behavioral desensitization of 10 affected combat veterans
(8 Vietnam, 1 World War II, and 1 post-Vietnam veteran). Subjects
were given several months of muscle relaxation training followed
by desensitization therapy. During the individual treatment sessions, stressful combat scenes were read to the veteran while the
therapist provided relaxation guidance. Pre- and posttreatment
physiologic measures taken while the veterans were faced with
these evocative combat scenes revealed substantial decrements in
anxiety arousal. (S)

Brende, J. O. (1985). The use of hypnosis in post-traumatic conditions. In W. E. Kelly (Ed.), Post-traumatic stress disorder and the
war veteran patient (pp. 193-210). New York: Brunner/Mazel.
    Presents a historical overview of the adaptation of hypnosis,
abreaction, and psychotherapy for treating combat-related symptoms in World War II combatants, as well as of their application
for treating PTSD in Vietnam veterans. (S)

Brende, J. O., & Benedict, B. D. (1980). The Vietnam combat delayed stress response syndrome: Hypnotherapy of "dissociative
symptoms." American Journal of Clinical Hypnosis, 23, 34-40.
    Presents a case report of the treatment of a Vietnam veteran
suffering symptoms of delayed stress. During the first phase of his
15-month treatment, he was treated with psychotherapeutic techniques. Hypnotic age regression techniques were used during the
second phase. Results indicate that the reexperiencing of prior
traumatic events in the context of a trusting therapeutic relationship led to an integration of the following affective components of the traumatic events: fear and helplessness; feelings of
betrayal, rage, and guilt; and anxieties over survival of a near-
death experience. (S)

Cavenar, J. O., Jr., & Nash, J. L. (1977). Narcoanalysis: The
forgotten diagnostic aid. Military Medicine, 142, 553-555.
    Following upon their previous publication (Cavenar & Nash,
1976) recommending narcoanalysis for treatment of Vietnam veterans with traumatic war neuroses, the authors review the history

of the use of narcoanalysis as well as indications, methodology, and choices of medication. They posit that it can be a useful diagnostic and treatment tool for military and civilian patients. (C)

Hogben, G., & Cornfield, R. (1981). Treatment of traumatic war neurosis with phenelzine. Archives of General Psychiatry, 38, 440-445.

Presents case histories of 5 veterans with traumatic war neuroses, ranging from 5 to 30 years' duration, which had not responded to antipsychotics or tricyclic antidepressants, or to psychotherapy with or without medication. Each veteran did show a profound, favorable response to phenelzine prescribed in conjunction with supportive psychotherapy. Phenelzine seemed to enhance psychotherapy by stimulating an intense abreaction that had not been achieved in earlier therapies, with or without psychotropic medication. Phenelzine is also a powerful inhibitor of REM sleep; it completely abolishes dream activity in doses of 60 mg or more. All 5 patients stopped having traumatic nightmares while taking phenelzine. (S)

Keane, T. M., & Kaloupek, D. G. (1982). Imaginal flooding in the treatment of a posttraumatic stress disorder. Journal of Consulting and Clinical Psychology, 50, 138-140.

Presents results of a treatment program for a Vietnam veteran suffering anxiety-related symptoms of PTSD. Treatment, which took place over a 22-day period of inpatient hospitalization, consisted of 19 sessions of the exposure technique of imaginal flooding using nightmares and "flashbacks" associated with the traumatic events. During treatment, self-monitored data, psychological test results, and psychological monitoring were used to assess treatment efficacy. A follow-up at 12 months indicated that the patient was measurably improved in adjustment as indicated by employment status, residential stability, emotional involvement, and reduced anxiety, nightmares, and flashbacks. (S)

Keane, T. M., Fairbank, J. A., Caddell, J. M., Zimering, R. T., & Bender, M. (1985). A behavioral approach to assessing and treating post-traumatic stress disorder in Vietnam veterans. In C. R. Figley (Ed.), Trauma and its wake: Vol. 1. The study and treatment of post-traumatic stress disorder (pp. 257-294). New York: Brunner/ Mazel.

Provides a conceptual model of PTSD based on the principles of behavioral learning such as Mowrer's two-factor learning theory and Stampfl and Levis's serial conditioning paradigm. The authors present a multimethod psychophysiological approach to the assessment of PTSD in Vietnam veterans and describe the use of stress management and imaginal flooding (implosive) therapy in their treatment. (S)

Kitchner, I., & Greenstein, R. (1985). Low-dose lithium carbonate in the treatment of posttraumatic stress disorder: Brief communication. Military Medicine, 150, 378-381.

Presents case studies of 4 Vietnam veterans effectively treated with low doses (300-600 mg/day) of lithium carbonate for PTSD symptoms of inappropriate anger, irritability, anxiety, and insomnia. Before treatment the authors observed the veterans to manifest mood swings that were milder than those associated with bipolar disorder. They thus suggest the presence of a subthreshold mood disorder in these traumatized patients. (C)

Kolb, L. C. (1985). The place of narcosynthesis in the treatment of chronic and delayed stress reactions of war. In S. M. Sonnenberg, A. S. Blank, Jr., & J. A. Talbott (Eds.), The trauma of war: Stress and recovery in Viet Nam veterans (pp. 211-226). Washington, DC: American Psychiatric Press.

Presents data from studies of veterans at a VA medical center who had symptoms suggesting the breakthrough of dissociated and strongly repressed affective states in addition to the typical symptomatology of chronic or delayed PTSD. In a modified narcosynthesis technique, study participants were exposed to an auditory recording of combat sounds to test for the presence of a conditioned emotional response. A videotape of the abreactive response (occurring in 14 of the 19 tested) was subsequently replayed to them to promote their reintegration of these affectively charged memories. A follow-up 2 years later revealed that only 1 of the abreacting patients had since experienced any major dissociative states or panic attacks. Conclusions remain tentative because the patients had also received various psychologic and biologic therapies. (S)

Kolb, L. C., Burris, B. C., & Griffiths, S. (1984). Propranolol and clonidine in treatment of the chronic post-traumatic stress disorders of war. In B. A. van der Kolk (Ed.), Post-traumatic stress disorder: Psychological and biologic sequelae (pp. 97-105). Washington, DC: American Psychiatric Press.

Presents results of a pharmacological study of 21 Vietnam combat veterans diagnosed as having chronic PTSD. The 12 who received propranolol and the 9 who received clonidine over 6 months reported substantial improvement in psychosocial adjustment, as well as reductions in nightmares, intrusive thoughts, explosiveness, and startle responses. The authors conclude that "usage of such adrenergic blocking agents attenuates the intensity of symptoms dependent upon somatization of the affects of rage, fear, and anxiety. To alleviate symptoms of guilt and shame, both psychotherapy and sociotherapy remain a necessity." They deduce that there is a subgroup of PTSD sufferers who have a persisting conditioned emotional response and for whom treatment requires the blocking or measurable attenuation of the abnormalities in the central adrenergic system.   (S)

Marafiote, R. (1980). Behavioral strategies in group treatment of Vietnam veterans. In T. Williams (Ed.), Post-traumatic stress disorders of the Vietnam veteran (pp. 49-72). Cincinnati, OH: Disabled American Veterans.
   Explains the principles and use of behavior therapy in facilitating group treatment for maladaptive behaviors in Vietnam veterans. These include the use of relaxation training for hyperalertness, "thought stopping" to relieve ruminations and intrusive imagery, and group reinforcement of social intimacy and emotional expression. Prescribing books (bibliotherapy) is also suggested as a valuable source of help for Vietnam veterans, and Marafiote provides an annotated list of self-help books.   (M)

Marshall, J. R. (1975). The treatment of night terrors associated with the posttraumatic syndrome. American Journal of Psychiatry, 132, 293-295.
   Describes three cases in which the frequency and intensity of night terrors associated with the posttraumatic syndrome were greatly lessened by administration of imipramine; in one case the night terrors disappeared completely. Marshall discusses possible explanations for this effect of imipramine, including the drug's arousal-preventing action. He believes the study of sleep EEGs in patients suffering from posttraumatic syndrome will prove fruitful. (MA)

Shen, W. W., & Park, S. (1983). The use of monoamine oxidase inhibitors in the treatment of traumatic war neurosis: Case report. Military Medicine, 148, 430-431.
   Discusses the apparent efficacy of monoamine oxidase inhibitors for treating postcombat nightmares, intrusive daytime combat "flashbacks," and explosive aggressivity using the clinical case of a 38-year-old veteran with a protracted and difficult psychiatric history over the 10 years since he returned from combat duty in Vietnam.   (C)

Silver, S. M., & Kelly, W. E. (1985). Hypnotherapy of post-traumatic stress disorder in combat veterans from WW II and Vietnam. In W. E. Kelly (Ed.), Post-traumatic stress disorder and the war veteran patient (pp. 211-233). New York: Brunner/Mazel.

Presents case examples to illustrate the use of hypnosis to facilitate recovery of buried, emotionally charged combat memories and to reduce anxiety in veterans with PTSD. The risks of using hypnotherapy are also presented. The authors compare World War II and Vietnam in terms of differences in the character of post-traumatic responses and the types of treatment appropriate to the veterans of each. (S)

Spiegel, D. (1981). Vietnam grief work using hypnosis. American Journal of Clinical Hypnosis, 24, 33-40.

Applies the theory and principles of hypnosis to assist Vietnam veterans with their unresolved war-related grief. Although such reactions are expectable in any war, many are delayed or disguised for these veterans because they have no experience of national meaning for this war. In Spiegel's opinion, hypnosis offers special promise for helping put these losses in perspective if the hypnotherapist offers a kind of grief work in addition to abreaction. Four case examples are provided. (C)

Walker, J. I. (1982). Chemotherapy of traumatic war stress. Military Medicine, 147, 1029-1033.

Reviews use of psychoactive medicines for treating residual symptoms in psychiatrically traumatized combat veterans. Intravenous sodium amytal and later sodium pentothal for "narcoanalysis" date back to before World War II and were thought to both promote abreaction and aid in distinguishing traumatic stress disorders from other latent conditions, such as schizophrenia, depression, or mild organicity. More recently, the literature describes positive results using monoamine oxidase inhibitors, tricyclic antidepressants, and antipsychotic agents. With some exceptions, benzodiazepines, sedative-hypnotics, and other soporific medications have more drawbacks than advantages for these veterans. Although it is not approved for such use, Walker reports effectiveness using propranolol (as an adjunct to psychotherapy) in relieving the somatic symptoms of anxiety. He discusses the uses, indications, and contraindications for these medicines, and emphasizes that no well-controlled studies have been done on the use of pharmacotherapeutic agents in treating residual traumatic combat stress symptoms. (C)

Yost, J. (1980). The psychopharmacologic treatment of the delayed stress syndrome in Vietnam veteran. In T. Williams (Ed.), Post-traumatic stress disorders of the Vietnam veteran (pp. 125-130). Cincinnati, OH: Disabled American Veterans.

Summarizes recommended psychopharmacologic approaches to residual symptoms associated with combat service in Vietnam. Drugs preferred by Yost are the benzodiazepines for anxiety or sleep disturbance and tricyclic antidepressants. He emphasizes a conservative approach, with medications prescribed only for veterans unresponsive to other modalities and with the goal of discontinuation as other treatments begin to have effect.   (C)

6   Institutional and Professional Responses

Adams, M. F. (1982). PTSD: An inpatient. American Journal of Nursing, 11, 1704-1705.

Discusses problems encountered among nursing personnel assigned to a 20-bed inpatient psychiatric unit specifically designated to treat Vietnam combat veterans. Staff problems included patients' mistrust of them as authority figures and the staff's subjection to demeaning sexual comments and derogatory remarks about the usefulness of female staff members as therapists. (S)

Bitzer, R. (1980). Caught in the middle: Mentally disabled Vietnam veterans and the Veterans Administration. In C. R. Figley & S. Leventman (Eds.), Strangers at home: Vietnam veterans since the war (pp. 305-323). New York: Praeger.

Notes that Vietnam veterans who have previously been considered ineligible because of having received an undesirable or general discharge ("bad discharge") are now presenting claims to the VA for disability ratings for service-connected mental disorders. In Bitzer's opinion, these veterans' disability claims are often wrongfully denied because many claimants were erroneously administratively discharged. He argues that their claims should be reconsidered favorably. Their primary mental disorders went unrecognized because, as a group, these men are especially prone to "act out" (and therefore were prone to be charged with misconduct by the military) and because military psychiatrists were serving more as agents for the service than for their patients. Further, some veterans' ability to cope with the pathogenic nature of the war was eroded by the Department of Defense policy to draft men with previously exempted lower mental categories ("Project 100,000"). Finally, Bitzer recalls that posttraumatic disorders often only become symptomatic as much as 5 years after the precipitating events and recommends a change in policy that would allow claims for service-connected disability to be greater than 1 year after discharge from the service. (S)

Blank, A. S., Jr. (1985a). Irrational reactions to post-traumatic stress disorder and Viet Nam veterans. In S. M. Sonnenberg, A. S. Blank, Jr., & J. A. Talbott (Eds.), The trauma of war: Stress and recovery in Viet Nam veterans (pp. 69-98). Washington, DC: American Psychiatric Press.

Discusses the ways in which clinicians and researchers have generally reacted to veterans of the Vietnam war and the concept of PTSD. This includes their failure to diagnosis and treat, their denial of the validity of the PTSD construct, their preference for a predisposition theory, and their generalized hostility and contempt toward Vietnam veterans and professionals who treat them. In some instances these "irrational" attitudes have stemmed from unresolved personal conflicts that intrude into the work with patients.   (S)

Blank, A. S., Jr. (1985c). The Veterans Administration's Viet Nam veterans outreach and counseling centers. In S. M. Sonnenberg, A. S. Blank, Jr., & J. A. Talbott (Eds.), The trauma of war: Stress and recovery in Viet Nam veterans (pp. 227-238). Washington, DC: American Psychiatric Press.
     Presents a historical review of the problems encountered by returnees from the Vietnam war, which led to the development of the unorthodox Vietnam Veteran Outreach Program within the VA. In addition to describing the therapeutic model followed, Blank discusses various aspects of the provided interventions: special considerations stemming from the unique features of the Vietnam experience and the impact of the character of the war on the veterans; additional staff training needs; use of "rap groups" and group therapy; indications and contraindications of psychoactive medications; the challenge of integrating psychological services with other types of assistance; stress reduction methods; and outreach strategies. He concludes by cataloging the services the outreach program offers.   (S)

Bonior, D. E., Champlin, S. M., & Kolly, T. S. (1984). The Vietnam veteran: A history of neglect. New York: Praeger.
     Explores public attitude and government policy with respect to the over 3 million veterans of the Vietnam war. The authors illustrate the predominantly negative trends in media coverage of the war and its veterans, document sustained inactivity and indifference by both the White House and Congress toward veterans' needs following the war, and provide evidence suggesting a conspiracy of the VA and traditional veterans' groups to exclude Vietnam veterans from benefits and participation: "When the war ended, quarreling U.S. institutions did not carry their dead from the battlefield, offered no dignity to their wounded, but simply withdrew, leaving those whom they implicitly regarded as irrelevant to make their own way home."   (C)

Dickman, H. R. (1972). The Veterans Administration and the Vietnam era. In R. S. Parker (Ed.), The emotional stress of war, violence and peace (pp. 226-234). Pittsburgh, PA: Stanwix House.
     In anticipating the post-Vietnam war upsurge in demand for VA services, Dickman reviews the extensive social impact made

through the VA's diverse and expanding programs developed over the past 25 years. He posits that the future adjustment problems of the veterans of this war will be similar to the adjustment problems facing large numbers of the population generally. Thus, social, behavioral, and occupational marginality arise from many interacting sources and will comprise a challenge to VA and community resources. Emerging VA programs are aiming at decreasing social marginality by combining principles of learning, clinical, and social psychology. For example, two different need-deficiency categories are proposed in lieu of traditional diagnoses with implications for greater VA-community cooperation. (C)

Early, E. (1984). On confronting the Viet Nam veteran. American Journal of Psychiatry, 141, 472-473.
        Briefly describes the problems involved in trying to verify the traumatic combat stories presented by Vietnam veterans during the course of assessment and treatment in light of disbelief by some authorities and professionals. Early cites the inadequacy of veterans' discharge papers as well as of VA personnel, who are not always capable of understanding the situation in Vietnam. He also points out that veterans often exhibit a great deal of emotion in relating their experiences and that for mental health professionals to express disbelief is to risk exacerbating the problem. (S)

Fuller, R. B. (1985). War veterans' post-traumatic stress disorder and the U.S. Congress. In W. E. Kelly (Ed.), Post-traumatic stress disorder and the war veteran patient (pp. 3-11). New York: Brunner/Mazel.
        Describes the history of the national political events surrounding attempts to establish a system to provide readjustment counseling for Vietnam veterans. These efforts began in 1972, but they failed to pass beyond the U.S. House of Representative's Veterans Affairs Committee to secure congressional approval until 1979. (S)

Furey, J. A. (1982). Post-traumatic stress disorder in Vietnam veterans: For some the war rages on. American Journal of Nursing, 11, 1694-1696.
        Discusses events leading up to the development of an in-service education program on PTSD for nursing personnel at a VA hospital. The five goals of the program are (1) to define and describe PTSD, (2) to identify the symptoms of PTSD, (3) to sensitize the nursing staff to the experience of the Vietnam veteran, (4) to identify the nursing implications and interventions in both the medical and psychiatric settings, and (5) to identify available hospital and community resources. (S)

Haley, S. A. (1974). When the patient reports atrocities: Specific treatment considerations of the Vietnam veteran. Archives of General Psychiatry, 30, 191-196.
     Certain aspects of the Vietnam war differentiated it from World War II and the Korean conflict: guerrilla tactics predominated, the war was undeclared and became increasingly unpopular, and for the first time the exposure to war atrocities committed by Americans became a national issue. Many Vietnam veterans reflect the impact of these differences in their conflicted attitudes toward their combat experiences and in their psychopathology. As a consequence of her evaluation and treatment of 130 Vietnam veterans (40 of whom acknowledged responsibility for acts of atrocity) at a VA outpatient clinic in 1969, Haley maintains that the veteran who reports such behavior presents a special therapeutic challenge in the treatment. Countertransference or natural feelings of revulsion and impulses to punish the patient must be continually monitored and confronted within the therapist. Case examples are provided. (C)

Haley, S. A. (1978). Treatment implications of post-combat stress response syndromes for mental health professionals. In C. R. Figley (Ed.), Stress disorders among Vietnam veterans: Theory, research and treatment (pp. 254-267). New York: Brunner/Mazel.
     Of 676 Vietnam-era veterans seen for intake at the mental hygiene clinic of the Boston VA between November 1974 and November 1975, 130 had served in Vietnam and, of those, 90 had been involved in combat. Records were reviewed for the presence of (1) depression, (2) explosive aggressive reactions, (3) sleep disturbances, (4) startle responses, (5) constriction of ego interests and adaptive functions, and (6) dissociative reactions. Among the 90 combat veterans, 67 had most of these symptoms, but only 30 had qualified as service-connected. The remaining veterans typically received a reactive diagnosis, yet informally received a diagnosis of "traumatic war neurosis" or "post-Vietnam syndrome" by the staff. These veterans were therefore denied disability status designation by the VA. Haley considers it ironic that those veterans the VA does treat (typically those with a depressive reaction diagnosis) most likely had extensive preexisting vulnerability rather than succumbed to overwhelming combat-generated stress. She speculates that the new PTSD diagnostic criteria in the DSM-III should help rectify nomenclature shortcomings.   (S)

Jacobs, J. B., & McNamara, D. (1986). Vietnam veterans and the Agent Orange controversy. Armed Forces & Society, 13, 57-80.
     Describes the evolving political and legal conflict between the VA and Vietnam veterans claiming disability benefits for perceived medical consequences of their exposure to Agent Orange. The authors review the history of the use of the herbicide in

Vietnam; survey the epidemiological data, which tend to refute these claims; and consider the sociopolitical implications of the continuing controversy. (C)

Keane, T. M., & Fairbank, J. A. (1983). Survey analysis of combat-related stress disorders in Vietnam veterans. American Journal of Psychiatry, 140, 348-350.
Presents results of a survey of mental health professionals in VA medical centers across the country to determine which conceptual frameworks were preferred in understanding the various problems of Vietnam veterans. Results indicated that psychiatrists were least likely to describe veterans' combat experiences as traumatic, less likely than social workers to claim that the specific events that occurred during Vietnam service were responsible for the veterans' current clinical problems, and more familiar than psychiatric social workers with the diagnostic criteria for PTSD. However, regardless of professional discipline, those with extensive experience working with PTSD patients were more likely to state that Vietnam experiences were responsible for current psychological problems; that the social support system upon return from Vietnam was a critical factor in the development of PTSD; and that combat has an enduring adverse psychological effect on combatants. Other findings include the consensus view that Vietnam veterans are more poorly adjusted than veterans of previous eras as well as more likely to seek compensation for psychological complaints. (S)

Kolb, L. C. (1982). Healing the wounds of Vietnam. Hospital and Community Psychiatry, 33, 877.
Comments on the plight of Vietnam veterans and notes the positive changes now taking place within the VA medical system to better deal with their special problems. (S)

Kubey, C., Addlestone, D. F., O'Dell, R. E., Snyder, K. D., Stichman, B. F., & Vietnam Veterans of America. (1985). The Viet vet survival guide: How to cut through the bureaucracy and get what you need--and are entitled to. New York: Ballantine Books.
Provides basic information regarding the nature of health and readjustment difficulties facing Vietnam veterans as well as a practical guide to understanding the various assistance policies and programs available from the government, especially the VA. Among subjects covered are disability compensation and death benefits; medical services; claims regarding Agent Orange exposure; psychological assistance, including for substance abuse; employment, education, and housing assistance; procedures for acquiring and correcting official records, including upgrading a discharge; claims and appeals procedures; veterans and the criminal justice system; and avenues for obtaining help or advocacy. (C)

Leventman, S. (1975). Official neglect of Vietnam veterans. Journal of Social Issues, 31, 171-179.

Contends that Vietnam veterans are disadvantaged in seeking assistance from the VA and other governmental agencies because of a bias toward veterans of earlier wars. For example, the VA expends over half its resources treating nonservice-connected medical conditions. Further, large numbers of Vietnam and Vietnam-era veterans were administratively discharged from the service under less-than-honorable conditions because of drug use or other disciplinary actions. Leventman underscores that the veteran who carries such a discharge is denied VA medical and educational benefits, and because many employers and institutions have been provided the information to decode his discharge papers, he also may be barred from vocational, educational, and other opportunities. Leventman agrees with P. Starr (1973) in recommending that less-than-honorable discharges be limited to those found guilty by court martial. He also strongly urges that VA benefits be reoriented toward serving younger veterans whose primary need is readjustment and that the government develop comprehensive programs in the areas of vocational, educational, and health assistance. (M)

Lopes, S. (1987). The wall: Images and offerings from the Vietnam Veterans Memorial. New York: Collins Publishers.

Presents a photojournalistic essay of the memorial, its Washington setting, and its visitors. From the photographs of those who come to remember and the excerpts from the notes and letters they bring, Lopes seeks to capture the responses of surviving Americans to this privately funded and initially quite controversial memorial and to the war it recalls. (C)

Scruggs, J. C., & Swerdlow, J. L. (1985). To heal a nation: The Vietnam Veterans Memorial. New York: Harper & Row.

Chronicles the intensely debated and always doubtful creation of the Vietnam Veterans Memorial, conceived by wounded Vietnam veteran Scruggs in 1979 and opened to the public in 1982. The project, funded entirely with private money, was continuously surrounded by the war's controversy. The book includes an appendix, which lists the names inscribed on the memorial to the 58,000 Americans who lost their lives in Southeast Asia during the war. (C)

Starr, P. (1973). The discarded army: Veterans after Vietnam. New York: Charterhouse.

Analyzes the interaction of human problems and social policy as they relate to patterns of (1) stress and adaptation of servicemen during and after Vietnam, and (2) corresponding military and governmental responses (especially questions of the adequacy of the VA). Topics addressed in this thoroughly documented and amply illustrated thesis include the peculiarly stressful nature of combat in Vietnam for American soldiers, the odyssey of Vietnam veterans and the overall operation of federal veterans' programs, problems of the severely injured, the compensation system, veterans' hospitals, the genesis of the military drug problem and drug addiction programs for veterans, the economic and social problems of readjustment, and the operation of the GI Bill. (C)

Stenger, C. A. (1971). The Vietnam era veteran. Counseling Psychologist, 2, 77-82.
    Reports the results of a VA study on the attitudes, values, and behaviors of its hospital staff regarding Vietnam-era veterans. Based on a descriptive survey, Stenger profiles the veteran, including his decreased willingness to accept authority; his expectation that authority will not be responsive to his need to be treated as an individual with a right to have a say in things that affect him; his sense of uncertainty and lack of optimism about life, with a consequent absence of direction or goals; his intense identification with his own age group; and his tendency to exercise less control over emotions and feelings. From this profile, Stenger provides 10 recommendations for VA hospitals to improve their health care delivery system for Vietnam-era veterans. (S)

Straker, M. (1976). The Vietnam veteran: The task is reintegration. Diseases of the Nervous System, 37, 75-79.
    Briefly reviews the literature on the frequency and basic causes of psychiatric breakdown following service in Vietnam. Straker's major point is that both the veteran and society must share the responsibility of reintegration without resorting to stigmatizing veterans as either victims or war criminals. He identifies the responsibilities of the VA for reintegrating veterans into society and describes the programs for Vietnam veterans offered by the Brentwood VA Hospital. He also presents clinical data relating to these programs, with the results of one clinical study failing to demonstrate significant differences between combat and noncombat veterans. (S)

Welch, C. E. (1984). The post-traumatic stress disorder syndrome for Vietnam veterans: The politics of etiology. Emotional First Aid: A Journal of Crisis Intervention, 1, 30-36.
    Reviews the psychiatric and political history of the establishment of PTSD as a diagnostic category and contrasts published interviews among Vietnam veterans with clinical reports in the professional literature. Welch contends that this entity was established in the aftermath of the Vietnam war especially to justify

eligibility for disability claims, but that its creation has led veterans and Americans generally to neglect to reconcile the consequences of U.S. involvement there.   (C)

7   Substance Abuse

Boscarino, J. (1979). Current drug involvement among Vietnam and non-Vietnam veterans. American Journal of Drug and Alcohol Abuse, 6, 301-312.
    Reports a study of drug and alcohol use self-reports among Vietnam veterans (N = 105) compared with a group of mixed veterans and nonveterans (N = 2,966) included in a 1975 national face-to-face survey. Results reflect that Vietnam veterans had higher levels of drug abuse primarily because they represented a higher risk group in that they were younger, more often male, and more educated than the general population. Analysis also revealed that Vietnam veterans did not have substantially higher levels of alcohol consumption once demographic differences were taken into consideration (although consumption was higher), thus refuting the notion of substance abuse substitution.   (C)

Branchey, L., Davis, W., & Lieber, C. S. (1984). Alcoholism in Vietnam and Korea veterans: A long term follow-up. Alcoholism: Clinical and Experimental Research, 8, 572-575.
    Draws attention to the limited research done on alcoholism in veterans and reports results of a study conducted with randomly selected Korean and Vietnam war-era veterans (N = 103) attending the dermatology and orthopedic clinics at a VA medical center. Along with information regarding drinking patterns, demographic data and military and combat exposure histories were obtained and existence of a psychiatric diagnosis was determined. The authors found that one third of these patients, who were attending clinics not devoted to the treatment of alcoholism, had alcohol-related problems, a prevalence far exceeding that found in the general population. An additional 19% had alcohol problem histories that were in remission. Alcohol dependency was greater among the Korean war veterans whereas alcohol abuse without dependency was higher for the veterans of Vietnam. A direct correlation was found between number of months of combat exposure and alcoholism status. In the alcoholic group, 14 patients (24%) were diagnosed as having PTSD. The authors underscore the need for increased clinical attention to this underserved group of veterans.   (C)

Brende, J. O. (1984). An educational-therapeutic group for drug and alcohol abusing combat veterans. Journal of Contemporary Psychotherapy, 14, 122-136.
    Advocates the use of short-term group treatment with an educational-therapeutic approach for veterans with substance abuse

problems. Using clinical material from an open-ended group of Vietnam veterans, Brende illustrates how substance abuse often represents the untreated veteran's attempt to control PTSD-related symptoms. These veterans used their group to work through significant war-related problems in phases: (1) dissolving detachment and gaining control of disruptive symptoms, (2) revealing death and dehumanization experiences, (3) discovering one's past "death of self" experiences, and (4) expressing grief. (C)

Craig, R. J., & Baker, S. L. (Eds.). (1982). Drug dependent patients: Treatment and research. Springfield, IL: Charles C. Thomas Publishers.
        Although not explicitly focused on the Vietnam war or its veterans, this collection of articles regarding the epidemiology and treatment of substance abuse draws extensively from experience within VA programs developed in the aftermath of the war. (See also M. D. Stanton, 1982.) (C)

Freudenberger, H. J. (1975). The psychology of the Vietnam veteran and drug addiction. Psychiatric Opinion, 12, 34-38.
        Describes the psychosocial adjustment problems of the Vietnam returnee addicts, including those that distinguish them from the more familiar street addicts. Their problems include deconditioning military indoctrination, cost differentials of supporting a habit in New York as compared with Saigon, and limitations in education and employment skills. Freudenberger details the lifestyle problems peculiar to Vietnam veterans and discusses the treatment problems that ensue. Veterans' addiction is seen as an attempt to escape the difficulties of Army life, service in Vietnam, and the stress of reentry into an indifferent society. (C)

Jelinek, J. M., & Williams, T. (1984). Post-traumatic stress disorder and substance abuse in Vietnam veterans: Treatment problems, strategies and recommendations. Journal of Substance Abuse Treatment, 1, 87-97.
        Draws on the extensive professional experience of the authors, both Vietnam veterans, to review the diverse clinical presentations of PTSD, especially those that include substance abuse. The authors highlight the need to understand the veteran's substance abuse patterns before selecting the treatment approach (i.e., treatment goals and strategies differ depending on whether substance abuse is used to suppress, exacerbate, or perpetuate PTSD symptoms). They also present an intake information outline, including critical substance abuse questions, and provide case examples. (C)

Johnson, B. D. (1978). Once an addict, seldom an addict. Contemporary Drug Problems, 7, 35-53.

Reviews studies bearing on heroin use patterns in contemporary America, especially those focusing on reported use by soldiers returning from Vietnam. Johnson interprets the data as indicating that chronic and persistent addiction is rarely the outcome of heroin use; that heroin is the illicit drug least apt to be tried; that while a small proportion of heroin users ever becomes addicted, an even smaller percent is addicted at any given time; and that an almost negligible number is apparently continually addicted for up to 3 years. Thus, "the results of these investigators not only challenge widespread myths about the addicting power of heroin, but disprove them for the most part." (C)

Keane, T. M., Caddell, J. M., Martin, B., Zimering, R. T., & Fairbank, J. A. (1983). Substance abuse among Vietnam veterans with posttraumatic stress disorders. Bulletin of the Society of Psychologists in Addictive Behaviors, 2, 117-122.

Presents results of interviews with 40 Vietnam veterans (both inpatients and outpatients) at a VA medical center who were diagnosed as suffering from PTSD. Sixty-three percent reported heavy and often abusive alcohol consumption. There was less reported use of other drugs such as marijuana (20%), amphetamines (5%), heroin (2.5%), barbiturates (2.5%), diazepam (2.5%), and LSD (0.5%). The authors suggest that the increase in alcohol abuse observed generally among Vietnam veterans may represent their efforts to cope with symptoms of PTSD. (S)

Lacoursiere, R. B., Godfrey, K. E., & Ruby, L. M. (1980). Traumatic neurosis in the etiology of alcoholism: Viet Nam combat and other trauma. American Journal of Psychiatry, 137, 966-968.

Presents case reports illustrating use of alcohol as self-medication for symptoms of PTSD (chronic anxiety, restlessness, insomnia, and recurrent frightening dreams) among Vietnam veterans. Repeated self-medication with alcohol resulted in tolerance and the need to increase consumption. Attempts to decrease consumption led to withdrawal symptoms, which exacerbated the initial PTSD symptoms. The authors conclude that a treatment approach for such cases of alcoholism that ignores the traumatic etiology will have less chance of success. They further suggest that alcoholism that begins secondary to a traumatic experience may persist after the traumatic neurosis is adequately treated. (S)

Martin, J. L. (1986). Effects of support on demoralization and problem drinking. In G. Boulanger & C. Kadushin (Eds.), The Vietnam veteran redefined: Fact and fiction (pp. 133-151). Hillsdale, NJ: Lawrence Erlbaum Associates.

Presents results of survey of Vietnam veterans ($\underline{N}$ = 1,381) that explored the value of interpersonal supports in determining mental health levels. The data indicate that combat veterans tend to be more reactive to the support characteristics of their interpersonal environment than either noncombatant veterans or nonveterans. They express more demoralization, but a supportive spouse or partner can reduce this effect. Overall, a positive social structure--that is, a combat veteran's frequent contact with supportive friends--mitigates against problem drinking, whereas frequent contact with a set of friends that does not include a confidant represents a social structure that promotes problem drinking. (S)

Mintz, J., O'Brien, C. P., & Pomerantz, B. (1979). Impact of Vietnam service on heroin-addicted veterans. American Journal of Drug and Alcohol Abuse, 6, 39-52.
    Presents results of a survey study of 59 Vietnam veterans and 34 age-matched non-Vietnam veterans who were admitted for heroin addiction at the Philadelphia VA hospital from May to November 1972. The Vietnam veteran sample reported that they began using heroin during their military service in Vietnam (to seek relief from fear and tensions of war), and indicated a significantly less negative attitude toward drug use than did the non-Vietnam veterans. The latter group said either that their military experiences had not affected their drug use or that their use was attributable to a lack of meaningful activity within the military. The war in Vietnam was not counted among their motivations. A 3-year follow-up showed no significant difference in readmission rate (32% for Vietnam veterans; 41% for non-Vietnam veterans). The authors compare the implications of these findings with those of previously published studies. (C)

Nace, E. P., & Meyers, A. L. (1974). The prognosis for addicted Vietnam returnees: A comparison with civilian addicts. Comprehensive Psychiatry, 15, 49-56.
    Compares 36 heroin-addicted Vietnam returnees with addicted civilian counterparts on the basis of independent variables reported in the literature to be of prognostic significance: socioeconomic status, family stability, education, employment, military service, and antisocial behavior. Findings generally support the hypothesis that the addicted Vietnam returnee appears to have a better prognosis than the chronic civilian drug addict and is also less likely to follow a pattern of chronic heroin addiction. (C)

Nace, E. P., O'Brien, C. P., Mintz, J., Meyers, A. L., & Ream, N. W. (1980). Follow-up of Vietnam veterans: II. Social adjustment. Drug and Alcohol Dependence, 6, 209-214.

As part of a larger study of substance abuse among Vietnam veterans (see Nace, O'Brien, Mintz, Ream, & Meyers, 1977), participants were divided into three groups according to their in-service narcotics use: frequent users ($\underline{n}$ = 98), occasional users ($\underline{n}$ = 55), and nonusers ($\underline{n}$ = 49). Through interviews conducted approximately 28 months after the veterans' return from Vietnam, researchers found that the three groups differed in the areas of employment/education, family adjustment, physical health, and depression. Further analysis revealed that only family adjustment and depression continued to correlate significantly with the Vietnam drug group after controlling for the influence of preservice variables. The authors interpret their findings to indicate that consideration of both preservice conditions and the veteran's Vietnam experience are necessary to understand his postservice adjustment problems. (C)

Nace, E. P., O'Brien, C. P., Mintz, J., Ream, N. W., & Meyers, A. L. (1977). Drinking problems among Vietnam veterans. Currents in Alcoholism, 2, 315-324.
      Reports findings regarding alcohol use patterns from a larger study of substance abuse and adjustment among 202 civilian veterans of Vietnam examined an average of 28 months after their return to the States in 1971 and 1972. Of that sample, 125 had been confined in a drug treatment center and 77 had been hospitalized in a conventional Army hospital at some time during 1971-72. Subjects underwent a semistructured interview, completed a Beck Depression Inventory, and provided a urine sample for testing. Data revealed that 39% of the sample reported drinking to a symptomatic degree and 50% reported being addicted to heroin while in Vietnam, but only 21% had used heroin since discharge. Those with drinking symptoms differed from those without primarily in reporting parental history of alcoholism, preservice patterns of problem drinking, frequent drunkenness in Vietnam, and histories of significant antisocial behaviors and polydrug use. Of the problem drinkers (the most severe category), 85% reported being addicted to heroin in Vietnam and, along with current alcohol abuse symptoms, were significantly more likely to be clinically depressed. Analysis of multiple correlations revealed that current drinking problems were significantly related to both narcotic use in Vietnam and preservice variables, but more so to the latter. Since leaving Vietnam, less than 3% of those with alcoholic symptoms have sought help for those problems. (C)

Nace, E. P., O'Brien, C. P., Mintz, J., Ream, N. W., & Meyers, A. L. (1978). Adjustment among Vietnam veteran drug users two years post service. In C. R. Figley (Ed.), Stress disorders among Vietnam veterans: Theory, research and treatment (pp. 71-128). New York: Brunner/Mazel.

Expands on the data and interpretations from a previously published study report (see Nace, Meyers, O'Brien, Ream, Mintz, 1977; Nace, O'Brien, Mintz, Meyers, & Ream, 1980; Nace, O'Brien, Mintz, Ream, & Meyers, 1977; O'Brien, Nace, Mintz, Meyers, & Ream, 1980) of 202 civilian Vietnam veterans (125 were drug positive on urine screening in Vietnam and 77 had been medical patients there) 2 years after their return in 1970-71. Alcohol-related problems in these veterans were extensive. Postservice criminality and narcotic use were accounted for primarily by preservice variables rather than by the use of narcotics in Vietnam. Alcohol use, marijuana use, and depression in the sample were related both to preservice variables and to the extent of heroin use in Vietnam. However, even though the Beck Depression Inventory highlighted the high level (32%) of depression among the sample generally, it did not reveal evidence of more extensive guilt, sleep disturbance, or irritability among the veterans who served in combat roles compared with those who were in support assignments. (C)

O'Brien, C. P., Nace, E. P., Mintz, J., Meyers, A. L., & Ream, N. W. (1980). Follow-up of Vietnam veterans: I. Relapse to drug use after Vietnam service. Drug and Alcohol Dependence, 5, 333-340.

Presents findings on current drug and alcohol use among a sample ($\underline{N}$ = 202) of Vietnam returnees who were interviewed approximately 2 years after their return from service in Vietnam in 1971 and 1972 (see Nace, O'Brien, Mintz, Ream, & Meyers, 1977). Study participants were divided by their reported narcotic use pattern in Vietnam as frequent users ($\underline{n}$ = 98), occasional users ($\underline{n}$ = 55), and nonusers ($\underline{n}$ = 49). Among the frequent users, 39% reported continued narcotic use post-Vietnam, as did 11% of the occasional users. Preservice variables were also found to correlate significantly with postservice drug involvement. Noteworthy was that other types of substances, such as alcohol and marijuana, were being used heavily by all three groups. (C)

Penk, W. E., Robinowitz, R., Roberts, W. R., Patterson, E. T., Dolan, M. P., & Atkins, H. G. (1981). Adjustment differences among male substance abusers varying in degree of combat experience in Vietnam. Journal of Consulting and Clinical Psychology, 49, 426-437.

Reports a study of 87 combat and 120 noncombat veteran participants in a substance abuse treatment program at a VA medical center. Combat-noncombat and within-combat group comparisons were made regarding the incidence and severity of postservice difficulties, demographic and family background factors, and current levels of psychopathology. Combat veterans reported significantly more PTSD symptoms than did noncombat veterans;

otherwise, these two groups did not differ in extent or type of substance abuse, demographic or family background factors, or other types of psychopathology. Within the combat group, heavy combat veterans reported significantly more PTSD, as well as more maladjustment on MMPI measures, than did those veterans with less combat experience. Present adjustment levels were not found to covary as a function of demographic or family background variables. Findings are interpreted as suggesting different treatment strategies for substance abusers with combat experience. The authors also argue for improved assessment and research techniques on this topic. (S)

Roberts, W. R., Penk, W. E., Gearing, M. L., Robinowitz, R., Dolan, M. P., & Patterson, E. T. (1982). Interpersonal problems of Vietnam combat veterans with symptoms of posttraumatic stress disorder. Journal of Abnormal Psychology, 91, 444-450.
      Presents results of a study of the adjustment of 274 Vietnam-era veterans seeking treatment for substance abuse. Veterans with evidence of PTSD were compared with a non-PTSD group of Vietnam combat veterans and a noncombat group of Vietnam-era veterans using MMPI scales, general measures of family and social adjustment, and measures of specific interpersonal problems. Results indicate that the PTSD group scored significantly higher regarding problems with intimacy and sociability than did either comparison group. They also scored higher on MMPI scales of paranoia, psychopathic deviance, social introversion, social maladjustment, family problems, and manifest hostility. The authors indicate that these results are not attributable to premilitary adjustment differences or to confounding demographic variables. (C)

Robins, L. N. (1974). A follow-up study of Vietnam veterans' drug use: The transition to civilian life. Journal of Drug Issues, 4, 61-63. (Official reports for this study are found in L. N. Robins (1973a). A follow-up of Vietnam drug users: Interim final report (Monograph Series A, No. 1). Washington, DC: White House Special Action Office for Drug Abuse; and L. N. Robins (1973b). The Vietnam drug user returns: Final report (Monograph Series A, No. 2). Washington, DC: White House Special Action Office for Drug Abuse.)
      Summarizes results of interviews and urine testing of 900 U.S. Army enlisted men who had served in Vietnam. Data were collected between May and September 1972, 8-12 months after their return to the States. Only 16% were still in the service at that time. "User" subjects (n = 449) were a representative sample of those whose urine was opiate positive when they left Vietnam; the remaining "general sample" represented all men who returned in September 1971. Of the general sample, 44% reported having tried some narcotic while in Vietnam (most often smoking heroin

mixed with tobacco or opium mixed with marijuana), and 20% described themselves as having become "addicted" there. Only 7% of
those reporting heroin use there had used heroin prior to their
arrival in Vietnam, and only 11% had had positive urines detected
at the time of their rotation home. About 5% of all men who have
returned from Vietnam have had some treatment for drugs in the
States--most often that mandated by the military. Robins acknowledges surprise at the study findings, confirmed with urine testing,
of the high proportion of men who reported addiction in Vietnam
(75%) but reported no continuation of addiction upon returning
home (only 7% reported addiction since their return). She comments, "The results of this study indicate that dependence on
narcotics is not so permanent as we had once believed. . . . Not
only did many of the addicted stop their drug use without any
special treatment at the time they left Vietnam but many of those
who continued use have not been readdicted." (See also Robins,
Davis, & Goodwin, 1974; Robins, Davis, & Nurco, 1974.)   (C)

Robins, L. N., Davis, D. H., & Nurco, D. N. (1974). How permanent
was Vietnam drug addiction? American Journal of Public Health, 64
(supplement), 38-43.
     Describes the authors' 1972 study (see Robins, 1974; Robins,
Davis, & Goodwin, 1974) and presents new findings. Among the
general sample, 43% admitted narcotics use in Vietnam, with 46%
of that group reporting addiction. However, both usage and addiction rates dropped dramatically upon return. In light of these
findings, the authors question public policies that force treatment
on all returning servicemen who yield positive urines in Vietnam.
(M)

Robins, L. N., & Helzer, J. E. (1975, October 27). Drug abuse
among Vietnam veterans--three years later. Medical World News,
pp. 44-49.
     This follow-up report (see Helzer, Robins, & Davis, 1975;
Robins, 1974; Robins, Davis, & Goodwin, 1974; Robins, Davis, &
Nurco, 1974; Robins, Helzer, & Davis, 1975) attempts to ascertain
whether a previously reported low rate of heroin addiction for
returning Vietnam veterans continued over their 3-year postreturn
period. Questions were also asked about the veterans' use of other
drugs (including alcohol). The low rate of heroin readdiction was
sustained, with more than 90% of those addicted in Vietnam es-
caping readdiction since returning home although 20% reported
some continued use. Other results include the finding that daily
use and interference with life were more commonly associated with
marijuana smoking and heavy drinking than with narcotics. The
authors point out that the then current U.S. government emphasis
on heroin addiction was prompting the neglect of other drugs,
which users report have caused more problems.   (M)

Rohrbaugh, M., Eads, G., & Press, S. (1974). Effects of the Vietnam experience on subsequent drug use among servicemen. International Journal of the Addictions, 9, 25-40.

Reports results of a study of self-reported drug use among three active duty samples (N = 1,743) surveyed at a large midwestern Army post in 1971. Results provided only limited evidence that drug use after return to the States was affected by military service in Southeast Asia. The authors contrast this with the many anecdotal reports of addicted Vietnam returnees. Several methodological problems are discussed, including the accuracy of self-report measures and the sampling bias caused by underrepresentation of drug users resulting from prior administrative separations for drug abuse. (M)

Roth, L. M. (1986). Substance use and mental health among Vietnam veterans. In G. Boulanger & C. Kadushin (Eds.), The Vietnam veteran redefined: Fact and fiction (pp. 61-77). Hillsdale, NJ: Lawrence Erlbaum Associates.

Reviews the literature on drug and alcohol use among Vietnam veterans and presents interview data on the current substance use of Vietnam and Vietnam-era veterans. Roth's data indicate that current use by Vietnam-era veterans does not significantly differ from that of nonveteran peers, and that Vietnam veterans are only slightly more likely than others to drink heavily. Neither military service generally nor specific exposure to drugs in Vietnam has affected current drug use of veterans. Similarly, exposure to combat has no identifiable effect on either current drug use or drinking rates of Vietnam veterans. However, preliminary results do suggest that combat veterans may be more likely than peers to drink heavily as a way of coping with episodes of anxiety and depression. (S)

Roy, R. (1983). Alcohol misuse and posttraumatic stress disorder (delayed): An alternative interpretation of the data. Journal of Studies on Alcohol, 44, 198-202.

Presents data from a reanalysis of the findings of a series of epidemiological studies conducted in 1977 under the auspices of the National Institute of Drug Abuse on a national probability sample of 3,322 adults. Previous findings had supported the conclusion that Vietnam veterans showed significantly higher rates of alcohol consumption and binge drinking than did Vietnam-era veterans. In this reanalysis, Roy calculated demographically adjusted means for alcohol consumption and binge drinking by pooling means for the combined sample of Vietnam and Vietnam-era veterans. Compared with those means calculated for nonveterans, the pooled means were not significantly different. Roy argues that the differences obtained must therefore reflect preexisting differences between Vietnam-assigned and non-Vietnam-assigned veterans; that is, the manner in which selection was made as to who went to combat accounts for the differences in alcohol use years later. (S)

Schnitt, J. M., & Nocks, J. J. (1984). Alcoholism treatment of Vietnam veterans with post-traumatic stress disorder. Journal of Substance Abuse Treatment, 1, 179-189.

Describes the clinical principles and practical approaches to the treatment of Vietnam veterans with both alcoholism and PTSD. Their program begins with the veteran's admission to a 28-day volunteer inpatient alcoholism milieu treatment unit for detoxification and stabilization. Use of psychoactive medications is avoided, and much emphasis is placed on strategies to raise his depleted self-esteem. While most therapeutic attention is focused on the veteran controlling his alcohol intake, the program also begins exploration of his underlying PTSD. Outpatient management is oriented toward group therapy, primarily with groups composed of PTSD and non-PTSD veterans with associated alcohol problems. The authors review the common transference and countertransference issues that arise in these groups, especially those issues that involve drinking. (C)

Solomon, G. F. (1971). Psychiatric casualties of the Vietnam conflict with particular reference to the problem of heroin addiction. Modern Medicine, 38, 199-201, 211, 215.

Notes that only 8 of 50 (16%) randomly chosen Vietnam veteran psychiatric admissions to the Palo Alto VA hospital in early 1970 had come to medical attention because of emotional problems while in the service. Solomon speculates that underrecognition of psychiatric dysfunction in Vietnam was due both to military procedures there (minimizing soldier complaints or reacting to emotionally troubled soldiers with disciplinary actions or administrative discharges) and to self-medication by soldiers with marijuana or opiates. He notes that late in the war, socially disadvantaged soldiers were overrepresented among the fighting forces. These soldiers faced the interacting stresses of alienation from their culture (due to both the breakdown in public consensus about the war and their generation's tendency not to accept the "rationalizations" provided by their elders) while participating in the "horrors of brutal, futile, apparently meaningless war." Solomon comments on veteran reentry problems (e.g., limited vocational opportunities and stigmatized social status) and speculates on the negative consequences, especially the strong likelihood of serious addiction. A spectrum of intervention strategies is explored. (C)

Stanton, M. D. (1982). Family therapy of drug dependent veterans. In R. J. Craig & S. L. Baker (Eds.), Drug dependent patients:

Treatment and research (pp. 141-152). Springfield, IL: Charles C. Thomas Publishers.

Describes clinical findings and treatment techniques that emerged from conducting family therapy with VA drug patients. The study population, half black and half white, were 45 VA patients aged 23-35 who were addicted to heroin for at least 2 years. The research findings report that the family structures of these patients were consistent with those of families of nonveteran drug addicts as revealed in other literature--for example, (1) there was usually a very close dependent mother-son relationship, (2) the father was distant and excluded, and (3) over half the fathers had drinking problems. The research findings further suggest that the addicted member was serving to keep the family-- especially the parents--together, and that the family system served to maintain the addiction. Stanton notes that it was extremely difficult to engage families in treatment. Nonetheless, the rate of engagement was two to three times that indicated in most published reports, and the overall treatment results were also superior. (C)

Van Kampen, M., Watson, C. G., Tilleskjor, B. A., Kucala, T., & Vassar, P. (1986). The definition of posttraumatic stress disorder in alcoholic Vietnam veterans. Journal of Nervous and Mental Disease, 174, 137-144.

Presents findings from a study of self-reported symptoms among 75 Vietnam veterans (20 were combat veterans) hospitalized at a VA medical center alcohol treatment unit. Following detoxification, a structured interview was conducted in which the veterans were asked about 16 DSM-III symptoms and 10 "post-Vietnam syndrome" complaints. Sixteen subjects met all DSM-III criteria for PTSD. The authors report strong validation for most DSM-III PTSD standards except for numbness to intimacy, constricted affect, memory impairment, problems concentrating, and survival guilt. Among the 10 post-Vietnam symptoms, only "lacking direction" correlated both with PTSD diagnosis and combat exposure. The consistency between these findings and those of other investigations of the validity of the PTSD diagnosis is discussed. (C)

Wish, E. D., Robins, L. N., Hesselbrock, M., & Helzer, J. E. (1979). The course of alcohol problems in Vietnam veterans. Currents in Alcoholism, 6, 239-256.

Assesses the preservice and subsequent course of alcohol problems in a group of Vietnam veterans compared with alcohol use in an age-matched sample of nonveterans during the same period. The matched subjects were interviewed using standardized questions about their drug use and behavioral and psychological adjustment during this specific period of their lives. Veterans reported significantly more alcohol problems both before and during military service. Both groups' alcohol problems dipped during the 1st year of the veteran's service but only veterans' use increased during the 2nd and 3rd year of service. Also studied was the relationship between the veteran's use of narcotics in Vietnam and his postservice alcohol problems. Heavy use of narcotics was associated with both a continued use after discharge and a resurgence of alcohol problems, although many veterans spontaneously discontinued narcotics use upon return. Situational factors contributed to a switch from alcohol to narcotics and back again during the preservice, service, and postservice periods, respectively. Most enlisted men were under their states' legal drinking age prior to service and were discouraged from using hard liquor while in Vietnam. On the other hand, narcotics were widely available in Vietnam but relatively scarce when they returned to the States, by which time most veterans in this sample were of legal drinking age. (M)

Wyman, L. P. (1978). Reentry stress perceptions of heroin using Vietnam era American soldiers while awaiting return to the civilian community. Dissertation Abstracts International, 38 (10-A), 6325.

Reports survey results using 25 identified opiate-using Vietnam-era soldiers in military drug abuse wards both before their reentry to civilian life and 3 months after their reentry. The study goal was to examine the relationship between anticipated problems and reported problems after reentry. The most significant changes occurred in the areas of reentry into peer groups, reentry into occupational groups, feelings of insecurity over reentry events, the loss of close friends, and the anticipations associated with engaging in criminal behaviors. Wyman concludes that a collection of services are necessary to reduce reentry stress and facilitate adjustment for veterans such as these. (C)

8   Special Groups

Becerra, R. M. (1982). The Hispanic Vietnam veteran: Mental
health issues and therapeutic approaches. In R. M. Becerra,
M. Karno, & J. I. Escobar (Eds.), Mental health and Hispanic
Americans: Clinical perspectives (pp. 169-180). New York: Grune
and Stratton.
    Presents case material supporting the argument that postwar
adjustment for Hispanic veterans is further complicated by lifelong
patterns of environmental stressors. Discrimination inside and outside the military, low socioeconomic status and other preservice
variables, and greater chances of serving in the military and especially in combat apparently lead to increased psychological vulnerability among Hispanics. Becerra suggests that individual psychotherapy and self-help "rap groups" that include other Hispanics are
therapeutic approaches for these veterans. (S)

Becerra, R. M., & Greenblatt, M. (1981). The mental health-seeking
behavior of Hispanic veterans. Comprehensive Psychiatry, 22, 124-
133.
    Seeks to understand, through structured interviews with a
randomly selected population of 234 Hispanic veterans and 295
non-Hispanic veterans, the apparent underutilization of VA
services by Hispanic veterans needing mental health assistance.
This survey showed that 24.4% of the Hispanic VA population were
mental health service users as compared with 22% of the Anglos.
The highest demand for such services among Hispanic veterans was
by those who served in the Vietnam period, whereas among the
Anglo group, it was by those who served in prior periods. The
survey indicates that mental health service use among Hispanics
and non-Hispanics is similar, suggesting a significant need for such
services among Hispanics and not a lower incidence of mental
health problems. Other data suggest that a high sense of cultural
identification may contribute to delays in seeking mental health
services by Hispanic veterans, but that use of folk healers, or
curanderos, was not a factor; instead, underutilization most often
resulted from either lack of knowledge about or lack of access to
mental health services. (C)

Boman, B. (1985). Post-traumatic stress disorder (traumatic war neurosis) and concurrent psychiatric illness among Australian Vietnam veterans: A controlled study. Journal of the Royal Army Medical Corps, 131, 128-131.

The cluster of depression, anxiety, irritability with unpredictable explosions of aggressive behavior, impulsivity, suicidal attempts, and substance abuse are included as associated symptoms under the DSM-III category of PTSD. This controlled study found that such features occurred with equal frequencies among one group of psychiatrically hospitalized Australian Vietnam veterans with PTSD and another group not so affected. Boman cautions against ascribing the full scope of a veteran's psychopathology to combat stress. (C)

Carney, C. M. (1985). Perceived symptoms among U.S. Army nurses: The effects of combat environment, gender, control, and social support. (Doctoral dissertation, The George Washington University). Dissertation Abstracts International, 46 (11-B), 4062.

Presents results of a study of long-term health correlates of active duty Army nurses who had prior exposure to a combat environment. Using a checklist of 75 symptoms, Carney compares current physical health reports from Army Nurse Corps veterans of the war in Vietnam (n = 361) with those of nurses assigned elsewhere during the conflict (n = 351). Multiple regression analyses of eight physical symptom categories revealed little difference between the groups. Among several explanations, the data supported a hypothesis that because of modern medical stabilization and evacuation capabilities, military medical personnel remote from the fighting may nonetheless undergo a similar level of stress as those who are there because of exposure to recent combat casualties ("psychological combat assignment"). Further, the Vietnam veteran nurses' reports of emotional and psychological difficulties in Vietnam were powerfully associated with increased symptoms. Noteworthy, however, is that some of this group suggested that their negative experiences in Vietnam were greatly offset by experiences that were the most personally and professionally rewarding of their careers. (C)

Carter, J. H. (1982). Alcoholism in black Vietnam veterans: Symptoms of posttraumatic stress disorder. Journal of the National Medical Association, 74, 655-660.

Discusses PTSD among black Vietnam veterans, arguing that a definitive diagnosis can be made only when recognition is given to the stress of racism as well as to that of war. Carter presents two case histories illustrative of PTSD in black Vietnam veterans, in which alcoholism is seen as an attempt to reduce feelings of inadequacy, pessimism, and uncontrollable rage. He concludes with a discussion of treatment approaches. (S)

Dewane, C. J. (1984). Posttraumatic stress disorder in medical personnel in Vietnam. Hospital and Community Psychiatry, 35, 1232-1234.

Speculates on premorbid and experiential factors that led to PTSD symptoms in Vietnam health personnel based on her 10 years of clinical experience with Vietnam veterans. She also describes clinical findings that are consonant with the PTSD diagnosis but that have unique features as a result of the conflicting experiences of caretaker, combatant, and survivor. (C)

Escobar, J. I., Randolph, E. T., Puente, G., Spiwak, F., Asamen, J. K., Hill, M., & Hough, R. L. (1983). Post-traumatic stress disorder in Hispanic Vietnam veterans: Clinical phenomenology and sociocultural characteristics. Journal of Nervous and Mental Disease, 171, 585-596.

A sample of 20 Hispanic-American Vietnam combat veterans was chosen from records of an East Los Angeles VA neighborhood health clinic between 1979 and 1980 for comparison with a Hispanic veteran control group and a sample of Hispanic veterans with DSM-III schizophrenic disorder. All subjects reported heavy Vietnam combat stress and met DSM-III criteria for PTSD. Most were very symptomatic and had significant social impairment. Methodology included use of the NIMH Diagnostic Interview Schedule, a social network questionnaire, and an acculturation rating scale for Mexican-Americans. Findings included that PTSD seemed not to be a discrete entity but instead mixed with symptom clusters cutting across various DSM-III categories; that highly symptomatic PTSD veterans reported smaller and more negatively experienced social networks; and that PTSD veterans appeared more alienated from their cultural heritage. The authors posit that "rap groups" alone may not constitute an adequate therapeutic approach compared with more formal psychiatric therapies. (C)

Fairbank, J. A., McCaffrey, R. J., & Keane, T. M. (1985). Psychometric detection of fabricated symptoms of posttraumatic stress disorder. American Journal of Psychiatry, 142, 501-503.

Fifteen Vietnam veterans with PTSD, and two control groups of 15 each who were instructed to fabricate PTSD symptoms, completed the MMPI. A discriminant function analysis of selected scale scores and an empirically derived decision rule successfully classified over 90% of the subjects. (MA)

Fendrich, J. M. (1972). The returning black Vietnam veteran. In L. J. Sherman & E. M. Caffey, Jr. (Eds.), The Vietnam veteran in contemporary society: Collected materials pertaining to the young veterans (sec. IV, pp. 72-79). Washington, DC: Veterans Administration.

Presents results of a study of readjustment patterns among black Vietnam veterans (N = 199). Findings from interview and survey data collected in 1968 include that the veterans' benefits available are inadequate. Generally, respondents report difficulty obtaining employment that will support them and their families. Measures of alienation suggest that a large minority of these veterans are highly alienated. Fendrich speculates that "if black disenchantment with white America intensifies, . . . black veterans could become the cutting edge of the black protest movement." (C)

Grant, B. L., & Coons, D. J. (1983). Guilty verdict in a murder committed by a veteran with post-traumatic stress disorder. Bulletin of the American Academy of Psychiatry and the Law, 11, 355-358.
    Vietnam-generated PTSD has gained visibility and attention from both mental health professionals and the general public, and has begun to surface as a successful legal defense against criminal responsibility for both violent and nonviolent crimes. The authors present a case in which such a defense was raised in a murder, but the defendant was subsequently found guilty despite the presence of the disorder. In that psychiatrists are increasingly being called upon to provide expert testimony in such cases, there is a need to differentiate personality traits unique to each individual from the characteristics of the disorder itself, and to determine the relevance of these to the specific circumstances of the crime. (M)

Hamilton, J. D. (1985). Pseudo-posttraumatic stress disorder. Military Medicine, 150, 353-356.
    Presents case histories of 3 patients who complained of PTSD symptoms from Vietnam combat service but whose allegations subsequently were proven to be fictitious. Hamilton provides guidance as to careful history taking and records review that will discern such discrepancies.   (C)

Harris, M. J., & Fisher, B. S. (1985). Group therapy in the treatment of female partners of Vietnam veterans. Journal for Specialists in Group Work, 10, 44-50.
    Describes the use of group therapy in a veterans outreach center in Portland, OR, for assisting the partners of Vietnam veterans.   (C)

Holloway, H. C., & Ursano, R. J. (1985). Viet Nam veterans on active duty: Adjustment in a supportive atmosphere. In S. M. Sonnenberg, A. S. Blank, Jr., & J. A. Talbott (Eds.), The trauma of war: Stress and recovery in Viet Nam veterans (pp. 321-338). Washington, DC: American Psychiatric Press.

Discusses how traumatic war experiences can become a powerful metaphor and organizing symbol in the communications of Vietnam veterans. The authors first provide an introduction to the nature of war and war experiences, and then present research findings on the effects of these experiences on Vietnam veterans who remained in the active military after service there. They emphasize the importance of understanding the effects of serving in the Vietnam war in terms of the veteran's social system (both micro and macro), the time course of events (both time of one's service in Vietnam and time of symptom onset), and the role of metaphor in the psychology of the individual. They conclude with suggestions for preventive programs to help soldiers develop coherent integrated accounts of their traumatic experiences. (S)

Johnson, L. (1980). Scars of war: Alienation and estrangement among wounded Vietnam veterans. In C. R. Figley & S. Leventman (Eds.), Strangers at home: Vietnam veterans since the war (pp. 213-227). New York: Praeger.

The Political Alienation Scale (PAS)--a multidimensional scale that measures frustration in readjustment to civilian life, a sense of political anomie or normlessness, rejection of prevailing social mores, and distrust of established political authorities--was sent to 256 randomly selected, previously wounded Vietnam veterans (response rate = 65%) in early 1973. The study focused on the relationship between veterans' present political alienation and estrangement, and several other factors including nature and circumstances of the wound, time since wound, type of entrance into the military, extent of commitment to the war, and military rank. Results showed that men who were drafted, who were not committed to the rationale behind the war, and who were not officers were eventually the most likely to be estranged from the polity. The actual wounding itself bore no strong relationship to subsequent levels of alienation. Some evidence did exist to suggest that moderately wounded veterans (notably single amputees) have particularly difficult readjustment problems. (C)

Jordan, H. W., Howe, G. L., Gelsomino, J., & Lockert, E. W. (1986). Post-traumatic stress disorder: A psychiatric defense. Journal of the National Medical Association, 78, 119-126.

Using a series of forensic case examples of Vietnam veterans, the authors review the array of legal, social, and psychiatric problems associated with PTSD. Particular attention is paid to various efforts by defense attorneys to obtain treatment as opposed to confinement in these cases. The authors provide guidance in distinguishing PTSD-derived deviant behaviors from those of primarily antisocial individuals who are incidentally veterans, and they encourage expert witnesses to become courtroom educators regarding the mental and behavioral aberrations that can result from traumatic situations such as combat. They note that--considering there are about 39,000 Vietnam veterans in state or federal prisons, 37,500 on parole, 250,000 on probation, and 8,700 awaiting trial--these distinctions have serious implications for the criminal justice system. (C)

Jurich, A. P. (1983). The Saigon of the family's mind: Family therapy with families of Vietnam veterans. Journal of Marital and Family Therapy, 9, 355-363.
     Describes problems arising within families of Vietnam veterans, especially those with symptoms of PTSD, and provides treatment strategies derived from these intrafamilial considerations. (C)

Kleiger, J. H. (1984). Chronic post-traumatic stress disorders among active duty Vietnam veterans: Case reports. Military Medicine, 149, 159-161.
     Presents 3 cases, all of whom had separated from the military following service in Vietnam and later rejoined. None had a history of significant preexisting psychopathology, character defects, or prior psychiatric treatment; all had sought psychiatric consultation after Vietnam; all maintained satisfactory performance records; and none had been in any legal or disciplinary trouble while in the service. Kleiger notes that when combat veterans seek help it may be for secondary symptoms of PTSD, such as substance abuse, marital discord, or depression, and that they may be reluctant to discuss combat-related emotional problems that developed while in the military. He recommends more research to discover the incidence and prevalence of PTSD within the active military, and he questions whether these patients should be treated by the military. An alternative might be to refer them to community programs that specialize in assisting Vietnam veterans. (C)

Lindy, J. D., & Titchener, J. (1983). Acts of God and man: Long-term character change in survivors of disasters and the law. Behavioral Sciences and the Law, 1, 85-96.
     Compares the psychological effects on survivors of the Buffalo Creek disaster with those on combatant survivors of the Vietnam war. Among survivors of the collapse of the Buffalo Creek slag dam in 1972, character changes included psychic constriction, denial, somatization, and survivor guilt. In the legal proceedings that followed, survivors received compensation for "psychic impairment." Among combatant survivors of Vietnam, a common character change included the failure to channel hostile impulses effectively. The authors present a case report in which a veteran's

experiences in Vietnam could explain subsequent assaultive behavior at work. (S)

Lipkin, J. O., Scurfield, R. M., & Blank, A. S., Jr. (1983). Posttraumatic stress disorder in Vietnam veterans: Assessment in a forensic setting. Behavioral Sciences and the Law, 1, 51-67. (Republished as J. O. Lipkin, A. S. Blank, Jr., & R. M. Scurfield (1985). Forensic assessment of post-traumatic stress disorder in Viet Nam veterans. In S. M. Sonnenberg, A. S. Blank, Jr., & J. A. Talbott (Eds.), The trauma of war: Stress and recovery in Viet Nam veterans (pp. 417-438). Washington, DC: American Psychiatric Press.)
    Reviews the nature of PTSD and the historical circumstances leading to its inclusion in the DSM-III. The authors consider special problems regarding the precision of diagnosis and particularly the assessment of PTSD among Vietnam veterans, and they discuss forensic determinations of Vietnam veterans. Salient factors include the influence of the veteran's entry into the military, his basic training experiences, his experiences in transport to and arrival in Vietnam, his military experiences in Vietnam, his contacts with Vietnamese civilians, and his homecoming. The authors also discuss critical dynamics involved in assessing a veteran, including attributes of the clinician. Finally, they present issues of legal disposition and treatment implications. (S)

Lynn, E. J., & Belza, M. (1984). Factitious posttraumatic stress disorder: The veteran who never got to Vietnam. Hospital and Community Psychiatry, 35, 697-701.
    Presents case reports of 7 patients admitted to the Reno VA Medical Center psychiatric unit complaining of Vietnam-related PTSD symptoms. All were found to have had no service in Vietnam. With the exception of 1 schizophrenic patient whose fabrications were part of a delusional system, all cases demonstrated subcomponents of Munchausen's Syndrome, malingering, or both. The authors point out the need for clinicians to be aware of factitious PTSD so that the patients' actual underlying psychopathology can be evaluated and treated. (S)

Maillet, E. L. (1972). The severely damaged veteran of the Vietnam war: Some problems in social role. In L. J. Sherman & E. M. Caffey, Jr. (Eds.), The Vietnam veteran in contemporary society: Collected materials pertaining to the young veterans (sec. IV, pp. 149-159). Washington, DC: Veterans Administration.
    Highlights the adaptational problems associated with the prolonged course of hospitalization and treatment, as well as with the altered social roles and capabilities, that befall the seriously wounded of the Vietnam war. Compounding the difficulties atten-

dant on being severely disabled in war in general are those associated with being a casualty of the divisive Vietnam war in particular. Such a veteran becomes doubly stigmatized, which profoundly
complicates his task of finding meaning in his personally disas-
trous experience. (C)

May, E. (1979). Inmate veterans: Hidden casualties of a lost war.
Corrections Magazine, 5, 3-13.
        Reviews evidence suggesting that a larger proportion of con-
finees in America's prisons and jails are Vietnam veterans than
has been recognized, and speculates on the likely influence of
combat service on the commission of their crimes. These prisoners
feel socially ignored and unjustly denied their veterans benefits.
Estimates of the prevalence of Vietnam-era veterans range as high
as 25% of inmates, with 7% having had war zone experience. May
notes that according to various studies, most veteran prisoners
have relatively less troubled backgrounds and have left the service
honorably; they are more likely to be first offenders and to have
been involved with drugs or other less serious crimes. Further, the
veteran prisoners are typically less disruptive than other prisoners,
with military training believed to have been a positive influence.
May discusses those special features of the Vietnam war that may
have contributed to their criminal behaviors, and he also describes
the various programs and initiatives designed to assist them. (M)

McCaughey, B. G., Kleiger, J. H., Reyes, A. F. C., Miller, A. C., &
Nathan, H. W. (1985). Treatment of active duty Vietnam veterans:
Some clinical observations (Report No. 84-51). San Diego, CA:
Naval Health Research Center.
        Summarizes clinical impressions from group therapy with
Vietnam veterans on active duty conducted at three Navy treatment facilities between 1981 and 1984. Although the authors vali-
date the fundamental posttraumatic clinical dynamics reported in
the treatment of civilian Vietnam combat veteran groups, they also
identify unique psychological defenses demonstrated by these veterans, such as remaining in the military in an effort to reexperi-
ence various gratifications experienced only in the combat theatre,
or resisting acknowledgment of painful feelings or disabilities on
the assumption that they would not be condoned by military superiors. The authors underscore the need for systematic research
on this underrecognized and undertreated group of veterans. (C)

McVicker, S. J. (1985). Invisible veterans: The women who served
in Vietnam. Journal of Psychosocial Nursing, 23, 13-19.
        Catalogs the varieties of stress that affected many of the
estimated 7,500 women who served with the military in Vietnam
throughout the war. McVicker also highlights aspects of the

woman veteran's reentry problems, which differ from those of the male veteran, and considers specialized treatment features that should be provided. (C)

Ott, J. (1985). Women Viet Nam veterans. In S. M. Sonnenberg, A. S. Blank, Jr., & J. A. Talbott (Eds.), The trauma of war: Stress and recovery in Viet Nam veterans (pp. 309-320). Washington, DC: American Psychiatric Press.
    Describes the problems encountered by female veterans of the Vietnam war, a population consisting primarily of nurses. Ott also discusses clinical problems associated with group therapy for women Vietnam veterans and makes suggestions for future research on issues confronting these veterans. (S)

Panzarella, R. F., Mantell, D. M., & Bridenbaugh, R. H. (1978). Psychiatric syndromes, self-concepts, and Vietnam veterans. In C. R. Figley (Ed.), Stress disorders among Vietnam veterans: Theory, research and treatment (pp. 148-172). New York: Brunner/ Mazel.
    Reports on a survey of 143 American soldiers who sought the services of an Army mental health clinic in Germany between October 1973 and May 1974. Included in the sample were 34 soldiers who had served at least one tour of duty in Vietnam. Subjects responded to two adjective checklists and a psychiatric symptoms checklist. Study findings detected no specific psychiatric symptomatology unique to those who served in Vietnam. Compared with the others, the Vietnam veterans were older, higher ranking, and more likely to be married, and they had had some previous contact with a mental health worker or institution. (C)

Parson, E. R. (1985a). The black Vietnam veteran: His representational world in post-traumatic stress disorder. In W. E. Kelly (Ed.), Post-traumatic stress disorder and the war veteran patient (pp. 170-192). New York: Brunner/Mazel.
    Discusses symptoms and inner experiences of black Vietnam veterans with PTSD (i.e., alterations in their representational world, which includes certain aspects of black self-identity). Parson also presents an overview of psychotherapy research with minority and low-income patients, which has applications for treating black Vietnam veterans. (S)

Parson, E. R. (1985b). The intercultural setting: Encountering black Viet Nam veterans. In S. M. Sonnenberg, A. S. Blank, Jr., & J. A. Talbott (Eds.), The trauma of war: Stress and recovery in Viet Nam veterans (pp. 359-388). Washington, DC: American Psychiatric Press.

Describes how racism and the stress of combat duty combined to make it especially difficult for black veterans to readjust successfully after serving in Vietnam. Parson provides information to assist mental health workers in effectively assessing and treating readjustment problems such as PTSD in black veterans. (S)

Paul, E. A. (1985). Wounded healers: A summary of the Vietnam Nurse Veteran Project, Military Medicine, 150, 571-576. (Project findings are also summarized in E. A. Paul & J. S. O'Neill (1986). American nurses in Vietnam: Stressors and aftereffects. American Journal of Nursing, 86, 526.)
     Describes the Vietnam Nurse Veteran (VNV) Project, in which 155 veterans were surveyed regarding Vietnam service stressors and aftereffects. The primary stressors identified by the 137 respondents (10.2% were male) included the young age and wound severity of the casualties cared for; the physical danger to which nurses were exposed; the brevity of military service prior to being sent to Vietnam (under 6 months); sexual harassment; and survivor guilt. Of the respondents, 38% complained of significant aftereffects including nightmares, "flashbacks," recurring physical problems, career problems, and depression. (C)

Pentland, B., & Dwyer, J. (1985). Incarcerated Viet Nam veterans. In S. M. Sonnenberg, A. S. Blank, Jr., & J. A. Talbott (Eds.), The trauma of war: Stress and recovery in Viet Nam veterans (pp. 403-416). Washington, DC: American Psychiatric Press.
     Discusses problems facing imprisoned Vietnam veterans. The authors posit that most of these veterans are not career or "outlaw" criminals but are individuals who have become disillusioned or otherwise affected by their war experiences. They discuss barriers to treatment within the prison environment, as well as the Veterans in Prison Program, a counseling program using an eclectic approach and incorporating a self-help model. They conclude that even minimal attempts at "inreach" counseling can help reduce recidivism. (S)

Pina, G., III. (1985). Diagnosis and treatment of post-traumatic stress disorder in Hispanic Viet Nam veterans. In S. M. Sonnenberg, A. S. Blank, Jr., & J. A. Talbott (Eds.), The trauma of war: Stress and recovery in Viet Nam veterans (pp. 389-402). Washington, DC: American Psychiatric Press.
     Discusses the unique problems experienced by Hispanic Vietnam veterans. These surround their Hispanic identity as American warriors, factors influencing that identity and PTSD, the diagnosis of PTSD in Hispanic veterans, the concept of machismo as it relates to guerrilla warfare, and treatment issues including Hispanic family involvement. (S)

Rothman, G. (1984). Needs of female patients in a veterans psychiatric hospital. Social Work, 29, 380-385.
    Reviews the psychiatric and medical care of female patients at a large VA psychiatric facility based on 69 interviews. Findings reveal that the women were satisfied with care in general but dissatisfied with unmet gender-specific needs (e.g., greater privacy, personal security, more comprehensive feminine medical care, and freedom from sexual harassment) in the predominantly male environment. These women complained of competition for rest room and shower facilities and the lack of pelvic examinations or instruction in breast self-examination. Rothman points out the importance of researching these issues in light of the increasing numbers of female veterans and the absence of published studies regarding their care. (C)

Sarkesian, S. C. (1976). An empirical reassessment of military professionalism. In F. D. Margiotta (Ed.), The changing world of the American military (pp. 37-55). Boulder, CO: Westview Press.
    Examines attitudes and perceptions of military professionals in the aftermath of the Vietnam war through a review of five recent empirical studies. The subjects of these studies consistently reflect feelings of alienation from the greater American society, which stem from the Vietnam war experience and from strong resentment that, whereas society through its politicians was at fault, the military (with the help of media bias) has been made the scapegoat. Sarkesian notes that the military, to reinforce and maintain its legitimacy, must share core values of society. This creates a predictable tension in America because society considers that the military exists to support democratic values, while professional military values are more authoritarian and bureaucratic in nature. Sarkesian concludes, "although it is unlikely that the profession will deliberately seek combat to restore its perceived status and influence, evidence of lost honor and self-deprecation reveals a serious dilemma within the profession." (C)

Schnaier, J. A. (1986). A study of women Vietnam veterans and their mental health adjustment. In C. R. Figley (Ed.), Trauma and its wake: Vol. 2. Traumatic stress theory, research, and intervention (pp. 97-132). New York: Brunner/Mazel.
    Presents results of a survey of 89 women who served in Vietnam as medical personnel. Results indicate that approximately one third of the stress symptom items were endorsed by 25% of the study participants. Also, of symptoms that arose between homecoming and 1 year after Vietnam, approximately 70% were reported as still present. Schnaier concludes that women serving in Vietnam may have undergone psychologically traumatic experiences; that there is evidence of mental health distress and PTSD among the women sampled; that the biographic-demographic factors indi-

cate significant differences from previously studied male veterans; and that there are positive, "growthful" experiences indicated by many of the women in this sample. (C)

Scrignar, C. B. (1984). Post-traumatic stress disorder: Diagnosis, treatment and legal issues. New York: Praeger.
    Presents Scrignar's behavioral approach to the general subject of psychic trauma and residual symptoms, and includes clinical and forensic considerations of affected Vietnam veterans. Scrignar speculates that the combination of widescale clinical neglect while in the service, ambiguities of national purpose regarding the war, and public shame toward veterans distorted the effect of the Vietnam conflict on combat veterans. In his opinion, these cases should categorically be classified as service connected. Case material is provided. (C)

Smith-Schubert, S. C. (1985). The relationship of sex role orientation to anxiety, depression and marital adjustment among women who are wives or partners of Vietnam veterans identified as suffering delayed stress. Dissertation Abstracts International, 46 (1-B), 315.
    Reports results of a study exploring the relationship of sex role orientation with psychiatric symptoms and marital adjustment among 106 wives or female partners of Vietnam veterans identified as having PTSD. Zung self-rating scales were used to measure anxiety and depression, and marital adjustment was measured with Spanier's Dyadic Adjustment Scale. Classification of sex role orientation was through use of the Bem Sex Role Inventory. Overall, the results showed these women to be experiencing symptoms, with most acknowledging anxiety and depression at clinical levels. Women with androgynous and masculine orientations showed lower anxiety and depression levels than those with feminine and undifferentiated orientations. (C)

Sparr, L. F., & Parkratz, L. D. (1983). Factitious posttraumatic stress disorders. American Journal of Psychiatry, 140, 1016-1019.
    Describes 5 patients, part of a growing number of young men who have reported an array of symptoms that suggest a diagnosis of PTSD. These subjects, all claiming to be Vietnam veterans, were treated at a VA medical center; 3 said they were former POWs. In fact, none had been POWs, 4 had never been in Vietnam, and 2 had never even been in the military; instead, all 5 suffered factitious disorders. The authors discuss the differential diagnoses and stress the value of verifying military histories. (MA)

Streimer, J. H., Cosstick, J., & Tennant, C. (1985). The psychosocial adjustment of Australian Vietnam veterans. American Journal
of Psychiatry, 142, 616-618.
    Reviews the case records of a random sample of 126 Austra-
lian Vietnam veteran inpatients, in which the diagnostic and background data were recorded and new DSM-III diagnoses were made.
Neurotic disorders accounted for 49% of the primary or secondary
diagnoses; only 10% of the overall sample had a primary diagnosis
of PTSD whereas 27% of the veterans who had seen combat had a
primary diagnosis of the disorder; and 29% were given a primary
diagnosis of alcohol abuse or dependence. The early developmental
environment of the overall sample frequently included poor parent-
child relationships, high rates of parental separation, and family
histories dominated by parental alcohol abuse. (MA)

Stretch, R. H. (1985). Posttraumatic stress disorder among U.S.
Army Reserve Vietnam and Vietnam-era veterans. Journal of Consulting and Clinical Psychology, 53, 935-936.
    Presents results from an epidemiological investigation of
PTSD among Vietnam and Vietnam-era veterans. Analysis of questionnaire data collected in spring 1982 from 935 randomly selected
Vietnam and Vietnam-era veterans assigned to U.S. Army Reserve
troop units nationwide reveals a PTSD rate for Vietnam veteran
reservists of 10.9%, which is midrange between estimates for
civilian (18%-54%) and active duty Army (5.1%) Vietnam veterans.
Results suggest that the quality of social support received during
Vietnam duty and the first year back may serve to either moderate or exacerbate PTSD symptomatology associated with combat
experience (e.g., Reserve membership may buffer reentry stress and
mitigate development of PTSD). (S)

Stretch, R. H. (1986a). Incidence and etiology of post-traumatic
stress disorder among active duty Army personnel. Journal of
Applied Social Psychology, 16, 464-481.
    Presents results from the first phase of a programmatic
research effort into the prevalence and severity of PTSD among
Vietnam and Vietnam-era veterans. Questionnaire data were collected from 238 Vietnam and 85 Vietnam-era veterans stationed at
a moderate-sized U.S. Army post on the East Coast in spring 1982.
Results indicate a significantly lower prevalence of PTSD than has
been reported in the literature among civilian Vietnam veterans.
Absence of social support during the first year back from Vietnam
appears to contribute more to the generation of PTSD symptomatology than does combat experience alone. Additional results
highlight the relationship between physical and psychological
health. (S)

Stretch, R. H., Vail, J. D., & Maloney, J. P. (1985). Posttraumatic stress disorder among Army Nurse Corps Vietnam veterans. Journal of Consulting and Clinical Psychology, 53, 704-708.

Presents results from an epidemiologic investigation of PTSD among Army nurse veterans. Analysis of questionnaire data from more than 700 Vietnam and Vietnam-era veterans still on active duty in the U.S. Army Nurse Corps reveals a current PTSD rate for Vietnam veteran nurses of 3.3%. This rate is comparable to that found among nonnurse active duty Army Vietnam veterans (5.1%) and is much lower than estimates (18%-54%) for civilian Vietnam veterans. Results suggest that danger and exposure to violence may be responsible for stress reactions such as PTSD among noncombatants. Additional results indicate that social support is an important moderator in the attenuation of PTSD.   (S)

Terry, W. (1972). Bringing the war home. In L. J. Sherman & E. M. Caffey, Jr. (Eds.), The Vietnam veteran in contemporary society: Collected materials pertaining to the young veterans (sec. IV, pp. 63-72). Washington, DC: Veterans Administration. (Reprinted from The Black Scholar, 1970, November.)

Dramatizes the broadening scope of racial tension and strife among the military in Vietnam by citing numerous examples from interviews with troops there and from official documents. Terry anticipates that the returning black soldiers, "schooled in the violent art of guerrilla war (and) fed up with dying in a war they believe is (the) white man's folly, (are) determined to earn their share of American opportunities even if that means becoming Black Panthers or turning to guns."   (C)

Ursano, R. J. (1981). The Viet Nam era prisoner of war: Precaptivity and the development of psychiatric illness. American Journal of Psychiatry, 138, 315-318.

Examines the role of preexisting personality structure in the development of psychiatric illness after POW experience using case studies of 6 repatriated Vietnam POWs who were coincidentally evaluated before their captivity. Findings indicate that predisposition to psychiatric illness is neither necessary nor sufficient for psychiatric illness to develop after repatriation. Personality changes reflect both adaptation to the captivity environment and the impact of the ego-ideal over that of the punitive elements of the superego. Thus, the findings can be explained more from the perspective of personality change than from that of psychopathology.   (MA)

Ursano, R. J. (1985). Viet Nam era prisoners of war: Studies of U.S. Air Force prisoners of war. In S. M. Sonnenberg, A. S. Blank, Jr., & J. A. Talbott (Eds.), The trauma of war: Stress and recovery in Viet Nam veterans (pp. 339-358). Washington, DC: American Psychiatric Press.

Presents data on follow-up evaluations of all Air Force POWs who were repatriated in 1973. Extensive psychiatric evaluations were conducted at the USAF School of Aerospace Medicine. Results supported the preeminence of the severity of stress over predisposing personality factors in the development of poststress psychiatric disturbances. Case studies of 6 POWs who had had pre-captivity psychiatric evaluations were selected for further study (see Ursano, 1981). Their analysis revealed that presence of or predisposition to psychiatric illness is neither necessary nor sufficient for psychiatric illness to develop following the extreme stress of POW captivity. (S)

Ursano, R. J., Boydstun, J. A., & Wheatley, R. D. (1981). Psychiatric illness in U.S. Air Force Viet Nam prisoners of war: A five-year follow-up. American Journal of Psychiatry, 138, 310-314.

Reviews the psychiatric status of the U.S. Air Force POWs, who experienced a profound degree of stress during the Vietnam war. This population has been monitored by an ongoing voluntary follow-up program from the time of repatriation through the following 5 years. Although no prior reports concerning U.S. Air Force Vietnam POWs suggest the presence of psychiatric consequences as a result of their war captivity, these data indicate a significant degree of psychiatric readjustment problems, which were greatest among POWs captured before 1969. These findings support the association of an unusually stressful environment with an increased incidence of psychiatric illness. (MA)

Van Devanter, L. M. (1985). The unknown warriors: Implications of the experiences of women in Vietnam. In W. E. Kelly (Ed.), Post-traumatic stress disorder and the war veteran patient (pp. 148-169). New York: Brunner/Mazel.

Interprets the extant but sparse research data, anecdotal information, and counseling experience of some therapists to indicate that many female Vietnam veterans experience persisting negative mental health effects from their service in Southeast Asia. Van Devanter proposes various programs of education and group therapy for these veterans. (S)

Walker, J. I. (1981b). Viet Nam combat veterans with legal difficulties: A psychiatric problem? American Journal of Psychiatry, 138, 1384-1385.

As of 1979, approximately 29,000 Vietnam veterans were incarcerated in state or federal prisons with several times that number on parole, probation, or awaiting trial. In anticipation of a growing tendency for attorneys to defend clients based on emotional problems consequent to war experiences in Vietnam, Walker discusses the differential diagnosis of PTSD and antisocial personality and provides case illustrations. (C)

Wesson, K. J. (1984). Expression of aggression and self-concept: A comparative study of incarcerated Vietnam combat and non-combat veterans. Dissertation Abstracts International, 45 (3-B), 1064-1065.
    Reports results of a study comparing personality traits of incarcerated Vietnam veterans (n = 43) and Vietnam-era veterans (n = 43) using a demographic questionnaire, the Tennessee Self Concept Scale (TSCS), and the Interpersonal Behavior Survey. Findings suggest that incarcerated combat veterans are more likely to be classified as sociopathic and that their aggression levels are significantly higher than those of incarcerated veterans who had not served in Vietnam. Overall, Vietnam-era veterans reveal lower self-concept scores than the population upon which the TSCS was normed. Wesson concludes that the experience of combat appears to have a lasting effect on postmilitary adjustment. (C)

Williams, C. M. (1980). The "veteran system" with a focus on women partners: Theoretical considerations, problems and treatment strategies. In T. Williams (Ed.), Post-traumatic stress disorders of the Vietnam veteran (pp. 73-122). Cincinnati, OH: Disabled American Veterans.
    Presents a "family systems theory" perspective to show how female partners are affected by veterans' problems and how their involvement in treatment can benefit themselves and their partners. Case examples are provided. (M)

Bleier, R., with O'Neil, T. (1975). Fighting back. New York: Stein and Day.

Presents Bleier's personal narrative about his induction into the military out of a professional football career, his military training and subsequent assignment to Vietnam in 1969 as a combat infantryman with the Army's 196th Light Infantry Brigade, his becoming wounded in combat, his struggle to recover, and his successful return to professional football after having been told he would be lucky if he could walk. (C)

Cleland, M. (1980). Strong at the broken places. Lincoln, VA: Chosen Books.

Presents the story of Cleland's return from Vietnam as a triple amputee, and of his successful readjustment as a veteran, which subsequently led to his appointment as head of the VA. Cleland highlights how his initial desire to return to the life he had known before Vietnam was frustrated by the great amount of personal change that had occurred. He indicates how this failure provided the means for him to create a new life for himself. (M)

Downs, F. (1984). Aftermath: A soldier's return to America from Vietnam, 1968. New York: Norton.

Presents the second part of Downs's reconstruction of the effects of his Vietnam combat experiences on his life (see Downs, 1978). This volume resumes the narrative on a day in January 1968, 4 months after his arrival in Vietnam, when his combat role was suddenly ended by a "Bouncing Betty" mine. This material covers roughly the first year of his recovery and rehabilitation and reflects his progression through the sequential echelons of military medical care in Asia and the United States. (C)

Egendorf, A. (1985). Healing from the war: Trauma and transformation after Vietnam. Boston: Houghton Mifflin.

Provides a subjectively oriented account of the various psychological and social distortions and transformations that were generated from participation in the war in Vietnam, and describes the consequent and often prolonged odyssey that many veterans have made, or need to make, in search of "healing." In order to understand what is traumatic about war experience for soldiers—especially those who fought in Vietnam—and for the nation, and to consider individual and societal approaches to restitution and enhancement (from "empowering" to "warriorship"), Egendorf weaves together observations from literature, insights from philosophers and from students of the mind and society, publications on the war in Vietnam and the Vietnam era in America, and his own personal travails and discoveries (from enlisted service in Vietnam as an intelligence case officer, participation in self-help "rap groups" with other disaffected Vietnam veterans, leadership of a large-scale study of Vietnam veteran adjustment, clinical experiences in counseling veterans and others, and his own readjustment difficulties).   (C)

Eilert, R. (1983). For self and country. New York: William Morrow.
    Provides a personal narrative of Eilert's year-long recovery from serious wounds received in Vietnam when, on November 26, 1967, he detonated a booby trap while leading a Marine squad on a combat patrol.   (C)

Howell-Koehler, N. (Ed.), with photographs by Baer, G. (1984). Vietnam: The battle comes home. Dobbs Ferry, NY: Morgan and Morgan.
    This photographic essay accompanies a collection of previously published essays by behavior and social scientists that seek to explain and validate the bewilderment and grief of veterans of the war in Southeast Asia as well as to describe their more common readjustment problems.   (C)

Keltner, N., Doggett, R., & Johnson, R. (1983). For the Vietnam veteran the war goes on. Perspectives in Psychiatric Care, 21, 108-113.
    Discusses some of the readjustment problems experienced by Vietnam veterans, including PTSD. Two of the authors provide their own personal case histories of readjustment difficulties. The article concludes with a discussion of various treatment techniques, including hypnotherapy, "rap groups," stress reduction techniques, and individual psychotherapy.   (S)

Kovic, R. (1976). Born on the Fourth of July. New York: McGraw-Hill.
    An autobiographical account of Kovic's odyssey from patriotic Marine to disabled antiwar activist.   (M)

Polner, M. (1968, November). Vietnam war stories. Trans-action, pp. 8-20. (Reprinted in R. J. Lifton (Ed.), (1970). America and the Asian revolutions (pp. 37-59). New Brunswick, NJ: Transaction Books.)

Presents the stories of Vietnam veterans based on interviews collected in 1967. Polner also interviewed several Army psychiatrists to gain their view of the impact the war had upon soldiers. Among his findings is that while many soldiers fought not for ideals but for survival, their idealism found later expression (for some) in antiwar political participation.   (M)

Polner, M. (1971). No victory parades: The return of the Vietnam veteran. New York: Holt, Rinehart and Winston.

Presents the story of the impact of the Vietnam war on 9 young veterans from lower middle- or middle-class backgrounds. These groups are evenly divided into "hawks" (war supporters), "doves" (opposed to the war), and "haunted" (troubled veterans). (M)

III SOCIAL AND INSTITUTIONAL CONTEXT

The Vietnam period in American life can be viewed against the backdrop not only of the social and political attitudes derived from the experience of World War II, but also of the technological advances of television coverage, the birth control pill, and nuclear parity between the great powers. More centrally, this volatile period in American history was especially notable for the intense and often militant challenges to traditional institutions (especially the military in Vietnam) by demonstrators from the civil rights and black-pride movements, the emerging New Left, and a dissenting youth counterculture--challenges that were themselves opposed by an equally fervent and reactive conservative sector. The prolonged war in Vietnam served as a rallying point, both pro and con, for the passions and ambitions of these groups, and it left those who chose or were directed to serve there in limbo with respect to what constituted justifiable use of force, or even what was regarded as patriotic behavior.

The selected references in this section provide a contextual framework for understanding the salience of the works represented in the previous two sections. These publications reflect on the antecedents, concurrent phenomena, and consequences that were likely to have affected the soldier as stress inducing or stress mitigating, or to have shaped his or her adaptation or maladaptation.

1   The Vietnam Era: Overviews, Analysis, and Bibliographies

Boettcher, T. D., with Halberstam, D., Buttinger, J., Hodgson, G., Aronson, J., & Fall, B. (1985). Vietnam: The valor and the sorrow--from the home front to the front lines in words and pictures. Boston: Little, Brown.
   Provides a historical review of the Vietnam war beginning with the 96-year French colonization of Vietnam and the subsequent Japanese occupation during World War II. The direct American involvement, ideologically justified as blocking the spread of communism, began in the mid-'50s with the introduction of American advisers to the government and military of South Vietnam for support against attacks from North Vietnam and insurgency from within its own population. The account proceeds through the commitment of U.S. combat troops in increasing numbers beginning in 1965 and the tortuous years of American combat activities, which were accompanied by mounting public protest in the States, to the military defeat and surrender of the Saigon government to North Vietnam in 1975 just 2 years after the negotiated withdrawal of American combat troops. (C)

Dougan, C., Lipsman, S., & the editors of Boston Publishing Co. (1984). The Vietnam experience: A nation divided. Boston: Boston Publishing Co.
   Part of a multivolume series providing a historical account of America's war in Southeast Asia and liberally illustrated with photographs, this volume describes the unfolding events that comprised the socially tumultuous Vietnam war era (1965-72). Thus it weaves together the military events from Vietnam with the increasingly radical and confrontational social and political crosscurrents that erupted: the black-pride and civil rights movements; the social reforms attempted in President Johnson's "Great Society"; youthful expressions of the "generation gap" as in the student protests, the "free speech movement," rising drug use, and the "counterculture"; and the demonstrations of the antiwar/peace and the draft resistance movements, which ultimately included members of the military and returning veterans. This review also considers the special roles of the media and public opinion polls as both reflecting and influencing the course of events. (C)

Emerson, G. (1972). Winners and losers: Battles, retreats, gains, losses and ruins from a long war. New York: Random House.

Emerson, a war correspondent for the New York Times in Vietnam (1970-72), pieces together a composite of the war's traumatic effect on society using interviews with Americans from varied settings whose roles during the war were quite diverse. (C)

Hebert, T. W. (1982). Vietnam booklist. Collinsville, CA: Vietnam Bookstore.
    Provides an annotated bibliography of over 500 books regarding the politics, policies, conduct, and consequences of the war in Vietnam. (C)

Horne, A. D. (Ed.). (1981). The wounded generation: Americans after Vietnam. Englewood Cliffs, NJ: Prentice Hall.
    Offers a collection of articles authored by men and women from the generation that participated in or opposed the war in Vietnam. Its retrospective viewpoint of the 1980s provides both a remembrance and a reassessment of the war. Horn combines various media presentations--including fiction, essay, articles, transcribed dialogue, and poetry--to "force us to confront again a constellation of truths that we may ignore only at our peril." Such contextual issues as the draft, the antiwar movement, and the readjustment of war veterans after the war are also included. (M)

Kendrick, A. (1974). The world within: America in the Vietnam years, 1945-1974. Boston: Little, Brown.
    Provides a social history and analysis focusing on the dramatic changes in America in the 1960s, with the war in Vietnam serving variously as both cause and effect: "Perhaps the most gangrenous aspect . . . was that it was accepted for so long and so phlegmatically by so many people." On its effects Kendrick writes, "In what began as a booby trap war Vietnam itself became the biggest booby trap of all for American pride and power." Concerning Vietnam he concludes, "The war fragmentized, demoralized, dispersed, corrupted and terrorized Vietnamese life and social structure far beyond the death, suffering and physical damage it caused." (C)

MacPherson, M. (1984). Long time passing: Vietnam and the haunted generation. Garden City, NY: Doubleday.
    Through interviews with over 500 people, MacPherson narrates the kaleidoscope of American memories, attitudes, and reactions to the war in Vietnam. (C)

Mantell, D. M., & Pilisuk, M. (Eds.). (1975). Soldiers in and after Vietnam (Theme issue). Journal of Social Issues, 31(4).

This dedicated special issue of this journal presents a collection of essays relating to the social and psychological issues of the war in Vietnam: soldier precombat training and indoctrination, special stresses of the combat environment, psychiatric breakdown among Army soldiers, the GI resistance movement and changing American attitudes toward the war, veteran reentry experiences and readjustment problems, and special issues pertaining to families of missing servicemen. (See also Bachman & Jennings, 1975; Egendorf, 1975; Eisenhart, 1975; Fiman, Borus, & Stanton, 1975; J. R. Hayes, 1975; Horowitz & Solomon, 1975; Jones & Johnson, 1975; Lifton, 1975b; Loh, 1975; Moskos, 1975; Pilisuk, 1975; Strayer & Ellenhorn, 1975.) (C)

Newman, J. (1982). Vietnam war literature: An annotated bibliography of imaginative works about Americans fighting in Vietnam. Metuchen, NJ: Scarecrow Press.
    Presents an annotated bibliography of related novels, stories, poetry, and drama. (C)

Peake, L. A. (1986). The United States in the Vietnam war, 1954-1975: A selected, annotated bibliography. New York: Garland Publishing.
    Provides over 1,500 thematically arranged citations regarding the war in Southeast Asia. Topic areas include the cultural and geopolitical origins of the war; political events and strategic decisions in the United States; tactical circumstances and events; personal accounts by participants; attitudes and influence of the media; the war's impact at home; and experiences of the POWs. Peake seeks to avoid selection bias in his reference choices despite the intense controversy surrounding the war. He notes in his introduction that America's involvement in Vietnam brought "a military defeat for the United States, international criticism of American policy and conduct of the war, a crisis within the American political system, and a tearing apart of the domestic fabric of the nation." (C)

Sherman, L. J., & Caffey, E. M., Jr. (Eds.). (1972). The Vietnam veteran in contemporary society: Collected materials pertaining to the young veterans. Washington, DC: Veterans Administration.
    Provides a collection of 52 works (some previously published) intended to reflect on the stress and strain of combat service in the Vietnam war, on veteran reentry and readjustment, and on service-connected physical and psychiatric disability, as well as on the contextual influence of the nation's attitude toward the war and its soldiers. (See also Allerton, Forrest, Anderson, Tischler, Strange, Imahara, Talbott, Housman, & Bourne, 1970; Bourne, 1972a; Caplan, 1972; Fendrich, 1972; Lifton, 1972b; Lumry &

Braatz, 1972; Maillet, 1972; M. D. Stanton, 1972b; Stuen & Solberg, 1972; Terry, 1972; Wyant, 1971, July.) (C)

Stromberg, P. L. (1974). Long war's writing: American novels about the fighting in Vietnam written while Americans fought. Dissertation Abstracts International, 35 (7-A), 4562. (University Microfilms No. 75-01627)
    Seeks to interweave political events, military events, and emerging literary works during and regarding the war in Vietnam. Through a critical synopsis of 46 novels about the war, Stromberg reveals changing patterns in perceptions and reactions of the soldier participants and American society. (C)

Wheeler, J. (1984). Touched with fire: The future of the Vietnam generation. New York: Franklin Watts.
    A West Point graduate and a veteran of Vietnam (1969-70), Wheeler reflects on his experiences through the war years and since, and reviews selected evidence from government, popular culture, journalists, and the media in general, as well as published accounts by other veterans, in order to understand the "interconnections and consequences of war-time events." Besides his USMA background and Vietnam service, Wheeler's perspective is shaped by his seminal roles in the Vietnam Memorial Fund and the Vietnam Veterans Leadership Program. He catalogs the often intertwined social and political movements of the '60s and the emerging group polarities, and he describes the consequent painful sense of alienation that affected this generation. Considering the underlying themes of the era to be idealization, creativity, anger, and the "feminization of the culture," he posits that emerging in the '80s from the '60s Vietnam generation is "the feeling of strength, maturity and available wisdom . . . (and that) this energy will begin to surge, and soon, and in graceful, tempered ways. We have been through a lot, but that experience empowers us." Also noteworthy in this volume is an appendix that chronicles the principal events of 1959-75. (C)

2   The Military Organization: Goals, Leadership, Methods, and Effects, Especially in Conducting the War in Southeast Asia

Baritz, L. (1985). Backfire: A history of how American culture led us into Vietnam and made us fight the way we did. New York: William Morrow.
    Provides a sociological interpretation of the historical, political, strategic, and circumstantial roots of America's failure in Vietnam ("how and why America became involved in its worst political and military defeat"). In searching out the cultural myths that drove and shaped it, Baritz notes the discrepancy between "the decency of the impulse (to be helpful to those less fortunate) (and) the bloody eagerness to kill in the name of virtue." He postulates that the war effort in Vietnam ("attempting to build a nation in our own image") was based on fundamental nationalistic myths as to our moral superiority and the supremacy of our technology and bureaucratic efficiency, and he considers it a critical mistake that we sought to wage war as if it was an ideological abstraction: "North Vietnam finally won its war because it was willing to accept more death than we considered rational." (C)

Bourne, P. G. (1967). Some observations on the psychosocial phenomena seen in basic training. Psychiatry, 30, 187-196. (Republished as: The military and the individual. In J. Finn (Ed.), (1971). Conscience and command: Justice and discipline in the military (pp. 137-158). New York: Vintage.)
    Provides observations that reflect on the psychological and group adaptive phases of a platoon (48 recruits) as it proceeded through the 9-week training cycle in 1965. Bourne defines the phases as (1) environmental shock--with recruits exhibiting the stunned, frightened behavior similar to that seen in survivors of physical or emotional disasters; (2) engagement--marked by mounting anger throughout the first 4 weeks of actual training, secondary to the extensive and all-encompassing hardships and degradations and the absence of personal rewards or acknowledgment; (3) attainment--marked by increasing feelings of individual competence throughout the last 4 weeks, coupled with a transformed identity built on military skills and confidence; and (4) termination--with euphoria based on an appreciation of personal accomplishment along with increased group cohesion of a functional nature. Incidence of upper respiratory illness tended to be limited to Phase 2. (C)

Butterfield, F. (1983, February). The new Vietnam scholarship. New York Times Magazine, pp. 26-35, 45-47, 52-58.
Relates the history of U.S. involvement in the Vietnam war from vantage points of recently published historical sources. In this succinct review, Butterfield sheds light on how it was that the American forces held the tactical initiative but never achieved the strategic initiative. (C)

Capps, W. H. (1982). The unfinished war: Vietnam and the American conscience. Boston: Beacon Press.
Seeks to clarify the historical, political, social, and military origins of the war and especially American motives and behaviors as the war progressed. One chapter ("The Combatants," pp. 78-104) traces, often through the remarks of participants, replacement of individual idealism and commitment with disillusionment and self-doubt. (C)

Cincinnatus. (1981). Self-destruction: The disintegration and decay of the United States Army during the Vietnam era. New York: Norton.
A historical review of the strategic and tactical decisions that led to the failures of Vietnam. Cincinnatus considers a wide and complex series of errors, from the initial failure to utilize historical precedent in conducting guerrilla warfare to the Army's later preoccupation with institutional self-perpetuation and self-aggrandizement. Woven throughout are references to the corrosive attitudinal and behavioral consequences affecting the soldiers and their relationships. (C)

Corson, W. R. (1974). Consequences of failure. New York: Norton.
Explores the social, political, and military aftereffects of U.S. military failure (as distinguished from military defeat) in Vietnam and the prospects for recovery of America's national pride and consensus. In a chapter devoted to "The Military Establishment" (pp. 74-105), Corson—a retiree from the Marine Corps and a veteran of World War II, Korea, and Vietnam—reviews the evolution of the military's broadscale demobilization problems with drug use, dissent, and race relations. He attributes these and other difficulties of the late-war period both to America's failure in Vietnam and to an "erosion of moral principle within the military." He refers to the rise in "fragging" incidents (assaults with explosives on military superiors) as a new servicewide form of psychological warfare and an aspect of institutionalized mutinous behaviors (along with sabotage, evasion of leadership responsibilities, and internecine conflict): "The potential for a mutinous refusal to carry out an order is so widespread that routine actions are being avoided by those in charge." Corson is highly critical of the ethics

of military officers of the late Vietnam period, who "continued to support a war in which human beings by the tens of thousands were slaughtered for no real military advantage." (C)

Eisenhart, R. W. (1975). You can't hack it little girl: A discussion of the covert psychological agenda of modern combat training. Journal of Social Issues, 31(4), 13-24.

　　Eisenhart shares his experiences as a Marine veteran in Vietnam to explain the process that led to his founding of the self-help project, "Flower of the Dragon" (Eisenhart, 1977). He illustrates how intimidation and attacks on sexual identity were used in basic training to achieve psychological control of recruits and to equate masculinity with fulfillment of the military mission. The emotional conflicts begun in training were often exacerbated by the Vietnam experience in which the soldier's trained aggressiveness was frustrated by the enemy's refusal to engage. Finally, he notes how the homecoming reception given them as veterans of an unpopular war did not offer the celebration conducive to reintegration into society that veterans of previous wars have received. (M)

Falk, R. A., Kolko, G., & Lifton, R. J. (Eds.). (1971). Crimes of war. New York: Random House.

　　Uses essays, historical legal documents, U.S. policy documents, and eyewitness accounts from the war in Vietnam to clarify the responsibility of leaders, citizens, and soldiers for criminal acts in war. According to the editors, this work was stimulated by the disclosures of the 1968 My Lai massacre as well as by mounting unofficial evidence pointing toward broadscale strategic and tactical war crimes by the American forces and their allies. They are unified in contending that the general criminal behavior of the troops in Vietnam is the predictable consequence of corrupt governmental and military policies. Lifton remarks, "My Lai illuminates, as nothing else has, the essential nature of America's war in Vietnam. . . . Atrocities are committed by desperate men--in the case of My Lai, men victimized by the absolute contradictions of the war they were asked to fight, and by the murderous illusions of their country's policy. Atrocity, then, is a perverse quest for meaning, the end result of a spurious sense of mission, the product of false witness" (p. 23). (See also Bourne, 1971; Livingston, 1969, September 20; Norden, 1971; Schell, 1968; Sterba, 1971.) (C)

Ferencz, B. B. (1968). War crimes law and the Vietnam war. American University Law Review, 17, 403-423.

　　Reviews the principles of international law established by the Military Tribunal at Nuremberg after World War II, and examines

the political and military circumstances leading to U.S. intervention in Vietnam. Ferencz considers the evidence attesting to the
conduct of military activities there and concludes that America is
not guilty of war crimes, crimes against peace, or crimes against
humanity, nor is its involvement in Vietnam unconstitutional. He
notes how certain ambiguities pertaining to conditions in Southeast
Asia make classification difficult: "International law has not yet
developed to a point where it clearly defines what constitutes a
Crime against Peace in conflicts which contain an explosive mix-
ture of nationalistic opposition to foreign domination, civil war
and social revolution." He also acknowledges that a drafted citizen
faces a dilemma in that, since "the Selective Service Act is a valid
exercise of Congressional power," refusal to be inducted is unlaw-
ful and invites prosecution in the civilian justice system. If, upon
entering the service, the new soldier then refuses to serve in
Vietnam, he likely will be convicted by military court martial. (C)

Fitzgerald, F. (1972). Fire in the lake: The Vietnamese and the
Americans in Vietnam. Boston: Atlantic--Little, Brown.
    Seeks to understand the fundamental nature of America's
"fruitless and immoral" war in Vietnam by tracing the unfolding
historical, social, political, and military features that led to the
collision between two such incompatible cultures. Among Fitzgerald's conclusions in this extensively documented work is that
"the civilians may neglect or try to ignore it, but those who have
seen combat must find a reason for that killing; they must put it
in some relation to their normal experience and to their role as
citizens. The usual agent for this reintegration is not the psychiatrist, but the politician. In this case, however, the politicians
could give no satisfactory answer to many of those who had killed
or watched their comrades being killed." (C)

Gibson, J. W. (1986). The perfect war: Technowar in Vietnam. New
York: Atlantic Monthly Press.
    Presents a critical analysis of U.S. assumptions, goals, poli-
cies, strategy, and methods that led to the foreign policy failure
and military defeat in Vietnam. Gibson especially faults America's
technologically based managerial approach: "Never was the 'other-
ness' of the foreign Other really questioned, nor was the social
world of the Vietnamese peasantry examined, nor were the terrible
contradictions and double-reality facing U.S. soldiers in the field
ever confronted." (C)

Hauser, W. (1973). America's Army in crisis: A study in civil-
military relations. Baltimore, MD: Johns Hopkins University Press.
    Explores the "identity crisis" within the U.S. Army of 1971 (a
crisis of "confidence," "conscience," and "adaptation" to American

social change) through empirical and theoretical considerations of three salient aspects: (1) recruitment policies and results--that is, the degree to which traditional military practices have actually altered the soldier's life-style, in contrast to civilian norms; (2) military professionalism--that is, the apparent current core value system of the armed services, especially in regard to war crimes, corruption, and careerism; and (3) degree of the military's isolation from civilian society--that is, measures of psychological and cultural distance, as well as the influence on the military of the burgeoning spillover of civilian issues of race and dissent, discipline and justice, and drugs. Hauser uses these three aspects as key analytic measures and outlines their contemporary features and historical antecedents. They are felt to reflect an army in urgent need of adaptive reform. They are likewise used to highlight similarities between the U.S. Army of 1971 and armies of other modern, Western, democratic, urban-industrial countries, which have undergone similar processes of adaptation as their societies experienced vast social change. (C)

Johnson, H., & Wilson, G. C. (1972). Army in anguish. New York: Pocket Books. (Originally published as a nine-part series in the Washington Post, 1971, September 12-21.)
    Discusses the decline of ethics, morale, and discipline in the U.S. Army during the latter period of the Vietnam war, the combination of which, in the authors' judgment, has created a crisis that threatens the Army's survival as an institution in its present form. The overview includes such issues as violence against superiors ("fragging"), racial conflict, drug abuse, and crime against soldiers on and off military installations. (M)

Just, W. (1970). Military Men. New York: Alfred A. Knopf
    Through detailed accounts of his site visits, journalist Just explores the character, disposition, motivation, and especially the reactions of those in the late Vietnam-era stateside Army to the declining American military, social, and political situation. He interviews soldiers at two Army infantry posts and cadets at the U.S. Military Academy at West Point. He also talks with representative senior sergeants, generals, retired officers, and successful officers who had not attended West Point. (C)

Karnow, S. (1983). Vietnam: A history. New York: Viking.
    This work, published in conjunction with public television's 1983 series on the war, covers the entire scope of events from the 1945 anti-French colonial uprising through the fall of the Saigon government to the communists in 1975. It especially focuses on the political and military events that occurred in Vietnam after the Americans arrived. A central theme is that America's leaders,

prompted as much by domestic politics as by global ambitions, carried the United States into Southeast Asia with little regard for the realities of the region, but that the conflict arose from and was ultimately decided by the forces of Vietnamese history. (C)

Lang, K. (1980). American military performance in Vietnam: Background and analysis. Journal of Political and Military Sociology, 8, 269-286.
     In this extensively documented sociological review of the "American fiasco in Vietnam," Lang uses comparisons from previous American wars as well as from the British conflict in South Africa and that of the French in Algeria ("both resembling the war in Vietnam as representing a disparity of strength between opponents with a major power employing its arsenal of modern weapons against an essentially guerrilla force"). He argues that, although much of the American troop disaffection, indiscipline, and dysfunction in Vietnam that followed the 1968 enemy Tet offensives is familiar in its form as a predictable demoralization reaction, it was nonetheless aggravated by organizational policies and the type of warfare being conducted. Further, the deviance so produced became politicized only through contact with the home front and crystallized along the more visible cleavages of race, risk, and career commitment to the military. Lang warns against seeking a single factor explanation for something as multifaceted as the overall performance in Southeast Asia. (C)

Radine, L. B. (1977). The taming of the troops: Social control in the United States Army. Westport, CT: Greenwood Press.
     Seeks to show how the U.S. Army functions generally to extend bureaucratic control in all its diversity and subtlety, and specifically to suppress resistance of its members. Examining the evolution of the Army's means of exercising leadership and discipline, as well as its institutions for mental health, military law and courts, and confinement, Radine argues that, throughout the Vietnam era and afterward, there has been an overall shift in Army controls from coercion to manipulation, and that the Army serves as a vanguard bureaucracy in developing new techniques of class control. (C)

Savage, P. L., & Gabriel, R. A. (1976). Cohesion and disintegration in the American Army: An alternative perspective. Armed Forces and Society, 2, 340-376.
     Contends that available statistics regarding the composition and performance of the U.S. Army during the Vietnam war compare unfavorably with those of the Wehrmacht in World War II and the French forces in Indochina. The authors further argue that the American Army's severe disintegration of primary group

cohesion and commitment "under comparatively minimal stress" in Vietnam was the direct consequence of reduced officer professionalism (as "expressed in the pervasive phenomenon of managerial careerism") and not of sociopolitical changes in American society. (See also Faris, 1977.) (C)

Shatan, C. F. (1977). Bogus manhood, bogus honor: Surrender and transfiguration in the U.S. Marine Corps. Psychoanalytic Review, 64, 585-610.
    Argues that the methods applied in classical Marine Corps basic training (as well as the ethos of the Corps more generally) serve as systematic attempts to "smash and recast" the recruit's personality through a process of institutionalized brutality. The ultimate goal is for him to surrender himself to military authority so as to be prepared to effect "depersonalized slaughter--(his) own or that of others." Shatan posits that "the loss of ego boundaries produced by this total assault enhance the possibility of future regressions side by side with dependency on the omnipotent officer." (C)

Sherrill, R. (1970). Military justice is to justice as military music is to music. New York: Harper & Row.
    Presents a series of case examples, including the Presidio "mutiny" trial and the court martial of Dr. Howard Levy, to demonstrate what Sherrill contends is the characteristic misuse of the military justice system by commanders to suppress legitimate dissent by service members. (C)

3 Men Facing the Military: Selection, Motivation, Indoctrination, Performance, Resistance, and Revolt

Atkinson, R. M. (1971). Ineffective personnel in military service: A critique of concepts and rehabilitation practices from a psychiatric viewpoint. American Journal of Psychiatry, 127, 1612-1618.

Ineffectiveness in military service has usually been shown to be the product of transactional psychosocial processes, although a contrary official attitude holds that it is the result of personality deficits. Rehabilitation practices vary widely in the armed services, often for reasons having little to do with the psychopathology of the ineffective individual. Atkinson concludes that with broader application of model military rehabilitation and crisis intervention programs, the armed services could profitably promote both organizational and individual effectiveness. (MA)

Badillo, G., & Curry, G. D. (1976). The social incidence of Vietnam casualties: Social class or race. Armed Forces and Society, 2, 397-406.

Through statistical comparison of Vietnam casualty statistics with variables of race, income, education, and parental occupation, the authors refute the allegation that the soldier's race was a prime determinant of his being a battlefield casualty. Examining data regarding 10 Cook County, IL, communities and using multiple regression analysis, they determined that those of lower socioeconomic origins, regardless of race, were overrepresented among the casualties. Further, they comment that among enlisted soldiers, the military assignment process, operating solely on efficiency principles, relied on criteria that were highly contingent on socioeconomic status origins to channel individuals from lower-class backgrounds into positions more susceptible to combat casualties. (C)

Barnes, P. (1972). The plight of the citizen-soldier. New York: Alfred A. Knopf.

Critiques the goals, policies, regulations, and methods of the military and offers recommendations Barnes believes will help it adapt to today's less militarily motivated citizen. (C)

Baskir, L. M., & Strauss, W. A. (1978). Chance and circumstance: The draft, the war, and the Vietnam generation. New York: Alfred A. Knopf.

Depicts how millions of young Americans responded to the
war in Vietnam. The emphasis is placed on documenting the numbers who served, who resisted, who were drafted, who were killed,
etc., based on the authors' extensive research. The following are
included among their findings: (1) although 27 million men were
draft eligible during the war years, only about a third served and
only 10% served in Vietnam; (2) of the 200,000 who were officially
charged for violating draft laws, only 3,000 ever went to jail; and
(3) although there were only 24 proven cases of desertion on the
battlefield, 20,000 men who served honorably in Vietnam "deserted"
upon return to the United States. (M)

Bell, D. B. (1979). Characteristics of Army deserters in the DOD
special discharge review program (Report No. 1229). Arlington, VA:
U.S. Army Research Institute for the Behavioral and Social
Sciences.
    Describes the characteristics and experiences of Army de-
serters participating in the Department of Defense Special Discharge Review Program (SDRP) and draws inference from the data
about desertion during the Vietnam era. Participants were divided
into two groups: those who lived in foreign lands while absent
without leave (AWOL) and those who did not. These groups, in
turn, were compared with other deserters and soldiers of the era.
Participants in the SDRP were not typical deserters of the time:
81% of them were exiles, compared with 1%-5% for the era as a
whole. The demographic profile of the exiles in the program was
quite different from that of the typical deserters and from soldiers, in general, of that era. For example, compared with soldiers,
the exiles were much more likely to be white, highly educated,
and high in mental ability. That finding was anticipated in view of
similar findings in a reanalysis of data from the Ford Clemency
Program. Exiles were also less likely to have served in Vietnam.
Compared with other deserters, they were much more likely to
have left the Army for antiwar reasons and to have planned to
desert rather than gone AWOL. In contrast, the nonexiled deserters resembled the "classic" deserter profile of this and previous
conflicts. These findings strongly suggest that the Vietnam era
produced more than one type of deserter, which should be kept in
mind when describing the era. (MA)

Borus, J. F., Stanton, M. D., Fiman, B. G., & Dowd, A. F. (1972).
Racial perceptions in the Army: An approach. American Journal of
Psychiatry, 128, 1369-1374.
    In order to assess racial attitudes and perceptions of Army
life, the authors developed and administered the Racial Perceptions
Inventory (RPI) to two widely different military populations
($\underline{N}$ = 471) (in 1970 and 1971). The findings demonstrate a significant difference in the racial perceptions of black and white sol-

diers at different positions in the Army chain of command, with black soldiers perceiving substantially more discrimination in the military. The authors discuss possible causes of this differential perception and the potential uses of the RPI to stimulate change in major social institutions. (A)

Cortright, D. (1975). Soldiers in revolt: The American military today. Garden City, NY: Anchor Press.

Seeks to document and analyze the GI resistance movement that flourished during the later part of the Vietnam era. This thoroughly documented historical account, motivated by Cortright's own service experiences as an antimilitary organizer, traces the rise in antimilitary incidents, the emerging resistance organizations, and the institutional responses against the salient contextual features of the times. Cortright argues for reforms that range from the discontinuance of U.S. "global interventionism" and the establishment of greater democratic control of the military, to the broadscale relaxation of service disciplinary policies "as a means of checking the arbitrary power of commanders" and the elimination of the "indignities and petty harassments of the military caste system." (C)

Datel, W. E. (1976). A summary of source data in military psychiatric epidemiology. Alexandria, VA: Defense Documentation Center (Document AD No. A 021-265).

Consolidates and summarizes historical data that in some instances predates World War I. The work reviews information on several indicators of neuropsychiatric disease among various U.S. military populations: (1) rate of disease diagnoses resulting from hospitalization, (2) rate of visits to outpatient facilities, and (3) number and proportion of beds occupied in hospitals. Army populations receive the greatest emphasis. Among the findings are that, beginning in the late 1960s and after a quiescence, the worldwide incidence of neuropsychiatric disease among Army personnel rose at the last observation point (mid-1973) to near the peak level seen during the Korean war (19.90 hospitalized episodes/1,000 persons/year); that the psychosis rate for worldwide active duty Army had never been higher than it was at the time of the last observation point (4.30/1,000 persons/year); that character and behavior disorder diagnoses also peaked at the same point in time; and that the proportion of Army hospital beds in the continental United States occupied for all psychiatric causes was greater in mid-1973 than it had ever been, including the so-called psychiatric disaster period of World War II. (C)

Finn, J. (Ed.). (1968). A conflict of loyalties: The case for selective conscientious objection. New York: Western.

Presents a collection of essays that argue for the establishment of policies and laws that would allow for selective conscientious objector exemption from service in the war in Vietnam.
(C)

Hayes, J. R. (1975). The dialectics of resistance: An analysis of the
GI movement. Journal of Social Issues, 31(4), 125-139.
Little attention has been given by social scientists to the
attempt by a minority of military personnel to create an antiwar,
antimilitary protest movement in the Vietnam-era military. The
purpose of this article is to briefly describe and analyze the GI
movement. Particular attention is focused on: (a) some of the
factors that were instrumental in the genesis and development of
the GI movement, and (b) the military's response to internal resistance. The article concludes with an assessment of the movement and a discussion of some of the reasons why the GI movement was less than successful in mobilizing resistance on a large
scale. (A)

Hayes, T. L. (1971). American deserters in Sweden: The men and
their challenge. New York: Association Press.
Describes the personal situations, attitudes, and assimilation
problems of Americans who became exiles to Sweden when they
deserted from the U.S. armed forces during the Vietnam era.
Characteristically, they contend that their actions were grounded
in morality and patriotism. (C)

Helmer, J. (1974). Bringing the war home: The American soldier in
Vietnam and after. New York: The Free Press.
Presents results of a sociological survey of "alienation"
among 90 Vietnam veterans. The subjects were chosen from
working-class backgrounds (as were most of those who fought and
died in the war), and comparisons were made among three equal
groups: members of the Veterans of Foreign Wars ("straights"),
members of the Vietnam Veterans Against the War ("radicals"), and
opiate dependents ("addicts"). Helmer interprets his data as indicating that the unprecedented rise in overt as well as indirect defiance of the military system (to include opiate use) in Vietnam
among those of lower rank was a working-class soldier's protest
(equivalent to the war resistance expressed by the relatively ex-
empt middle-class youth at home), and that the war only served to
precipitate a crisis in the longer-term alienation of the working
class, pushing them into rebellion and revolt. Moreover, he believes his finding "shatters conventional wisdom about the
character of the American fighting man" and challenges the
prevalent notion that primary-group solidarity in combat explains
away all combat motivation. (C)

Hoiberg, A. (1980). Military effectiveness of Navy men during and after Vietnam. Armed Forces and Society, 6, 232-246.

Presents a study of correlates of effectiveness in Navy personnel from 1966 through the 1970s. Hoiberg includes a review of relevant statistics and concludes that service effectiveness relates to variations in the interaction of individual character and ethics, environmental factors, and the organizational climate. (C)

Johnston, J., & Bachman, J. G. (1971). Young men look at military service. Ann Arbor, MI: University of Michigan, Institute for Social Research.

Compares results of a survey of draft-eligible men, conducted in spring 1969 and again in summer 1970, that inquired about their plans and attitudes toward military service. Among their findings the authors note that the majority shifted from identifying with U.S. political and military policies in Vietnam to feeling alienated from the greater society, the government, and U.S. involvement there. An anti-Vietnam position was highest among those who expected to be drafted or planned to join the Reserves or National Guard and lowest among those who intended to enter the service as officers. (C)

Killmer, R. L., Lecky, R. S., & Wiley, D. S. (1971). They can't go home again. Philadelphia: Pilgrim Press.

Describes various circumstances, motivations, and adaptations of U.S. draft resisters and deserters who left America for Canada to avoid military service and protest U.S. combat activities in Southeast Asia. (C)

Killmer, R. L., & Lutz, C. P. (1972). The draft and the rest of your life. Minneapolis, MN: Augsburg.

Explains the policies and procedures of the Selective Service System and is intended to serve as a guide for draft-eligible men regarding their legal and extralegal (draft evasion) options. (C)

Kline, C. L., Rider, K., Berry, K., & Elrod, J. M. (1971). The young American expatriates in Canada: Alienated or self-defined? American Journal of Orthopsychiatry, 4, 74-84.

Presents findings of a study of 30 military refusers, 10 of whom were deserters, and the wives of the 16 who were married. All subjects resided in Canada in landed immigrant status (Canadian government statistics included 18,000 such men). Although the study methodology is unspecified, the authors report the group as being predominantly white, middle class, Anglo-Saxon Protestant, with high school or college education, and without evidence of psychiatric or characterologic disturbance. Families of origin were generally stable. In the authors' opinion, their decisions to emigrate to Canada were "ego-preserving" and development-promoting solutions to a life crisis in which "cooperation with the Selective Service meant dehumanization and sacrifice of selfhood." None regretted the decision to reject military service and the "decaying American society" to come to Canada. (C)

Loh, W. D. (1975). National loyalties and amnesty: A legal and social psychological analysis. Journal of Social Issues, 31(4), 157-170.
This essay discusses some of the legal doctrines and social psychological concepts relevant to amnesty. From statutes, precedents, and case law, it is argued that national loyalty is an important underlying policy consideration in amnesty. National loyalty can be operationalized in terms of attitudinal measures of national commitment. Questions of policy and research are raised concerning how different types of national commitment held by different war resisters might predispose their acceptance or rejection of an amnesty proposal. (A)

Mantell, D. M. (1974). True Americanism: Green Berets and war resisters--A study of commitment. New York: Teachers College Press.
Presents results of interviews with 50 male U.S. citizens (25 Green Berets and 25 war resisters) to study the origins and course of development of personal violence, nonviolence, and subsequent participation in political events. Questionnaires were also administered to provide background information on their social and sexual development, as well as on their relationships with family, friends, and authority figures. Mantell interprets the data as showing that the different attitudes toward violence between these groups can be explained by contrasting their early training and environment, particularly differences in family background. (M)

Martin, R. (1986). Who went to war. In G. Boulanger & C. Kadushin (Eds.), The Vietnam veteran redefined: Fact and fiction (pp. 13-24). Hillsdale, NJ: Lawrence Erlbaum Associates.
Reviews the military selection process since colonial times. Analysis of data from Vietnam does not support the argument that combat status was assigned on class lines or that proportionately more blacks than whites were sent to Vietnam or were involved in heavy combat. Differential casualty rates along class and racial lines are more easily understood when rank rather than occupational assignment is considered. (S)

Moskos, C. C., Jr. (1970). The American enlisted man: The rank and file in today's military. New York: Russell Sage Foundation.

Reviews historical trends, recent survey data, and participant-observation data collected between 1965 and 1967 with American military units in Vietnam, Germany, Korea, and the Dominican Republic to define the dominant patterns of relationships, attitudes, combat motivations, and reactions to antiwar activists among contemporary enlisted soldiers. Regarding combat motivation in Vietnam during these years, Moskos posits that it "arises out of the linkages between individual self-concern, primary group process, and the shared beliefs of soldiers." Included in the latter is a "latent ideology" of devotion to American ideals as well as an exaggerated masculine ethic, which fosters the initial motivation to enter combat but recedes once the harsh realities of warfare are confronted. (Includes previously published material by Moskos, 1969, November.) (C)

Osborne, J. K. (1971). I refuse. Philadelphia: Westminster.
    Presents Osborne's account and personal reflections on his arrest, conviction, and incarceration for refusing to serve with the U.S. Army. (C)

Peterson, P. B. (1974). Against the tide: An argument in favor of the American soldier. New Rochelle, NY: Arlington House.
    Presents results of various studies of changes in attitudes, beliefs, and preferences within certain Army subgroups. Data include analysis of the relevant literature; Peterson's personal observations as an Army infantry officer; interviews of Army personnel; and questionnaire results. Using the Job Analysis and Interest Measurement (JAIM) instrument, Peterson surveyed 4,008 U.S. Army soldiers and veterans between the years 1966 and 1972. Subgroups included those in Officer Candidate School (OCS) and the same individuals 3 years later; enlisted infantrymen serving in Vietnam in 1969 and upon their return to the States; individuals staying in the Army and those leaving it; and Army students attending the U.S. Army War College. In general, Peterson interprets his findings as refuting the often publicized prejudicial stereotypes of soldiers as oppressed, "brainwashed," violent automatons and of military professionals as inept, naive, or manipulating autocrats. (C)

Regan, D. J. (1981). Mourning glory: The making of a Marine. Old Greenwich, CT: Devin-Adair.
    Interwoven with memories from his two combat tours in Vietnam (1965 and 1968), Regan presents a chronicle of his Marine Corps basic training. His overall emphasis is on how extremely difficult it was to preserve his identity through the ordeal: "They (sought) to destroy utterly our notion that we were unique individuals capable of and desiring self-determination (so that we

could) look boldly into the face of death and conquer the gut-deep panic that results." (C)

Rivkin, R. S. (1970). G.I. rights and Army justice. New York: Grove Press.

Seeks to encourage soldiers who would challenge military authority by providing advice as to how to use relevant laws and regulations and by teaching them how to exploit discrepancies between military regulations and actual practice. (C)

Stapp, A. (1970). Up against the brass. New York: Simon and Schuster.

Presents a personal account of Stapp's experiences as a college draft resister and later as an enlisted soldier in the Army (1966-69) who organized resistance activities with the American Servicemen's Union. (C)

Stevens, F. (1970). If this be treason. New York: Peter H. Wyden.

Describes and analyzes results of interviews with over 50 draft evaders from various regions of the country. Through their accounts, these men reveal similar stages of increased aversion toward serving in the war in Vietnam as their Selective Service System options narrowed. Their ultimate decision to evade the draft is typically troubled by the feeling of having no honorable alternative. (C)

Tauber, P. (1971). The sunshine soldiers. New York: Simon and Schuster.

A personal narrative of the author's basic military training with the Army Reserve. Tauber joined the reserves to avoid service in Vietnam and is devoted to obstructing military authority and indoctrination, a system he views with suspicion and disdain. (C)

Blair, J. D., & Bachman, J. G. (1976). The public view of the military. In N. L. Goldman & D. R. Segal (Eds.), The social psychology of military service (pp. 215-236). Beverly Hills, CA: Sage Publications.

Reports findings of a national survey conducted in late 1972 through early 1973 assessing the public view of the military. The survey was based on two samples: (1) 1,855 civilians age 16 and older, and (2) 2,522 Navy personnel (stratified as to be representative of naval ship and shore stations). Both samples supported a general factor of promilitary sentiment; that is, individuals expressing positive attitudes on one aspect of preferences or perceptions were likely to express positive attitudes on other aspects as well. Variations within the sample tended to be along lines of age and education, with young college graduates being the most negative toward the military. Few differences were found between veterans and nonveterans, with veterans likely to rate the military in the same way they evaluated their own service experience. In sum, the authors state, "our measure of Vietnam dissent did not show the overwhelming rejection of the war generally reported in poll findings. . . . The military organization and the role it plays in society are still positively evaluated by the average person." (M)

Braestrup, P. (1977). Big story: How the American press and television reported and interpreted the crisis of Tet 1968 in Vietnam and Washington (2 vols.). Boulder, CO: Westview Press.

Provides a comprehensive review and critique of the press coverage of the war, especially its role in interpreting the enemy's 1968 Tet offensives and evoking a reversal in public and political support for the government and the military. (C)

Fanning, L. A. (1976). Betrayal in Vietnam. New Rochelle, NY: Arlington House.

Provides a critical account of the influence of the antiwar movement, especially in Congress. (C)

Hallin, D. C. (1984). The media, the war in Vietnam and political support: A critique of the thesis of an oppositional media (Abstract). The Wilson Quarterly, 8, 25-26. (Original article published in the Journal of Politics, 1984, February, University of Florida, Gainesville.)

Having surveyed 779 television network news reports on the war that were broadcast between August 1965 and January 1973, Hallin found marked changes in television news coverage after the communists' surprise 1968 Tet offensives. Prior to then, positive television news assessments of U.S. prospects in Vietnam outnumbered negative ones by 10:1; afterward, the ratio was roughly 1:1. Overall, editorializing by television newsmen was rare (8%), with reporters relying as heavily on government spokesmen after Tet as they had earlier and rarely questioning their reliability. In sum, Hallin argues that television coverage of Vietnam changed not because newsmen were suddenly at odds with their government, but because the nation's political leadership was increasingly divided, reflecting the dissolving consensus behind the U.S. war effort. (C)

Halstead, F. (1978). Out now!: A participant's account of the American movement against the Vietnam war. New York: Monad Press.

Provides a detailed and factual insiders' history of the radical antiwar movement from its earliest protest demonstrations against American intervention in Vietnam in spring 1964 as the number of U.S. military personnel exceeded 20,000. Included in the chronology are various descriptions of movement activities and achievements that were designed to undermine military activities in Vietnam by influencing the soldiers assigned there. Halstead's bias regarding America's intentions in Vietnam is acknowledged throughout the work: "In reality, U.S. intervention had a thoroughly imperialistic character. The colossus of world capitalism hurled its military might without provocation against a small and divided colonial nation thousands of miles away struggling for self-determination and unification." Further, he shares the leftist ideology of many of the movement's leaders: "The prolonged civil war in South Vietnam thereby proved to be an integral part of the international confrontation between the upholders of capitalism and the forces moving in a socialist direction that has been unfolding since the October 1917 Bolshevik revolution." (C)

Heath, G. L. (Ed.). (1976). Mutiny does not happen lightly: The literature of the American resistance to the Vietnam war. Metuchen, NJ: Scarecrow Press.

Summarizes the chronology of the development of the Vietnam war resistance movement from 1964 through 1972 and provides documentation (flyers, leaflets, letters, reports, manuals, etc.) of the beliefs, goals, and activities of over 100 resistance groups, many organized on university campuses. According to Heath, these selected materials, with their "eloquence, integrity, bitterness, and desperation, (give testimony for) one of the great moral, political, and military agonies of our time." The volume also includes a selected bibliography of over 700 references "that illuminate the context and substance of The Resistance to the United States' misadventure in Vietnam." (C)

Hollander, N. (1971). Adolescents and the war: The sources of socialization. Journalism Quarterly, 48, 472-479.
    Reports survey results of high school seniors in 1969 as to questions regarding the sources of their attitudes about the war in Vietnam (i.e., "political socialization"). The dominant source mentioned by the most respondents was television, with newspapers and magazines following in importance. Hollander notes, "for this vital political issue the role of the family as a source appears to have vanished. . . . The new parent is the mass media." (C)

Huntington, S. P. (1976). The soldier and the state in the 1970s. In F. D. Margiotta (Ed.), The changing world of the American military (pp. 15-35). Boulder, CO: Westview Press.
    Using survey and other data, Huntington reviews the vicissitudes in American civil-military relations during this century to include the aftermath of the Vietnam war. He notes that public sentiment toward the American military in the early Vietnam war period was an extension of the cold war pattern and represented a nontraditional toleration of the military. The 1960s witnessed a momentous and dramatic "democratic surge" in American public life, causing a renewed commitment to the traditional ideals of equality, liberty, democracy, and openness in government, and a concomitant challenging of the authority of established political, economic, and social institutions. This brought the period to a close, with the prolonged Vietnam war serving to galvanize anti-military sentiment as well as to raise the question of the role of military force in a foreign civil war (quoting Moskos, "anti-militarism has become the anti-semitism of the intellectual community"). Further, the draft brought into the military this "democratic surge," with its challenge to established authority, counterculture, and racial tensions: "instead of being tolerated by liberal society, the military establishment was being invaded by it." Finally, Huntington points out that strong tendencies existed within the armed services in the late 1960s and early 1970s to adopt life-styles and human relations similar to these civilian patterns, thereby reducing traditional concepts of rank, discipline, and authority (e.g., "The Army wants to join you!"). (C)

Keniston, K. (1968). Young radicals: Notes on committed youth. New York: Harcourt Brace and World.
    Builds a psychological profile of the committed radical of the American New Left through interviews with 16 young (average age 23) resistance leaders and observations of their activist movement

over the summer of 1967. Explanatory considerations include the interaction effects of background, early family experiences, and social influence more generally, as well as later developmental events juxtaposed with the historical context. Keniston, who is himself an avowed radical, acknowledges that his is not a neutral study and expresses his sympathy with the subjects of his research in their sense of urgency to bring about an end to the war in Vietnam. (C)

Mueller, J. E. (1971). Trends in popular support for the wars in Korea and Vietnam. American Political Science Review, 65, 358-375.

Analyzes the patterns of American popular support for these two wars based on responses to national opinion polls over their respective courses. In the case of the Korean war, conclusions regarding the extent of popular support were believed to be confounded by the pervasive anticommunist sentiment of the times, which led to an overriding desire to support the political leadership of the country. However, a general downward trend was measurable, with a marked drop after the Chinese entered the war in 1950. But unlike the Korean war, the war in Vietnam had no clear-cut beginning. For most Americans it first became significant in 1965 with the massive influx of U.S. troops and the sustained bombing by American planes. Support peaked late in that year and showed a much more gradual decline than in Korea. The data find supporters for both wars "disproportionately among the affluent, the better educated, and--contrary to popular wisdom--the young." The decline in popular support for both wars is explained as a logarithmic function of the number of casualties sustained. While it is commonly thought that the Vietnam war was more unpopular than the Korean war, that impression must in part be considered as a function of its doubled duration. The data do not suggest that the opposition to the Vietnam war was more extensive than that to the war in Korea. (M)

Mullen, R. W. (1981). Blacks and Vietnam. Washington, DC: University Press of America.

Traces black America's evolving attitudes as reflected in the speeches and published remarks of prominent black orators and public figures through the course of the war in Vietnam. These attitudes were at first limited to civil rights goals, but they subsequently broadened to include widespread opposition to the war because blacks identified with dark-skinned Asian "brothers" who were perceived as also victims of white America's neocolonial genocidal policies. Mullen regrets that there remains fractionalization within today's black community in the wake of the war but is hopeful that future political unity may center around the more resolute returning black veterans. (C)

Powers, T. (1973). The war at home: Vietnam and the American people, 1964-1968. New York: Grossman Publishers.
     Provides a history of America's social and political upheaval in response to U.S. foreign policy and combat activities in Vietnam. Powers chronicles the evolution of the antiwar movement from its beginnings in the early 1960s, springing from the civil rights and student free speech movements. He seeks "to show how the opposition created and then organized itself, and to demonstrate the ways in which it finally forced (President) Lyndon Johnson to abandon his chosen policy." (C)

Sanford, N., & Comstock, C. (Eds.). (1971). Sanctions of evil: Sources of social destructiveness. San Francisco: Jossey-Bass.
     Presents a group of articles that reflects the evolution of social destructiveness--that is, how dehumanization occurs, how sanctions for evil come to exist, and how people cooperate in doing harm or in failing to prevent it. Central to editors' argument is the notion that most social destructiveness is done by people who believe they are justified in doing what they do and regard their victims as un-entitled to basic human rights. The book's focus is on the period of the mid-1960s and the war, and it particularly owes its inception to reactions to the My Lai massacre in 1968. The authors posit that social destructiveness can be reduced by organized self-enhancement among victim groups, by avoiding the pathology of defensiveness, and by going beyond prevention through promotion of humanitarian values and cooperation among future generations. (M)

Schuman, H. (1972). Two sources of antiwar sentiment in America. American Journal of Sociology, 78, 513-536.
     Reviews published measures of public opinion toward the Vietnam war and hypothesizes that, because they peaked at different points in the war, the college-related protests and the wider public disenchantment have sharply different characteristics. Schuman tested this hypothesis through interviews in 1971 with a cross-section of Detroit adults (N = 1,263) and a small sample of University of Michigan students (N = 236) who had previously expressed opposition. Thematic analysis of the responses revealed two separate objections to the war: a moral one, primarily voiced by the student population; and a pragmatic one of somewhat lesser intensity, voiced by the general population and based on the failure to achieve a military victory. Moreover, among the more educated, especially the younger individuals, there was greater moral criticism of government action in Vietnam, while among the less educated, objection was more in terms of danger to American lives. Women were more likely than men to mention "people killed or injured" as reasons for their objection. Blacks appeared to be concerned less with winning the war and more with the idea that

the war is racist and genocidal. Regarding the prospect of America's involvement in a future war, twice as many of those voicing pragmatic objections (50%) would involve themselves in one as those voicing moral objections (25%). (M)

Stern, L. (1978). America in anguish, 1965 to 1973. In A. R. Millett (Ed.), A short history of the Vietnam war (pp. 3-12). Bloomington: Indiana University Press. (Originally published in the Washington Post, 1973, January 28.)

Reviews the history of rising public and, later, political opposition to America's war in Southeast Asia, and provides examples of increasingly agonized Americans seeking to express their defection from the government and its policies. Stern sees a strong association between the increasing stridency of the antiwar protests and the widening effect of the draft. He also underscores as instrumental the role of television, which intruded the war into American homes, vividly portraying the "devastation that was being inflicted on a remote peasant society" as well as impressing upon viewers the "spectacle of Americans dying and bleeding in the mountains and paddies." (C)

Teevan, R. C., & Stamps, L. W. (1973). A motivational correlate of Viet Nam protest group members. Psychological Reports, 33, 777-778.

Using projected stimulus slides, researchers gave the Hostile Press motivation test to 39 men and women who were active protesters of the U.S. military policy in Vietnam and to 60 nonprotesters. The instrument and method were designed to measure "fear of failure" as a motivator--that is, presence of an overly hostile, paranoid, defensive attitude toward authority figures and tasks in conjunction with the subjects' ambitiousness. The protest group had significantly higher Hostile Press scores than the nonprotest group. The authors interpret the data to suggest the protesting individuals are reacting to the externally imposed restrictions placed upon them by the U.S. government and the Vietnam policy with a form of generalized aggression; in other words, the demonstrations and other protest activities serve as an anxiety-releasing activity. (C)

Waterhouse, L. G., & Wizard, M. G. (1971). Turning the guns around. New York: Praeger.

The authors, who joined forces as fellow members of Students for a Democratic Society, describe their intense objections to the motives and methods of the military and its leaders, as well as their efforts on behalf of the G.I. resistance movement of the late '60s and, later, the protest activities of the Vietnam Veterans Against the War. (C)

Zaroulis, N., & Sullivan, G. (1984). Who spoke up?: American protest against the war in Vietnam 1963-1975. Garden City, NY:
Doubleday.
    Presents a detailed, elaborate, and thoroughly documented
history of the antiwar movement that evolved in America in opposition to U.S. political and military activities in Southeast Asia.
The authors recount the themes, personalities, and events that
shaped the collective protest, which was "unique in human history," and they underscore its importance "not because it stopped
the war, which it may or may not have done, (but) because it ex-
isted (and serves to remind) Americans that times come when citizens can and, indeed, must challenge their government's authority." The authors note that despite the considerable efforts of the
government to discredit and sabotage the dissent, it persisted:
"(T)he Movement survived nevertheless because, in the end, it
spoke for America. It had traveled from the fringes of American
politics into its very heart. The antiwar movement saved the
nation's honor, and saved it not easily but by speaking truth to
those who did not want to hear." (C)

Ziferstein, I. (1967). Psychological habituation to war: A socio-
psychological case study. American Journal of Orthopsychiatry, 37,
457-468.
    Contends that American citizens have regressed, becoming
uncritical of government leaders who have enlarged the war-
making role in Vietnam. This has been effected by such administration practices as barely perceptible gradual escalation, news
management, intimidating public addresses designed to encourage
citizens to overrely on the omniscience of government, and confusion of citizens through excessive or complex justifying details.
The resultant combination of cognitive dissonance and the individual's tendency to suppress dissent has led to a "confused and
helpless infant-citizen who finds comfort in leaving all decisions
to the father figures." Ziferstein recommends several steps in
"sociotherapy" for this collective condition. (C)

5   Youth Revolt and Student Dissent

Altbach, P. G., & Laufer, R. S. (Eds.). (1972). The new pilgrims: Youth protest in transition. New York: David McKay.

This collection of previously published social science essays examines the development and nature of the student protest and youth revolt that escalated throughout America in the late '60s and early '70s. The contributors tend to agree that this movement constitutes a spread from issues orientation in the early '60s to a generational protest movement, and that this occurred primarily due to failures in the civil rights movement and disaffection with the Vietnam war. They note the resultant fusion between political protest and cultural radicalism and explore the structural features of contemporary society that foster the isolation of the student movement. More specific to the war, in "The Revolution as a Trip: Symbol and Paradox" (pp. 251-266), B. G. Myerhoff describes and analyzes the student protest activities occurring at American University in 1970 in response to both the Cambodian invasion and the slaying of Kent State and Jackson State students. The volume also includes a selected bibliography by K. Keniston and M. Lerner on student protest (pp. 313-326). (C)

Bachman, J. G., & Jennings, M. K. (1975). The impact of Vietnam on trust in government. Journal of Social Issues, 31(4), 141-155.

Trust in government dropped dramatically during the late 1960s and early 1970s. Data spanning this period are presented from two nationwide studies of young males. The results show that views about the role of the United States in the Vietnam War played a substantial part in the decline in government trust; however, actual service in the armed forces did not seem to produce a disproportionate drop in that trust. Along a number of other dimensions distinctions emerged between those who did and did not serve; nevertheless, the similarities outweighed the differences. (A)

Bahnson, C. B. (1972). Psychoanalytic theory and problems of contemporary youth. In J. H. Masserman (Ed.), Science and psychoanalysis: Vol. 21. Research and relevance (pp. 237-242). New York: Grune and Stratton.

Uses psychoanalytic theory to define and understand contemporary youth. Bahnson posits that they reject society and its values as being inhuman, destructive, and irrelevant to human needs; particularly disavowed is the value of delaying or giving up immediate need gratification in the service of society. Repression defenses have been replaced by regression defenses with an emergence of more primitive social patterns characterized by hedonism and by oral and narcissistic withdrawal coupled with a magical outlook on life. Youths are not adopting culture-syntonic defensive patterns of sublimation, intellectualization, and displacement because they perceive them to be dishonest. The result is antimilitarism and rejection of the Vietnam war with redirection of aggressive drives toward targets within our society. (C)

Fendrich, J. M. (1974). Activists ten years later: A test of generational unit continuity. Journal of Social Issues, 30(3), 95-118.
    This study focuses on the generational unit born out of the student protest movement. Three groups were selected for the study: (a) former civil rights activists involved in protest demonstrations during 1960 and 1963, (b) former students who had been involved in student government politics during that time, and (c) former students who had taken no part in institutional or noninstitutional politics. The major dependent variables are political attitudes and political behavior eight to eleven years after the student protest. Using path analysis, it was found that the level of student activism had major direct and indirect effects on political attitudes and behavior. Together with other exogenous and intervening variables, student activism accounted for 55% of the variance in political attitudes and 42% of the variance in political behavior. (A)

Flacks, R. (1967). The liberated generation: An exploration of the roots of student protest. Journal of Social Issues, 23(3), 52-75.
    Presents the results of Flacks's research into the sociopsychological roots, especially regarding family socialization, of the surprising rise in student radical protest activity. From his two studies--one a set of interviews conducted with 50 registered student activists and their parents in the summer of 1965, the other consisting of interviews with samples of recent protesters ($\underline{n}$ = 65) and antiprotesters ($\underline{n}$ = 35) in May 1966--Flacks found that the protesting students in general were from urban, highly educated, Jewish or irreligious, professional, and affluent families that exhibited permissive child-raising attitudes. Although the students are more "radical" than their parents, the parents are also more liberal than those of the controls: "Activists and their parents tend to place greater stress on involvement in intellectual and aesthetic pursuits, humanitarian concerns, opportunities for self-expression, and tend to de-emphasize or positively disvalue personal achievement, conventional morality and conventional religiosity." According to Flacks, the protest arises from the students' perceived discrepancy between what they were taught at home and what they experience from their increasing contact with bureaucratic institutions. (C)

Gerzon, M. (1969). The whole world is watching: A young man looks at youth's dissent. New York: Paperback Library.

Explains and argues the attitudes and beliefs that led to the spreading social protest and alienation among contemporary American youth. The central theme is their revolt against the myriad of identity-destroying influences in today's impersonal and technological society. Gerzon, himself a young activist (age 20), remarks, "The cynics were alienated socially because of their distrust of mass society; the activists were alienated politically by the hypocritical values of adult society; the hippies were alienated psychologically by the socially patterned frustrations of modern society . . . (and all were) alienated spiritually by the absence of meaningful character ideals." (C)

Gitlin, T. (1987). The sixties: Years of hope, days of rage. New York: Bantam.

Presents a critical account of the '60s social upheavals, especially the dissent and counterculture of the young, from the vantage point of a leader of one of its most prominent and radical reformist movements, Students for a Democratic Society. (C)

Gottlieb, D. (1970). The rise and fall of the American teenager: A more personal view of the sociology of American youth. Youth and Society, 1, 420-436.

Traces how the structure of society has fostered the creation of a youth culture (in the 1960s). While this phenomenon is not unique to America, industrialization, with its increased affluence and extended period of socialization in educational institutions, provides the time and resources for youth to form their own group distinct from the adult population. This separateness or 'generation gap' engenders a unique set of values and some degree of alienation from the larger society. Gottlieb notes that, traditionally, society has been quicker to adapt to technological changes as opposed to social changes and urges that government and social scientists develop a realistic analysis of youths and their prospects for the future. (M)

Hartocollis, P. (1969). Young rebels in a mental hospital. Bulletin of the Menninger Clinic, 33, 215-232.

Describes an incident of protest and threatened walkout by young patients at the C. F. Menninger Memorial Hospital in 1968. Hartocollis notes its similarity to the spreading rebellion on college campuses and comments that the patient-leaders were college students prior to their hospital admission. He sees the protests of this new generation and these patients as representing a "fundamental force, building up momentum underneath . . . as a crisis of values in our society." He highlights the apparent reversal of roles between the traditional critics (parents or parental surrogates) and those criticized (youth), and further posits that in this hospital crisis, those who outwardly objected to the dissenters were motivated by suppressed sympathies. His recommended solution is engagement short of losing oneself in the involvement: "Such involvement, no longer for the purpose of controlling the situation, enabled us to experience the existing problems, the (patients') frustrated needs and unspoken anxieties." The consequent exchange had the value of enabling the staff to respond to the patients' apparently legitimate concerns, even if not welcoming their "latent" needs. (M)

Horn, J. L., & Knott, P. D. (1971). Activist youth in the 1960's: Summary and prognosis. Science, 171, 977-985.
    Depicts the modal personality of the 1960s youth activist, as distinguished from the alienated "hippie," based on a synthesis of earlier studies. These youth were typically a minority faction of university students from middle- to upper middle-class backgrounds. Studies show that many had formed a close identification with their parents' values. This was often fostered by the parents' love-oriented child-rearing methods (of Dr. Benjamin Spock), which discouraged physical discipline and promoted instead a reasoning attitude with the child. Their fathers' occupations tended to be predominantly socially rather than financially oriented, and politically liberal. The academic achievement of their families was above average. The authors note that "activists were found to score high on tests that indicate a liking for intellectual activities, independence of thought, and openness to ideas." Yet these commendable characteristics are found in an individual who also lacks the experience and resulting wisdom necessary to offer solutions to society's problems and who has consequently become absorbed in dramatizing society's inconsistencies and problems. The authors suggest that this youthful creativity and energy will not yield its maximum social benefit without the offer from the established members of society of an invitation to apprenticeship. (M)

Hughes, H. S. (1969). Emotional disturbance and American social change, 1944-1969. American Journal of Psychiatry, 126, 21-28.
    Reflects on the social tumult of the late '60s and reviews the evolution of the political alienation of young adults as consisting of three successive stages departing from the more confident World War II generation. These shifts within successive youth generations apparently began as a reaction to the inquisition atmosphere of the '50s McCarthy era, passed quickly through the politically committed early '60s phase, and broadened into today's confrontative militant one with "its juxtaposition of anarchism and preemptory silencing of opponents, its peculiar blend of political puritanism and personal license, its cult of 'confrontation' as a

quasi-religious act of witness." Hughes sees in this retrospection a theme of "cumulative disenchantment, a slow seepage of faith in the conventional American pieties" for American youth. More generally within contemporary society he notes a mounting illiberal social mindset, which seems to echo these antiestablishment youth sentiments, looks to psychiatry to heal a "sick society" (implying an absence of individual responsibility), and heralds a cultural tack in which psychiatry's traditional reflective and open stance may be increasingly rejected in favor of a "new all-or-nothing" style that is equally as repressive as the McCarthy period. (C)

Keniston, K. (1967). The sources of student dissent. Journal of Social Issues, 23(3), 108-137.
        Generalizes about the varieties, origins, and consequences of the upsurge in student dissent, based on a review of relevant dissertations and on Keniston's own research. Dissenters are a small vocal minority (about 5% of students) within a "silent" but sympathetic generation of college undergraduates. They participate in demonstrations to draw attention to matters of political, social, or ethical injustice, including the war in Southeast Asia. Keniston faults the stereotype of the dissenter as a maladjusted and alienated bohemian who is attracted to socialist political ideas, and he similarly warns against confusing the apolitical and socially alienated dissenting student ("hippie"), who he considers to be psychologically disturbed, with the socially committed political activist or protester. These "new" activists are still optimistic in their view of society, and they echo the liberal values of their families. Keniston analyzes the collection of personal, social, and historical factors that apparently have combined to increase the frequency of politically motivated activities on American campuses. (C)

Morrison, J., & Morrison, R. K. (1987). From Camelot to Kent State: The sixties experience in the words of those who lived it. New York: Times Books.
        Presents edited interviews with over 50 individuals who lived various roles and activities representative of the socially tumultuous '60s decade. Several recount their military experiences in Vietnam. (C)

Nicholi, A. M. (1970). Campus disorders: A problem of adult leadership. American Journal of Psychiatry, 127, 424-429.
        The psychological determinants of campus disorders can in part be understood in terms of unresponsive and inaccessible adult leaders in the home, the university, and government. A fundamental problem centers around the failure of these adult leaders to listen to youth, to spend sufficient time with them, and thus to recognize and affirm their worth as human beings. Nicholi dis-

cusses various levels of emotional response evoked in students by the remote leader and, based on this formulation, offers eight specific recommendations for working effectively with youth. (A)

Seligman, D. (1969, January). A special kind of rebellion. Fortune, pp. 66-69, 172-175.

Explores the likely causes and consequences of the shift among college students from the "silent generation" of the 1950s-early 1960s to the dissidents of the late 1960s as measured by a series of polls, including a recent Fortune-Yankelovich survey. Seligman notes that although only 2% of college youth are highly visible activists, roughly 40% of their peers hold similar views ("protest prone"), signifying a true generation gap. Of the larger group, approximately half endorse the belief that the United States is a sick society and acknowledge a loss in faith in democratic institutions, and two thirds endorse civil disobedience to promote their causes, especially antiwar protests and draft resistance. (C)

Slater, P. E. (1970). The pursuit of loneliness: American culture at the breaking point. Boston: Beacon Press.

Provides social analysis of the "domestic upheaval now taking place in America." Slater notes the increased radicalism of the draft resistance movements, peace demonstrations, black militancy, hippie communes, and student protests, and he posits that the underlying "somewhat amorphous counterculture" is overtaking the conventional "scarcity-oriented technological culture." He considers the war in Vietnam to be an outgrowth of America's traditional competitive-technological culture: "We engage in the mass slaughter of innocent persons by the most barbarous means possible." Further, he argues that, as a result of accelerating and frustrating technological changes, "Americans have lost their manhood and their capacity to control their environment" and have focused on the enemy in Vietnam as a scapegoat. Slater advocates a purposeful "reversal of our old pattern of technological radicalism and social conservatism." (C)

Starr, J. M. (1974). The peace and love generation: Changing attitudes toward sex and violence among college youth. Journal of Social Issues, 30(2), 73-106.

The period of the sixties marked the emergence of a distinctive generational ideology among a substantial segment of American youth. This "peace and love" ideology featured a high degree of age group consciousness and unique integration of life style and political concerns, the psychological foundation for which was laid by the increased differentiation of age roles and de-differentiation of sex roles associated with advanced industrial development. The expansion of higher education, emergence of the multibillion dollar youth market, and growth of the mass media provided the means by which many such youth were able to achieve consciousness of their common interests and join active generation units with distinctive styles of expression. The war in Indochina constituted the traumatic episode which differentiated the various age groups in America and galvanized the middle class, college segment of the youth cohort into action. (A)

Wangh, M. (1972). Some unconscious factors in the psychogenesis of recent student uprisings. Psychoanalytic Quarterly, 41, 207-223.

Presents collective psychodynamic and developmental theories to explain the diffuse, disorganized, yet prevalent antiauthority/ antimilitary attitude of the youth of the late '60s. Wangh speculates that this generation's departure from the typical periodic revival of idealization of the soldier-hero as a displacement for oedipal tensions is the result of reawakened, shared anxieties secondary to having grown up in the uncertain period of surface testing of nuclear devices. Thus, extensive repression and reaction formation characterize the generation's total disavowal of aggressiveness and represent necessarily drastic defenses to counteract the compound anxieties of age-appropriate revival of oedipal fantasies plus the apocalyptic fantasies. Their predictable regressive reactions include a retreat into mystical religions of universal love, screaming lights and noise, and drugs. (C)

Yankelovich, D. A. (1972). The changing values on campus: Political and personal attitudes of today's college students. New York: Washington Square Press.

Explores the prevailing mood on American college campuses using a 1971 national sample survey of attitudes among college students (N = 1,244) sponsored by the John D. Rockefeller III Fund. Yankelovich notes changing trends by comparing these findings with those from similar surveys he conducted in 1968, 1969, and 1970. He interprets the student movement as being a search for a new moral faith; thus, the trend among these students is to reject the dominant mode of thinking in America (as represented by technology, rationalism, and traditional middle-class sensibility) and to embrace a philosophy that "elevates nature and the natural to the highest position." He discusses 18 overlapping meanings of this "new world view" as expressed in his findings and notes that although the student movement is typically identified with the Left and political radicalism, many of its leading ideas have deep roots in conservative tradition. Prominent in the 1971 findings is that student cynicism and frustration seem to have replaced some the commitment to political revolution seen rising in the previous three surveys, while the somewhat separate though overlapping cultural revolution seems to be continuing undiminished. (C)

Yankelovich, D. A. (1974). <u>A study of American youth</u>. New York: McGraw-Hill.

Presents survey results from 2,516 noncollege youths, including 176 Vietnam veterans. Generally the findings reveal that between 1969 and 1973, a dramatic shift occurred among American youth away from accepted attitudes regarding authority and conformity. Compared with nonveterans, Vietnam veterans showed (1) twice the unemployment rate, (2) lower general morale, (3) more pessimism about the future, (4) greater estrangement from American society, (5) less strictness in their moral viewpoint, and (6) less traditional and more liberal thinking regarding social and political questions.   (C)

6   Drug Use: In Uniform and Among Civilian Peers

Baker, S. L. (1971). Drug abuse in the United States Army. Bulletin of the New York Academy of Medicine, 47, 541-549.
    Reviews the statistical evidence documenting the rising prevalence of illicit drug use within the youth culture in general and within the military over the previous 10 years. Baker also reviews the evolution of the policies and programs within the Army regarding treatment, rehabilitation, retention, and criminal prosecution of drug users. (C)

Black, S., Owens, K. L., & Wolff, R. P. (1970). Patterns of drug use: A study of 5,482 subjects. American Journal of Psychiatry, 127, 420-423.
    Reports results of a drug use survey administered to 5,482 active duty enlisted men in 56 separate Army units in the United States between January and April, 1969. Of that sample, 27% reported having used marijuana, amphetamines, LSD, or heroin; and of those 1,243 drug-positive soldiers, 26% had used LSD and 5% had used heroin. The authors note that because of the large size and variation in background and education of this group of physically and socially functional men, these results may more accurately reflect drug use incidence than those of any previously reported studies. (C)

Brown, C. C., & Savage, C. (Eds.). (1971). The drug abuse controversy. Baltimore, MD: National Educational Consultants.
    Presents the professional perspectives of a diverse and distinguished group of physicians and social scientists who seek to clarify the salient historical, dynamic, and ethical issues pertaining to the "drug explosion" in contemporary American culture. This collection constitutes the proceedings of a symposium of the same name held in October 1970. (C)

Brunner, J. H., Coles, R., & Meagher, D. (1970). Drugs and youth: Medical, psychiatric and legal facts. New York: Liveright.
    Defines and explains various psychological, medical, and legal facets of the controversial "drug scene" spreading widely among American youth, primarily the use of marijuana, hallucinogens, and heroin. The authors take pains to assure the reader of their neutrality: "(Our intention is that this book) . . . not be viewed as yet another mass of credentials designed to shower a rightfully in-

quiring public with rhetoric and to lead that public toward a neat clearcut 'position.' We frankly don't have one and want to say so here and now."   (C)

Callan, J. P., & Patterson, C. D. (1973). Patterns of drug abuse among military inductees. American Journal of Psychiatry, 130, 260-264.

A questionnaire concerning drug abuse was administered to 19,948 new military inductees over a 6-month period (January-June 1971). Almost one third of the subjects had used drugs, but most were casual users. Marijuana and hashish were most frequently used. There were higher rates of use among college dropouts and men from unstable families, urban areas, and families with high incomes. Although there was little racial difference in overall drug use, nonwhites used amphetamines, barbiturates, and heroin twice as much as whites, while whites tended to use marijuana, hashish, and hallucinogens.   (MA)

Calogeras, R. C., & Camp, N. M. (1975). Drug abuse and aggression. Bulletin of the Menninger Clinic, 39, 329-344.

Drawing on their experiences in Europe during 1971-72, the authors elaborate a psychodynamically oriented formulation of the heavily drug-abusing soldiers seen there. They contend that the abusive use of psychoactive drugs by the soldier-adolescent (in the developmental sense) derives special meaning because of the setting of the closed system of military subculture. As a reaction-formationlike "instant defense," the drug experience both (1) regressively recapitulates early passive-aggressive themes providing sadomasochistic gratification, and (2) deflects the aggressive drive into largely self-destructive channels. These soldiers typically have strong predisposing early object losses and consequent ego fragility. They use drugs as an introjective experience to promote a feeling of reunion with the early maternal object along with massive denial of her negative aspects (with the free aggression attached to military leaders). Two cases, one of whom served previously in combat in Vietnam, are provided.   (C)

DuPont, R. L., & Greene, M. H. (1973). The dynamics of a heroin addiction epidemic. Science, 181, 716-722.

Uses statistics from clinical and law enforcement sources to describe the heroin addiction epidemic in the District of Columbia that began in 1966 and peaked in early 1972. Observations include that the age of first use of heroin (as reported by 55% of 13,000 treatment program patients) was 16-20 years old, and that the peak year of first use was 1969. In seeking to explain the decline of heroin use and addiction, the authors focus on three features: (1) increased availability of treatment programs, (2) vigorous local, national, and international law enforcement efforts to reduce the supply, and (3) development of an antiheroin attitude in the community. (C)

Froede, R. C., & Stahl, C. J. (1971). Fatal narcotism in military personnel. Journal of Forensic Science, 16, 199-218.

Reviews the history of drug abuse in military populations, especially among American soldiers, since the Civil War, and presents the demographic, pathologic, and toxicologic characteristics of all cases of fatal narcotism in military personnel ($\underline{N}$ = 174) filed with the Armed Forces Institute of Pathology between 1918 and the first half of 1970. The majority of deaths occurred in the Asian theatres in nonwhite males aged 18-25 and in the three lowest pay grades. Most resulted from drug overdose or hypersensitivity, rather than from the medical complications of narcotic addiction. The rates before and during the mobilization years of World War II are insignificant; they are followed by a slight rise in the closing phases of the war. In 1951-53, an extraordinary increase in deaths occurred, primarily among troops assigned in Korea. A similar marked elevation emerges in 1969-70, and while these rates are not statistically pure, they lead the authors to predict a significant increase in drug abuse among the military population assigned in Southeast Asia during the remaining demobilization period. (C)

Greden, J. F., & Morgan, D. W. (1972). Amnesty's impact upon drug use: A pre/post study. American Journal of Psychiatry, 129, 392-394.

Reports on a survey to determine patterns of drug use and attitudes toward treatment that was conducted shortly before a drug abuse control program was established throughout the Army. Eight months after the program was begun, the survey was repeated using a similar population at the same stateside military installation. Comparison of the surveys revealed no immediate beneficial effects of the program. Reports of previous drug use had increased, the number of those who intended to use nonopiate drugs in the future had increased, willingness to seek treatment remained unchanged, and a great deal of skepticism still prevailed. (MA)

Greden, J. F., Morgan, D. W., & Frenkel, S. I. (1974). The changing drug scene: 1970-1972. American Journal of Psychiatry, 131, 77-81.

Authors used the same questionnaire to survey drug use at a stateside military installation in 1970, 1971, and 1972. Over the 3 years, the percentage of respondents reporting previous drug use increased. Figures on amount of use and number of current users also increased. For most drug types, the increases occurred between 1970 and 1971; heroin use, however, increased each year. The usefulness of specialized short-term drug treatment programs is questioned. (MA)

Gunderson, E. K. E., Russell, J. W., & Nail, R. L. (1973). A drug involvement scale for classification of drug abusers. Journal of Community Psychology, 1, 399-403.
    Describes development of a drug involvement screening instrument from data derived from Navy and Marine enlisted men (N = 590) admitted to the U.S. Naval Drug Rehabilitation Center (July-December 1971). The authors report that the instrument is easy to score and is successful in differentiating degrees of drug involvement over a wide range. They also note that this population may be unique in that 54% of the sample reported heavy use of heroin while assigned in Vietnam, and they speculate that scoring adjustments may be necessary when the instrument is used with other populations. (C)

Hauschild, T. (1971). Marijuana. Military Medicine, 136, 105-109.
    Reviews recent studies on the effects of marijuana, especially considering observations from Vietnam. Psychosis following marijuana use in small amounts has been reported in those with a predisposition to mental illness, but acute brain syndrome is nonetheless correlated with dosage and can occur in anyone. Marijuana has also been found to increase the likelihood of using other drugs, especially when marijuana is unavailable; to result in time and space distortions; and to lead to lethargy and apathy. Typical signs and symptoms of intoxication (e.g., thickened speech, blurred vision, poor concentration, impaired thinking, and a dreamlike, floating state) are associated with marijuana use. Further, there is no evidence to support contentions that it enhances creativity or resolves mental or emotional problems. (C)

Khantzian, E. J., Mack, J. E., & Schatzberg, A. F. (1974). Heroin use as an attempt to cope: Clinical observations. American Journal of Psychiatry, 131, 160-164.
    Suggests that addicts' use of opiates represents a unique and characteristic way of dealing with ordinary human problems and the real world around them. Through five case reports (including one of a Vietnam veteran who smoked heroin while stationed in Vietnam), the authors illustrate how addicts resort to drugs because they have failed to develop symptomatic, characterologic, or other adaptive solutions to stress. In addition, they describe how the pseudoculture of the addict plays a part in filling his social vacuum and providing an alternative to his failure to establish meaningful attachments to other people. The implications for treatment are considered. (C)

Krippner, S. (1972). Marijuana and Viet Nam: Twin dilemmas for American youth. In R. S. Parker (Ed.), The emotional stress of war, violence and peace (pp. 176-225). Pittsburgh, PA: Stanwix House.

Explores the coincident phenomena of mounting marijuana use and rising antiwar sentiment among American youth. In this scholarly essay Krippner opines that, although the evidence indicates that military service in Vietnam or association with returning soldiers promotes accelerated involvement with marijuana among today's youth, marijuana use (as is the case with political alienation) affects only a minority. Further, the public's worry regarding its use represents a social scapegoating in which attention is diverted away from the more critical social ills (racial strife, overpopulation, poverty, and the threat of nuclear attack), which produce today's widespread stress, anxiety, and alienation. (C)

Mizner, G. L., Barter, J. T., & Werme, P. H. (1970). Patterns of drug use among college students: A preliminary report. American Journal of Psychiatry, 127, 15-24.

In a large survey of college student drug use in the Denver-Boulder metropolitan area, almost one third of the students admitted to having used illegal drugs. The most commonly used illegal drug was marijuana, which had been used by 26% of the students. Amphetamines had been used by 14% and LSD by 5%. The authors explore attitudes toward drug use and drug legislation as well as mood states and reasons for drug use. Patterns of drug use are contrasted with a variety of demographic variables and with different college and university characteristics. (MA)

Nace, E. P., Meyers, A. L., Rothberg, J. M., & Maleson, F. (1975). Addicted and nonaddicted drug users: A comparison of drug use patterns. Archives of General Psychiatry, 32, 77-80.

Presents data collected through interviews with 101 stateside multidrug-using soldiers, including 18 Vietnam veterans, regarding drug usage patterns. Analysis revealed little difference between heroin-using soldiers (n = 68) and demographically similar multidrug-using but nonaddicted peers (n = 33). Relatively few differences in drug usage patterns were reported before the onset of heroin addiction, and what differences there were indicated more extensive and more progressive drug use among the nonaddicted users. The authors interpret these data as refuting a "stepping-stone hypothesis" of heroin addiction. Within a few months after first heroin use, those who did not become addicted returned to their preheroin experimentation levels of drug taking while the addicted group maintained an escalating pattern of opiate use. (C)

Nail, R. L., Gunderson, E. K. E., & Arthur, R. J. (1974). Black-white differences in social background and military drug abuse patterns. American Journal of Psychiatry, 131, 1097-1102.

Reports on data gathered regarding the drug use patterns and social backgrounds of 833 Navy enlisted men (764 white and 69 black) admitted to a drug rehabilitation center (July 1971 to October 1972). The typical subject was 20 years old, had served roughly 2 years on active duty including a tour in Southeast Asia, and was of the lowest enlisted ranks. Black subjects reported better school adjustment, less delinquency, and fewer difficulties in their home lives than did whites. They had used heroin more frequently than whites but were less involved with hallucinogenic drugs. The authors suggest that different cultural patterns may underlie the drug abuse behaviors of the two groups: white users seem to be expressing new varieties of delinquent or antisocial behavior while blacks are following long-established subcultural patterns of drug use. (MA)

Nowlis, H. H. (1969). Drugs on the college campus. New York: Doubleday.

Presents results from a 1967 national workshop series that included college and university deans, counselors, and health directors and was sponsored by the National Association of Student Personnel Administrators. In this distillation the participants offer observations on the medical, psychological, social, and legal complexities of the college "drug problem." (C)

O'Donnell, J. A., Voss, H. L., Clayton, R. R., Slatin, G. T., & Room, R. G. W. (1976). Young men and drugs: A nationwide survey (Research Monograph No. 5). Rockville, MD: National Institute on Drug Abuse.

Presents the preliminary report of a nationwide study of psychoactive drug use by young men. Interview data were obtained from 2,510 men (20-30 years old) between October 1974 and May 1975. Noted among the findings was that the peak period of the drug epidemic was 1968-72 or 1969-73 for all drugs except alcohol; that for most drugs, half or more of the users used the drug less than 10 times; that use of any of the nine drug classes was associated with use of all the others; that veterans, regardless of where they served, show no higher rates for current drug use than nonveterans; and that there is no indication of any recent decline in the annual prevalence of use of any drug, with the possible exception of psychedelics. (C)

Rothberg, J. M., Holloway, H. C., Nace, E. P., & Meyers, A. L. (1976). An application of stepwise discriminant analysis to the characterization of military heroin dependents, illicit drug users, and psychiatric patients. International Journal of the Addictions, 11, 819-830.

Describes use of a variation of stepwise linear discriminant function analysis to explore the significance of 28 drug use and 23 nondrug use variables extracted from interviews with soldiers seen at mental health clinics (N = 44) and drug treatment centers (N = 101) at four stateside military posts between December 1970 and January 1972. Among the drug user group, further analyses were conducted to distinguish between those who acknowledged heroin dependency (n = 68) and those with other drug abuse problems (n = 33). The authors report their findings, conclude that this method of analysis is useful in identifying variables that discriminate between the samples under study, and discuss implications for future research on drug abuse behavior. (C)

Sapol, E., & Roffman, R. A. (1969). Marijuana in Vietnam. Journal of the American Pharmaceutical Association, 9, 615-619.

Reviews results of a drug use survey of enlisted soldiers (N = 584) departing Vietnam in 1967 (Roffman & Sapol, 1970) and compares the prevalence rates found among these soldiers (e.g., 31.7% report use of marijuana at least once) with those reported in published studies among university students. The authors note a similarity and deduce that "simply being in Vietnam may not be the most relevant explanation of some marijuana use among soldiers who are assigned there." (C)

Tennant, F. S., Jr., Preble, M. R., Groesbeck, C. J., & Banks, N. I. (1972). Drug abuse among American soldiers in West Germany. Military Medicine, 137, 381-383.

Reports results of a drug survey administered to 3,553 U.S. Army soldiers in West Germany in 1970-71. Findings include that 46% of those surveyed acknowledged use of some illegal drug at least once (95% used marijuana and hashish); users estimated drug use in their units to be 25%-35% higher than did nonusers; and 65% indicated drug use prior to starting military service. The authors note that the overall incidence of drug abuse in this population is similar to that reported for soldiers in Vietnam (45%) and for stateside college students. Additional data on drug use were obtained from over 400 interviews with drug abusers and a review of 100 consecutive drug-related hospital admissions. The authors describe the symptoms of chronic hashish use and summarize data concerning drug-related hospitalizations and deaths. Whereas physical dependence on heroin or barbiturates was rare among identified users, the use of hashish, amphetamines, and "downers" generated definite medical and psychiatric problems. (C)

Wilbur, R. S. (1974). The battle against drug dependency within the military. Journal of Drug Issues, 4, 11-31.

Reviews the evolution of Department of Defense (DOD) policies, initiatives, and results in seeking to counteract the rapid rise in addictive drug use by American service personnel in the early 1970s. Wilbur, then assistant secretary of defense, credits the accelerated technological development and worldwide use of random urine drug screening, as well as the DOD policy of law enforcement and disciplinary exemption for identified drug users, for the notable reduction in drug use within the military and among returnees from Southeast Asia. He highlights the extensive success of military rehabilitation and treatment programs, and notes that the serviceman "caught up in drug abuse" is radically different and more easily treatable than the typical street addict: "He was instead a young average American who succumbed to the heavy pressures of family separation and loneliness, ready drug availability, and who was the product of the drug culture which permeates our society."   (C)

Wyant, W. K., Jr. (1971, July). Coming home with a habit. The Nation, pp. 7-10. (Reprinted in L. J. Sherman & E. M. Caffey, Jr. (Eds.), (1972). The Vietnam veteran in contemporary society: Collected materials pertaining to the young veterans (sec. IV, pp. 187-194). Washington, DC: Veterans Administration.)

Reviews the recent history of Department of Defense, administration, and congressional efforts to determine the scope of the drug abuse problem within the military, especially among the troops assigned in Southeast Asia, and to plan and coordinate preventive and rehabilitative initiatives.   (C)

7   The Soldier and His Family: Crosscurrents of Stress

Bey, D. R., & Lange, J. (1974). Waiting wives: Women under stress. American Journal of Psychiatry, 131, 283-286.
    Describes the normal reactions of 40 wives of noncareer Army soldiers to the abnormal stress of their husbands' assignment to Vietnam. The authors note that little has been done to reduce the stress family members experience when a husband is ordered to combat. They suggest that studies of this group be undertaken and that special programs be developed for their benefit. (C)

Brandon, H. (1984). Casualties: Death in Vietnam; anguish and survival in America. New York: St. Martin's Press.
    Explores the impact of the war in Southeast Asia through transcripts of interviews with surviving relatives and friends of 16 soldiers who died there. (C)

Brown, P. C. (1984). Legacies of a war: Treatment considerations with Vietnam veterans and their families. Social Work, 29, 372-379.
    Reviews the psychological symptoms noted to still affect many veterans years after their tours in Vietnam (e.g., intrusive thoughts, "flashbacks," and nightmares of traumatic combat experiences; persistence of the "psychic numbing" that was adaptive while in Vietnam; painful feelings of guilt and depression related to shameful feelings from taking part in a war that society condemned; and anger) and catalogs the various behavioral difficulties that apparently stem from them (e.g., social isolation, substance abuse, suicide, violent outbursts, and divorce). Brown especially focuses on how these reactions disturb the veteran's functioning as a family member, and he provides a rationale for a modified family therapy. This treatment begins individually so that both the veteran and his wife can have the opportunity to identify their values and needs before confronting the impact his difficulties have had on their relationship. Subsequent participation in support groups of similarly affected couples is therapeutic in that it provides both veterans and their wives with encouragement, nurturance, and positive reinforcement. Wives also gain greater empathy for their husbands' traumatic experiences by reviewing prescribed books and films on the war. (M)

Cahoon, E. P. (1984). An examination of relationships between post-traumatic stress disorder, marital distress, and response to therapy by Vietnam veterans. Dissertation Abstracts International, 45 (4-B), 1279.

Reports results of a survey of 60 Vietnam combat veterans and their spouses who participated in a 7-week couples group that focused on basic communication skills. Study results corroborated the utility of the Vietnam Era Stress inventory. Severity of PTSD strongly correlated with standardized self-report measures of anxiety and marital distress. Overall, spouses expressed more willingness to participate in conjoint treatment than the veterans. However, higher levels of PTSD correlated with the veterans' preference for separate treatment. Postgroup treatment ratings included improvements in global satisfaction and communication, lower anxiety, increased ability to cope, and fewer PTSD symptoms. (C)

Canter, S. (1986). Women friends of men. In G. Boulanger & C. Kadushin (Eds.), The Vietnam veteran redefined: Fact and fiction (pp. 153-164). Hillsdale, NJ: Lawrence Erlbaum Associates.

Explores environmental and personal characteristics that encourage or discourage friendships between the men of the Vietnam generation and women, and discusses how these men's friendships with women differ from friendships with other men and how those differences affect quality of life. (S)

Carroll, E. M., Rueger, D. B., Foy, D. W., & Donahoe, C. P., Jr. (1985). Vietnam combat veterans with posttraumatic stress disorder: Analysis of marital and cohabitating adjustment. Journal of Abnormal Psychology, 94, 329-333.

Reports results of a study comparing indices of self-reported cohabitation and marital adjustment in help-seeking Vietnam combat veterans with PTSD (n = 21) and without PTSD (n = 18), and in veterans with minimal combat experience (n = 21). The PTSD group reported significantly more problems with both expressiveness and aggressiveness toward their partners, and with adjustment in the relationship in general, but they did not differ from the other groups on measures of intimacy and affectionate behavior. Premilitary adjustment, response style, or demographic distinctions were not correlated with these differences. The authors discuss implications of these findings for treatment planning. (C)

Centers for Disease Control Vietnam Experience Study. (1988). Health status of Vietnam veterans: III. Reproductive outcomes and child health. Journal of the American Medical Association, 259, 2715-2719.

Reports additional findings from a multidimensional assessment of the health of Vietnam veterans (see CDC Vietnam Experience Study, Parts I and II, 1988). Vietnam veterans reported more adverse reproductive and child health outcomes than did non-Vietnam veterans. However, children of Vietnam veterans were not more likely to have birth defects recorded on hospital birth records than were children of the control group. (MA)

Colbach, E. M. (1970). Psychiatric criteria for compassionate reassignment in the Army. American Journal of Psychiatry, 127, 508-510.

A significant number of active duty Army personnel request reassignment based on the psychiatric condition of a family member. Often the attending physician predicts dire consequences if the request is not granted. Lack of awareness of current Army policy for judging these requests leads to much false hope and to resultant anger and disappointment. (A)

DeFazio, V. J., & Pascucci, N. J. (1984). Return to Ithaca: A perspective on marriage and love in post traumatic stress disorder. Journal of Contemporary Psychotherapy, 14, 76-89.

Describes types of difficulties in forming satisfactory partnerships seen among Vietnam Vet Center populations and provides metapsychological explanations that take into account both the distortions of the veterans' character development as a result of military service (i.e., a product of the level of combat stress experienced and the "psychotic effects of combat," the lowered morale in Vietnam in the later years of the war, and the tendency for the military to be a "homosexual society" that insists on conformity and encourages the "externalization of aggression") and the personality vulnerabilities they brought into the military (i.e., a product of the younger age of soldiers who served in Vietnam, the plasticity of the adolescent personality, and the degree to which infantile dependence characterized the individual before his tour in Vietnam). Implications for treatment are discussed, especially that which includes partners. (C)

Figley, C. R., & Sprenkle, D. H. (1978). Delayed stress response syndrome: Family therapy indications. Journal of Marriage and Family Counseling, 4, 53-59.

Describes PTSD symptom development in Vietnam veterans as representing a type of chronic catastrophic stress reaction. The authors further elaborate on special implications for treatment within a family therapy program. (C)

Gonzalez, V. (1970). Psychiatry and the Army brat. Springfield, IL: Charles C. Thomas.

Presents a series of clinical studies of military children to illustrate common stresses on military children and the relationship between stress--primarily that resulting from extended father absence--and reaction. Paradoxically, the return of the father became more of a crisis than his departure, especially for the adolescent. Gonzalez considers the impact of frequent family moves and culturally mixed marriages. He also describes difficulties in adapting to the military father's death or injury. Finally, he presents an overview of the medical and psychiatric help available to military families. (C)

Herndon, A. D., & Law, J. G. (1986). Post-traumatic stress and the family: A multimethod approach to counseling. In C. R. Figley (Ed.), Trauma and its wake: Vol. 2. Traumatic stress theory, research, and intervention (pp. 264-279). New York: Brunner/Mazel.
    Describes effects of PTSD on Vietnam veterans and their families, and some treatment approaches used within the VA. For most veterans, 10 or more individual therapy sessions are provided to develop sufficient ego strength to benefit from a group experience. The next 3-4 sessions focus on the veteran's general adjustment and difficulties. The following 3-4 sessions deal with the meanings he has ascribed to his experiences in Vietnam and to his reentry into civilian life. Group counseling for veterans' wives provides education about combat experience, PTSD, and how PTSD can hamper a marital relationship. From this, specific problem areas in the marriage are targeted for change. Couple groups are then conducted so that veterans and wives can share feelings and expectations. (S)

Hunter, E. J., den Dulk, D., & Williams, J. W. (1980). The literature on military families, 1980: An annotated bibliography. Colorado Springs, CO: USAF Office of Scientific Research.
    Contains over 480 references on military family literature. The majority of those that relate to the war in Vietnam are regarding POW/MIA families. (C)

Lieberman, E. J. (1971, April 19). War and the family: The psychology of anti-grief. Modern Medicine, pp. 179-183, 191.
    Notes that although over 250,000 Americans lost an immediate family member in Vietnam, the war seems to have lacked public acknowledgment and grief. Lieberman considers that a social-psychological "anti-grief" has instead predominated as the nation's mode of denying the realities of modern-day warfare (i.e., stoic detachment is valued and mourning is considered to be unmanly, a loss of self-control, and a threat to the good of society). He underscores that in the service of growth and adaptation, grieving for these losses is necessary to allow for ambivalences toward the dead person to be "faced, worked through, and integrated." The war widow and disabled veteran must "first mourn that missing

part of their lives, in order to reconstitute their lives on a meaningful basis." (C)

Lieberman, E. J. (1971). American families and the Vietnam war. Journal of Marriage and the Family, 33, 709-721.
Using demographics and statistics from previous American wars, Lieberman describes the impact of war on the family, including problems surrounding the death or wounding of fathers, father absence, divorce, gender-linked roles, and resocialization of veterans. The Vietnam conflict is regarded as unique in that it had high levels of socioracial discrimination consequent to the draft, poverty among lower ranking servicemen, and a greater proportion of disabled or poorly adjusted veterans. The mounting divorce rate among military families, veteran antipathy toward the war, and veteran perceptions of a lack of public and governmental support lead Lieberman to recommend increased government expenditures. (C)

MacIntosh, H. (1968). Separation problems in military wives. American Journal of Psychiatry, 125, 260-265.
Reports results of a study of 63 service wives complaining of psychiatric symptoms resulting from separation from their husbands because of his military duties. They were compared with a control group of 113 women displaying similar symptoms but without such separation as a factor. The separated wives were significantly younger, more often married to enlisted servicemen, less educated, and more often Army rather Air Force wives. Among them, 30% requested their husbands be reassigned back with them (a request that was significantly less common, however, among women with husbands serving in Southeast Asia). MacIntosh advocates discouragement of this alternative to mitigate against "regression" of military wives and their adoption of a "sick role" while "denying the social reality of being a military wife." He also emphasizes the great need for accessible psychiatric treatment for separated military wives. (C)

Marrs, R. (1985). Why the pain won't stop and what the family can do to help. In W. E. Kelly (Ed.), Post-traumatic stress disorder and the war veteran patient (pp. 85-101). New York: Brunner/Mazel.
Uses case histories of 3 Vietnam combat veterans to illustrate how the family is affected by the veteran's attempts to cope with his experiences in Vietnam. Marrs presents guidelines for communication between the veteran and his family, and catalogs problems faced both by the veteran's partner and by the veteran as described by his partner. (S)

Rosenheck, R., & Nathan, P. (1985). Secondary traumatization in children of Vietnam veterans. Hospital and Community Psychiatry, 36, 538-539.

Discusses the potential for intergenerational transmission of PTSD from veterans traumatized in combat in Vietnam to their children. The authors use an illustrative case example of "secondary traumatization" in a 10-year-old boy, and note that, in their clinical experience, such a child, "exposed to these 'reliving' experiences in a traumatized parent, identifies with the parent and experiences in fantasy the same kinds of events his parent actually lived through. In an attempt to imitate and identify with the adults on whom they depend, these children internalize a frightening reality far removed from them in space and time." (C)

Silver, S. M., & Iacono, C. U. (1986). Symptom groups and family patterns of Vietnam veterans with post-traumatic stress disorders. In C. R. Figley (Ed.), Trauma and its wake: Vol. 2. Traumatic stress theory, research, and intervention (pp. 78-96). New York: Brunner/Mazel.

Reviews and expands on a previously published study of the validity of the DSM-III diagnosis of PTSD and of the relationship between family functioning and PTSD symptoms (Silver & Iacono, 1984). Surveyed were 405 Vietnam veterans seeking counseling from Disabled American Veterans (DAV) Vietnam veteran outreach centers; 63 veterans who were not in Vietnam served as controls. Factor analysis of the PTSD symptoms provided substantial empirical support for PTSD as a single disorder. Depression and aggressive behavior, however, emerged as more cardinal, rather than associative, to PTSD. Also analyzed were questions regarding family functioning. Variables comprising marital family life accounted for the greatest amount of variance in extent of symptoms. Further, symptom onset correlated significantly with both incidence of marriage and birth of the first child. (S)

Stanton, M. D., & Figley, C. R. (1978). Treating the Vietnam veteran within the family system. In C. R. Figley (Ed.), Stress disorders among Vietnam veterans: Theory, research and treatment (pp. 281-290). New York: Brunner/Mazel.

Media sensationalism regarding drug use and violence among some veterans has impressed the public that this behavior is typical of all veterans. This has contributed to veterans attempting to disown their veteran status and avoiding professional assistance for adjustment problems. Further, the authors note that stress reactions in general are enmeshed within the interpersonal context of family reactions and that families themselves are sources of stress as they pass through progressive stages (e.g., marriage, birth of first child, etc.). These varying patterns develop over time and can potentially aggravate or mitigate the veteran's stress, depending how much he maintains close physical and psychological ties with his family of origin and/or his marital partner. If these ties are close, the family members should be included as part of the therapeutic plan. The family therapist can also help in explaining the nature of the problem to the children as well as in determining its impact on them. (M)

Tanay, E. (1976). The Dear John syndrome during the Vietnam war. Diseases of the Nervous System, 37, 165-167.
      Reviews the theories of psychological reactions to separation and loss in an attempt to explain the apparent increase in personal rejection notifications, especially patently hostile ones, received by soldiers in the Vietnam theatre compared with those in previous wars. Tanay notes that there is ordinarily a social prohibition against withdrawing affection from soldiers at war, with society providing compensatory gratifications to the women left behind. However, "the Vietnam war provided almost none of these bond-reinforcing mechanisms." Thus, "the widespread hostile or ambivalent attitudes towards the war posed an additional stress for those affected by military separation." Tanay provides policy recommendations consistent with these observations. (C)

Williams, C. M., & Williams, T. (1985). Family therapy for Viet Nam veterans. In S. M. Sonnenberg, A. S. Blank, Jr., & J. A. Talbott (Eds.), The trauma of war: Stress and recovery in Viet Nam veterans (pp. 193-210). Washington, DC: American Psychiatric Press.
      Orients the mental health worker to the use of "family systems theory" in assessing and treating Vietnam veteran families in which the veteran is experiencing symptoms of PTSD. Key characteristics of veteran families are presented as well as the effects of systems and socialization on them, especially wives. The authors present guidelines for treatment in spousal groups along with specific strategies for working with Vietnam veteran families in general. They conclude by describing a multimodal approach to treatment that integrates family therapy with therapies from other perspectives. (S)

Zunin, L. M. (1969, October). Why did our husbands have to die? Coronet, pp. 32-38.
      From his work with widows of servicemen killed in action in Vietnam (Zunin & Barr, 1969, June 15), Zunin describes the attitudes of these women, how they cope with their loss, how they manage the loneliness of their lives without their husbands, and what they envision for their future. He also refers to the children's reactions and on how the wives and children work together to adjust following their loss. (C)

Zunin, L. M., & Barr, N. I. (1969, June 15). Therapy program aids servicemen's widows. U.S. Medicine, pp. 6, 31.
Two Navy psychiatrists describe results of an experimental group therapy program, Operation Second Life, designed to assist volunteer wives of servicemen killed in action in Vietnam. Group leaders used a Gestalt psychotherapy perspective with a group composed of officers' widows between 25 and 35 years of age. Four crucial periods that exacerbate grief were commonly observed: the time they would have joined their husbands for R&R (rest and relaxation) leave had he survived; the time the husband's remains arrived (sometimes long after death occurred); the time of the husband's scheduled return; and the times of the return of American POWs. It was found that most women of the group were very patriotic, had strong religious feelings, idealized their marriages, and did not indulge in self-pity. The program helped them to accept their loss and their own reactions to it, face their problems squarely as "singles," and begin a second life without bitterness.   (C)

8   Ethical Positions in Military and Civilian Medicine and Psychiatry

American Psychiatric Association Board of Trustees. (1971). Official actions. American Journal of Psychiatry, 128, 138-139.
Details for its membership a set of official position statements pertaining to the American involvement in the war in Vietnam and the attendant stateside protest activities. For example, "That the Board of Trustees of the APA wishes to add its voice to that of the great masses of the American people who have so firmly expressed their agony concerning the war in Southeast Asia. Also, as psychiatrists we have specialized deep concern about its grave effects on morale and on the rise of alienation, dehumanization, and divisiveness among the American people. Therefore: The Board hereby expresses its conviction that the prompt halt to the hostilities in Southeast Asia and the prompt withdrawal of American forces will render it possible to reorder our national priorities to build a mentally healthier nation." (C)

Barr, N. I., & Zunin, L. M. (1971). Clarification of the psychiatrist's dilemma while in military service. American Journal of Orthopsychiatry, 41, 672-674.
Posits that psychiatric practice in the military differs qualitatively from civilian psychiatry: (1) the primary allegiance of the psychiatrist is to the military rather than to the patient; (2) patient-psychiatrist confidentiality is lacking; (3) the transference relationship is distorted; (4) traditional treatment goals may result in increased symptomatology; (5) practitioners may suffer similar environment-based stresses as the patients; (6) practitioners have potential control over military aspects of the patients' environment; and (7) many patients evidence significant manipulative intent because of the greater potential for secondary gain. The authors warn that research conclusions from within the military are not always applicable because of these differences. (C)

Barr, N. I., & Zunin, L. M. (1973). The role of the psychiatrist in the military service. Psychiatric Opinion, 10, 17-19.
Recommends that military psychiatrists be redesignated psychiatric military officers (PMO) in order to highlight the institutionalized deviance from civilian practice standards. Such factors as lack of confidentiality, emphasis on returning disordered patients to duty and conformity, and the unavoidable real role the PMO has in the military organization of his patient serve to create medical, ethical, and moral dilemmas for the psychiatrist,

distortions in the transference, and tendencies for patients to try to maximize secondary gain through manipulation. Lack of clarification of these differences in role not only leads to confusion and inefficiency for drafted psychiatrists, but also creates unnecessary hostility and resistance in them.   (C)

Bey, D. R., & Chapman, R. E. (1974). Psychiatry: The right way, the wrong way, and the military way. Bulletin of the Menninger Clinic, 38, 343-354.
     Bey, who served in Vietnam as a division psychiatrist, and Chapman seek to clarify the "vast differences" in assumptions, structures, and practices of military psychiatry under wartime conditions from those of the civilian psychiatrist. The authors present 15 such differences that support the preeminence of collective societal goals over those of the individual, and they specifically counter those who would criticize the methods of military psychiatrists as dehumanizing and unethical by commenting "that war is indeed immoral," with all citizens becoming responsible by participating, even if indirectly, in seeking to destroy the enemy.   (C)

Brown, D. E., Jr. (1970). The military: A valuable arena for research and innovation (Editorial). American Journal of Psychiatry, 127 (supplement), 511-512.
     Seeks to temper the growing professional opposition toward military psychiatry by reminding readers of the long history of valuable contributions made to the practice of civilian psychiatry by those providing psychiatric care in the military services.   (C)

Clausen, R. E., Jr., & Daniels, A. K. (1966). Role conflicts and their ideological resolution in military psychiatric practice. American Journal of Psychiatry, 123, 280-287.
     The military psychiatrist may experience conflict between his roles as psychiatrist and as military officer in several ways. The necessary change in emphasis from psychotherapy to consultation may run counter to his previous training and preference. Patients referred to him may suspect him of being a "company" man while line officers may regard him as patient- rather than service-oriented. The authors point out that a useful ideology for military psychiatry may be drawn out of various guidelines for conflict resolution pertaining to the entire Medical Corps, and they apply these to the specific conflicts likely to be encountered by the military psychiatrist.   (A)

Daniels, A. K. (1969). The captive professional: Bureaucratic limitations in the practice of military psychiatry. Journal of Health and Social Behavior, 10, 255-265.

From policy documents and interviews with military psychiatrists, Daniels describes a critical conflict of interest that is inherent in the practice of military psychiatry. She catalogs the elements comprising the embracing network of organizational constraints and influences that serves to shift the military psychiatrist's definition of the clinical situation (a "transfer of loyalties") away from civilian emphasis on the patient's perspective to that of the military organization and its need to enforce discipline. She alludes to these shifts as the "costs of captivity" for the military psychiatrist and posits that they arise from the extensive expectancies of the military as well as from the ambiguous nature of psychiatric nosology as modified and employed in military regulations. (C)

Dubey, J. (1967). Military psychiatrist as social engineer. American Journal of Psychiatry, 124, 52-58.
Examines the social (professional) roles of the military psychiatrist with special attention to the uses and misuses of power, the dilemma of loyalty divided between the individual patient and the community, and the complications of the social impact of psychiatric diagnoses. This article reflects some of the mounting social consciousness of the Vietnam era. Also notable is that Dubey offers ethical dilemma solutions. (C)

Frank, I. M., & Hoedemaker, F. S. (1970). The civilian psychiatrist and the draft. American Journal of Psychiatry, 127, 497-502.
A study of 11 patients who presented with psychiatric symptoms after receiving induction or activation notices revealed that their chief motivation was to obtain a letter recommending deferment. The authors discuss the ethical question of psychiatrists' volunteering their services to young men seeking deferment to express their own opposition to the Viet Nam conflict and offer suggestions to the civilian psychiatrist who is called on to evaluate a patient for the draft. (See also Roemer, 1971.) (A)

Friedman, H. J. (1972). Military psychiatry: Limitations of the current preventive approach. Archives of General Psychiatry, 26, 118-123.
Provides a critical essay arguing that overly coercive attitudes and methods of contemporary military leadership undermine the adjustment of soldiers (especially the numerous soldiers with limited ego skills). Friedman also posits that critical deficiencies in prevailing clinical emphasis within military psychiatry (with its reliance upon primary prevention) lead the psychiatrist to neglect the clinical needs of the patient/soldier and became instead "the overseer of a system of social control which is distinctly nonmedical in its character." Case examples are provided. (C)

Gibbs, J. J. (1973). Military psychiatry: Reflections and projections. Psychiatric Opinion, 10, 20-23.

Reviews diverse opinions regarding the ethical and practical questions that face the practice of psychiatry in the uniformed services. Gibbs believes that the controversy surrounding military psychiatry stems from a basically unresolvable moral issue and that ardent critics are attempting to express strong emotions under the mantle of scientific rationality. He emphasizes that the challenge from within the military from drafted civilian psychiatrists is useful in urging continued representation of the needs of the individual in contrast to the priorities of the military institution.   (C)

Hastings Center Report. (1978, April). In the service of the state: The psychiatrist as double agent (special supplement). Washington, DC: The Hastings Center Institute of Society, Ethics and the Life Sciences.

Reports on a conference (March 24-26, 1977), cosponsored with the American Psychiatric Association, that explored conflicting loyalties of psychiatrists, especially those functioning within institutions. Included is a section devoted to "moral dilemmas in military practice" (pp. 3-6), which provides an opportunity for the participants (A. K. Daniels, W. Gaylin, D. Mechanic, A. Stone, G. Klerman, E. Freidson, M. Sabshin, P. Friedman, and J. Marmor) to reflect on such dilemmas as they were shaped by the Vietnam war and the heightened humanism of the 1960s and 1970s.   (C)

Hayes, F. W. (1977). Lest we forget. Military Medicine, 142, 263-267.

Using selected worldwide and theatre prevalence figures depicting military personnel attrition caused by psychiatric and behavioral problems in World War II, Korea, and especially Vietnam, Hayes reminds readers of the critical force conservation role historically played by military psychiatrists using combat psychiatric principles developed in World War I. He further notes rising trends in diagnosable mental disorders in the ranks of the current armed forces, which are faced by diminishing numbers of well-trained psychiatrists, and makes suggestions regarding the indoctrination of physicians and military leaders in time-tested principles of effective leadership and preventive mental health.   (C)

Kirshner, L. A. (1973). Countertransference issues in the treatment of the military dissenter. American Journal of Orthopsychiatry, 43, 654-659.

Delineates various antitherapeutic attitudes (e.g., denial, isolation, identification, and projection) that Kirshner has seen among military psychiatrists faced with dissenting military patients and suggests that they stem from the psychiatrists' own unre-

solved identity issues. Kirshner underscores the developmental necessity for the late adolescent soldier, like all adolescents, to
challenge his authorities and the requirement that the military
psychiatrist assist him in resolving his conflicts. Kirshner acknowledges that these psychiatrists are under real institutional pressures
to punish or exclude the nonconforming serviceman, and he sees
parallels in the increasing pressures on psychiatrists generally to
resolve society's dilemmas. (C)

Liberman, R. P., Sonnenberg, S. M., & Stern, M. S., with Brown,
D. E., Jr. (1971). Psychiatric evaluations for young men facing the
draft. American Journal of Psychiatry, 128, 147-152.
     Describes the experiences of the three primary authors in
conducting civilian psychiatric evaluations of 147 young men anticipating the draft. The authors report that the material they elicited generally led to a clinical impression of unsuitability for
military service. The patients tended to be either anxious, depressed, goal-directed individuals who were strongly resistant to
authority, or withdrawn, aimless dropouts; 96% were subsequently
exempted from the draft. The authors feel that civilian psychiatrists have a responsibility to maintain their patients' health, and
often this is incompatible with military service. In discussing the
presented material, Brown, while endorsing the evaluation guidelines used, comments that some of the psychopathology of these
men more likely represented situational anxiety and depression;
that studies of psychiatrists' predictions have shown them to be
often inaccurate, especially as to successful service performance;
and that to be more accurate, screening psychiatrists must be familiar with the adaptational tasks faced by the patient anticipating
entrance into the military. (C)

Locke, K. (1972). Notes on the adjustment of a psychiatrist to the
military. Psychiatric Opinion, 9, 17-21.
     Posits that psychiatrists who serve with the military are sys-
tematically induced to betray their individualist values so they will
instead cooperate in dehumanizing the GI and prosecuting the war.
The military psychiatrist is thus transformed into "a soft police-
man, a pacifier, an institutional ombudsman, a mystifier and the
official stereotyper and narcotizer." Locke, who served a stateside
tour with the Army beginning in 1969, describes his "third alternative" solution to the military psychiatrist's ethical dilemma: active
participation in the GI (antimilitary) movement. (C)

Moskowitz, J. A. (1971). On drafting the psychiatric "draft" letter.
American Journal of Psychiatry, 128, 69-72.
     Using four case examples, Moskowitz illustrates negative psy-
chological reactions present in some young men seeking deferment

from serving in the armed forces on psychiatric grounds. He provides recommendations for avoiding iatrogenic mental illness (e.g.,
if the psychiatrist "disagrees with the war or identifies with his
patient, he might tend to write a letter that would magnify the
patient's symptoms"). (C)

Ollendorff, R. H., & Adams, P. L. (1971). Psychiatry and the draft.
American Journal of Orthopsychiatry, 41, 85-90.
     Portrays a mounting crisis on American college campuses by
drawing on the authors' experiences providing mental health services for students at the University of Florida. The alarm derives
from their observation of growing numbers of nihilistic, alienated,
and emotionally conflicted middle-class students who reflect preoccupation with, fear of, and contempt toward military conscription.
According to the authors, this situation "corrupts" the civilian
psychiatrist, who feels increasingly "powerless and angry" in trying
to convince the Selective Service of the need to grant draft exemption to this burgeoning group of physically fit but neurotic
young men who properly need psychotherapy and rehabilitation instead of military discipline. Equally corrupted is the opposing
"establishment" psychiatrist who "declares as fit everybody who is
not dead." The authors are especially scornful of physicians who
anonymously cooperate with draft boards: "Doctors will be 'called'
more and more for their unthinking political stands made in the
guise of professionalism." (C)

Perlman, M. S. (1975). Basic problems of military psychiatry: Delayed reaction in Vietnam veterans. International Journal of Of-
fender Therapy and Comparative Criminology, 19, 129-138.
     Argues that military psychiatry should be reformed because
of its inattention to persistent or latent PTSD in combat veterans.
Based on studies demonstrating persisting PTSD among veterans of
prior wars and psychiatric casualties of natural disasters, as well
as on his own clinical observations of neglected post-Vietnam psychiatric symptoms in individuals who had previously been screened
by Navy psychiatrists, Perlman concludes there is a "blindness" in
military psychiatrists, which stems from the organization and
structure of military psychiatry. Besides barriers to diagnosis
resulting from the veteran's disinclination to talk about his experiences as well as communication difficulties arising from class
differences between the psychiatrist and his soldier-patient, military psychiatrists are further hampered by their own reluctance
to acknowledge the cruel acts committed by members of the American military, a group with whom they identify; by the absence of
privileged communication for military psychiatry; and by the tendency for post-Vietnam readjustment symptoms to be expressed in
antisocial and antiauthority behaviors (i.e., disciplinary infrac-
tions), or in neurotic symptoms that may be compensable condi-

tions and thus retained by combat veterans because of secondary gain. (C)

Robitscher, J. (1980). The powers of psychiatry. Boston: Houghton Mifflin.
Reviews the social role of psychiatry in general and includes various references to role dilemmas for the psychiatrist within the military and for civilian psychiatrists who encounter individuals seeking psychiatric exemption from military service. In a chapter entitled "How Psychiatrists Usurp Authority: Abortion and the Draft" (pp. 302-318), Robitscher asserts that, as with psychiatric exceptions to legal restrictions for women seeking abortion, deliberate mislabeling of draft-eligible young men as sick by psychiatrists during the Vietnam era represented a major deviation from scientific standards so that social goals could be achieved. He notes that the psychiatrists themselves justified such a political deviation from medical standards because they felt it was in the service of a higher morality. (C)

Roemer, P. A. (1971). The psychiatrist and the draft evader (Letter). American Journal of Psychiatry, 127, 1236-1237.
Reacting to Frank and Hoedemaker (1970), Roemer expresses his opposition to the Vietnam war and the "established order," and asserts that it is not possible for any psychiatrist to be "objective" when faced with someone asking for a letter to get him out of the draft. In his own experience, because he was candid in such evaluations, the patients did not need to present themselves as "crazy" for an honest professional opinion to be generated and forwarded to the military authorities. (C)

Sullivan, P. R. (1971). Influence of personal values on psychiatric judgement. Journal of Nervous and Mental Disease, 152, 193-198.
Presents results of a study of the disposition patterns of 8 Navy hospital-based psychiatrists over a 6-month period in early 1968. Study participants were distinguished by the degree of their agreement (using a scalar 0-3) with six personal value statements about obligation and commitment to military service (including one question about the morality of America's involvement in Vietnam). The 4 psychiatrists with the highest scores (suggesting "collectivist" values, i.e., agent of the military) returned a significantly higher proportion of their patients back to military duty following hospitalization than did the 4 psychiatrists with the lowest scores (suggesting "individualist" values, i.e., agent of the patient). Sullivan discusses the implications of these findings in terms of the inevitability of a psychiatrist's personal values influencing his or her medical judgment--obviously within the military but also, more subtly, in civilian practice. Case material is provided. (C)

Veatch, R. M. (1977b). Soldier, physician and moral man. In R. M. Veatch (Ed.), Case studies in medical ethics (pp. 61-64). Cambridge: Harvard University Press.
     Reviews elements of testimony in the court-martial of Capt. Howard B. Levy, a drafted Army physician who refused to provide medical training for Vietnam-bound troops because he believed such skills would perpetuate an unjust war. The case raises the critical question of how a physician can reconcile his obligation to society with his obligation to those directly affected by his practice of medicine. It also raises the question of whether he is obligated by universal moral requirements or by the morality of his profession.   (C)

Weitzel, W. D. (1976). A psychiatrist in a bureaucracy: The unsettling compromises. Hospital and Community Psychiatry, 29, 644-647.
     Using interviews with 9 psychiatrists who recently entered the Army, Weitzel seeks answers to questions raised by Daniels (1969) regarding potential conflicts of interest in the military psychiatrist. Among his study participants he notes three modes of professional adjustment, which he perceives as unsatisfactory attempts at compromise in the face of the dilemmas inherent in practicing psychiatry for the Army: (1) alignment with official Army views ("identification with the aggressor"); (2) compartmentalization of roles in an attempt to meet the expectations of both the soldier-patient and the Army; or (3) rejection of a military identity ("acting out"). He concludes that "when psychiatrists are placed in situations in which they must reconcile an organization's administrative goals and an individual patient's needs they must inevitably compromise both." Although this work does not specifically refer to the recently concluded American war in Vietnam, the sentiments Weitzel examines evidently reflect the tumult in American society following that war-weary period.   (C)

Index of Authors

Boldface indicates primary references: the individuals listed appear as authors or editors of the specific work abstracted. Lightface indicates secondary references: the individuals listed either are cited or cross-referenced in the abstract itself or are authors or editors of a source in which the abstracted work is contained or from which it was reprinted.

About the Authors

NORMAN M. CAMP, M.D., has received specialized training in psychiatry, child and adolescent psychiatry, and psychiatric analysis, and is currently Associate Professor in the Department of Psychiatry at the Medical College of Virginia. During his twenty years as a psychiatrist with the U.S. Army, he was assigned to Vietnam, Europe, and various U.S. posts as well as at Walter Reed Army Medical Center and Walter Reed Army Institute of Research. His articles regarding the provision of psychiatric services have appeared in numerous periodicals. He is the author with C. M. Carney of the forthcoming *Painful Memories and Crushing Burdens: U.S. Army Psychiatrists in the Vietnam War* (Greenwood Press).

ROBERT H. STRETCH is a Research Psychologist and a Major in the U.S. Army Medical Service Corps. He is currently Scientific Liaison Officer for the U.S. Army Medical Research and Development Command at the Defence and Civil Institute of Environmental Medicine, Toronto. He has been researching the psychosocial adjustment of Vietnam veterans for the past nine years.

WILLIAM C. MARSHALL is a consultant to a program for the mentally retarded in Maryland. He received his Master of Arts degree in Clinical Psychology from Western Michigan University and was research assistant to Dr. Camp at Walter Reed Army Institute of Research.